Music Representation and Transformation in Software

Donald P. Pazel

Music Representation
and Transformation in Software

Structure and Algorithms in Python

 Springer

Donald P. Pazel
Fishkill, NY, USA

ISBN 978-3-030-97471-8   ISBN 978-3-030-97472-5   (eBook)
https://doi.org/10.1007/978-3-030-97472-5

This Springer imprint is published by the registered company Springer Nature Switzerland AG
The registered company address is: Gewerbestrasse 11, 6330 Cham, Switzerland

Preface

Introduction

Suppose you have an interest in programming computer music and need a starting point. Perhaps you have tried various music applications or tools, such as mixers, production systems, or notation systems, but feel a need to dig deeper, to be more hands-on and work with music fundamentals. Perhaps you have familiarity with concepts of musical notes, keys, chords, scores, and other music elements, but you don't know where to begin in designing and programming about them, let alone translating them to MIDI®[1]. You want to be able to put all those elements to work through programming, but you need direction to get to that next killer music app that you have in mind. This book guides you to that sweet spot of developing and using your programming skills to design and build systems about music.

However, this book does more than provide that kind of instruction. This book takes the reader on a journey through music concepts in an organized approach that develops music essentials, from the concepts of tone, pitch, and time, through notes, intervals, chords, and scores while at the same time interpreting these elements as software artifacts. As these many concepts are covered, we do so with close attention to the organization of and relationships amongst these concepts and reflect those as Python classes and objects, and so learn about music from a software design viewpoint. By this process, we approach this design in a logical and structured way.

The objective for doing this is to make music theory elements programmatically accessible. The resulting software should allow you to be able to code in the language of music, letting you to think primarily in musical concepts about your programming objectives, while leaving various music calculations, such as key or chord construction, transparent. That is the point behind the software discussion on music representation in the first part of this book.

The second part of the book is devoted to music transformation algorithms. These transforms comprise an interesting application of music representation for modifying music through key change, melodic reflection, and much more. This part of the book is more academic and has more of a research feel. However, the connection to programming prominently remains with discussions grounded in

---

[1] MIDI is a registered trademark of the Association of Manufacturers of Electronic Instruments (AMEI).

implementation details and software structure considerations. We hope the reader finds inspiration in this section for novel applications or advanced interests in the wide area of computer music research.

The Origin of this Book

The origin of this book has its roots in the late 90's. At that time, I had the honor of being a member of a computer music research team at IBM®[2] TJ Watson Research Center in New York. This department should not be confused with being a club of musicians that jammed after work. Rather, the Computer Music Center (CMC) focused on MIDI-based composition software and real-time music modification as full-time work in the Mathematics Department of this esteemed IBM research center. The department was technically and principally led by computer music veterans Danny Oppenheim and Jim Wright. During my tenure there we constructed MusicSketcher [1], a prototype application that demonstrated a wide range of music transformational capability, including dynamic chord replacement, and harmony preserving dynamic note shifts, and other capabilities. These transformations went by the name Smart Harmony [2]. My work experiences in this department served as an introduction to computer music, MIDI, and various music tools. The novelty and creativity behind the work there was very impressive, and I found the talks, works, and efforts there stimulating in ideas.

Many years and many different careers later, along with finally having freedom of time, I decided to take a fresh look at a few ideas in computer music research, but now in the context of some 20 to 30 years of technological change. The prior work with which I was familiar was preserved in papers and memory. This forced me to think through from scratch the foundations for music representations and transformational capabilities. Additionally, instead of using C/C++ as we had years earlier, I now have access to Java or Python, computer languages with which I have become more adept through my professional industrial experiences. Computing hardware also improved considerable over time. Further, VST®[3] digital audio provided advanced capability in MIDI rendering and provided access to rich sound samples which are currently plentiful in the market.

I considered building on an idea for music collaboration that I thought about while I was in the CMC long ago [3]. The idea was to allow multiple people to log into a group-based music session, choose instruments, insert riffs or melody lines, and dynamically modify them in real time collaboratively. As I moved forward on this idea, the effort took on many technical challenges. Firstly, and most importantly, I needed a rich flexible music representation with functionality that translates into MIDI and music performance dynamics. While I thought this was my main concern, I quickly learned that there are many other critical features outside of music to address. As this project was designed to have a web-based front end and significantly, real-time collaborative interaction, it required a coordinating server as well. After much effort, I achieved a prototypical result that was very close to what I wanted. Multiple players could engage in music performance through a web interface as a shared experience, much in the way I envisioned. A tune is composed on a shared (web-based) screen using selectable multi-measure music fragments stitched together. The players take on different instrument roles, say one on drums, another guitar, etc. Once the playback started, each player controls their instrument's pitch (while automatically maintaining harmony) and volume levels. The tempo and harmony (chords) are also adjusted in real time through a special "conductor" role. A server takes care of all the interactivity and music dynamics, and ensures the players are relatively synchronized to a unified experience.

As these features became demonstrable, the key question became "Where to go from here?" A question that remains unsettled still. Even as I contemplated the work's uncertain future, there remained a nagging consideration that I had reluctantly been putting off and needed to consider.

---

[2] IBM is a registered trademark of International Business Machines.

[3] VST is a trademark of Steinberg Media Technologies, GmbH.

The problem which with I struggled was that this project was simply too massive for one person to contain within reasonable time. Although initially I focused on building a proper music representation, I quickly became absorbed with server architecture details, distributed playback algorithms, client synchronization, web interfaces (JavaScript), and general maintenance. Quickly, the core music representation became brittle and sketchy with the load of work. What started as a music project, became more of a "soup to nuts" web application project, a terribly interesting one, but one that left scarce time and energy for addressing the increasingly insufficient core music representative and transformative issues on which I wanted and needed to spend much more time and energy.

I took a break from the project for reflection, to reexamine the work that had been done, determine how to improve upon it, and see to where that circumspection leads. As I realized early on, music representation is a deep and interesting software modeling exercise in itself. The intuitive concepts of music require rigorous definition. The closer I looked, it seemed that although we are generally adept with many music concepts like intervals, scales, chords, and the like, our understanding of these are somewhat superficial and at times not so well structured, if not incomplete, and rough around the edges. It's like the many skills we adopt from rote learning. We work with certain skills daily but don't think deeply about them nor even understand their foundations with much clarity. Looking at the music representation I had developed, I found needless complexity that seemed to come more from lack of foundation (from admittedly a rush to get that component finished as an expense for other needs) than say sloppy code.

Yet another important aspect surfaced, that music representation comes with a set of algorithms that are in fact, genuinely interesting. The computation of scales, computing interval end notes, and similar, are interesting topics, that in a thought-provoking way made me question how as a musician I had done those things, and if there are better ways to think about those topics, especially, when designing software to manipulate them. As an example, the notion of time in music is interesting, that along with the varied temporal representations comprises an interesting study, including the conversions of one temporal representation to another. It is interesting to think about the properties of a musical note, to question why we limit to specific durations, and pitches. These are just a few examples of what came to light. It speaks to the larger issue of questioning our understanding of music, what restrictions might be too rigid, and if anything can be done to lessen those restrictions.

I never returned to that initial distributed application. Instead, I decided to focus on music representation, the related foundational algorithms, and eventually to music transformational issues, from the perspective of a software engineer and to some degree, a mathematician. This turn of focus resulted in a sizeable body of study and code that is detailed in this book. The result is a far more fulfilling adventure than I could have imagined.

This experience is what led me to writing this book. After years of working solely on music representation, and years looking at how to build transformational algorithms with that representation, I thought I would share that experience here in hopes of motivating others to carry on and perfect that effort and inspire people towards efforts in computer music.

Prerequisites and Approach

Readers are expected to have basic programming skills, and some familiarity with Python. This includes familiarity with computational statements, logical structures such as if and loop (for/while) statements, and function or procedure definitions with calling protocols, including parameter passing. Also, a familiarity with the concepts of list and dictionary (or maps), embodied as Python lists and maps or dicts, is also assumed. Unlike many topical introductory books with claims to programming or a specific programming language training, this book assumes basic programming skills in Python. If needed, there are many excellent books for learning Python such as [4] [5] or online references such as [6].

The reader should have some loosely defined notions of musical elements. That is, the reader should have notions about what notes, intervals and chords are. However, the book is built around introducing all these concepts in a methodical structured way. So, unlike the programming prerequisites, the music prerequisites are less strict.

Object-Oriented design skills are not required but are a critical part of the book's teachings. This book places a heavy emphasis on learning object-oriented (O-O or OO) design and thinking. Designing in an object-oriented manner forces one to step back from a problem space, and pull apart the concepts and their dependencies, and make judgments on how to approach a programming task. It forces developers to:

- code a software model that clearly maps to the problem domain's conceptual model, and in a sense, "talks in its terms".
- reflect relationships and dependencies directly in the software model that are relevant in the domain's conceptual model.
- keep in mind efficiencies and inefficiencies, or limitations of programming artifacts used in the software model.
- stretch for generality where needed, but within reasonable bounds.

What the reader should realize is that like with so many software endeavors, the software design process never ends. This is particularly so with the music domain, with, for example, the introduction of different instruments, different styles of music, and so forth, each introducing their own conceptual needs. We do not claim to present in this book the best possible music representation but do believe this model goes a long way on generality and will change over time to be more inclusive, and to introduce the reader to software design in the object-oriented style.

Since music many times involves calculations, especially involving dynamics over time, some mathematics is involved. The reader should be able to understand simple equations for calculations and similar and be capable of translating these into code.

What this Book is Not About

As important as describing what this book is about, is mentioning what it is not about. Importantly, this is not a book about music notation, nor how to build music notation software. Music notation for sure is important and related to the topic of this book. Notation concerns the visual and textual communication of music content and instruction for performance. Consequently, notation incorporates a mapping of music concepts to text/symbol and/or visa-versa. This book's concern is with embodying music concepts as software model objects, something more abstract that could be useful in building a music notation system but is not one in and of itself. By the way, there are numerous exemplar music notation systems on the market: Dorico®[4], Sibelius®[5], Notion®[6], and Finale®[7] to name a few. As a warning to more ambitious readers, building a music notation editor is a herculean effort. Entire teams of developers and testers are actively devoted to such endeavors with extensive time and resource commitments by a few companies.

Secondly, this is not a book about building MIDI rendering software. MIDI and some of its important aspects and translation of music models to MIDI are described in detail here and provide a useful

---

[4] Dorico is a registered trademark of Steinberg Media Technologies GMbH.
[5] Sibelius is a registered trademark of Avid Technology Europe LTD.
[6] Notion is a registered trademark of Presonus Expansion, L.L.C.
[7] Finale is a registered trademark of MakeMusic, Inc.

educational introduction for readers interested in learning about MIDI. However, construction of MIDI rendering software is a topic unto itself and is outside the scope of this book.

Intended Audience

A wide variety of readership is envisioned for this book. Primarily it is for students to accelerate their software development capabilities in designing and building music software. With that, we offer the following thoughts for the varied reader constituency:

Students

Students should take seriously the technical prerequisites. It is important to be able to program procedurally in some programming language. If you already know Python, fine. If not and you pick up programming languages easily, fine. However, knowing the basics of Python is the expectation of this book. The book also delivers an introduction to object-oriented principles and how to program to them in Python. The book applies object-oriented principles to varied music elements and accelerates in depth rapidly. The algorithms, even in the representation section at times can be complex and intricate, and in some cases are expressed in mathematical formulae which the user should be able to understand and translate to code.

In a few instances, advanced computer science concepts are discussed, for example, red-black trees and constraint engines. Students need not understand the implementations of these concepts in detail, but should concentrate in understanding the features they provide, how to use them, their interfaces, and chiefly their strengths and limitations. The more intrigued student may want to invest more time on theory and implementation details in these areas.

While the primary focus for entry-level students should be on the representation part of the book, the transformation part could be of great interest and well-worth reading. It comprises a combination of practical applications of music representation and an introduction to constraint management. Students, if not guided by an instructor, should read through the transformations and at least understand what they contribute musically, and understand them technically as best can. Reading through the many examples should help in providing this understanding.

For representation chapters, the end of chapter questions are mostly for provoking thought about the range in complexity of what is presented. The student is encouraged to read through the questions and select a few (if not assigned by the instructor) to think through as best can. For the transformation chapters, each chapter ends with a "final thoughts" section which highlights both positive and less than positive aspects of the chapter's topic. It is meant to be thought provoking, and fuel for further efforts.

Instructors

Instructors can consider using this book for a one semester course on computer music programming. The representation part could easily occupy a semester. For classes comprised of students with lower-level programming skills, the instructor could augment the course with a robust Python review. That said, it is recommended to spend a good deal of time on object-oriented concepts and how to code Python to an object-oriented methodology. After that, the book can be followed chapter to chapter with the idea of introducing new music concepts in succession, along with representation and coding principles.

If the semester has more time to offer, one can consider introducing topics from the transformation section, with at least a guide through the transformations and examples. The constraint engine itself can be technically demanding for students, and the instructor can defer on its implementation details, and instead highlight its interface and usage. The constraint engine is an interesting topic, and advanced students may want to consider augmenting or working with it as an advanced project in this or other domains.

Practitioners

Practitioners may come to this book for a variety of reasons, and in a variety of ways. If you want to learn how to approach object-oriented programming with computer music as a domain, then a straightforward read is recommended. Otherwise, treating it as a reference text, picking and choosing chapters in the representation section is useful.

As for the transformation section, there are many topics from which to choose. A few of the transforms make use of the constraint engine, but many don't. It is a matter of looking through the transform types to determine which topics might be of interest.

Experienced Researchers

Experienced researchers may generally find the representation section less interesting than the transformation section, except perhaps for the later chapters of the representation section concerning variable dynamics and harmony representation. We would expect this audience to be more interested in the transformation section of the book, on which there are a wide range of topics to study and expand upon.

Regarding the Musical Examples

The reader will find an abundance of musical examples. While music written on a page is not as satisfying as listening to it, there are several ways to listen to them.

- Use the score to midi conversion code discussed in this book to generate MIDI files and play the examples on a MIDI player of choice.

- Although not covered in this book, there is a primitive VST host referenced in the code base that can be used with Python interface code in the code base.

- The author found copying generated music to a notation application with playback is very practical and useful, and allows for quickly changing an example's dynamics, tempo, etc.

- Hands-on playing examples on a musical instrument.

The author is aware that many books of this type go through great effort to provide support for MIDI playback. The decision was made to invest effort on the main ideas of this book on music representation and transformation, even at the expense of not providing what would at best be a poorly functional MIDI playback software package that would only detract from the learning experience.

About the Software

As a bonus this book is associated with an accessible software package that reflects the work of this text. This software can be found at:

https://github.com/dpazel/music_rep

This software package reflects the class hierarchy and details described throughout this text. It is covered by MIT license with no guarantees nor warranties.

Readers are encouraged to copy the code locally to their computers and use a programming IDE like Eclipse®[8] or PyCharm®[9] to review the code while working through related sections of the book. Importantly, please review the "readme" file which instructs which related software packages (Python packages) are required for the code to build and run. There are ample unit tests as well in the package that the reader may find useful towards understanding the code and concepts. The code base uses some interesting external packages which should be educational and useful to software engineering students.

It is emphasized that running examples in debug mode may be the best way for learning and exploring the ideas in this book.

Bear in mind that the software was developed from a research viewpoint. The conceptual model on music was developed with two ambitions. One was to develop a music software model that encapsulates in logical development most basic music theoretical elements. Also, the model's developmental aim is to provide a foundation capable of enabling transformations, and in doing so prove strong enough to sort out a transform's strengths and limitations that a simpler model might not be able to do.

However, the code is less than industrial in strength and robustness! That is, one is likely to find missing features or outright errors, or even some intentional missing elements meant for exercises. The code may occasionally be improved upon over time, so it would be in the readers' interests to periodically check for updates.

It is my hope that readers find this book more than helpful in their programming or music careers or general educational endeavors, but also find the book thought-provoking, stimulating, and encouraging for interests in computer music programming and research.

To all who venture here, Best of Luck!

Donald P Pazel,

Fishkill, NY

January 2022

---

[8] Eclipse is a registered trademark of Eclipse Foundation, Inc. Ref. http://www.eclipse.org

[9] PyCharm is a registered trademark of JetBrains s.r.o. Ref. https://www.jetbrains.com/pycharm

Acknowledgements

Parts of this text were produced using the MusiSync font, © 2001, 2008 by Robert Allgeyer, SIL Open Font License[10]. Also, the overwhelming majority of musical examples were constructed in and figures extracted from personal Dorico projects.

There are many people who introduced me to the study of computer music, and the problems and issues behind representing music in software. Of course, much of that starts with the Computer Music Center members at IBM Watson Labs and especially to Danny Oppenheim and Jim Wright who together embodied the spirit and mind of the project, and Robert Fuhrer, as well as the manager David Jameson, our fearless tester David Speck, and Jim Cate in a production role. However, a special thanks to Steven Abrams who as the newly minted manager at the time, served as a crucial catalyst and contributor for ideas and progress that resulted in pulling together the best ideas in the group, including Smart Harmony. Many of these ideas provided inspiration for the follow-on work in this text, and a few of those seed ideas are borrowed and cited appropriately. I offer my thanks and appreciation to Dr. William R. Pullyblank for sponsoring that effort as part of his Mathematics department.

Many thanks go to Aries Arditi for many directional conversations and for his review and suggested changes to the document, and similarly to Daniel Spreadbury and Roger Dannenberg for their kind reviews. Also thanks to Dr. Stephen Andrilli of LaSalle University for his continued encouragement, and to Brian Hinman for his sage counsel.

Also, I would be completely lost in this endeavor were it not for the strong musical influences in my life. I studied piano for many years with Ralph Burkhart who taught me the foundations of music theory, music performance technique, and music appreciation. Also Dr. Ruth Schonthal taught me foundations and appreciation for music composition. Both Ralph and Dr. Schonthal are now gone and are very much missed. I hope they understood how totally in awe of them I am. After many years of absence from piano, in recent years I continued piano study with Jennifer Gallant Lopez who led me to an awakening of a renewed appreciation of great music and performance. Also, many thanks to Amy Baglione for introducing me to the rudiments of jazz and beyond.

A special thanks to Ralf Gerstner, executive editor at Springer, for taking on this book and for his patient shepherding and steady hand through the publication process.

Some influences are long lasting and unforgettable, and come from a different and indeed magical time of my life. I am deeply indebted to Br. Hugh Albright of LaSalle University, Philadelphia. His ethereal yet profound way of conveying the beauty of mathematical abstraction left a lasting influence, and a life-long love and respect for mathematics. As well, Dr. Thomas Kriete of the University of Virginia taught me the importance of rigor and clarity of presentation for instruction. I am grateful for their belief in me. I could only hope that some of those influences show through here.

And the best for last, with love for my wife Joan for the time and patience for making this book happen. My love and best friend forever!

---

[10] The SIL Open Font License is completely free for personal and commercial tasks. And you don't need to pay any single penny for utilizing them commercially. Also, if you get some other license like OFL, Public domain, and 100% free. They are also free for commercial uses.

Contents

Contents

Contents

Contents

Contents

Part 1: Representation

The first part of this book focuses on the representation of music in software. We begin with a more precise definition about the meaning of the phrase "representation in software". Whenever software applications are designed, be they music applications, billing systems, or internet chat rooms, etc., they are broken down at a conceptual level to account for the discrete concepts or entities involved. For example, invoices, bills, customers in billing systems or participants and discussions in chat rooms, etc. are discrete concepts that are the subjects of their respective applications. Each of those entities can be further broken into two key constituents, namely data properties, and algorithmic logic which we refer to as methods. For example, for a representative entity for a person, data properties might include name, address, and age. Methods might include accessing or changing these data properties. What is important is that the data always remains consistent during an application's execution lifetime. For example, ensuring the address is correct for the name.

A method is usually referenced by a signature consisting of a method name descriptive of what the method does, a set of input data, and one or more data that is returned. The set of method signatures for an entity usually divides into strictly internal, meaning it maintains the data consistency even when changed, or external, meaning it is meant to be used by other entities or generally by the application itself.

Discovering the conceptual elements of an application, and further refining each by data property and methods is what is meant by the term 'representation in software' and is further embodied in the process known as object-oriented (OO) design. The opening chapter of this part of the book describes OO design and discusses OO programming in the Python programming language.

The topic of this part of the book concerns representation in software for the main elements found in music theory. Anyone who has attempted to build a music-based software project is aware of how difficult it is to capture the complex conceptual space of music into software. For example, a note is a basic entity in music theory that is encapsulated by data properties including pitch frequency, duration, and volume. One immediately comes across an increasingly complex set of artifacts that add to the context of a note. Among these are key, time signature, and tempo. Add upon that, chords, measures, voices, and so forth, of which note is a part, and the complexity multiplies. Following so, we are eventually led to score representation, including processes for complex changes such as in time signatures, tempos, and so forth. There is a hierarchy of music concepts, each layer built upon the lower until we see the full conceptual space that defines a knowledge base about music, often referred to as music theory.

Translating these entities into a structured, accurate, and flexible software model is not an easy task. There are decisions to be made on the conceptual model as structure, the key entities, and their dependencies. That is, how does one represent or code all that information using a programming language, and after that, using that representation, how does one program towards application goals. Each misstep, however small, may not necessarily lead to inoperable code, but rather inflexible code, where doing even the easiest of changes requires, for example, overly complex coding changes. One may also find suspicious infrequently used procedures that depend on multiple sources of information for perhaps partial calculations, which overall seem to stick out like a sore thumb in the code base.

The objective of this part of the book is to provide direction to this discussion, to build a music software model from basic concepts and build towards more complex concepts. Chapter by chapter we introduce new music concepts and break each apart into data properties and methods. The goal is that by the end of this book section, we will have developed a relatively complete library of music elements in software that can be practically useful and for experimentation and provide a foundation for the advanced work found later in the transformation part of the book.

1 Software Modeling and Object-Oriented Design

Software design has been an ever-evolving craft since the beginning of programming. As software systems became more complex there was more need for discipline in crafting software and organizing it. It became clear that strict procedural designs and use of data structures, although effective, could lead to code that easily fractures under the strain of changes, through carelessness or lack of foresight. Looked at another way, the early programming languages had no implicit capability to assist with enforcing design principles.

Object-oriented design is a paradigm for programming that evolved primarily through the 1970's and into the 1980's. At a simplistic level, the basic idea behind this paradigm is to think of a software system as a set of concepts or entities, and for each define a set of data properties that encapsulate the entity, and as well, a set of procedure-like logic that allow the entity to regulate or maintain consistency of those data properties, and a set of procedure-like logic that provides public access from other concepts or generally. This approach has been adopted by many programming languages including Smalltalk, C++, and Python, to name a few, and each has inherent support structures and features for object-oriented design. The design concepts become actualized as classes within which are defined the data properties and logic methods.

The point of using object-oriented design is to consolidate application data and processes into well-defined conceptual silos as design. The development becomes more logical as it adheres to the problem space more precisely at a conceptual level. In using object-oriented design, as we will see, there are decisions to make about class definition and related class hierarchies, data property and method definition and so forth. Over time, object-oriented programming has evolved into a rather large topic. However, many of the basics are easily stated and illustrated. It is beyond this text to develop object-oriented design theory in detail here. Instead, the basics are described in this chapter, and further aspects are introduced as needed later.

In this book, we take a journey towards building an object-oriented model for music using the Python programming language. However, at the same time, we look at music theory very deeply, even to the point of including some modern music concepts, such as 8 tone scales, and cluster chords. With that, we transform music theory to software within a broader context, and in doing so, guide ourselves through a set of decisions and problems in doing the related software design and implementation.

1.1 Object-Oriented Design by Example

For a hands-on introduction to object-oriented design, we explore a simple example comprised of a few related entities from a hypothetical and simple banking system. In this system we have accounts of different types for different purposes. We have accounts for credit cards, checking, and savings. Furthermore, suppose our imaginary bank offers two types of credit card accounts, Z1, and Z2. Also,

© The Author(s), under exclusive license to Springer Nature Switzerland AG 2022
D. P. Pazel, *Music Representation and Transformation in Software*, https://doi.org/10.1007/978-3-030-97472-5_1

suppose there are two types of checking accounts, basic and enhanced. A diagram depicting the relationships amongst these entities is shown in Fig. 1.1. Keep in mind that this diagram aims to facilitate design, indicating what entities are envisioned in our application and how data and code is organized. The design diagram is abstract in showing the definitions of the application's entities and relationships, and not actual instances of the entities. In programming, we instantiate the definitions in that many Accounts, many Checking accounts, and so forth, based on these definitions are created. Building these kinds of diagrams is common practice in program design.

The hierarchical diagram shows a box for each entity type discussed above, along with relationship arrows described below. Let's look at the element of this application more closely.

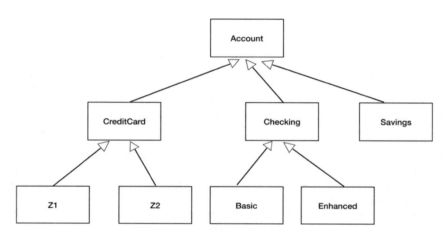

Fig. 1.1 Example Object-Oriented Design

Class: Instead of entity we will use the word **class**, which relates more to its programming embodiment described later. Classes represent the conceptual elements that comprise our system. It is abstract in the sense that classes are descriptive or defining elements. For example, there is only one class definition for 'Account', which describes its data and behavior. However, in an actual application, there will be many account **objects** or **instances** based on that definition. Each instance holds real data with behaviors based on actual data values and code. This bundling of related data on a common conceptual entity is called **encapsulation**.

Properties and Methods: With class being a defining element, at the detail level, a class is composed of **properties** and **methods**. It is easiest to think of properties as data definitions. For example, in the case of the class Account, one would have a property that names or identities the owner of the account and name that property 'owner'. Other properties include the date the account was opened, called 'opening date', and the property 'status' of the account with values like open, closed, frozen, and so on. Properties are defined data holders related to what the class conceptually represents.

Methods on the other hand, can be thought of as calculations or actions related to the class that either other classes can invoke, or that can be invoked external to any class. Returning to the class Account example, invoking change_owner(), would provide a means to change ownership of the account. More than simply a name setting action, change_owner() verifies the identity of new owner, as well as checks if the new owner has permission to ownership and related business role to it, and so on. Get_Credit_Line() is another method requiring various calculations depending on the type of account, balances, and so forth. Many methods and properties may be openly accessible, or **public**, to the application. Others may be strictly internal to each class, or in that sense **private**. These accessibility characteristics, public or private, are referred to as **data protection** values. Methods are specified in the form of a **signature** which provides the name of the method, and the names of both input and output data.

Inheritance: The arrows between classes in the diagram can best be thought of as denoting "is a" relationships between the source class and the target class. For example, "Checking is a kind of Account" or "Basic is a kind of Checking (Account)", the "Z1 credit card is a CreditCard (Account)", and so forth, are clearly marked in the diagram by arrows. Each arrow indicates **inheritance**, that one class has the same properties and methods of another and may likely include additional properties or methods. In an inheritance relationship, the class at the base of the arrow is called a **subclass** in relationship to the class at the arrowhead called the **superclass**. What this means is that all the properties and methods of the superclass, for example Account, are also part of say, a Checking (account), the subclass. Similarly, Account's properties and methods are included in CreditCard and Savings. Superclasses like Account reduce duplication of data definitions and method implementations for its subclasses. This makes development much easier since changes and enhancements to superclasses automatically bind to their subclasses.

Interface: An **interface**, like a class, is a summary of data properties and methods, but unlike a class are not directly instantiated. Classes **implement** interfaces, in that when so indicated, the classes further define the interface's data properties and methods. Many classes can implement the same interface. In that way, interface provides a form of multiple inheritance, allowing instances of different implementing classes to be identified by the interface semantics only. An interface should not be confused with a class definition wherein the semantics or meaning of these characteristics is laid out, described, and even coded as properties and methods. In fact, interface instances are not created by themselves but only in as much as an implementing class is created. What is important about interfaces is that they encapsulate a set of data properties and methods that can be accessed through the implementing class. The interface mechanism varies across programming languages. Java provides interfaces to be used at user discretion. Python and C++ do not. In these latter cases, the class definitions themselves are in a sense, de facto interfaces. The point behind the notion of interface whether by interface semantics or by class definition, is that in both cases there is an identifiable encapsulation of accessible data and methods that can be used as a source for coding activity.

Polymorphism: The object-oriented feature of **polymorphism** has several different meanings. Inheritance relates to a kind of polymorphism, in as much as, for example, CreditCard, Checking, and Savings are subclasses of Account, and wherever an Account instance can be used, usually so can Account's subclasses of CreditCard, Checking, and Savings. In that sense, inheritance leverages a kind of polymorphism. A more commonly held notion of polymorphism is when a class can have several methods of the same name but with different parameter types or numbers of parameters that serve to distinguish which method is invoked by calling arguments. As a simple example, the Checking class may have several method implementations for the method deduct(). In one, deduct(owner_name, amount), a deduction for some amount is made by a specific owner of the account. In another, deduct(amount), a deduction is made anonymously on an account.

As mentioned earlier, object-oriented design is a kind of science to itself. The brief introduction above hardly scratches the surface. For more information, reference [7], [8]. A visual representation of many concepts in object-oriented design can be found in the study of Unified Modeling Language or UML. The inheritance arrow in the above diagram is the UML symbol for inheritance for example. A reference for UML is [9]. Finally, to see object-oriented design in light of practice for commonly used programming motifs, refer to the study of programming patterns [10].

1.2   A Concise Introduction to Python Classes

The Python programming language offers ample semantic structures for implementing object-oriented design and programming. In this chapter, we outline Python's object-oriented semantics starting with the class statement, which is the main declarative for defining a class. The class statement typically includes the following definitional statements in this order:

```
class ClassName(subclass_1, subclass_2, ... ):    # Class Declaration Header
    class_data1 = value                           # Class Static Data Definitions
    class_data2 = value

    def __init__(self, args, ...):                # Class Instance Initializer
        self.instance_data1 = value               # Instance Data Definitions
        self.instance_data2 = value

    def method1(self, args, ...):                 # Method Definitions
    def method2(self, args, ...):
```

- *Class Declaration Header:* This statement provides the name of the class being defined, along with a list of class names of other defined classes to serve as superclasses. When no superclasses are specified, the default is the Python system class "object". So far, we have only explored classes with only one superclass, and for this text that will typically be the case. However, a class can have multiple superclasses, and pick up the properties and methods of all the superclasses. Such a situation is called *multiple inheritance*. Multiple inheritance has some complexity and must be defined with care especially in cases where the subclasses share similarly name methods or data. Further discussion on multiple inheritance can be found below.

- *Class Static Data Definitions:* A class can define *static* data variables proper to the class itself, and independent of class instances. That is, although we may create many class instances, there is only one value for each of these class data variables, that is, the static values being singular to the class itself. Access is made through **ClassName.class_data1**, for example.

- *Class Instance Initializer:* When a class is instantiated to an instance, that instance requires proper initialization, with application dependent default values for instance data, and for possibly building ancillary data for proper instance behavior. That initialization is implemented in the class's __init__() method. In code, the __init__() method is automatically invoked at instance creation, e.g., **a = ClassName(args).** The first variable in the signature of __init__(), *self*, is a reference to the new instance. Additional parameters may be specified for supplemental value input to assist in initialization. While, the __init__() method is invoked to initialize a class instance, note that the subclasses also require initialization as well, and this is achieved by the subclass's __init__() invoking the __init__() methods of each superclass.

- *Instance Data Definitions:* **Instance data** refers to the class variables that on an instance-by-instance basis hold values for that instance. They come into existence usually on first usage, as opposed to a formal declaration of name and type found in many programming languages. Instance data access is made through the reference **self.instanceData1**, for example. While instance data variables can be defined in any method for an instance, doing so in __init__(), as a policy, establishes an expectation as to where to find all instance data definitions and their initial settings.

- *Instance Method Definitions:* Class **methods** define class behaviors. Each class definition provides a set of method definitions. A method definition consists of a method name along with a set of parameters which together defines the method signature, and an implementation as code. As for the parameters, the first parameter is "self", which for the instance access refers to the class instance itself. Note that, when called, "self" is not explicitly passed, e.g., **instance.method1(args)**. It is worth noting that while method signatures must be unique, methods can be defined with the same name provided the signatures are unique, e.g., deposit(dollars) verses deposit(dollars, for_account_name).

- *Class and Static Methods:* Python provide two method variants that have a more global nature, in that they are called independent of any class instance. In both cases, there is a signature as described. A class method's signature has, instead of "self", a "cls" variable as first parameter which references the Python class object itself. The other parameters are as before. A class method is called, e.g., **class.method_namer(args)**. Static methods on the other hand have neither self nor cls as a first parameter. They are called by object or class as before, but the again the first argument is neither self nor cls.

Properties

On the topic of instance data definitions, the related topic of Python ***properties*** is worth highlighting. While instance variables are accessible by name both inside or outside the class definition, sometimes getting and setting an instance variable to some value might require additional processing above and beyond merely accessing the instance data directly. However, accessing instance variable data along with the additional processing through new user defined methods would only add to the complexity of class usage. Python properties is a feature that provides for that extra processing while maintaining simple user access to instance data. An outline for defining properties is as follows:

```
@property
def account_name(self):
    # Additional processing
    return self.name

@account_name.setter
def account_name(self, name):
    # Code to determine the name value
    self.name = new_name
    return
```

The decorator '@property' is used to declare the getter method, while @name.setter prefixes the setter method. In usage, for example, one simply calls **instance.account_name** to get the account name, and **instance.account_name='Valerie'** to set the account name.

Multiple Inheritance

In regards to multiple inheritance, it is important during object instantiation to not only initialize the main object, but each instantiated superclass by calling the __init__() method for each superclass. Consider the following modification on the Account class example. In this case, suppose Account inherits from both Bank and Client. In that case, Account's initialization includes initializing data for both Bank and Client. When an Account is constructed, full data of each is expected in Account's __init__() signature, and the Account must then pass the appropriate initialization data to the superclass' initialization methods.

Following along to this example, we have Account derive from, or more specifically, inherit from the classes Bank and Client. This is a case of multiple inheritance. A sketch of how to specify this in Python is given below.

```
class Account(Bank, Client):

    def __init__(self, bank_record_data, client_record_data):

        Bank.__init__(self, bank_record_data)
        Client.__init__(self, client_record_data)
```

We see in this example the two superclasses for Account are Bank and Client and are specified in the class definition. Also, the __init__() for Account has two additional arguments, one an unspecified amalgam of data about the bank, and one about the client, which are used to initialize Bank and Client respectively. Observe that the __init__() methods for both Bank and Client are called with the respective initialization data within the Account constructor. This is a very important step as it fills in critical data for the superclass instance for each class.

Python supports many of the characteristics of object-oriented design touched upon earlier, such as encapsulation, inheritance, and polymorphism. However, there is little to no data protection except by convention[11]. Regarding interface, it effectively consists of the data variables and methods defined in the class and is not a separate abstraction. Nonetheless Python does provide more than adequate object-oriented support for implementing object-oriented design.

This concise description of Python classes goes a long way toward understanding how to use them, and to understand how they are used in the context of this book. Further features of Python classes are discussed as they arise in the text. As always, one can refer to the many excellent textbooks on Python, such as [4] [5], for further information.

1.3   What Can Go Wrong in Object-Oriented Design

Any attempt to debate software design methodologies or discuss comparisons are met with strong opinions and perhaps heated discussion. Besides object-oriented, there are other design methodologies such as functional design, procedural design, and data-driven design. We will not discuss alternatives here but remain focused object-oriented design.

Considering prior discussion, one naturally wants to know if object-oriented design has problematic aspects, or pitfalls to avoid in its usage. We discuss two items along that line. One involves being overly motivated by object-oriented design ideals, and the other concerns coping with the inherent complexity one finds in applications/systems design no matter what methodology is seized upon, that OO design is not a panacea.

Over Abstraction

In looking at an application's data as class definitions, one might be tempted to detail the layers of abstraction to an extreme – wherein all application data must live within a large-scale object type schema. It is very easy when designing in abstraction, to derive many abstract layers even non-obvious ones, to glean additional relationships amongst object types, with additional data to track or methods to construct, not for relevance to the application, but for the sake of completeness. One outcome, for

---

[11] One often finds in Python that protected or private data is prefixed with a single underscore, and methods with two underscores. This is simply a convention for protected data access, and not an outright enforcement.

example, is for the class hierarchy to expand from say three layers deep to five layers deep, even though the initial model sufficed for the application. Some objects that were single inheritance become multiple inheritance, and so forth. Sometimes these kinds of expansive architectures are quite necessary, and sometimes they only burden the schema and coding effort needlessly, and in the end make an architecture that becomes difficult to navigate with some largely useless design enclaves.

This happens many times on a first encounter with object-oriented design, when novices "see objects everywhere", and end-up coding to an ideal instead of a practical application. Perhaps the best practice is that when deriving class schemas, watch for object types, relationships and inheritances that lack relevance to the needs of the application and/or do not fill any application needs. At that point, it is good to reconsider the current and future goals of the project design. As one simple example, if a system designer feels a need to derive their own integer or real number class, it might be a good time to retreat and question the true necessity for making that kind of decision and judge the necessity of that impact across the application, now and in the future.

Correcting a schema after first application release can be a difficult and thankless task, especially when removing these kinds of design elements.

Concurrency and Side-effects

It is important as well to not confuse the benefits of object-oriented design with general coding practice. Depending on the application, you still must deal with for example, concurrency issues. You still must deal with potential side-effects sometimes stemming from processing side-effects, e.g., unexpected data value changes during transactions. These don't go away simply because you use object-oriented design, and sometimes a correct object-oriented design to address these issues can be difficult.

Still Requires Good Practice

This leads to the final consideration, that object-oriented design is not a panacea for treating all the ills of programming. Many of those remain. We might point out, that even within the confines of object-oriented design, you should be encouraged to devise meaningful class, variable, and method names, and avoid cramming too much semantics into one place, for example, a Python file, i.e., putting multiple classes into a single file.

While much has been accomplished in programming and program design over the last few decades, application/system design and coding remain difficult tasks, and require skill, continual diligence, and attention.

1.4   The Meaning of Music Representation

Building on the prior sections, the term 'music representation' has two aspects. For one, it means articulating the comprehensive set of music theory concepts, their semantics, and their relationships. In another, it means the embodiment of these concepts as software design classes, class relationships, their associated data properties, and methods. In this book, music representation is a software modeling exercise, with a focus on thinking and detailing the translation of music concepts to object-oriented terms.

What this means is that music concepts such as tone, pitch, scale, and chord are to be defined as Python classes. In all cases, it involves detailing and defining the data each class holds, as well as their behaviors as methods. These classes become constituents to a class hierarchy. Among other things, this exercise involves examining which music concepts are more fundamental than others, and which music concepts are derivative concepts of others, and so forth. In all, translating music theory into Python classes is a rigorous effort and a very rewarding one. It forces one to be reflective about domain concepts, to detail what they mean, and how music concepts relate to each other. It forces one to fill in knowledge gaps, and to acknowledge edge cases that are often overlooked, towards building a complete and consistent view of the domain.

Music students should find this study interesting in that it necessarily entails rigorous definition of music theory concepts, even to the point of articulating with precision the most fundamental ideas. For example, what distinguishes tone from pitch? Many times, terms like these are used loosely and inter-changeably, perhaps with meaning inferred from usage context. Here however, each concept, like any of these, is defined with precision and accuracy. It is an essential point in software modeling that concept definitions have well-defined semantics.

Computer science students accustomed to working with class hierarchy definitions will appreciate this rigorous formalism on music theory.

2 The Chromatic Scale and the Diatonic Foundation

Among the most fundamental concepts of music training and music theory education are the sounds of different tones or pitches[12] on one or more instruments. We come to know and identify them and distinguish similarities and differences among them both within and across instruments. Eventually we see them in larger coherent organizations, understanding tonal relationships in broader terms, such as intervals, scales, and chords. Due to certain unvarying and recognizable characteristics about pitches, these larger concepts have a marked stability that make music possible across the space of instruments. With the help of educators, we learn the formal and larger organization of these concepts in what we call *music theory*, and further apply this theory in music composition, analysis, and performance.

We begin our musical journey similarly with a focus on tones and pitches, and likewise explore their structure around the chromatic scale as our starting point. From the chromatic scale, we look at seven tones that become the foundation for naming all tones. As we will see later, these primitives build a foundation for further music theoretical artifacts such as intervals, scales, chords, etc.

We begin with a brief informal survey of Western music foundations by examining the Pythagorean scale and its subsequent evolution. Our exploration continues to the 12-tone equal-tempered chromatic scale which defines the space of tones and pitches that will be used throughout the text. We develop the diatonic or 7-tone structure that is imposed on the chromatic scale as a larger concept we term "the diatonic foundation". This structural relationship between diatonic tones and the chromatic scale is core to the foundations of scales, intervals, and chords that are discussed in detail later.

We finally pivot to the software modeling viewpoint, developing tone and pitch Python classes as the foundation of music representation in software. Subsequent music concept representations are built upon the representations defined here. This co-development of music theory and software representation returns throughout the remainder of the book.

2.1 The Pythagorean Scale

The history of defining tones and creating pitches for music traces back to antiquity. A pitch has a frequency measured in cycles per second, which can be imagined as the vibrational rate of a plucked string, say, as in a harp. For our starting point, the Grecian ideas on tone and pitch, in the context of the Pythagorean scale[13], represents a case for building a suite of consonant or agreeable sounding pitch/frequencies based on vibrational frequency ratios.

---

[12] In informal discussion tones and pitches are many times used synonymously. Later these are more precisely defined.

[13] So named as being attributed to the famous Greek mathematician Pythagoras.

D. P. Pazel, *Music Representation and Transformation in Software*, https://doi.org/10.1007/978-3-030-97472-5_2

The construction of this ancient scale is based on creating pitches with frequencies based on fractions or ratios one pitch's frequency relative to another pitch's frequency. This is sometimes referred to as an interval, however, intervals have a more precise meaning discussed later. Select a pitch of some frequency as a root pitch. For the root pitch, intervals relative to the root based on doubling that frequency were considered in some sense related, of having a strongly discernable sameness. Other ratios to the root pitch were also noted as significant. In particular, the root pitch's frequency multiplied by 3/2 corresponding to a pitch a ***perfect fifth*** interval higher to the root was considered important. Two pitches a perfect fifth apart were consider in some sense pleasing and were given the characterization ***consonant***, as were many pitches with intervals expressed as ratios of small integers, e.g., 3/2, 4/3, 6/5.

The root pitch frequency multiplied by 2/3 is the frequency of the ***perfect fourth*** to the lower identical root (1/2 the root frequency). Accordingly, the frequency a perfect fourth above the root is 4/3 (2 * 2/3) of the root frequency.

The process for generating a Pythagorean scale is based on using the perfect fourth and fifth intervals just discussed. It involves generating 7 tones successively using each interval, and applying some appropriate powers of 2 or 1/2 to the frequencies to contain the generated pitches within twice the root's pitch frequency, that is, making the pitches' resulting ratios contained in the ratio range [1 .. 2]. This results in deriving a sequence of notes between the two pitches considered nearly synonymous. In other words, it derives a scale.

As a demonstration of Pythagorean scale derivation, consider Fig. 2.1 below which outlines the derivation of the Pythagorean 12 tone scale. (We use standard note annotations here for referential purposes only.)

							2/3 ←——|——→ 3/2					
Gb	**Db**	**Ab**	**Eb**	**Bb**	**F**	**C**	**G**	**D**	**A**	**E**	**B**	**F#**
64/729	32/243	16/81	8/27	4/9	2/3	1	3/2	9/4	27/8	81/16	243/32	729/64
128/729	64/243	32/81	16/27	8/9	4/3			9/8	27/16	81/32	243/64	729/128
256/725	128/243	64/81	32/27	16/9						81/128	243/128	729/256
512/729	256/243	128/81										729/512
1024/729												

Fig. 2.1 Pythagorean scale derivation using the factor 3/2 successively to the right, and 2/3 to the left. Each column shows the doubling or halving necessary to get the ratio to within one octave, i.e., within the interval [1 ... 2].

Starting at C we derive pitches a perfect fifth higher in succession to the right until F#, making 7 notes. Then, starting at C, we derive the pitches a perfect fifth lower in succession to the left until Gb, again making 7 notes. This gives a total of 13 pitches. The frequencies are normalized to C having a ratio 1. According to construction, all the derived pitch ratios must be in the interval [1 .. 2]. To achieve this, after applying the appropriate multiplier for the pitch ratio, we then reduce the pitch by applying sufficient factors of 1/2 (or 2 for fifths lower) so that the resulting ratio per pitch lies in [1 .. 2]. (Shown in each column) We get our final 13 pitches. Then, sorting the resulting ratio values we have the resulting scale shown in Fig. 2.2.

In total the construction produces 12 tones, akin to the Western 12 tone chromatic scale. However, there is an issue. In the derivation of the 7 tones in each direction, there are two tones, F# and Gb, that are quite close in ratio values but not the same. Ideally, we would like these to match to make a perfect scale that we could repeat at double or half the root, and so forth. This misalignment causes problems, which in that time were relieved with various pitch omissions [11]. In any case, despite its consonant sounds, the Pythagorean scale is a flawed if not problematic scale system for music.

Fig. 2.2   Pythagorean Scale Ratios,final ratios after reduction in Fig. 2.1

```
C  - 1
Db - 1.05
D  - 1.13
Eb - 1.19
E  - 1.27
F  - 1.33
F# - 1.42, Gb - 1.40
G  - 1.5
Ab - 1.58
A  - 1.69
Bb - 1.78
B  - 1.90
```

The eventual solution involves altering the factors to make the pitches in some sense "evenly spaced", while preserving the notion of consonant sounds that the ratio approach of the Pythagorean scale achieved. As we will see, the eventual solution was to have identical ratios for any two consecutive ascending pitches. This leads us to the discussion of the equal-tempered chromatic scale.

2.2   Just Intonation and Equal-Tempered Chromatic Scales

The awkwardness of the Pythagorean scale was addressed in several ways. A technique called *just* or *pure intonation* was developed that in some ways is a brute force technique to make the scales work by constructing the other 11 pitches from the root pitch using interval ratios consisting of small whole numbers, which are considered consonant as discussed above.

Fig. 2.3   Just Intonation Ratios - small number ratios are a basis for just intonation tuning.

```
C  - 1/1
C# - 16/15
D  - 9/8
Eb - 6/5
E  - 5/4
F  - 4/3
F# - 7/5
G  - 3/2
Ab - 8/5
A  - 5/3
Bb - 9/5
B  - 15/8
```

Fig. 2.3 shows ratios used for just intonation. The downside of this approach is that some instruments so tuned will only sound good in the key to which it is tuned. Using other tones as keys will be out of tune, and so the instrument needs to be re-tuned for other keys [12] (See exercise 2.4.1.)

Following to just intonation is the notion of *well-tempered* tuning, in which slight perturbations on pitch tuning achieve making major and minor keys sound good on a keyboard. There are many such schemes, with mixed results. Reference Werckmeister temperaments [13] for an example.

A variant of well-tempered tuning that eventually found widespread acceptance is *equal-temperament*, resulting in an improved tuning scale over ancient scales in avoiding consonance issues, while providing pitch consistency across octaves. The idea behind well-tempering is that through 12 tones, any two consecutive ascending tones have identical ratios, namely $2^{1/12}$, or roughly 1.059, while by necessity successive octave pitches have a ratio of 2. The successive multiplication of each pitch's frequency by $2^{1/12}$ for the successor pitch's frequency results in evenness in the tonal space, while at the same time approximating reasonably well the ancient ratio-based pitches providing consonant sounds. The scale ratio uniformity also provides stability of tuning for other keys, i.e., one tuning is good for all keys, avoiding the problems of just intonation, in addition to those of the Pythagorean approach. This 12-tone equal-tempered system is sometimes referred to as 12-EDO or 12-TET.

Why 12 notes and not 10 or 15? In part at least, the answer is that 12 solves an optimization problem that, remarkably, preserves the benefits of the just intonation consonant pitches while avoiding its deficits. In reference to Fig. 2.3, it turns out that "the twelve-tone equal-tempered scale is the *smallest* equal-tempered scale that contains all seven of the basic consonant intervals to a good approximation — within one percent — and contains more consonant intervals than dissonant intervals."[14] [14]

Furthermore, a 12-tone pitch set based on a root pitch can be extended to lower or higher pitch ranges using the same equal-tempered ratio thereby extending to a larger range of pitches. For the purposes of this book, any range of pitches derived in this manner from the 12-tone equal-tempered scale is called a ***chromatic scale*** and is the foundation for the tonal space referenced throughout the remainder of the book.

While the above provides a constructive means for computing chromatic pitches, the precise pitch range of chromaticism must be determined. More precisely:

- What is the frequency range of the chromatic scale that we will consider? That is, what are the lowest and highest pitch frequencies?

- Is there one frequency that can be selected as a tonal center for the chromatic range, from which all other pitch frequencies can be derived using the equal-tempered ratio of $2^{1/12}$?

Knowing the answer to the second question, lower and higher pitches are easily computed. But how many? Where does it start and end?

The answer to the second question, based on tuning standards, is 440hz[15] [15], which is what we know as the A above middle C, notated as A4. As to the first question, there is no definitive answer as each musical instrument is constrained to specific natural ranges. However, the range of the modern standard keyboard is broad, well established and encompasses the pitch ranges of nearly all other commonly used musical instruments. The keyboard range is from 4 octaves below A4 to 4 octaves above middle C (C4), for a total of 88 individual pitches based on the equal-tempered scale. Notationally, these refer to A0 and C8 respectively. We refer to any two successive pitches of these 88 pitches as being a ***semitone***, or ***half-step*** apart.

As an exercise for understanding the chromatic scale structure introduced above, we break down a pitch reference as tone and octave and address how to index each pitch in the chromatic scale. We then show how to compute between the pitch's reference structure and its index in the chromatic scale.

As there are 12 sequential chromatic pitches per frequency doubling, the 88 semitones are divided into adjacent groupings, each comprising 12 consecutive semitones. The convention we use is for each group to start on a C pitch. Each group is called a ***chromatic partition*** or simply ***partition***, or ***octave***. In this manner, any semitone in the chromatic scale can be designated by a combination of an octave number and a 0-based[16] offset into the partition. We assume octave numbering is also 0-based in such

---

[14] The basic consonant intervals are octave, perfect fourth, and fifth, major and minor third, and major and minor sixth.

[15] Hz or Hertz is a unit of frequency taken to be one vibrational cycle.

[16] 0-based means the first offset is 0. In 1-based, the first offset is 1.

a way that C4's octave is the fourth octave. We call this pair of numbers the pitch's ***chromatic location***, i.e.,

(octave number, offset in octave)

Expressed as chromatic locations, the chromatic scale then comprises the pitches:

(0, 0), (0, 1), ... (0, 11), (1, 0) ... (1, 11), (2, 0) ...

Using this notation, the standard keyboard range is from (0, 9), the lowest A on the keyboard, to (8, 0), the highest C on the keyboard. Again, we use 0-based numbering for octave and tonal offset, i.e., partition 0 is the first partition, and semitone 0 is the first pitch C. Note that (4, 0) corresponds to middle C, and (4, 9) to the A above middle C that is usually 440hz, as mentioned earlier.

Looking at this another way, the pitches in the chromatic scale are sequential and so can be counted or indexed, again 0-based. Going with that scheme, (0, 0) corresponding to index 0, and A0 or (0, 9) having index 9. Fig. 2.4 shows these relationships.

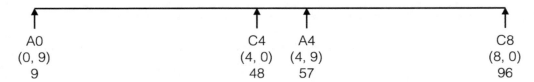

Fig. 2.4 Chromatic Scale and Pitches
Showing the layout of the chromatic scale and the placement of significant chromatic pitches.

Conversions between chromatic location and index are based on the formulas:

$$(octave, offset) = 12 * octave + offset \qquad (2.1)$$

$$index = (\frac{index}{12}, \qquad index \% 12) \qquad (2.2)$$

The division by 12 above is integer division, meaning use the integer part and discard the fractional part or remainder.

To clarify on terminology, in discussing ***tones*** we are talking about any of the 12 semitones of an octave, regardless of octave. For example, the 3rd tone (D) refers to the 3rd semitone in any partition. Consequently, there are only 12 tones. ***Pitch,*** however, references both the partition number and the tone's offset. Recapping, tone references to the offset in any octave location, but pitch is a precise chromatic location.

2.2.1   The Chromatic Scale Representation

The prior chromatic scale discussion provides an entry to discussion about software representation and its Python code embodiment. We consider the construction of the ChromaticScale Python class and translate the location/index conversion logic given above to code.

To start, there is no reason to have multiple instances of a ChromaticScale. There is only one, and we can reference it as a single object with global access. With that in mind, we develop the ChromaticScale class as a *static class* meaning that it contains only static methods and constants. There is an argument that static classes make for a less preferable representation of global characteristics, and that instead, non-class (i.e., global function) based code would be a qualitatively less complex representation with equal efficiency. However, for pedagogical purposes, we generally insist on looking at the world in terms of classes and class instances. Besides, global static data and methods wrapped as a class provide a consolidation of related global elements under a unified theme or concept. The class provides a global singular reference point for related activity and data. Furthermore, doing so preserves viewpoint consistency over the entire code base, wherein everything is viewed through an objectified lens.

The ChromaticScale class is of limited use in the code base and exists mainly to summarize the topics of this chapter as well as easing into case studies of Python classes for musical elements. More experienced programmers may ask why not used the singleton design pattern (refer to [10]) for the implementation. The answer is that the topic here does not require that level of complexity. For example, this class does not rely on more complex superclasses, nor does it require cloning or the like.

A portion of the ChromaticScale class definition is shown below. The class consist of constants that are static to the class as well as a number of methods which are also static. In the case of the methods, the Python decorator "@staticmethod" declares that the following method is static for the class. As with chromatic locations discussed earlier, we represent pitches as Python tuples of numbers (octave, offset). The methods above replicate the two conversion formulas (2.1) (2.2) presented earlier.

```python
class ChromaticScale:

    NUMBER_OF_SEMITONES = 12
    CHROMATIC_START = (0, 9)
    CHROMATIC_END = (8, 0)

    CHROMATIC_FORM = r'([0-8]):(10|11|[0-9])'
    CHROMATIC_PATTERN = re.compile(CHROMATIC_FORM)
    . . .
    @staticmethod
    def location_to_index(pitch):
        return ChromaticScale.NUMBER_OF_SEMITONES * pitch[0] + pitch[1]

    @staticmethod
    def index_to_location(index):
        return index // ChromaticScale.NUMBER_OF_SEMITONES, index %
            ChromaticScale.NUMBER_OF_SEMITONES

    @staticmethod
    def parse_notation(notation):
        n = ChromaticScale.CHROMATIC_PATTERN.match(notation)
        if not n:
            return None
        return int(n.group(1)), int(n.group(2))
```

Several constants related to chromatic scale are defined including:

- NUMBER_OF_SEMITONES: indicates the number of equal-tempered tones in a chromatic scale octave.

- CHROMATIC_START, CHROMATIC_END: in tuple notation denotes the chromatic locations (octave, offset) for the start and end tones of the full chromatic scale

- SEMITONE_RATIO: denotes the value $2^{1/12}$, which is the multiplier to derive a tone's frequency from its predecessor tone's frequency.

This class introduces a powerful Python means for converting strings to binary information that can be used within representational objects or for calculations. This technique is used frequently in the code base. In this simple case, we convert a textual pitch location expression into a Python tuple for chromatic scale reference. For example, we can parse the text "4:6" (meaning octave 4, offset 6) into the Python tuplet (4, 6). Python regular expressions are discussed thoroughly in [16]. The pattern for this case is held by static variable CHROMATIC_FORM as r'([0-8]):(10|11|[0-9])'. The 'r' means the text should be understood as a regular expression. This expression can be read as "start with an integer between 0 and 8, followed by a ':', followed by an integer between 0 and 11".

The seemingly odd positions of 10 and 11 in the regular expression simply give parsing precedence to 10 and 11, where if placed after [0-9], the parser would pick up 1 and ! on the second 0 or 1. The regular expression is then processed or "compiled" into a Python pattern, the result of which is held by CHROMATIC_PATTERN. The static method parse_notation() takes a string input, matches it against the pattern, and returns the chromatic location, octave and offset, as a Python tuple (after conversion from string to integer).

Here is a simple example of these static methods' usage:

```
location = ChromaticScale.parse_notation("4:9")      # parse "4:9" to tuplet (4, 9)
print(location)
index = ChromaticScale.location_to_index(location) # convert (4, 9) to 57
print(index)
loc = ChromaticScale.index_to_location(index)        # convert 57 to (4, 9)
print(loc)

(4, 9)
57
(4, 9)
```

To see further examples of ChromaticScale usage, the reader is encouraged to read, run, and step through the corresponding test file test_chromatic_scale.py.

2.3   Tones, Pitches, and the Diatonic Foundation

The diatonic foundation is a way of viewing the chromatic scale through a subset of seven specific tones, with the remaining five being modifications of those seven. It provides a tonal reference system, and an organizing tonal filter, that provides a foundation for diatonic scales (e.g., major, minor) and more. The origin of this filter is not clear but may be related to following from C in major 5ths until, with the exception of B, only dissonant sounds are encountered.

Fig. 2.5 shows seven distinct semitones per chromatic 12-tone octave. These tones are labelled solely with alphabet letters, in order {C, D, E, F, G, A, B}, and for referential purposes here are called the *basic diatonic tones*. The remaining five tones are considered *augmented tone* variations of the neighboring basic tones. All 12 tones are called *diatonic tones*. Each labeled tone is identically positioned within each octave. In other words, the same label assignments (basic and augmented) are made to the tones in each octave. It should be noted that any 12 consecutive semitones, regardless of first tone's location, is called an octave as well. This convention works well for scales introduced later, but in the context of the discussion here, octaves have C for their first tone.

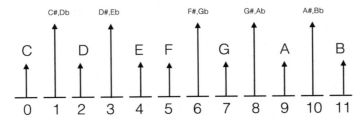

Fig. 2.5 Tonal Positions in the Diatonic Foundation. This figure shows seven basic diatonic tones (shorter arrows) along with the remaining five tones (longer arrows being chromatic modifications to the seven.

The position of the basic diatonic tones, i.e., C through B, over a 12-tone octave is given by a list of distinct semitone offsets {0, 2, 4, 5, 7, 9, 11} from the beginning of the octave, which correspond to {C, D, E, F, G, A, B}. The remaining five tones arise through augmentations of neighboring basic tones. The standard *augmentations* are given by the symbols {bb, b, #, ##} which correspond to { -2, -1, 1, 2} semitone offsets respectively. These specify deviations on basic tones to derive the augmented tones.

More precisely, a diatonic tone is specified by a basic diatonic tone label (e.g., C, D, ...) in combination with any one or none of the augmentation symbols (e.g., Ab, C#). For example, F## is a diatonic tone based on F and the ## augmentation. This tone's chromatic offset is 5(F) + 2(##) = 7, and Gb is chromatic offset 7(G) - 1(b) = 6. For completion, but not shown in the above diagram, for C there is Cb, Cbb; for B, B# and B##.

Based on the above arguments, diatonic tones are not unique to chromatic offset. In other words, a chromatic offset may correspond to several tones. To list a few, for offsets 3 and 6 respectively,

D# == Eb == Fbb, F# == Gb == E##

The tones in these equivalences are called **enharmonic tones**. While the existence of enharmonic tones may seem problematic, or at worst a flaw to the diatonic system, they provide a solid foundation for scale construction. Later we will see which enharmonic is used for a tone in a scale is contextually based and logical and determined by the type of the scale within which one is working.

It is important to point out that the diatonic foundation as described here is a fixed conceptual structure that provides a map of pitches to sound frequencies, an ordering and structuring of tones within all octaves and for all pitches, along with tone and pitch naming. It is a foundational artifact for the rest of music theory as described here. While its layout is observed to be identical to the C major scale, that is in fact incidental. Major scales are constructed relative to any pitch on the diatonic foundation.

Each octave starts on C and comprises a collection of 12 diatonic tones. Octaves are numbered 0, 1, 2 ... The terms chromatic partition, partition, and octave are often used interchangeably and that usage should be noted particularly in the Python code.

The combination of an octave with a diatonic tone is called a **diatonic pitch**. A textual representation for a pitch is "tone:octave"[17]. For example, middle C is "C:4" and the standard A 440hz pitch is "A:4". An equivalent tuple-based representation more suitable for programming and algorithms is the **diatonic location** representation of (octave, diatonic pitch), such as (5, C#), (3, D), (6, Fbb), etc., which will be seen later.

---

[17] This is synonymous to what is known as Scientific Pitch Notation (ref. ref. https://en.wikipedia.org/wiki/Scientific_pitch_notation).

For example, computing a chromatic index from a diatonic location becomes:

(octave, tone) —> (octave, (basic_tone, augmentation))

   —> (octave, (basic_tone_partition_offset, augmentation_offset))

   —> 12 * octave + basic_tone_partition_offset + augmentation_offset

For example,

(4, Db) —> (4, (D, b))

   —> (4, (2, -1))

   —> 4*12 + 2 - 1 = 49

Finally, the C tone-based orientation for octaves on chromatic partitions is common practice, say, as opposed to making A the start[18]. We point out that for ***transposed instruments***, such as horns in F, etc. that at least notationally, a score marking for C sounds other than given by our discussion. For example, for a horn in F, a C in a score is a marking for F. In many ways, transposed instruments illustrate the importance of defining a diatonic foundation as a basis for sounds/frequencies, as opposed to, say, scales which are simply relative overlays over the diatonic foundation tones and pitches that is shown later. We will not dwell on this topic right now. Transposed instruments are more fully discussed later.

2.3.1   Diatonic Tone Representation

The class DiatonicTone represents individual tones without regard to octave. This is our first presentation of a non-static music related entity. That is, the user creates instances of DiatonicTone, each with its own identity and characteristics. Reference tonal_model/diatonic_tone.py in the code base.

```
class DiatonicTone(object):
    # Constructor
    def __init__(self, diatonic_name):
        diatonic_info = DiatonicTone.parse(diatonic_name)
        if not diatonic_info:
            raise Exception('Illegal diatonic pitch specified {0}'.format(
                                                        diatonic_name))

        self.__diatonic_letter = …
        self.__augmentation_symbol = …
        self.__diatonic_symbol = self.diatonic_letter + self.augmentation_symbol
        self.__diatonic_index = …
        self.__augmentation_offset = self.__tonal_offset = …
        self.__placement = …
```

We begin by looking the data DiatonicTone keeps per instance that defines what a diatonic tone represents, shown above. The constructor takes the name of the tone as string, parses it, using a parser much as was introduced in ChromaticScale. Looking inside the constructor code we see seven fields define the object. With that, we have the following fields:

• **__diatonic_letter**: the letter part of the tone e.g., the C in C#.

• **__augmentation_symbol**: The augmentation part if any, e.g., the # in C#.

---

[18] This is surprising given the significance of the A:4 tuning mentioned earlier.

- **__diatonic_symbol**: a standardized textual format for the tone, e.g., C#, using upper case for the diatonic letter, even if specified as "c#" in constructor input.

- **__diatonic_index**: index of diatonic letter, e.g., C—>0, D—>1, E—>2, etc.

- **__augmentation_offset**: numerical value of augmentation, e.g., bb—>-2, ##—>2.

- **__tonal_offset**: chromatic offset of the diatonic letter plus the augmentation_offset.

- **__placement**: the actual position (offset) for the note on a 12-tone partition. See below.

The distinction between tonal_offset and placement is very important and deserves explanation. Diatonic locations can sometimes 'spill over' to neighboring octaves, as we will see with pitches. For example, Cb:5 is identical to B:4, and B#:5 is identical to C:6. The attribute tonal_offset provides an offset relative to the start of an octave. In that case, Cb has -1 as the tonal_offset, and 12 for B#. Placement indicates which of the 12 tones (origin 0) in an octave the tone represents, accounting for tonal_offsets that are out of the [0, 11] range. In this case Cb is 11 (B), and B# is 0 (C). The attribute tonal_offset is useful in calculations across the full chromatic scale, especially for determining the actual octave a pitch is in. The attribute "placement" on the other hand precisely points out the correct tone regardless of partition.

```
class DiatonicTone:
    # Basic diatonic tone letters.
    DIATONIC_LETTERS = list('CDEFGAB')
    # Regex used for parsing diatonic pitch.
    DIATONIC_PATTERN_STRING = '([A-Ga-g])(bbb|bb|b|###|##|#)?'
    DIATONIC_PATTERN = re.compile(DIATONIC_PATTERN_STRING)
    # Diatonic C scale indices
    DIATONIC_INDEX_MAPPING = {'C': 0, 'D': 1, 'E': 2, 'F': 3, 'G': 4, 'A': 5, 'B': 6}
    # Semitone offsets for all diatonic pitch letters
    CHROMATIC_OFFSETS = {'C': 0, 'D': 2, 'E': 4, 'F': 5, 'G': 7, 'A': 9, 'B': 11}
    # All augmentations in text representation
    AUGMENTATIONS = ('bbb', 'bb', 'b', '', '#', '##', '###')
    AUGMENTATION_OFFSET_MAPPING={'': 0, 'b': -1, 'bb': -2, 'bbb': -3, '#': 1,
                                '##': 2, '###': 3}
    DIATONIC_OFFSET_ENHARMONIC_MAPPING = {
        0: ['C', 'B#', 'Dbb'],
        1: ['C#', 'B##', 'Db'], …
```

Diatonic tone includes several constants that are useful across the code base, such as:

- **DIATONIC_LETTERS**: the list [C, D, E, F, G, A, B].

- **DIATONIC_INDEX_MAPPING**: giving the index of a diatonic letter.

- **CHROMATIC_OFFSETS**: giving diatonic letters to chromatic offset.

- **AUGMENTATIONS**: listing the valid set of augmentations as string.

- **AUGMENTATION_OFFSET_MAPPING**: mapping augmentation (string) to a displacement value.

- **DIATONIC_OFFSET_ENHARMONIC_MAPPING**: For each offset, the set of enharmonic diatonic symbols.

The reader can look over the set of methods provided by DiatonicTone. Of note is the inclusion of overrides to __eq__(), __ne__(), and __hash__(). These are useful for comparing tones for identity.

The concept of *diatonic distance* is useful later. Given two tones, tone1 and tone2, the diatonic distance from tone1 to tone2 is the number diatonic letters from tone1 to tone2, less 1. An orientation is assumed that tone2 succeeds tone1. For example, the diatonic distance from C to D is 1. The same is true for Cb to Db. The diatonic distance from E to D is 6 with the diatonic letters path being [E, F, G, A, B, C, D]. The formula in Python for diatonic distance is simply:

$$diatonic\_dist = (tone2.diatonic\_index - tone1.diatonic\_index) \% 7 \qquad (2.3)$$

as Python always computes a positive modulus, in precisely the way that this distance semantics requires.

2.3.2   DiatonicToneCache

A total of 49 unique DiatonicTone instances can be constructed. Later when we construct Note's we will create many diatonic pitches, each pitch having a diatonic tone. Doing so results in needlessly high storage allocation. Since the 49 instances of tones never change, it would be better if diatonic tones could be reused throughout the code base.

A cache for DiatonicTones provides a means for reuse. The point of having a cache is that all diatonic tones can be created once and referenced and retrieved by their diatonic symbol.

The DiatonicToneCache class is a singleton class. This class has only one instance. The instance is created exactly once and never exposed, but only used as a caching mechanism for accessing tones by name. DiatonicToneCache has only one property, __diatonic_map, a python dictionary, mapping the diatonic tone's symbol to its DiatonicTone instance, e.g., Eb, to the instance of DiatonicTone for Eb.

The map's key is based on text normalized to lower case. So, diatonic tones are retrieved by first lower casing the input text. With that requirement, requests for Eb and eb return the same tone.

```
class DiatonicToneCache:
    DIATONIC_CACHE = None

    def __init__(self):
        self.__diatonic_map = {}
        self.__build_diatonics()

    @staticmethod
    def get_cache():
        if DiatonicToneCache.DIATONIC_CACHE is None:
            DiatonicToneCache.DIATONIC_CACHE = DiatonicToneCache()
        return DiatonicToneCache.DIATONIC_CACHE

    @staticmethod
    def get_tone(tone_text):
        cache = DiatonicToneCache.get_cache()
        return cache.get_cache_tone(tone_text)

    def get_cache_tone(self, tone_text):
        return self.__diatonic_map[tone_text.lower()]
```

```
def __build_diatonics(self):
    for ltr in DiatonicTone.DIATONIC_LETTERS:
        for aug in DiatonicTone.AUGMENTATIONS:
```

A few implementation details of DiatonicToneCache are shown above. The class has a map (__diatonic_map) as described earlier and populates it with all the legal tones. The static method get_cache() creates the cache singleton and puts it in the static variable DIATONIC_CACHE (Why? See exercise 2.4.11). The static method get_tone() is commonly called, and first calls get_cache() to get the cache, then queries the map for the diatonic tone by symbol name in lower case.

Finally, the method __build_diatonics() populates the diatonic map by looping over all letters over all augmentations and mapping the lower case diatonic symbol to the created DiatonicTone.

2.3.3   Diatonic Pitch Representation

DiatonicPitch represents a diatonic tone in the context of a specific octave. This class is non-static, which like DiatonicTone means that instances are created. Looking at its properties, we have:

```
class DiatonicPitch(object):
    def __init__(self, octave, diatonic_tone):
        self.__octave = octave

        if isinstance(diatonic_tone, DiatonicTone):
            self.__diatonic_tone = diatonic_tone
        else:
            self.__diatonic_tone = DiatonicFoundation.get_tone(diatonic_tone)
        self.__chromatic_distance = 12 * octave + self.diatonic_tone.tonal_offset
```

DiatonicPitch has three properties:

- **__octave**: the octave of the pitch.

- **__diatonic_tone**: the DiatonicTone instance for the tone.

- **__chromatic_distance**: the chromatic distance of the pitch, or index in semitones relative origin 0. This is a useful calculation to have completed and have readily accessible for later use in the code base.

Note that the initializer code has unusual semantics around the second argument, diatonic_tone. In many cases, it is useful to construct the pitch by specifying that argument in string format, e.g., "D#" or given as a DiatonicTone instance. The "if" check using the system method "isinstance" decides which representation of tone was passed via diatonic_tone.

Overloading the diatonic_tone argument like this is not necessarily good practice. Testing instance types can become a maintenance headache as other tone representations are considered. However, Python does not offer much help in this situation having only a single signature for __init__(). One approach is for __init__() to take three parameters: octave, tone as string, and tone as object, using named parameters for the latter two, as well as default values. Requiring only one of the last two arguments as not None requires further code checking.

Another approach is to add an alternative static construction method with parameters octave and say, tone as a DiatonicTone instance. Then you use standard or alternative construction means depending on what is wanted. However, the disadvantage is that the user must recall or know about the alternative construction means. Each way of approaching this problem has advantages and disadvantages which a designer/coder must weigh. Here type checking for string or DiatonicTone within the constructor is sufficient and convenient enough to use in this case.

Like DiatonicTone, DiatonicPitch includes a string parser to facilitate creating DiatonicPitch using strings. The string should be specified in the following format:

(letter)(augmentation_symbol) : (octave)

Examples include C:4 or c:4, Db:6, etc. The diatonic pitch object is created in the following manner:

diatonic_pitch = DiatonicPitch.parse(string)

The regular expression and parsing logic are given below:

```
DIATONIC_PATTERN = re.compile(r'([A-Ga-g])(bbb|bb|b|###|##|#)?:?([0-8])')


@staticmethod
def parse(diatonic_pitch_text):
    if not diatonic_pitch_text:
        return None
    m = DiatonicPitch.DIATONIC_PATTERN.match(diatonic_pitch_text)
    if not m:
        return None     diatonic_tone = DiatonicToneCache.get_tone(m.group(1).upper() +
                                    ('' if m.group(2) is None else m.group(2)))
    if not diatonic_tone:
        return None
```

The logic is relatively straight forward. The tone is first obtained, and the pitch is created. The key aspect of the logic is obtaining the parsed string's elements for calling arguments. Examples of creating DiatonicPitch are shown below:

```
pitch = DiatonicPitch(5, 'Eb')
print(pitch)
pitch = DiatonicPitch.parse('Fb:3')
print(pitch)
```
```
Eb:5
Fb:3
```

2.4   Exercises

2.4.1 Consider the just intonation consonant intervals:

    a.   2:1 octave
    b.   3:2 perfect fifth
    c.   4:3 perfect fourth
    d.   5:3 major sixth
    e.   5:4 major third
    f.   6:5 minor third
    g.   8:5 minor sixth

Compare these in ratio to the corresponding intervals in the 12-tone well-tempered scale. Determine an overall error estimate between these scales based on these tones.

2.4.2 Write a static method to find the nearest equal-tempered pitches below and above an input frequency. Pick one as the closest and quantify why it is the closest.

2.4.3 Construct other tempered scales and explore their accuracy to the consonant intervals of exercise 2.4.1, and to the 12-tone equal-tempered scale.

2.4.4 Build a sinusoidal sound generator in Python, and try various frequencies based on both Pythagorean and well-tempered scale to see how they compare aurally.

2.4.5 A static class is an example of singleton class, however using statics in this manner is typically not the way singletons are constructed. Discuss alternatives, their strengths, weaknesses, and practical considerations.

2.4.6 Design and build the diatonic tone cache as an incremental cache, that is, as a cache where new tones are added only on first creation. Can the cache be fully initialized at program load as opposed to first use using Python? If so, how?

2.4.7 In the code for DiatonicTone, is there any need to override __eq__, __ne__, and __hash__?

2.4.8 Much like tones have a cache, design and build a cache for diatonic pitches. Build one version with all members added on initialization, and another version that adds members incrementally (see exercise 2.4.6) with usage. Discuss the pros and cons of each approach.

2.4.9 Look carefully at DiatonicFoundation.map_to_diatonic_scale. What is the function of the map DiatonicFoundation.ENHARMONIC_OCTAVE_ADJUSTMENT_MAPPING? Hint: look at the enharmonic equivalences.

2.4.10 Discuss any issues regarding transposed instruments, and how/if the classes in this chapter need to address these issues.

2.4.11 Python uses a garbage collection scheme for freeing memory. The user rarely is required to explicitly free class instances, arrays, or the like. Why are DiatonicTones in the cache safely never freed in an application run lifetime?

2.4.12 Research the 24 equal tempered tonal system, 24-TET or 24-EDO, and discuss strengths, weaknesses, and considerations in composing or performing with them.

3 Intervals

Music intervals are conceptually significant in music theory. They provide a foundation for other musical concepts, including scales, and chords. Simply stated, intervals categorize relationships between two pitches. In doing so they define a qualifying connection between chromatic and diatonic degrees that proliferates throughout music theory.

The study of intervals can sometimes be very confusing. For example, there are defining rules regarding intervals with the same diatonic distance but qualitative sound differences, e.g., major, minor, that at times seem to make intervals less than formal, and more subjective in meaning. Much of this may be based on viewing intervals as an artifact of the diatonic major scale, that scale tones are in a sense perfect or major, and others less so. (Scales are a topic in themselves with their own complexities that will be studied later.) In this text, we do not pursue the approach of defining intervals through the diatonic major scale. Instead, by introducing intervals as a derivative of the diatonic foundation introduced in chapter 2, one sees intervals as a lexicon for tonal qualification differences along the chromatic scale and diatonic foundation that should simplify and bring order to this topic. That approach is something more foundational than seeing them only in the context of one kind of scale.

We begin this chapter with defining intervals and their characteristics. We distinguish simple from compound intervals and cover the basics of interval inversion. The discussion follows closely to traditional basic music theory. We then turn to a deeper analysis of intervals that expands upon the introductory discussion and extends our understanding of intervals. This includes a discussion of the interval negation and reduction, and finally interval addition.

Lastly, we move this analytical view to code where theory becomes practice and explore the Python Interval class and its defining characteristics, and how complex interval operations are implemented in Python.

3.1 What is a Music Interval?

An interval qualifies a relationship between two pitches, a starting pitch and an ending pitch, usually but not necessarily with the starting pitch lower than the ending pitch. Intervals are useful for:

- describing a quality relationship between two pitches, one relative to another, e.g., major, minor, perfect.

- defining a consistent descriptive template for pitch comparison across the chromatic scale, regardless of starting and ending pitch.

- being a building block for richer musical concepts such as scales and chords.

D. P. Pazel, *Music Representation and Transformation in Software*, https://doi.org/10.1007/978-3-030-97472-5_3

The intervallic relationship between two pitches is expressed as a combination of their diatonic distance and quality. For example, we have "perfect fifth", "minor third", "major sixth", and "octave". More precisely, an interval specifies a sound quality, e.g., perfect, minor, etc., and a diatonic distance, e.g., fifth, third, etc.

Intervals are not defined to specific pitches, but as relative relationships amongst pitch pairs based purely on their separation and quality. In other words, many pairs of chromatic pitches can have the same interval relationship. With that kind of relative identity, intervals provide a characterization for the qualities of sounds two pitches can produce together. Furthermore, as we will see, intervals can be defined as a combination of diatonic and chromatic distances, nicely formulating intervallic sound quality as a purely quantitative function of both parameters.

The quantitative part of an interval is called *interval distance*, much like diatonic distance as defined in the class DiatonicTone and is the number of diatonic tones (letters) between the start and end pitches. The interval distance is usually specified as an ordinal (that is, a positive integer) origin 1, and for this immediate discussion is limited to 1st, 2nd, 3rd, 4th, 5th, 6th, 7th, 8th.

Interval quality relates to something close to subjective observations about the interval's sound like happy, sad, spacey, etc. Five interval qualities are recognized:

Major (M), Minor (m), Diminished (d), Augmented (A), Perfect (P)

For the purposes of this text, we use the notation "q:d" for an interval, where

$$q \in \{d, m, M, P, A\}, d \in \{1,2,3,4,5,6,7,8\} \qquad (3.3.1)$$

For example, P:5 is a perfect fifth, and m:7 is a minor seventh. The 1st is also referred to as *unison* while an 8th is an *octave* which are qualitatively perfect, and so are denoted P:1 and P:8 respectively.

Not all combination in (3.3.1) are permissible. The rules for permitted interval types are:

- Of the 8 diatonic steps, the perfect (P) distances are the 1st, 4th, 5th and 8th.

- The remaining distances of the 8 diatonic steps are major (M).

- The perfect and major intervals are based on the chromatic distances $\{0, 2, 4, 5, 7, 9, 11\}$ introduced in 2.3.

- Minor (m) is one semitone less than a major,

- A diminished (d) is 2 semitones lower than a major, or one semitone lower than a perfect.

- An augmented (A) is 1 semitone higher than a major or perfect.

Note that there are no intervals P:3, P:6, etc. Also, there are no m:4, m:5, M:4, M:5 intervals and the like.

The quantitative measure that distinguishes intervals with the same interval distance, e.g., M:6, m:6, is their chromatic offsets. Consider the chromatic distances for the perfect and major intervals. The semitone distances $\{0, 5, 7, 12\}$ correspond to P:1, P:4, P:5, and P:8. The distances $\{2, 4, 9, 11\}$ correspond to {M:2, M:3, M:6, M:7}. While interval distance is only diatonic distance measured in diatonic steps, the interval quality is accounted for by variations in chromatic distances. Thus M:6 and m:6 are both 6ths, but with different chromatic distances, 9 and 8 respectively, accounting for the differing tonal qualities.

To demonstrate the deceptive nature of interval qualification and why chromatic offset alone is insufficient for categorization, contrast the interval P:5 from C to G, to the interval B to Gb. The chromatic differences in both cases are the same, 7, but the diatonic differences are not. C to G is a P:5 but B to Gb is d:6. Some might defer this as merely an issue with enharmonic equivalence, that Gb is really F#. But the notion of interval is actually quite precisely based on both kinds of distances that also has an impact on how one interprets notes enharmonically, i.e., that even enharmonic notes function differently in the context of intervals.

To recap on definition, an interval consists of two parts:

- A diatonic distance, giving the number of diatonic tones covered between two pitches irrespective of tonal augmentations.

- An interval quality designating quality of combined tones, that alternatively can be specified with chromatic distance.

All 28 possible intervals within an octave are listed in Table 3-1 below. Note that in this text we will continually reference intervals by diatonic distance and quality. However, they can as well be parameterized in terms of diatonic distance and chromatic distance. For computational purposes within a software implementation, this latter parameterization is far preferable.

The inclusion of octave (diatonic distance 8) in the interval table is interesting for several reasons. One is that the 8th diatonic pitch is in the succeeding octave! The reason for including the last octave note is practical, as it is common in music to speak of octave relationships along with the qualifications of octave sounds.

Intervals wherein the diatonic distance is within or at an octave are called *simple intervals*. Simple intervals repeat every octave, independent of starting tone.

Interval	Diatonic	Chromatic	Interval	Diatonic	Chromatic
d:0	1	-1	d:5	5	6
P:1	1	0	P:5	5	7
A:1	1	1	A:5	5	8
d:2	2	0	d:6	6	7
m:2	2	1	m:6	6	8
M:2	2	2	M:6	6	9
A:2	2	3	A:6	6	10
d:3	3	2	d:7	7	9
m:3	3	3	m:7	7	10
M:3	3	4	M:7	7	11
A:3	3	5	A:7	7	12
d:4	4	4	d:8	8	11
P:4	4	5	P:8	8	12
A:4	4	6	A:8	8	13

Table 3-1 28 simple intervals along with diatonic and chromatic distance parameters.

Another interesting aspect of intervals is that due to the chromatic augmentations, some intervals can 'spill' out of the range of an octave. On the low end, the d:1 (diminished unison) goes below the octave, and A:8 (augmented octave) goes outside above the octave.

It should be noted that d:1 is somewhat controversial in the literature and is not universally recognized. It is the only interval that swings to the opposite direction of how other intervals are defined. That is, it has a negative chromatic distance whilst the others are positive or 0. This causes complications and making sense of this in the broad picture of intervals is a goal for later discussions.

An aspect of Table 3-1 of interest and importance is that it identifies computational functions regarding diatonic and chromatic distances, as well as interval type. For example, we clearly see interval type specified by diatonic and chromatic distance[19]:

$$f: (diatonic\_distance, chromatic\_distance) \rightarrow Interval\ Type \qquad (3.3.2)$$

Also, chromatic distance is a function of diatonic distance and interval type:

$$f(diatonic\_distance, IntervalType) \rightarrow chromatic\_distance \qquad (3.3.3)$$

While noting that these kinds of relationships (3.3.2), (3.3.3) may seem to be an exercise in incidental knowledge, it helps in understanding the interval concept, and in the complexities of building a software system knowing these can at times prove very useful.

3.1.1   Compound Intervals

When diatonic distances exceed octave boundaries, e.g., 9th, 10th, 11th, 12th, 13th, ..., intervals are called *compound intervals*.

Here are several notable aspects about compound intervals:

1) Octave diatonic distances are 8, 15, 22, and so forth.

2) Compound intervals reduce to simple intervals by eliminating sufficient octaves. For example, P:12 is P:8 + P:5. So, P:12 is based on P:5. For our discussions, we call P:5 the ***reduction*** of P:12. Calculations for reduction follow in a later section.

Fig. 3.1 shows examples of compound intervals.

Fig. 3.1 Compound intervals and reductions

In the first measure we have examples of a major 10th and minor 13th respectively. To the right is the reduction of these to major 3rd and minor 6th respectively. The difference is mainly in sound, where the 10th is more "open" sounding and the 3rd has more of a "closed" sound.

---

[19] The function notation $f: (a, b) \rightarrow c$ can be read to mean that for each combination of a and b values, there is exactly one c value.

Compound intervals extend the range of interval definition and are frequently used by composers to achieve improved or unique sound qualities. Their importance will be felt later when we consider intervals as computational objects in intervallic arithmetic.

3.1.2   Interval Inversion

Intervals as presented thus far indicate pitch relationship with an orientation from a lower pitch to a higher pitch. Inversion simply provides their relationship with the pitches reversed. Given two pitches of an interval, the inversion of their interval is obtained by switching the upper and lower pitches, or in other words, using the end pitch as the start of the interval, and the starting pitch as the end. For simple intervals, this is achieved by moving the lower pitch an octave higher.

Fig. 3.2: Simple intervals and their inversions.

The relationships between intervals and their inversions are illustrated in Fig. 3.2. The first interval is a major 3rd. The inversion next to it is a minor 6th. It is constructed by moving the C:4 to C:5 as the higher note. The 2nd example is a perfect 4th, E:4 to A:4. The inversion is a perfect 5th and like the first example is constructed by moving A:4 to E:5. It is important to point out that the inverted interval is only a characterization of pitch separation generally, and in these examples, inversions are not in any way fixed to the pitches from which they are derived, i.e., a P:5 is a P:5 regardless of the pitch on which it starts.

The concept of interval inversion is important for several reasons:

- Inversions show up in chord inversions, wherein a note other than the root becomes the lower note, and so influences the sound of the chord.

- As a means for computing the start tone of an interval by using its inversion to find its end.

The rule for inverting simple intervals is as follows. Given an interval (n, t), where n is the diatonic distance, and t is the interval quality, the inversion is (9 - n, t') where t' is determined from t by the mapping:

$$M \rightarrow m, m \rightarrow M, d \rightarrow A, A \rightarrow d, P \rightarrow P \qquad (3.3.4)$$

Table 3-2 shows all possible interval inversions within the first octave. Notice the symmetry of the inversions, which, by the way, nicely accommodates the diminished unison. The application of the inversion operation to compound intervals is taken up later.

3.2   Interval Analytics

The discussion of intervals above, aside from some notational novelties, is very much in line with traditional teaching. In this chapter, we extend upon what has been presented to achieve a broader view of intervals as a computational system with interval computational objects. At the same time, we fill in gaps from the earlier discussion regarding compound intervals, unisons, and inversion. Doing so provides a richer and fuller context and preparation for interval representation and computation in Python

D:1→A:8	D:5→A:4
P:1→P:8	P:5→P:4
A:1→d:8	A:5→d:4
D:1→A:7	D:6→A:3
m:2→M:7	M:6→M:3
M:2→m:7	M:6→m:3
A:2→d:7	A:6→d:3
d:3→A:6	D:7→A:2
m:3→m:6	m:7→M:2
M:3→m:6	M:7→m:2
A:3→d:6	A:7→d:2
d:4→A:5	d:8->A:1
P:4→P:5	P:8→P:1
A:4→d:5	A:8→d:1

Table 3-2 Inversions

In Table 3-1 intervals and their diatonic and chromatic distances are presented. We saw that intervals are fully characterized by two integers, namely diatonic distance, and chromatic distance. In the following we will rely on that characterization of an interval, often designated here as a pair (d, c). To simplify computation and unlike in Table 3-1, d is given in origin 0, that is, P:5 = (4, 9), wherein d is 4, not 5. Similarly, the value c is 0-based. If we need the interval type, it can be easily computed from Table 3-1, mindful that the table uses origin 1 for diatonic distance.

3.2.1 Negative Intervals

For two given pitches, intervals in practice are constructed with a positive orientation. By that we mean that the starting pitch is lower than the ending pitch. In that sense, the interval is 'positive' by going from a lower to higher pitch. In examples where, for example, the objective is to compute the starting pitch from an interval's end pitch, the orientation is still framed positively by virtue of calling one pitch the start and the other the end, typically with the starting lower than the ending.

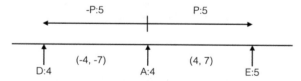

Fig. 3.3 Negative intervals. This figure contrasts "-P:5" with "P:5" along with respective numerical representations.

We introduce the notion of a negative orientation for an interval wherein the start pitch is higher than the end. In that case, we count diatonic and chromatic distances in the negative direction. This is the meaning of ***negative intervals***.

This situation is highlighted in Fig. 3.3. P:5 goes from A:4 to E:5, while -P:5 starts at A:4 and goes to the lower D:4. To clarify though, just bear in mind that counting diatonic steps follows that of the diatonic foundation mentioned in the prior chapter, but in reverse. The results may seem counterintuitive. Consider the case of the interval -M:2 starting pitch C:4. The downward diatonic count (1) gives B. However, the chromatic count (2) gives you Bb, and in the lower register making it pitch Bb:3! The point being, for this case, is that end points of negative major intervals may take you to different tones sets than you might find in end points of their positive counterparts.

In terms of representation, if I = (d, c) is an interval then:

$$Neg(I) \equiv (-d, -c) \qquad (3.3.5)$$

From (3.3.5)[20] it is easy to see that Neg(Neg(I)) = I, for any interval I. An interesting example is the unison interval wherein -d:1 = A:1 as well as -A:1 = d:1.

3.2.2   Interval Reduction

A compound interval is a combination of a simple interval with additional distance in octave units. For example, P:12 can be seen as P:8 + P:5. That is, P:12 is really a P:5 with a single octave extension. Knowing this makes P:12 relatable to the simple interval P:5. **Reduction** is an interval operation that computes P:5 given P:12. More precisely, reduction reduces an interval by octaves to a simple interval of the same sign.

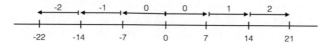

Fig. 3.4 Interval mark offs, both positive and negative

Reduction is a relatively simple computation, once you determine how many octaves are involved, which is purely determined by the diatonic distance, see Fig. 3.4. Recall that there are 7 diatonic tones in an octave (origin 0). So, octaves are covered in blocks of 7 consecutive diatonic pitches. In short, we can map diatonic distances to octave ordinals as in Equation (3.3.6).

$$Oct(d) \equiv 0 \; if \; d = 0 \; else \; ((abs(d) - 1) \; // \; 7) * sign(d) \qquad (3.3.6)$$

In Equation (3.3.6), abs(d) is defined as taking the absolute value of d, and sign(d) means use the sign of d, which is 1 for d=0 or positive and -1 for negative.

Reduction then is a simply a case of removing the octaves both diatonically and chromatically from the interval parameters as shown in Equation (3.3.7):

$$Red(I) \equiv Red((d, c)) \equiv (d - 7 * Oct(d), c - 12 * Oct(d)) \qquad (3.3.7)$$

A couple of simple examples follow:

Red(M:14) = Red((13, 23)) = (13 − 7*1, 23 − 12 * 1) = (6, 11) = M:7

Red(-m:16) = Red((-15, -25)) = (-15 − 7*(-2), -25 − 12 * (-2)) = (-1, -1) = -m:2

---

[20] Note the symbol ≡ is used to mean "is defined as". Here the operator Neg() is being defined.

3.2.3   Inversions

In this section we show the computational mechanics of interval inversion starting first with simple intervals then compound intervals. We further consider negative simple intervals and negative compound intervals.

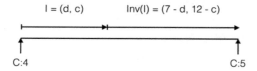

$$I = (d, c) \qquad Inv(I) = (7 - d, 12 - c)$$

C:4   C:5

Fig. 3.5 Inversion calculation

We begin with examining the inversion of a simple interval I. Let I = (d, c) with diatonic and chromatic distances d and c respectively. Being a simple interval, $0 <= d <= 7$, and $0 <= c <= 12$. The inversion is just the complement of the octave as illustrated in Fig. 3.5. The formula for computing the inversion of simple interval I is:

$$Inv(I) \equiv Inv((c,d)) \equiv P{:}8 - I = (7,12) - (d,c) = (7 - d, 12 - c) \qquad (3.3.8)$$

For example, Inv(d:6) = (7 - 5, 12 - 7) = (2, 5) = A:3.

Consider next the case of computing inversions of negative simple intervals. When taking the inversion of a negative interval, one wants the result to be semantically similar to that of positive intervals. That is, you should get the same resulting interval, however, to be consistent, the result should be a negative interval. For positive simple interval I,

$$Inv(-I) \equiv Inv(-(c,d)) \equiv -P{:}8 + I = (-7 + d, -12 + c) \qquad (3.3.9)$$

For example, Inv(-d:6) = (-7 + 5, -12 + 7) = (-2, -5) = -A:3

When working with compound intervals, be they negative or positive, the inversion formula is similar, but also applicable to the above cases:

$$Inv(I) \equiv sign(I) * P{:}8 - Red(I) \qquad (3.3.10)$$

Equation (3.3.10) says, that the inversion of a compound interval is the interval that complements the first octave based on its reduction, and is positive if the input is positive, and negative otherwise. One way of thinking about it, is that no matter how many extra octaves are involve, the inverse relates only to the octave "farthest out" to the end. The bottom line, and what is important, is that the complement of an interval has the same 'complementary' sound that we have in simple inversions within a single octave. This example works through the calculations for -P:12:

Red(-P:12) = Red(-(11, 19)) = Red((-11, -19)) = (7 - 11, 12 - 19) = (-4, -7) = -P:5

Inv(-P:12) = -P:8 – Red(-P:12) = -(7, 12) - (-4, -7) = (-7 + 4, -12 + 7) = (-3, -5) = -P:4

3.2.4   Interval Addition

With the interval operators introduced, one might sense a convergence to a 'kind of' an arithmetic on intervals, over the extended (i.e., including negative) interval range. We introduce interval addition and subtraction in this section. However, we qualify this arithmetic because not all additions and subtractions are possible. Despite this limitation, for the most part, the arithmetic is feasible and practical.

We begin by defining the two operations on two intervals I = (d, c) and J = (e, f)

$$I \pm J \equiv (d \pm e, c \pm f) \qquad (3.3.11)$$

Equation (3.3.11) serves as a straightforward definition. Addition can simplistically be imagined by laying out intervals end to end with the end of I adjacent to the start of J and taking the full resultant interval as the answer. For subtraction imagine the end of I adjacent to the end of J and take the interval from the start of I to the start of J. Refer to Fig. 3.6.

Fig. 3.6 Illustrations of interval addition (left) and subtraction (right).

Note that P:1 acts like 0 in addition:

I + P:1 = (c, d) + (0, 0) = (c, d) = I

Table 3-3 shows a subset of additions within the first octave in tabular form.

+	P:1	M:2	m:3	M:3	d:4	P:4	P:5	M:6	M:7
P:1	P:1	M:2	m:3	M:3	d:4	P:4	P:5	M:6	M:7
M:2	M:2	M:3	P:4	A:4	d:5	P:5	M:6	M:7	A:8
m:3	m:3	P:4	d:5	P:5	d:6	m:6	m:7	P:8	M:9
M:3	M:3	A:4	P:5	A:5	m:6	M:6	M:7	A:8	A:9
d:4	d:4	d:5	d:6	m:6	X	d:7	d:8	m:9	m:10
P:4	P:4	P:5	m:6	M:6	d:7	m:7	P:8	M:9	M:10
P:5	P:5	M:6	m:7	M:7	d:8	P:8	M:9	M:10	A:11
M:6	M:6	M:7	P:8	A:8	m:9	M:9	M:10	A:11	A:12
M:7	M:7	A:8	M:9	A:9	m:10	M:10	A:11	A:12	A:13

Table 3-3 Partial addition table for intervals within first octave

Notice that d:4 + d:4 = X. This is a case where the resultant interval not a valid interval:

d:4 + d:4 = (3, 4) + (3, 4) = (6, 8) = ?:7

A diminished 7th is (6, 9). So, (6, 8) is not a valid interval. In the extension of the table to other intervals, especially diminished intervals, this situation arises more frequently. However, especially when dealing with major, minor, and perfect summands, addition and subtraction is a practical operation. We find more utility in these operations when we get to scales and chords.

3.2.5   Afterword on Interval Operators

Mathematical minded readers would note that the set of intervals appear to take on a familiar operational semantics found in group theory. Recall that a set G of elements and a binary operator, say $*$, is a *group* if the following hold:

1.   Closure: for all $a, b \in G, a * b \in G$.

2.   Associativity: for all $a, b, c \in G, a * (b * c) = (a * b) * c$.

3.   Identity: $\exists i \in G$ *such that* $\forall a \in G, i * a = a * i = a$.

4.   Inverse: $\forall a \in G, \exists a' \in G$ *such that* $a * a' = a' * a = i$.

In the case where the group is *abelian*, we add the condition:

Commutativity: $\forall a, b \in G, a * b = b * a$.

Many of these conditions appear to be met by interval. Addition is a binary operator, P:1 appears to behave like an identity, and each interval has a negative which acts like an inverse. Associativity and commutativity properties appear to hold. However, the set of intervals is not a group. Firstly, additive closure does not hold as shown by the example d:4 + d:4. Also, addition is in fact not associative. However, this is not due of a case wherein the two side of the associativity equation yield different answers, but due of the non-closure of the additive operator (see exercises).

Despite these short comings in not being formally a group, that does not mean that interval addition is impractical. As mentioned, there are many cases that work fine, especially when limited to major, minor, and perfect intervals as summands. Minor and diminished intervals can cause issues as seen. Interval addition's effective use is seen in later chapters.

For readers interested in further study of group or field theory, there are many outstanding references, most notably [17], [18], [19].

3.3   Interval Representation and Implementation

The Python class representation for Interval is defined with two classes, IntervalType and Interval. The former defines the interval qualities of Major, Minor, Perfect, etc. The latter capture the concept of an interval and provides support for the operative dynamics defined in this chapter.

```python
from enum import Enum
class IntervalType(Enum):
    Major = 1
    Minor = 2
    Diminished = 3
    Augmented = 4
    Perfect = 5
```

IntervalType is simply a Python enumeration[21]. In this case the five types are equated with 5 sequential integers. This is typical for defined enumerations, although there are other ways to do this. Note that IntervalType inherits from Enum to make the class an enumeration. Within the class definition you will find a method that converts the enumeration type to the string shorthand introduced earlier, i.e., "M", "m", "d", "A", "P". This is used for printable output purposes.

Looking at the class Interval, the constructor __init__() takes two arguments, a diatonic distance as integer origin 1, and an interval type as given by an IntervalType enum value.

```python
class Interval(object):

    def __init__(self, diatonic_distance, interval_type):
        self.__interval_type = interval_type
```

---

[21] Python added enumeration support in version 3.

```
self.__diatonic_distance = …
self.__chromatic_distance = …
```

Interval is based on three properties:

- **__interval_type**: the interval type of the interval, as given by the IntervalType enum.

- **__diatonic_distance**: the diatonic distance covered by the interval, origin 0. This value can be negative for negative intervals.

- **__chromatic_distance**: the number of semitones covered by the interval, which can be negative for negative intervals.

Chromatic_distance is computed from the input arguments. The diatonic distance is passed as an origin 1 integer, as that is normal usage convention. However internally, we use origin 0, as that is more convenient for calculations. Interval retains these three values which are exposed to the user as properties, holding diatonic_distance in origin 0.

Note in the code that Interval has several tables to assist in checking and constructing intervals. INTERVAL_MAP in particular maps a diatonic_distance, chromatic_distance pair to IntervalType within an octave.

We also mention that Interval provides a second means for construction, the static method create_interval() which takes 2 pitches, and returns the Interval from the first to the second, as shown below.

```
def create_interval(pitch_a, pitch_b)
```

3.3.1   Negation, Inversion, and Reduction

The dynamics of interval negation, inversion, and reduction are discussed in 3.2. The implementation details track close to those dynamics earlier discussed. In examination of the code, the reader may note the care that is taken in making these kinds of calculations, which are not covered here. However, what is noteworthy is that each of these operations returns a new Interval instance, as opposed to changing the interval itself. Keeping each Interval instance immutable is yet another decision point about which an implementer needs to weigh the trade-offs.

The impetus for maintaining immutability over modifying the original is that operations like these are more likely to be used in sequence and incrementally, taking the intermediate results to apply to other operations. For example, when we look at addition, we might do the following:

interval_1 = interval.reduction() + interval.negation()

The semantics should be clear for what is wanted, but if interval itself was changed by reduction() and then by negation() one obtains a quite different semantics and result. Other reasons for immutability are given in 3.3.2.

3.3.2   Interval Addition and Operator Overloading

As in other languages, Python allows operator overloading. That is, one can define the behavior of operators, for example addition (+) , to allow a new semantics based on operand types. We explore how this is done with addition defined over Intervals. We begin with the intervals I_1, I_2, I_3 in the following:

$$I_3 = I_1 + I_2.$$

We first look at some code to perform the addition:

```
@staticmethod
def add_intervals(a, b):
    diatonic_count = a.diatonic_distance + b.diatonic_distance
    chromatic_count = a.chromatic_distance + b.chromatic_distance
    b_dc = diatonic_count % 7
    b_ct = chromatic_count - 12 * (diatonic_count // 7)
    return Interval(diatonic_count + 1, Interval.INTERVAL_MAP[(b_dc, b_ct)])
```

The static method add_intervals(a, b) defined in class Interval returns the sum of Interval instances a and b. Straight forward calculations are made for the new diatonic instance and chromatic distance. Also of note is a reduction calculation on these values in order to use INTERVAL_MAP to acquire the result IntervalType. Finally, a new summed interval is returned, with the diatonic distance passed to Interval in origin 1. The logic is very direct. However, note that in the code, there is another step to verify that the summation interval is valid using b_dc and b_ct.

To get to the goal of redefining addition to work with Interval instances, we have to overload, that is supplant Interval's native __add__() method. This method is easy to overload, especially with the add_intervals() method discussed above doing the hard work.

```
def __add__(self, interval):
    return Interval.add_intervals(self, interval)
```

This comprises the basics for an example of operator overloading in Python. Of course, there are many other details that go into an actual production implementation. For example, the data type of the interval argument should be checked to see if it is an Interval instance. Operator overloading can be an immense help in simplifying coding, providing the capability of expressing complex calculations through simple expressions.

Python provides many other possibilities for useful operator overloading. In class Interval, for example, the native method __iadd__() is overloaded. This allows one to express an in-[place add like this:

$I += Interval.parse('P:5')$

Other operator overload possibilities include, __sub__, __mul__, __div__ for subtraction, multiplication, and division, along with respective in-place methods as explained for __iadd__.

Class Interval also overloads the equality operator __eq__(). By default, in Python, an equality comparison of two intervals, I==J, returns true only when in fact I and J are the same interval instance. So, if one compares two distinct instances with value P:5, they are not the same. Overloading __eq__() provides a way to make that version of equality work. Similarly for the "not equals" comparison, !=, we overload __ne__(). See below for details.

```
def __eq__(self, other):
    return self.is_same(other)

def __ne__(self, other):
    return not self.is_same(other)

def is_same(self, other_interval):
    ...
    return self.interval_type == other_interval.interval_type and \
```

The __hash__() method overload provides for the creation of a hashcode for an object. It is important to make a class type reliably "hashable" in order to use its instances in a dictionary or set. These would not work for Interval in its default implementation. The rules for defining hashcode calculations are:

1. Over an instance's lifetime, the hashcode value must not change.

2. Instances that obey the intended definition of equality must have the same hashcode values. On this, __eq__() and __hash__() must agree.

3. The hashcode value should be based on immutable values.

In part, because of 3, operations on Intervals should return new distinct instances and not mutate the chromatic distance, diatonic distance, or interval type of an Interval instance. The code uses the hash-code value based on the interval instance's text representation as shown below.

```
def __hash__(self):
    return hash(str(self))
```

3.3.3   Exceptions

We mentioned earlier that interval addition can incur closure violations. That is, it is possible that two intervals cannot be added together. In code, one way to handle this situation is to throw an exception. For example, in add_intervals(), we have:

```
if (b_dc, b_ct) not in Interval.INTERVAL_MAP:
    raise Exception('Illegal Addition {0} + {1}    ({2}, {3})'.format(a, b,
                                              diatonic_count + 1,
                                              chromatic_count))
```

In this case, we detect that the interval is invalid based on IntervalMap values. The response shown is to raise a Python exception. In raising an exception, it is particularly important to provide a clear message about the reason for the exception. In this case, we include in the exception a string containing the textual representation of the two summands, as well as the resultant diatonic and chromatic distances. These are important clues for software developers to use to detect and fix errors. This is especially important as this error could arise as an intermediate result in a complex expression of interval arithmetic evaluation and the message provides the identities of the intervals in the offending calculation.

On the other side of this circumstance, the calling application code must be prepared for the possibility of an exception, and not assume that the potentially offending logic works all the time. In these cases, the code should be designed with "try ... except" clauses. Here is one example:

```
try:
    interval = I + K
except Exception as e
    print(e)
    # Take recovery actions
```

The idea is to bracket the logic that can raise exceptions between "try" and "except", and on failure, the code should deal with the error and take remediative actions. In an application every similar situation is unique ranging from simplistic like above or to entire application failure and recovery design architectures for handling exceptions of all kinds.

3.3.4   Computing Start and End Pitches

Much of Interval class comprises implementation of the interval dynamics described in this chapter. However, there are two methods of note that speak to interesting kinds of music algorithms and computations. These include computing the antipodal end pitches of an interval. For an interval, one deals with computing the end pitch given the start pitch, and another to compute the start pitch given the end pitch.

Consider the case of computing the end pitch from the starting. The gist of the logic is to compute the non-augmented end pitch using the diatonic distance. The logic then computes the augmentation to the pitch to encompass the chromatic distance. The diatonic pitch is then constructed.

```python
def get_end_pitch(self, pitch):
    diatonic_dist = pitch.diatonic_distance() + self.diatonic_distance
    tone_index = diatonic_dist % 7
    end_pitch_string = DiatonicTone.get_diatonic_letter(tone_index)
    end_pitch_octave = diatonic_dist // 7

    chromatic_dist = pitch.chromatic_distance + self.chromatic_distance
    normal_pitch = DiatonicPitch(end_pitch_octave, DiatonicFoundation.
                        get_tone(end_pitch_string))

    alteration = chromatic_dist - normal_pitch.chromatic_distance
    end_pitch_string += DiatonicTone.augmentation(alteration)

    return DiatonicPitch.parse(end_pitch_string + ':' + str(end_pitch_octave))
```

A trick for computing the start from end tone is by negating the interval and computing the end pitch:

```python
def get_start_pitch(self, pitch):
    return (self.negation()).get_end_pitch(pitch)
```

3.4   Examples

There are several ways to create intervals. One is by constructor, another by a parser over textual interval representations, and finally by specifying the interval with start and end pitches. These are illustrated in the following:

```python
interval = Interval(5, IntervalType.Perfect)
print(interval)
interval = Interval.parse("m:10")
print(interval)
interval = Interval.create_interval(DiatonicPitch.parse("a:3"), Diaton-
icPitch.parse("f#:4"))
print(interval)
P:5
m:10
```

The following example of interval addition and subtraction and their in-place forms are self-explanatory:

```
i1 = Interval(5, IntervalType.Perfect)
i2 = Interval.parse("M:3")
interval = i1 + i2
print(interval)
interval = i1 - i2
print(interval)
interval += i2
print(interval)
interval -= i2
print(interval)
```
```
M:7
m:3
P:5
-
```

Lastly, here are examples of computing the start and end of an interval:

```
interval = Interval(5, IntervalType.Perfect)
pitch = interval.get_end_pitch(DiatonicPitch.parse("F#:5"))
print(pitch)
pitch = interval.get_start_pitch(DiatonicPitch.parse("C:5"))
print(pitch)
```
```
C#:6
F:4
```

3.5   Exercises

3.5.1 Pick a scale with which you are familiar. Compute the intervals pitch-to-pitch, for an octave. Then recompute the scale pitches using only the pitch-to-pitch intervals. Do the same for various roots to see if the scales are produced correctly.

3.5.2. As in exercise 3.5.1, but this time, compute the intervals of each pitch relative to the scale's root. Then recompute the scale pitches using only the root-to-pitch intervals. Do the same for various roots to see if the scales are produced correctly.

3.5.3 Modify the addition/subtraction operations on DiatonicPitch to compute the antipodal pitch of an interval given the starting or end pitch. For example, for interval I and starting pitch P, develop the operation: P + I to produce the end pitch. Similarly, implement subtraction for P − I to produce the starting pitch. Discuss the semantics for I + P and I − P to see if they make similar sense.

3.5.4 Create a cache for intervals that span octaves -2 to 2 inclusive. Integrate the cache's usage into the create_interval() and parse() methods. Optionally, add a static method to Interval called get_interval() which acts like the constructor but uses the cache.

3.5.5 Show that the set of intervals under addition is not associative, that is, find a case where A + (B + C) != (A + B) + C, for intervals A, B, C.

3.5.6 By analyzing the behavior of diatonic and chromatic distance in class Interval, provide an explanation of the root cause of interval additive failure.

3.5.7 For compound intervals, inversion is defined so that the result is a simple interval. Consider if there are other definitions for inverse that preserve the "extra octaves".

3.5.8 Carefully examine the intervals -d:1, -P:1, and -A:1. How do these relate to A:1, P:1, d:1 respectively. What is the impact of these cases for negative intervals, interval identity, if any?

3.5.9 Suppose we redefine intervallic addition so that illegal additions use a locally min/max interval for its result. For example:

m:3 + m:3 = (2, -1) + (2, -1) = (4, -2) → d:5, instead of being illegal,

and similarly for additions that exceed augmented intervals. How does this definition affect commutativity, associativity, closure, etc.

4 Modality, Tonality, and Scales

Composers and musicians have discovered many interesting patterns or relationships within the 12-tone chromatic scale. Among these some take the form of tone patterns within an octave and replicated across all octaves, what we commonly refer to as keys or scales. Scales are a mainstay of Western music. It is often the first musical concept beginning students learn, and later becomes a daily fixture in composition, performance practice, and improvisation.

In this chapter we explore how scales are constructed, by first examining how scale types, or modalities, are defined as relationships between diatonic and chromatic offsets as a pattern. We re-examine modality's definition using intervals, and with that build a framework for defining and working with modalities. An extensive, familiar, and varied set of modalities is defined and examined through this modality framework. We then look at algorithms to compute the tones for any modality.

Tonality arises as a means to overlay modality patterns across the chromatic scale with a 'focus' on a given tone or key. When applied to a range of pitches across the chromatic scale, tonality produces an organization of pitches based on the modality with a focal tone, what we frequently refer to as a scale. This chapter looks at how pitch scales are constructed from tonality, that is, algorithms to compute pitches across a range of the chromatic scale for a given tonality.

Finally, we again look at this framework as a Python class structure. We consider the interactions between modality and tonality as classes and algorithms for computing scales.

4.1 Modality and Tonality

Modality is a cornerstone of music theory by which we define tone sets, or more precisely tone patterns[22] relative to an arbitrary starting tone. There are many ways to select sets of tones. However, we restrict ourselves to defining modality as a simple pattern of tones within a 12-semitone sequence or chromatic octave of fixed offsets from an arbitrary starting tone. The selection is stable and consistent in that for a starting tone, the same set of tones is selected for any subsequent or preceding chromatic octave in the chromatic scale.

This definition of modality provides us with standard scales such as major, several varieties of minor, and modal scales. It is also the foundation for various, less common scales such as whole-tone, blues, and pentatonic, to name a few. The flexibility of this modality definition allows scales to have more or less than the seven (diatonic) tones with which we are most familiar.

---

[22] The definition of modality may vary across references. In our usage, we mean scalar patterns. This is not to be confused with the concept of modal scales, e.g., Ionian, Dorian, Phrygian, etc. These are discussed as modes later in this book.

© The Author(s), under exclusive license to Springer Nature Switzerland AG 2022

D. P. Pazel, *Music Representation and Transformation in Software*, https://doi.org/10.1007/978-3-030-97472-5_4

4.1.1   A Traditional Approach to Modality

We begin with defining modalities with a basic, straightforward approach, traditional in nature, much as when most of us first learned scales. That is, we look at modality as defining a calculation on successive chromatic tones using a pattern expressed in terms of numbers of half-steps and a succession of letterings, independent of starting tone. For example, Eb major is computed as Eb, then 2 semitones to F, then 2 semitones to G, then 1 semitone to Ab, and so forth until we recycle back to Eb, and start all over again across successive chromatic octaves.

Making this approach more formal, each modality has an identity or name, that we will call a **modality type**. Examples include 'major', 'minor', 'whole-tone', etc. Modality provides a means for computing tones that belong to its modality type, independent of starting tone. As a general formula, we do this using two specifications:

1) **Chromatic Specification**: A means for specifying successive tones within a chromatic octave. Typically, this is achieved with a half-tone/full-tone sequence pattern, as we showed earlier.

2) **Lettering Specification**: A consistent means of letter assignment in a chromatic octave. That is, assigning any of A through G to the modality tones in a chromatic octave. More precisely, per modality type, regardless of initial tone, the tone-to-tone lettering increments are the same. Of course, appropriate augmentations, e.g., b, #, bb, ##, are made based on chromatic specification. For diatonic scales, lettering is implicitly assumed to include all diatonic letters in sequence with appropriate augmentations.

Modality then is a template, pattern, or specification for computing a set of tones. The combination of a modality and an initial tone to which the pattern is applied is called a **tonality**. The result of applying a modality to an initial tone produces a **tone set** also called a **scale**. Put another way, modality can be viewed an algorithm that, for an assumed but non-specific first tone, provides the calculations for other tones in succession, or iteratively. The chromatic specification is used to compute successive tones, and the lettering specification to name each tone, with appropriate augmentation.

For the chromatic specification, the means for identifying the tone subset within a 12-semitone sequence is given as a sequence of semitone offsets $\{o_1, o_2, ..., o_n\}$ called **chromatic** or **semitone offsets**, where the offsets are applied in succession for scale tone generation. That is, given an initial tone, the next is o_1 semitones after that, the next is o_2 semitones after that, and so on. The last tone generated is o_n semitones after the penultimate tone, and as a requirement to the definition of modality, that last tone would be the same as the first tone again for the next 12 semitone sequence.

The lettering specification ensures scales are consistently lettered across octaves regardless of initial tone. In traditional scale computations, successive tones take successive diatonic letters, as diatonic scales have 7 tones meaning that all letters are covered. However, less common modalities like the whole-tone scale uses 6 tones from the set 'CDEFGAB'. In this case, some letter in 'CDEFGAB' is skipped in tone lettering. When we say, "the lettering is consistent", what is meant is that for any whole-tone scale, regardless of initial tone, the relative letter skipped is the same, e.g., 2nd, 3rd, etc. Similarly, for modalities that require letter duplication, as is the case for octatonic scales, a consistent lettering policy insists on duplicating a diatonic letter and expect the same relative letter duplicated for whichever selected starting tone.

As an example of this process, the incremental chromatic offsets for the major modality are $\{2, 2, 1, 2, 2, 2, 1\}$. Based on this, Fig. 4.1 shows these semitones offsets on a 12-semitone chromatic octave. For example, assigning C to 0, we see the resulting tone scale is $\{C, D, E, F, G, A, B, C\}$. As an aside, take note of the chromatic distances from the root, in this case, $\{2, 4, 5, 7, 9, 11, 12\}$.

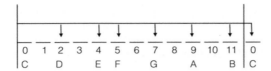

Fig. 4.1 Semitone sequence for major scale's chromatic consistency.

This set of **cumulative offsets** is easily computed from the incremental semitone offsets and provides an alternative way to compute the scale tones in lieu of using the incremental offsets. See exercise 4.5.1.

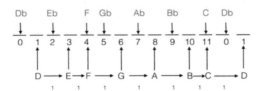

Fig. 4.2 Diatonic offsets determine scale lettering.

Lettering or *diatonic offsets* specification is much like that of semitone offsets just observed. It comprises a list of incremental letter offsets applied to the diatonic letters. For example, the major modality has the lettering offsets {1, 1, 1, 1, 1, 1, 1}. Referencing Fig. 4.2, given Db Major as root, we have: {Db, Eb, F, Gb, Ab, Bb, C}, meaning for each tone we bump the lettering forward by 1 giving {D, E, F, G, A, B, C, D}. For each scalar tone so lettered, an appropriate augmentation is required to align each tone with its chromatic position calculated from the semitone offsets. The incremental offsets and diatonic offsets, combined in this way, well-define modality.

For those primarily familiar with diatonic scales like major and minor, lettering consistency may seem too obvious in that all letters are used in succession. However, outside diatonic scales, the issue becomes important. For example, pentatonic modality has 5 tones per scale, leading to question which two diatonic letters should be skipped? For octatonic modality, there are 8 tones. Which 'letter' should be doubled? There are several ways to make these determinations. However, for the purposes of this text, we insist that the lettering is consistently applied per modality type regardless of starting tone as described above. This consistency provides an intervallic consistency described in the next sections. This provides a uniformity to tonal scale construction and interval calculation which becomes clearer as we change approach to this topic in the next section.

4.1.2   An Intervallic Approach to Modality

The traditional approach to defining modality, presented in the prior section, is simple, easy to teach, and interestingly extends very well to non-diatonic modalities like the pentatonic and octatonic. However, designing chromatic and diatonic offset tables can easily lead to problematic situations.

Consider the half-whole tone octatonic modality defined by these chromatic and lettering offsets:

offsets: {1, 2, 1, 2, 1, 2, 1, 2}

lettering: {1, 1, 1, 0, 1, 1, 1, 1}

With a lead tone of C, we get the scale {C, Db, Eb, Fb, F#, G, A, Bb, C}. While at quick glance this looks like an octatonic scale, eventually one notices the internal interval Fb—>F#[23]. There is no unison interval variant for that pair of tones (recall we are not allowing double augmented intervals). These types of situations are easily incurred with managed coordinated lists. One remedy for this modality is the following:

offsets: {1, 2, 1, 2, 1, 2, 1, 2}

lettering: {1, 1, 1, 1, 0, 1, 1, 1}

giving {C, Db, Eb, Fb, Gb, G, A, Bb, C} wherein all incremental intervals are well defined.

Rather than working with carefully synchronized lists of offset specifications, suppose we define modality based on intervals. After all, intervals are literally composed of chromatic offsets and diatonic lettering offsets, e.g., M:3 is 4 semitones and 2 diatonic letters. So, a single list of intervals is essentially a combination of chromatic and diatonic offsets. While it is still the case that inconsistencies as described earlier can still occur, at least one starts from a simpler, solid foundation than cumbersome synchronized offset lists.

For our first example of using intervals to define modality, we again look at the major modality and construct it using a sequence of intervals:

{P:1, M:2, M:2, m:2, M:2, M:2, M:2, m:2}

We call these intervals the modality's **_incremental intervals_**. The algorithm behind its use is that given a starting tone, we iteratively traverse the list's intervals to produce the successive tones from the last tone produced and so on, with the requirement that the last tone is the same as the first tone. Using the C tone as a starting point, we easily compute the tonal scale {C, D, E, F, G, A, B, C}.

While that works perfectly, we could alternatively express the modality in **_root-based intervals_**, that is, intervals starting with the root tone and ending at each scale tone. These intervals are relevant for chord construction, for example. In the prior case, we have as root-based intervals:

{P:1, M:2, M:3, P:4, P:5, M:6, M:7, P:8}

The root-based intervals are easily computed from the incremental intervals, and visa-versa, using interval addition and subtraction, which the reader is encouraged to explore.

There are good reasons to adopt an intervallic definition for modalities over the traditional teaching. First, it uses the foundational music concept of intervals as its basis, as opposed to coordinated offset lists. Secondly, its root-based interval aspect is highly relevant to chordal definition. Note that while the intervallic approach does not spare us from the aforementioned modality design issues, it is a more facile framework than offset lists for checking interval-related issues.

4.1.3   Counterexamples

While the intervallic approach to modality definition has clear foundational benefits, there are issues about which one should be aware.

One may be led to believe that a modality composed with incremental intervals would naturally have valid root-based intervals. Similarly, one may believe a modality with valid root-base intervals leads to a valid set of incremental intervals. Neither statement is correct, and the following counterexamples demonstrate both cases.

---

[23] It is important for all intervals to exist within a scale so they can be used to specify chords for the scale.

We first explore a counterexample to valid incremental intervals producing valid root-based intervals. Consider the modality constructed from the incremental intervals:

{P:1, m:2, m:2, m:2, M:2, M:2, M:2, A:2}.

Basing the modality on the C tone, we get the tone set:

{C, Db, Ebb, Fbb, Gbb, Abb, Bbb, C}

Amongst several issues, note that there is no valid root-based interval for C to Fbb!

For the converse case, consider the modality defined by the root-based intervals:

{P:1, d:3, M:6, M:7, P:8}

So, for C as root tone, we have the tone set {C, Ebb, A, B, C}. In attempting to produce the incremental intervals we have the case of Ebb to A for which there is no valid interval!

So, valid incremental intervals do not guarantee valid root intervals, and visa-versa.

Our final counterexample illustrates yet another false assumption related to root-based and incremental intervals. The false assumption is that even when incremental and root intervals are valid, that all other intervals are valid within the modality. Consider the tone set:

{Bb, C#, D, Eb, Fb, Gb, Ab, Bb}

produced by the incremental intervals {P:1, A:2, m:2, m:2, m:2, M:2, M:2, M:2} and root tone Bb. The root-based intervals are:

{P:1, A:2, m:3, d:4, d:5, m:6, m:7, P:8}.

Even with this consistency, we have the internal interval C#→Fb which is an invalid interval.

For a given modality, when the incremental and root intervals can be successfully derived from each other, and additionally, all intermediate intervals in the scale are valid, the tonal scale is called *perfect* for the purposes of this text.

It is preferable but not required for modalities to be perfect. Music is an art and open to originality, and one can compose music with modalities however defined. The point is that perfect modalities make working with them easier, at least in the classical sense and in other contexts, especially when we are assured that all intermediate intervals exist[24].

Common varieties of modalities along with their incremental intervals can be found in Appendix A.

4.1.4   Modes, Derived Modalities and Modal Index

A set of modalities referred to as *modes* or sometimes the *medieval church modes* are a set of modalities that, in common usage, derive from the major modality. Modes enjoy significant use in music generally and are very well known. For example, given the C major scale, we have the following modes:

- Ionian: {C, D, E, F, G, A, B}

- Dorian: {D, E, F, G, A, B, C}

- Phrygian: {E, F, G, A, B, C, D}

---

[24] Sometimes practical the way around this, in compositional practice, is to use enharmonic representations for tones. For example, C#-->Fb can be realized by C#→E (m:3) or Db→Fb (m:3).

- Lydian: {F, G, A, B, C, D, E}

- Mixolydian: {G, A, B, C, D, E, F}

- Aeolian: {A, B, C, D, E, F, G}

- Locrian: {B, C, D, E, F, G, A}

It should be clear that each derives from the C major scale by starting the scale on a different tone from C major, a pattern general enough to apply to any major scale. More generally, it is a technique that can be applied to any modality.

The derivations of incremental or root-based intervals for the modes are not given here but can be easily calculated. Instead, we focus on the generalization of this technique to arbitrary modalities. For a given modality, we know the pattern produces an ordered set of tones of fixed number. We introduce the concept of ***modal index*** as part of the definition of modality to indicate which of the generated tones should be considered the ***lead tone***, sometimes also called ***tonal center***. In the above example, the modality is major, and the 7 modes are indicated by modal index 0, 1,2, 3, 4, 5, 6. So, for dorian mode above, the modality is major, the modal index is 1, the ***basis tone*** for the tonality is C, but the ***root tone*** is D.

Another application of modal index can be found in the pentatonic modality. In this case, major, Egyptian, minor blues, major blues, and minor are simply different modal indices of the major pentatonic modality.

It is important to note that the seven modes given for the major modality are of such significance that they are considered modalities of their own (with modal index 0), even though they are modal derivatives of major. That is, we provide a dorian modality of mode 0, even though major modality with modal index 1 is the same modality.

4.2   Modality and Tonality Representation

At first thought, software representation of modality and tonality should be quite simply designed as a two-class system based on the following parameters:

- **Modality**: having an identifier (name), defining incremental intervals, along with a modal index, the value of which should be 0 by default.

- **Tonality**: having a modality and the specification of a diatonic tone serving as the first tone of its scale.

Logically and structurally, this is correct, but it is only where the work begins. We mention a couple of other relevant issues:

- The modalities mentioned earlier, such as major, minor, etc. are very common and useful. Any of these well-known modalities should be easily acquired without needing to explicitly construct by passing incremental intervals or other defining structures.

- The concept of modal index adds a level of complexity to the Modality class structure. A non-zero modal index means there is a distinct modality that serves as a basis for the derivation of the modal modality. This is a complication implying a non-trivial algorithm within the modality class to produce the incremental intervals and related properties properly.

And of course, there is a need for relevant data type and consistency checking at construction. Moreover, we would like sufficient flexibility in the design to allow users to define their own modalities and tonalities, with as little difficulty as possible.

4.2.1   Defining and Creating Modality

We take the above-mentioned issues in turn, but for now we consider the elements involved in building the Modality class. Definitionally modality requires a type or name, a set of incremental intervals, and a modal index. In chapter 3, we used a Python Enum to cover interval types. The Python Enum is very useful, but it is non-mutable, meaning we cannot dynamically add or delete enum types, which would be useful for user defined modalities. In this case, we will define "a kind of enum" that will allow us that flexibility:

```python
class ModalityType(object):
    def __init__(self, name):
        self.__name = name
    @property
    def name(self):
        return self.__name
    def __eq__(self, other):
        ...
        return self.name == other.name
    def __hash__(self):
        return self.name.__hash__()
```

This code for ModalityType is simple enough and easy to use for modality type creation, e.g., ModalityType("Major"). Of course, it is useful to override both equality and hash methods to ensure we can compare ModalityType instances and use them as keys in dictionaries and sets. This is often overlooked but ensures two instances with the same name are considered the same, and either can key/map to the correct value in dictionaries.

A modality definition also requires a defining list of incremental intervals. Since we have many known modalities to specify, one of the easiest and accessible means to specify them is as a string list, e.g.,

['P:1', 'M:2', 'm:2', 'M:2', 'M:2', 'M:2', 'M:2', 'm:2']

As a convention we specify P:1 as the first interval, and the last interval should compute the same tone as the starting tone but on the chromatic octave above the start. The string representations can be converted into Interval instances with the method Interval.parse().

Finally, bundling modality type and defining intervals to one place, we package both into a class called ModalitySpec. This is helpful for definitional purposes, for example, defining all known modalities as static data. ModalitySpec is created with a ModalityType and an interval string list of strings as discussed. We do not bundle modal index into this mix, as that is more a variational property of core modality that belongs as a parameter to Modality itself. Modality is constructed from an instance of ModalitySpec and a modal index (which defaults to 0). Using this Python class system, an example of creating a modality is as follows:

```python
from tonalmodel.modality import ModalityType, ModalitySpec, Modality

modality_type = ModalityType('my_modality')
incremental_interval_strs = [
    'P:1', 'm:2', 'M:3', 'm:2', 'm:2', 'M:2', 'A:2'
]
modality_spec = ModalitySpec(modality_type, incremental_interval_strs)
modality = Modality(modality_spec)
```

4.2.2   System Modalities

Let us address the first issue cited above, that of how to facilitate creating common *system modalities*, e.g., major, minor, pentatonic, etc. The class Modality can be used to build any modality specified by a modality type and the incremental intervals, both of which are found in ModalitySpec. Commonly used ModalitySpec's can be categorized, for example diatonic (major, minor), Pentatonic, Octatonic, etc. By creating a Modality subclass for each of these categories, we can include their ModalitySpec's as constant instances per category. As a convenience we provide specialized constructors to pass simply ModalityType and modal index (default 0), e.g., DiatonicModality(ModalityType.MelodicMinor). This gives us the following Modality subclasses.

- **DiatonicModality**: Comprises major and all minor scales, as well as the modal scales.

- **PentatonicModality**: Contains 5 pentatonic scale definitions.

- **OctatonicModality**: Contains half-whole and whole-half variants.

- **WholeToneModality**: Each tone is M:2 apart.

- **BluesModality**: Major and minor.

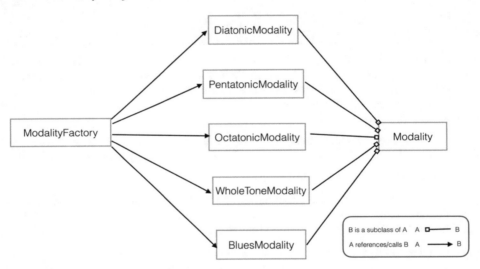

Fig. 4.3 Modality Inheritance and ModalityFactory registrations.

All of this is simply for organizational purposes. For example, if one had several modalities that fit into some modality category, you develop a category-named subclass of modality, and include the ModalitySpecs there, and so on. This aspect of the design is illustrated in Fig. 4.3. We will get to ModalityFactory later, but for now we see the five subclasses of Modality that define these system modalities.

Again, in case the point of all this is not clear, this design approach provides a much more convenient way to construct the system or common modalities, while at the same time preserves a means for user-specified modality, which will be explored in more detail later.

Using this software machinery, we can simply construct common modalities. Here are a few examples:

```
from tonalmodel.diatonic_modality import DiatonicModality
from tonalmodel.modality import ModalityType
from tonalmodel.pentatonic_modality import PentatonicModality
```

```
diatonic_modality = DiatonicModality.create(ModalityType.Major)
pentatonic_modality = PentatonicModality.create(ModalityType.EgyptianPentatonic)
```

4.2.3   Modality Factory

The Modality subclasses mentioned above make creating common modalities easier, but leaves the user needing to find the appropriate categorical class to create common modalities. That is, to create Major, you must import DiatonicModality; for pentatonic, PentatonicModality, etc. This is where ModalityFactory comes in. With ModalityFactory one only needs specify a modality type and optionally a modal index to create a modality. For example:

```
from tonalmodel.modality_factory import ModalityFactory
from tonalmodel.modality import ModalityType, Modality

major_modality = ModalityFactory.create_modality(ModalityType.Major)
pentatonic_modality_mode_1 = ModalityFactory.create_modality(ModalityType.MajorPenta-
```

The ModalityFactory class is a static class with a method to create a modality for a specified modality type. It is a variant of the design pattern Abstract Factory as found in [10]. The static method ModalityFactory.create_modality(modality_type, modal_index) is used to create the modality of a specified type. For that to work however, that type along with its ModalitySpec must be registered into ModalityFactory.

To elaborate, ModalityFactory maintains a dictionary keyed by ModalityType with value ModalitySpec. The register_modality(type, spec) static method provides a means for classes like DiatonicModality, and others to register type and spec as a setup step[25] towards making their modalities accessible via ModalityFactory. This is indicated in Fig. 4.3. The method create_modality() simply looks up the spec from the type, and so along with the modal index, creates the modality. If the type is not in the dictionary, the static class throws an exception.

Here is an example of how to set up a custom modality type:

```
from tonalmodel.modality_factory import ModalityFactory
from tonalmodel.modality import ModalityType, ModalitySpec, Modality

MY_MODALITY = 'my_modality'
modality_type = ModalityType(MY_MODALITY)
incremental_interval_strs = [
    'P:1', 'm:2', 'M:3', 'm:2', 'm:2', 'M:2', 'A:2'
]
modality_spec = ModalitySpec(modality_type, incremental_interval_strs)
ModalityFactory.register_modality(modality_type, modality_spec)
modality = ModalityFactory.create_modality(ModalityType(MY_MODALITY))
```

---

[25] In this case, modality registration to ModalityFactory occurs at library load before user code is executed. Depending on intended use and systems, the code for registration may need to be in ModalityFactory itself.

4.2.4   Modal Index, Incremental Intervals, and Tonal Scale

Modality builds a modality using a ModalitySpec and a modal index. For non-zero modality index, the incremental intervals should be reordered circularly so that scales can be computed with the initial tone corresponding to the modal index.

The reordering of the incremental intervals is visually demonstrated in Fig. 4.4. The diagram shows the incremental interval list for the Major scale on top. The modal_index here is three, which is Lydian mode.

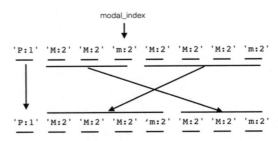

Fig. 4.4 Resetting Incremental Intervals to Modal Index

The blocks of intervals are moved as indicted in the figure, with P:1 leading the new interval list. For the most part, this is an exercise in recycling the list. The reader should attempt outlining the code with an eye towards maintaining the indexing correctly. The code can be found in the constructor for Modality, which at the same time, computes the root interval list.

For a second algorithm involving modality, consider given a modality and a root tone, generate the remaining tones of the scale in that modality starting with the root tone. Given a modality and its root-based intervals, the calculation is rather simple. [In fact, far simpler than if we worked with cumbersome chromatic and diatonic offset counts.] Each tone is acquired by computing the end tone from a root interval:

```
def get_tonal_scale(self, diatonic_tone):
    tones = []
    for interval in self.root_intervals:
        tones.append(interval.get_end_tone(diatonic_tone)
    return tones
```

Note the following example of usage based on the modality of the prior example:

```
modality = ModalityFactory.create_modality(ModalityType(MY_MODALITY))

tones = modality.get_tonal_scale(DiatonicFoundation.get_tone('Eb'))
print('[{0}]'.format(','.join(str(tone.diatonic_symbol) for tone in tones)))
[Eb,Fb,Ab,Bbb,Cbb,Dbb,Eb]
```

4.2.5   Tonality Representation

The representation of tonality is a combination of a modality and a diatonic tone representing the first tone of the tonality. This information is sufficient for constructing the more familiar tonalities with modal index 0. Non-zero modal index can be specified in the construction. To facilitate Tonality construction, we provide three ways to construct them:

```
# Use a modality instance (includes modal_index) and first scale tone
# (string or DiatonicTone)
Tonality(modality, first_tone)
# Use a modality type, first scale tone (string or DiatonicTone), and modal_index
Tonality.create(modality_type, first_tone, modal_index=0)
# Use a basis first tone (string or DiatonicTone), modality type, and modal_index
Tonality.create_on_basis_tone(basis_tone, modality_type, modal_index=0)
```

The following is useful Tonality instance information:

- **modality_type**: The type of the modality behind the tonality.

- **modality**: An instance of Modality.

- **diatonic_tone**: The first tone of the tonal scale

- **annotation**: The tonal scale starting with the diatonic_tone argument. This is computed by the Modality method get_tonal_scale() discussed earlier.

- **basis_tone**: The first diatonic tone for the modality exclusive of modal_index (as if modal_index=0).

All of these are computed in the Tonality constructor:

```
def __init__(self, modality, diatonic_tone):
    self.__diatonic_tone = diatonic_tone
    self.__modality_type = modality.modality_type
    self.__modality = modality
    self.__annotation = self.modality.get_tonal_scale(self.diatonic_tone)
    self.__basis_tone = (self.annotation[:-1])[-self.modal_index]
```

The calculation of basis tone is interesting. [:-1] clips off the final tone, and the negative index [-self.modal_index] locates the correct basis tone. The curious reader will find stepping though this calculation useful.

The following example shows three ways to create E-Dorian tonality:

```
from tonalmodel.modality import Modality, ModalityType, ModalitySpec
from tonalmodel.tonality import Tonality
from tonalmodel.modality_factory import ModalityFactory

tonality_a = Tonality(ModalityFactory.create_modality(ModalityType.Major, 1), 'E')
tonality_b = Tonality.create(ModalityType.Major, 'E', 1)
tonality_c = Tonality.create_on_basis_tone('D', ModalityType.Major, 1)

print('{0}:  [{1}]'.format(tonality_a,
                            ','.join(tone.diatonic_symbol
                                for tone in tonality_a.annotation)))
print('{0}:  [{1}]'.format(tonality_b,
                            ','.join(tone.diatonic_symbol
                                for tone in tonality_b.annotation)))
print('{0}:  [{1}]'.format(tonality_c,
```

```
                    ','.join(tone.diatonic_symbol
                        for tone in tonality_c.annotation)))
    -----------------------------------------------------------------------
D-Major E(1):   [E,F#,G,A,B,C#,D,E]
D-Major E(1):   [E,F#,G,A,B,C#,D,E]
D-Major E(1):   [E,F#,G,A,B,C#,D,E]
```

4.2.6   Pitch Scales

We demonstrated earlier the generation of tonal scales, which are represented by the "annotation" property of Tonality. However, to generate pitch-based scales, the computation involves applying that annotation over a range of the chromatic scale. While that capability can be built directly into the Tonality class, we will look at an alternative design. It would be useful to design pitch scale to include information about the tonality and chromatic range specified to build them, the parameters that produce that scale. By packaging the resulting scale with its generating input, we can build multiple pitch scales, each nicely packaged with its generative context from which one can query their constructive contextual elements. To do this, we make pitch scale a class of its own.

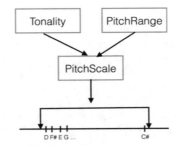

Fig. 4.5 PitchScale with input Tonality and PitchRange

Towards that end, we introduce a couple of helpful classes, shown in Fig. 4.5. PitchRange, based on Range, allow us to specify a range for pitches on the chromatic scale. The class PitchScale builds and retains a computed scale as well as the tonality and pitch range used to create it.

PitchRange is a subclass of Range, which is a very simple but practical class. It retains two integer properties, start_index and end_index, with start_index <= end_index. This class represents a range of integers from start_index to end_index, inclusively. PitchRange specifies a range as beginning and ending chromatic scale indices. To specify the range using textual scientific pitch notation, use the create() method.

Finally, PitchScale takes instances of Tonality and PitchRange and builds the scale based on the tonality that fits into the specified range, that is, the set of modality-based DiatonicPitches that maximally fits within the range, and accessible through the data property PitchScale.pitch_scale.

The relevant constructors from this discussion are:

```
PitchRange(start_chromatic_index, end_chromatic_index)
PitchRange.create(start_spn_as_text, end_spn_as_text)      # spn equals, e.g., "C:4"
PitchScale(tonality, pitch_range)
```

The algorithm for generating a pitch scale that adheres to a given pitch range is relatively straight forward. The tonality provides the tonal scale which serves as a template for the pitch scale. The gist of the algorithm is to find the starting pitch based on the tone in the tonal scale closest but higher to the start of the chromatic range. The others are found by cycling incrementally through incremental intervals whilst tracking chromatic index, until the loop is out of the bounds of the chromatic range.

The algorithm is sketched below. The function lowestInRange() finds the first Tonality tone in the chromatic range, along with its chromatic index. The convenience of using intervals is that in getting the end pitch, the correct octave number is computed, which otherwise would be a messy calculation to include within this code.

```
function build_pitch_scale(tones, incremental_intervals, chrm_range):
    (tone_index, chrm_index) = lowestInRange(tones, offsets, chrm_range)
    scale = [DiatonicPitch(partition_of(chrm_index),
                           tones[tone_index].diatonic_symbol)]
    prior_pitch = scale[0]
    while True:
        tone_index += 1
        if tone_index > len(self.tone_scale) - 1:
            tone_index = 1 # skip 0 as that should be P:1
        incremental_interval = incremental_intervals[tone_index]
        current_pitch = incremental_interval.get_end_pitch(prior_pitch)
        if current_pitch.chromatic_distance > chrm_range.end_index:
            break
        scale.append(current_pitch)
        prior_pitch = current_pitch
    return scale
```

As an example, suppose we want all the pitches of D melodic minor within a range C:4 to C:6 (inclusive). The following code provides a solution:

```
from tonalmodel.tonality import Tonality
from tonalmodel.modality import ModalityType, SYSTEM_MODALITIES
from tonalmodel.pitch_range import PitchRange
from tonalmodel.pitch_scale import PitchScale

pitch_range = PitchRange.create("c:4", "c:6")
tonality = Tonality.create(ModalityType.MelodicMinor, 'D')
pitch_scale = PitchScale(tonality, pitch_range)
print('Scale = [{0}]'.format(', '.join(str(pitch)
                              for pitch in  pitch_scale.pitch_scale)))
----------------------------------------------------------------------------
Scale = [C#:4, D:4, E:4, F:4, G:4, A:4, B:4, C#:5, D:5, E:5, F:5, G:5, A:5, B:5]
```

4.3   Exercises

4.3.1 Design, develop, and write algorithms to compute root-based intervals from incremental, and vice versa.

4.3.2 ModalityType takes a string argument to identify the modality. However, ModalityType is case sensitive. That is, while the string 'Major' gives you the Major modality, 'major' is unrecognized. How can ModalityType be altered to make construction case insensitive?

4.3.2 Explore what happens when you apply non-zero modal indices to a modal modality, for example the Aeolian of the Dorian modalities. Calculate a modal composition table over all possibilities. Is this composition commutative, e.g., Locrian of Phrygian = Phrygian of Locrian?

4.3.3 Design and/or develop a modality checker that validates a modality defined by a set of incremental intervals, that checks for valid root intervals, and valid internal intervals. What is the runtime expression for the algorithm?

4.3.4 Augment Range, PitchRange, and PitchScale so that chromatic ranges can be specified with start >= end, and thereby construct the pitch scale in descending order.

4.3.5 Explore the meaning of modalities and tonalities whose range is beyond an octave, e.g., having scales that are 12 or 15 tones with some note distances beyond an octave. Discuss design alterations for modality and tonality to accommodate those scales.

4.3.6 In octatonic scales, the A:1 is used to duplicate a diatonic letter. Explore other octatonic scales with A:1 in other positions in the incremental interval sequence, and validate the resulting scale, i.e., validate root-based and internal intervals.

4.3.7 Devise an operation to combine two PitchScales into one. Under what conditions would the combination operation be legal, e.g., same tonalities? Devise an operation to take a subrange within a Pitch-Scale.

5 Time in Music

In developing a music model, we need to measure time for marking music events positionally and for measuring event durations. By music events we mean many well-known musical objects such as notes, measures, beats, and so forth. All of these have an aspect concerning duration and time-based position in a piece of music. In this chapter, time in music is defined in different ways with different metrics. We focus on three meanings of time in music, their representations and discuss their differences. While these approaches to temporal representation are different and measure time in different metrics, they nonetheless can be converted one to the other, and the algorithms for those conversions are discussed.

It may seem odd to discuss time even before we discuss a proper definition of note, or even a framework for scoring. However, how time is defined in music is foundational to those items and can be defined before digging deeply into them.

We begin with an overview of three types of time measurement in music. The primary focus is on a time definition based on common note duration measurement, what we call whole note time. We discuss and define two artifacts that relate to and impact time measurement, namely time signature and tempo. We then show how to convert whole note time into actual time and vice versa. We also look at time quantified in terms of measures and beats, and its conversion to/from whole note time. We finish with a discussion of various software representational issues related to time in music, and how to approach them in Python.

5.1 Three Notions of Time in Music, an Introduction

As music listeners, we are usually use minutes or seconds, or even milliseconds, to mark musical events, or in gauging the length of a piece of music. We term this temporal measure as ***real time*** or ***actual time***. This temporal measure is of great importance in digital audio, where we care about marking music locations as real time measurements. This measure is used in coordinating music with non-music media, especially in soundtrack spotting in film scoring. However, compositionally, real time measurement is less important, as real time can vary significantly in performance interpretations of a score, making actual time imprecise for definitively marking a musical event's location in a music score.

While this is noted here and important for the reader to understand, time variability due to interpretive performance parameters is not considered in this discussion. For us, actual time is strictly parameterized by a score's markings, which we define precisely later. So analytically, the combination of beat, tempo, and note length all constitute elements that factor into, for example, a note's duration in actual time, as well as to the actual time of a musical event's location.

D. P. Pazel, *Music Representation and Transformation in Software*, https://doi.org/10.1007/978-3-030-97472-5_5

For musicians and composers, music event marking is typically based in a combination of measure and beat, for example measure 35 beat 2. Beat is usually a count of some note type, e.g., quarter note, per measure. In this text we refer to this form of time in music as **beat time**. More formally, it is a combination of measure number and beat number, indicated as (measure, beat). The beat number can be represented fractionally to increase the resolution of position within a measure.

A more homogeneous and consistent way to measure time in music is to accumulate a measure of sequential note durations from the start of the score. This measure is in units of whole notes, including fractional values of whole notes. For example, in a 3/4-time signature, the measure boundaries occur on {0, 3/4, 3/2, 9/4, ...}. For the purposes of this text, we refer to time in this sense as **whole note time (wnt)** or simply **whole time (wht)**, named after note's duration unit with the whole note measured as 1. Whole note time is the most uniform of the above-mentioned time measures and is the primary focus of discussion.

5.2   Whole Note Time: Measuring Time in Fractions

It is common practice to mark music event locations by measure and beat within a score. For example, the bridge on some song may occur on beat 1 of measure 45. Many times, measures are numbered on written scores, and the music event location is easily located between bar lines. However, there are problems with using measure/beat as a measurement from a representation viewpoint. The principal objection is its lack of uniformity. A score can change time signature many times in a score, meaning that either or both of beat definition and number of beats per measure can change. The point is that measures may not be uniformly defined in a piece of music, with the definition of beat and number of beats changing many times throughout the score up to any music event of interest. In any measurement scheme, it would be better to have a measurement that is more uniform or homogeneous over an entire score, avoiding potential issues as in beat and measure counting.[26] For software systems about music, a uniform measure for time provides consistency and reliability for representation purposes.

Fortunately, a uniform measure is readily apparent. We use the whole note as a unit of measurement and define the location or position of an event in terms of whole (or fraction of whole) notes from some starting position. As mentioned, we call this whole note time or whole time for short. This form of measurement is quite ideal, especially for software. Firstly, it is a uniform measure being based on the whole note whose value is taken as 1. Secondly, the whole note value of an event position is independent of tempo and time signatures that may change along the way to the event. Thirdly, and conveniently, in using whole time, event and note positions are based on the same measurement units used for note duration, e.g. eighth, quarter, half notes.

In this text, we will use **position** to indicate the whole note time of an event measured from some given reference point, by default, the beginning of a score. We use the term **duration** to indicate the length of some musical entity, e.g., note, sequential set of notes, etc., in whole note time.

As an example of whole note time usage, consider the following musical sequence of notes:

The duration values for the notes are clearly,

- 1/8 for the eighth
- ¾ for the dotted half

---

[26] We explore measure and beat as a measurement device later.

- ¼ for the quarter

- 3/16 for the dotted eighth

- ¼ for the rest

Adding these values in order, the positions for each note are:

- 0 for the eighth note

- 1/8 for the dotted half note

- 7/8 for the quarter note

- 9/8 for the dotted eighth

- 21/16 for the rest

Whole note time is represented as rational numbers, or fractions. Especially for software, the beauty of this representation is that it is exact while at the same time avoids issues with floating point approximation. Consider the following simple case:

The full duration of this three-note sequence is 1/4, making each note with duration 1/12. With that, the positions of the three notes are {0, 1/12, 1/6}. Note that adding duration 1/12 to the last note at 1/6 gives ¼, representing the full duration for the triplet. Whole note time is exact and precise, and well suited for software.

Looking ahead, position and duration, while based on WHT rational numbers, have their own semantics for operational interactions, which becomes a kind of arithmetic. Using p and d for position and duration WHT value types respectively, we have rules like:

- $p = p + d = d + p$, the sum of a position and duration is a position.

- $d = p1 - p2$, the difference of two positions is a duration.

- $d = r * d$, for rational r, r times duration is a duration.

Details of this arithmetic system are discussed later and its implementation is found in the referenced source code.

5.3   Time Signature and Tempo

Our goal in this chapter is to convert among whole time, beat time, and actual time, and to develop algorithms to do these conversions. While whole time is ideal for software, actual and beat time is best for user facing information, say during performance. So, having these conversions is meaningful.

Setting the stage for these algorithms, we derive a simple relationship involving whole time, beats and tempo. Music scores provide connections among these metrics by identifying beat note duration (found in time signatures) and tempo. What this means is that we have a beat note whose duration is in whole time units, and a tempo in beats per minute, which together provide a gateway to the conversion algorithms we seek. To be more explicit, assume we have the following values:

- M = some quantity of whole note time to convert to actual time.

- beat_duration = whole time value for a beat.

- tempo_rate = beats per minute.

Based on these three values. The actual time T is given by (5.1)

$$T = \frac{\frac{M}{beat\_duration}}{tempo\_rate} = \frac{M}{beat\_duration * tempo\_rate} \tag{5.1}$$

T is measured in minutes. For music software, T is usually measured in milliseconds. This unit has stronger affinity with computer music systems, as it is more compatible with sound production systems that use that measurement unit. That's why you may note the factor 60 * 1000 used to convert minutes to milliseconds found later on.

By the way. the inverse of this equation, (5.2), is useful for converting actual time into music time, and will be referenced later in this chapter.

$$M = T * beat\_duration * tempo\_rate \tag{5.2}$$

5.3.1   Time Signature

Time signature specifies a combination of beats per measure and beat type. For example, a 3:4 time signature specifies 3 beats per measure, where a beat is a quarter note. The '4' however is just a short-hand for a 1/4 whole note time value for the beat duration. We use the notation TS(beats, beat duration) to specify a time signature. For the prior example, we have the time signature TS(3, 1/4) meaning 3 beats per measure where the beat value is ¼ (quarter note) in whole time value. The ¼ implies a beat note of a quarter note.

For time signature specification in software, it can be argued that it would be better to simply specify a duration value for the beat, instead of the note shorthand. This generalizes the notion of time signature, as there is no constraint on the beat value being a standard note duration value, nor derivative thereof.

The value of this representation is best seen in compound time signatures[27] where the beat duration and beat note are different. For example, the 6:8 time signature could be specified as TS(2, 3/8) which provides an accurate beat measurement, which is not the case for TS(6, 1/8).

5.3.2   Tempo

Tempo is a beats per minute specification. By default, it specifies beat rate for the beat note specified in a time signature. So, for a 4:4 time signature, tempo defines the beats per minute in terms of quarter notes per minute.

However, for compound time signatures in which the beat is effectively in 3's of the time signature defined beat, one typically finds a tempo specification like this:

♩. = 50

This means that a duration of a dotted quarter or 3/8 should be taken as the 'de facto' beat value with 50 beats per minute. As an example, the time signature may be 12:8. So while the tempo indicates a beat value of 3/8, the time signature has an explicit 1/8th note beat. In that case, the tempo is effectively

---

[27] A compound time signature is one wherein the measure time is divided by three into equal beat parts, e.g. 6:8 become 2 3/8 parts.

150 for 1/8th notes. Of course, this is rarely computed possibly except for metronome setting, as explicitly the true beat is 3/8.

Nonetheless, a generalized conversion of this nature could be handy for our algorithms. More explicitly, given a tempo A for a given beat duration A, we want to compute the equivalent tempo B for a different given beat duration B. Given the following:

- tempo_A = the given tempo

- beat_A = the beat duration for tempo_A

- beat_B = a different beat duration

- tempo_B = the equivalent tempo for the beat_B

We have:

$$tempo\_B = \left(\frac{beat\_A}{beat\_B}\right) * tempo\_A \qquad (5.3)$$

This effectively gives the identical tempo rate but for a different beat value.

That the note value given in tempo does not need to be the same note value in the time signature is an unfortunate conflict. As noted, most of the time these two specifications are identical, but are not required to be so. Nonetheless, it is easy to convert a tempo beat value to the beat specified in the time signature using (5.3), if needed.

5.4   Whole Time / Actual Time Conversions

In this section we explore algorithms for converting whole time to actual time and vice versa. Unlike our derivation in earlier equations, we consider a more complex context wherein the time signature and/or tempo may change over time. To start, we assume that we have a list of time signatures and a list of tempos with their respective whole-time positions in ascending order, and that these map on a musical whole note timeline as shown in Fig. 5.1.

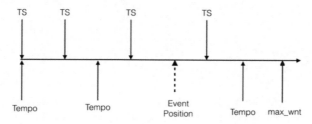

Fig. 5.1 Whole note timeline with time signature and tempo events.

Fig. 5.1 shows a timeline in whole time units with a series of time signature (TS) and tempo (Tempo) changes in order with precise whole note positions. Also, an arbitrary event is shown at a distinct position on the timeline. The objective of this discussion is to compute the actual time for the event. We make the following assumptions:

1. The timeline starts at 0, with an initial time signature and tempo setting.

2. Time signatures and tempos are intermixed in whole time.

3. For a tempo setting, we assume it uses a beat setting based on the immediately prior time signature.

4. A time signature change cannot be made outside of a measure boundary defined by the prior time signature. For example, on 3:4 → 5:8, the change can only be made at the end of the 3rd beat of a 3:4 measure.

5. All measures have duration based on the preceding time signature, i.e., number of beats times duration, except for the first which can have a smaller duration. That value is called the *pickup*. The last measure need not be full beat value.

6. There is a value, max_wnt, that represents the whole time value for the end of the score.

The algorithm for converting whole note time to actual time is sketched below in pseudo-code. In summary, the algorithm identifies all the whole-time based segments defined by the time signature and tempo event boundaries, finds the segment that contains the given event position for conversion, then adds the actual time of all the segments before that segment, and finally adds the actual time up to event position within the last segment.

```
wnt_to_actual(TS[], Tempo[], max_wnt, event_position)
    wnt = min(event_position, max_wnt)
    E = merge(TS, Tempo, max_wnt)      # time ordered merge of TS and Tempo and max_wnt
    setCurrent(E[0]) setCurrent(E[1]) # Set time sig and tempo - so two calls
    i = 1 S = 0
    while i < len(E):
        wnt_diff = wnt - E[i] if event_position in (E[i+1],E[i]) else E[i+1] - E[i]
        translated_tempo = current_tempo.effective_tempo(currentTS.beat_duration)
        S += wnt_diff / (currentTS.beat_duration * translated_tempo)
        if event_position in (E[i+1] - E[i]):
            break;
        setCurrent(E[i + 1])
        i++
    return S


setCurrent(e)
    if e instanceof(TS)
        currentTS = e
    elif e instanceof(Tempo)
        currentTempo = e
```

We note several details about the algorithm. First the set of time signatures TS[] and Tempo[] are merged into a single set E[] ordered by their whole time positions. The last element is a position element representing max_wnt. The event position to convert, given by the input variable "event_position', is trimmed to be the min of the given position and the maximum music time of the timeline. That way, position is contained in exactly one of the segments defined by E[]. setCurrent() is a routine to set either the currentTS or currentTempo for segment computation.

Finally, the tempo method "effective_tempo()" converts the tempo from the tempo beat to the time signature beat to normalize on using the current time signature beat tempo in calculations. The algorithm details are self-explanatory.

The algorithm for converting actual time to whole note time below is very similar in that it runs through the whole note time segments defined by the time signature and tempo boundaries. Each segment duration is converted to actual time and added to a running actual time sum. The segments whole time also has a running sum. That actual time running sum proceeds over the segments until the segment that contains the given actual time is found. The residual actual time for that segment is converted back to whole note time, which is added to a running sum of whole note time. Note that the algorithm returns the full whole note duration of the music when the actual time exceeds that of the full music.

The two algorithms are relatively straight forward and are meant to convey a basic computational strategy of computing some version of time one way or another by traversing the segments defined by the time signature and tempo boundaries. These algorithms run in linear time proportional to the number of time signatures and tempo changes. A far more efficient scheme is possible, found in the code base, and discussed later in the chapter.

```
actual_to_wnt(TS[], Tempo[], max_wnt, time_pos):
   E = merge(TS, Tempo, max_wnt);
   setCurrent(E[0]); setCurrent(E[1]);
   i = 1 AT = 0 WNT = 0
   while i < len(E) - 1:
       wnt_diff = E[i+1]-E[i]
       translated_tempo = current_tempo.effective_tempo(currentTS.beat_duration)
       at_diff = wnt_diff / (currentTS.beat_duration * translated_tempo)
       if apos in [AT, AT + at_diff]:
           WNT += (AT + at_diff - time_pos) *
                        (currentTS.beat_duration * translated_tempo)
           break;
       AT += at_diff;
       WNT += wnt_diff
       setCurrent(E[i + 1])
       i++;
```

5.5   Whole Time / Beat Time Conversion

In this section, we look at how to convert beat time to/from whole note time. We make the same assumptions as in the prior section, regarding the whole-time timeline marked by time signature and tempo events. The beauty of having this conversion is that together with the prior conversion algorithms, whole note time, beat time, and actual time are all inter-convertible by transitive composition. See Fig. 5.2.

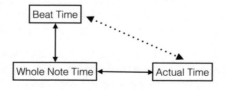

Fig. 5.2 Transitive interaction with conversions.

The algorithm for converting beat time to whole note time only needs to consider the time signature changes over the music timeline. Much like the prior algorithms, this one proceeds over the boundary segments, but only those defined by the time signatures and the maximum whole note time argument. A complication however concerns a possible pickup value, which is given in whole note time, and indicates a partial measure at the beginning of the timeline. This has an effect on measure/beat numbering. Typically, with no pickup, the initial measure is notated at BT(0, 0). But for non-zero pickup, the initial beat is non-zero. For example, with a 3:4 initial time signature, and a pickup beat 1/2 (half note) in duration, the first beat is BP(0, 1), meaning the initial beat of measure 0 is beat 1 (origin 0).

```
bt_to_wnt(TS[], pickup, max_wnt, bp):
    E = merge(TS, nil, max_wnt)
    if pickup > 0:
        pickup_beats = pickup / E[0].beat_duration
        prior_bp = BP(0, E[0].beats_per_measure - pickup_beats)
    else:
        prior_beats = 0
        prior_bp = BP(0, 0)
    prior_ts = E[0] Swht = 0

    for i in range(1, len(E)):
        num_beats = (E[i].position - prior_ts.position) / prior_ts.beat_duration
                             - pickup_beats
        num_measures = int(num_beats / prior_ts.beats_per_measure) +
                          (1 if pickup_beats > 0 else 0)
        measure_tally += num_measures
        current_ts_bp = BP(measure_tally, 0)
        if bp in [prior_bp, current_ts_bp]:
            Swht += ((bp.measure - prior_bp.measure)*prior_ts.beats_per_measure +
                      (bp.beat - prior_pb.beat)) * prior_ts.beat_duration
            break
        else:
            Swht += ((current_ts_bp.measure - prior_bp.measure)*
                                    prior_ts.beats_per_measure +
                      (current_ts_bp.beat - prior_pb.beat)) *
                                    prior_ts.beat_duration
        prior_ts = E[i]
        pickup_beats = 0
    return Swht
```

The algorithm is straight forward, moving time signature to time signature, computing the beat time position for each. If the input argument beat position lies between the beat position of the prior time signature and the current, then we truncate the beat position to prior time signature beat position and convert to whole note time, add to the whole note time sum, and do an early exit.

Throughout the loop, a sum of whole note time across time signature segments is maintained. The algorithm executes in time linear to the number of time signatures. While that is typically low, the algorithm can be improved using precomputed segment conversions. This is given in the code with runtime $O(\log(n))$.

The algorithm for converting whole note time to beat position is easier than its converse.

```
wht_to_bp(TS[], pickup, max_wnt, p):
    E = merge(TS, nil, max_wnt);
    if pickup > 0:
```

```
        pickup_beats = pickup / E[0].beat_duration
        prior_bp = BP(0, E[0].beats_per_measure - pickup_beats)
    else:
        prior_beats = 0
        prior_bp = BP(0, 0)
    prior_ts = E[0] Swht = 0


    for i in range(1, len(E)):
        diff_wht = (p.position if p in [Swht, E[i].position]
                            else E[i].position) - prior_ts.position
        num_beats = diff_wht / prior_ts.beat_duration
        num_measures = num_beats // prior_ts.beats_per_measure
        residual_beats = num_beats % prior_ts.beats_per_measure
        bp += BP(num_measures, residual_beats)
        if p in [Swht, E[i].position]
            return bp
        else:
            prior_bp = bp
            Swht += diff_wht
            prior_ts = E[i]
    return bp
```

Whole time is summed over segments until the segment containing the event's whole note time is found. A simple conversion to beat time is made over the differential in whole note time. The algorithm uses a shorthand '+' operator for adding beat positions together, the reader should realize that that includes measure carryover on the beat units, i.e., add 1 to measures when the summed beats exceed the beats per measure of the prior time signature. For example, in time signature 3/4:

$(5, 1) + (3,2) = (9, 0)$.

Again, this algorithm runs in linear time, but can be redesigned to run $O(\log(n))$, where n is the number of segments.

5.6   Representational Considerations

The focus of this chapter is in defining types for time in music, namely whole time, actual time, and beat time. We discussed algorithms to convert from one type to another. We introduced whole note time that behaves linearly across music, and in that sense is more stable than the other types, making it useful as a software representation of time for music. While the conversion algorithms are the center piece of the chapter, beneath them lie a number of other representational topics of interest that we will see much more later.

From that perspective, we look closely at how to represent time for music in software. Principally, we consider its numerical representation, primarily for whole note time. Based on that representation, the concepts of duration and position figure largely in the remainder of this text, and so their representations as computational objects are examined in some detail.

Finally, we examine the software development of the conversion algorithms. We approach these somewhat differently from the instructional approach taken earlier, and in a way that runs faster than linear to the number of segments defined by time signature and tempo events. We delve into the support software structures that achieves that runtime.

5.6.1   Whole Note Time Representation

As discussed in the text, whole note time is based on music note durational values, with 1 being a whole note, 1/2 a half, etc. If whole time is represented by real or decimal numbers, we eventually run into accuracy issues, especially with notes whose durations require infinite precision, values like 1/3 or other. For example, for a quarter note split into 7ths, each with a duration of $1/28 = 0.0357142...$, seven of these add to 0.2499999. Results can vary across programming languages. This type of accuracy issue, once incurred, only proliferates, and causes issues with comparative operators and whole number boundaries.

Whole note time values are then best represented as rational numbers or fractions. The software representation for whole note time in Python is the Fraction class from the "fractions" module. This representation provides all the essential support needed for working with whole note time values as fractions, including addition, subtraction, multiplication, and division support. A quick example illustrates its accuracy.

```
from fractions import Fraction
a = Fraction(1, 7)
b = a + a + a + a + a + a + a
print('a={0} b={1}'.format(a, b))

a=1/7 b=1
```

The class Fraction also takes care of reduction to lowest terms automatically, so the numerator and denominator are generally numerically well behaved, i.e., keeping numerator and denominator values low.

5.6.2   Position and Duration

Position and duration arise frequently in music representation. The semantic intention behind position is to designate a place or event location in a score in whole time. Duration indicates an extent in whole time. Consequently, fractions are used extensively representing whole time values in the Python classes Position and Duration.

Fig. 5.3 Position/Duration Addition

+	p	d	i	f	r
p	x	p	p	p	p
d	p	d	d	d	d
i	p	d			
f	p	d			
r	p	d			

The reason behind having these two classes, is that many times, we will be interested in using whole time to designate a location in music, such as a music note's position, within some larger context, like a score. Duration is used to indicate a difference in two positions, the whole note time difference between the two, or for the length of a note. As indicated by this discussion, duration has no reference frame and is effectively a relative value, but position does. Position and Duration have distinctions in purpose.

We mention this explicitly because Position and Duration form a kind of arithmetic or calculus. In that regard, we use Python's ability to overload operators much like we did with Interval. The simple case of addition is shown in *Fig. 5.3*. Here, additive type rules are shown with p=position, d=duration, i=integer, f=rational/fraction, and r = real. Note that p + p is not illegal as an operation, as both have reference frames, but p + d is simply augmenting a position. The cases for adding amongst integers, rational numbers, and reals is important for consistency's sake and some facilitating utility but are not relevant to this discussion.

Designing and developing a complete calculus across new data types can be tedious, as many cases need to be addressed in code for each operator. Besides addition, there are cases for implementing subtraction, equality, and for all the relational operators, e.g., ==, >=, <, ... In addition, it is useful to override inline operators like:

position += duration

duration *= 2

The importance of providing comparator operations, e.g., duration >= 5, goes beyond allowing inline comparisons but also, behind the covers, allows sorting operations.

Construction of a Position or Duration object is simply to pass the numerator and denominator or a Fraction, e.g., Position(6, 8), Duration(Fraction(1, 12)). In both cases, the class has one property, namely the Python Fraction produced by the constructor and its arguments.

The following shows construction and related operator usage:

```
from timemodel.duration import Duration
from timemodel.position import Position


p = Position(13, 8)
d = Duration(3, 4)
p0 = p + d
p1 = p - d
print('{0} = {1} + {2}'.format(p0, p, d))
print('{0} = {1} + {2}'.format(p1, p, d))


p += Duration(1, 8)
print('p={0}'.format(p))
d = Duration(1, 4) + d
print('d={0}'.format(d))
```
```
19/8 = 13/8 + 3/4
7/8 = 13/8 - 3/4
p=7/4
d=1
```

As a final word on this topic. When implementing operator overloads in Python, there are several overload methods that make the calculus more complete. Besides __add__() consider overloading __iadd__() to implement the '+=' operator. Also, __radd__() supplements native type addition support with examples like '4 + Position(1, 4)'. Examples of both are shown above. Similar variants exist for other operators.

5.6.3   Beat Position

Beat position is a simple wrapper for measure number, an integer, and a beat number relative to the measure's beginning, a Fraction. Like Position, BeatPosition also implements relational operators to support sorting.

However, BeatPosition has no corresponding BeatDuration, nor arithmetic type operations, in part because these artifacts are dependent on a broader context containing time signatures. See the exercises for further related information. Here are some examples of BeatPosition

```
from timemodel.beat_position import BeatPosition

bp = BeatPosition(5, 2)
print(bp)
bp1 = BeatPosition(4, 5)
print(bp > bp1)
```
```
BP[5, 2]
True
```

5.6.4   TimeSignature and Tempo classes

TimeSignature and Tempo are Python classes for time signature and tempo respectively which were mentioned in the preceding algorithms.

The class TimeSignature's constructor takes two parameters:

- **number_of_beats**: an integer indicating the number of beats per measure.
- **beat_duration**: the duration of the beat which can be specified as any of Fraction, Duration, or TSBeatType, an enum with values Whole, Half, Quarter, Eighth, Sixteenth.

Outside of this, the class is basically a descriptive entity.

The class Tempo's constructor takes two parameters:

- **tempo**: the beats per minute (BPM) of the tempo beat. This can be any of an integer, Fraction, or TempoType, an enum with values, Larghissimo, Lento, Largo, etc.
- **beat_duration**: the tempo beat duration which is specified as a Duration.

A few examples follow:

```
from structure.time_signature import TSBeatType, TimeSignature
from structure.tempo import Tempo, TempoType

ts = TimeSignature(3, TSBeatType.Quarter)
print(ts)
tempo = Tempo(TempoType.Adagio, Duration(1, 4))
print(tempo)
```
```
TS[3, 1/4]
Tempo[71, 1/4]
```

In practice, we use the classes TimeSignatureEvent and TempoEvent to associate the TimeSignature and Tempo object to specific position values. For multiples of either, these events can be collected into a list-like Python class called EventSequence which contains special event accounting properties useful in some contexts. An example involving TimeSignature follows (with similar for Tempo):

```
from timemodel.time_signature_event import TimeSignatureEvent
from timemodel.event_sequence import EventSequence

ts_line = EventSequence([TimeSignatureEvent(TimeSignature(3, Duration(1, 4)),
                                            Position(0)),
                         TimeSignatureEvent(TimeSignature(2, Duration(1, 8)),
                                            Position(6, 4))])
```

5.6.5 The Time Conversion Algorithms

The TimeConversion class embodies all the conversion algorithms. The algorithms rely on several setup arguments including lists of time signatures and tempos, a max whole note time for the music, and a whole note duration for a pickup if there is one. Access to these conversion algorithms requires the construction of a TimeConversion instance. Its arguments include:

- **tempo_sequence**: an EventSequence of TempoEvents.

- **time_sig_sequence**: an EventSequence of TimeSignatureEvents.

- **max_pos**: Position instance of maximum whole time.

- **pickup**: Duration instance of pickup in whole time.

Construction is as follows:

```
time_conversion = TimeConversion(tempo_sequence, time_sig_sequence, max_pos, pickup)
```

With a TimeConversion instance, any of the four conversion algorithms can be invoked multiple times or in combinations. These include:

- **position_to_actual_time(wnt_position)**: converts the whole-time position to actual time.

- **actual_time_to_position(actual_time)**: converts actual time to whole time.

- **bp_to_position(beat_position)**: convert beat position to whole time.

- **position_ot_bp(wnt_position)**: convert whole time to beat position.

Unlike the algorithms discussed earlier, the TimeConversion class makes extensive use of dictionaries or maps to facilitate calculation. The gist of all the algorithms is to determine some measure of time on the last segment containing the given event position but within the last segment for some time signature and/or tempo. Once knowing that, the remaining calculation is simply a conversion using the time in that last segment to the event position.

To implement this kind of solution, we build four maps:

- **ts_mt_map**: maps whole time position to time signature

- **ts_time_map**: maps actual time position to time signature

- **tempo_mt_map**: maps whole time position to tempo

- **tempo_time_map**: maps actual time position to tempo

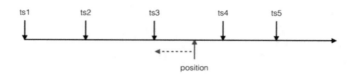

Fig. 5.4 ts_wnt_map layout

To better see how this approach works, consider the ts_mt_map. For a time signature and its whole time position, an entry is made mapping that whole time position to the time signature. Fig. 5.4 shows an instance of this map with five time signature entries with a mapping of their whole time position to the TimeSignature instance itself. Of significance, the dictionary provides a floor() method by which given a whole time position, returns the TimeSignature instance just prior to position (as well as the time signature instance). Floor() is a very useful method for finding the prior TimeSignature instance. Further, it runs in O(log(n)) time, where n is the number of entries.

Another feature of our map is the ability for it to act as a reverse map. For example, given a tempo instance, to find its actual time, use:

```
tempo_actual_time = tempo_time_map.reverse_get(tempo)
```

Both of these useful map features, floor() and reverse_get() are not found in map as found in the default Python library. The code base contains class OrderedMap which does this and is discussed further in Appendix B.

We conclude with illustrating how all this technical discussion comes together in computing position_to_actual_time() in the TimeConversion class. The combination of these computational assistive maps and their features essentially reduces the computation of actual time to that of converting the value delta_wnt.

It is fair to say that this approach offloads a large part of the runtime complexity of the algorithms in sections 5.4 and 5.5 into the class constructor in building the maps. The benefit to this approach however is in the reuse of that initialization for fast computation during conversion, to something like O(log(n)) where n is the number of time signatures or tempos.

```
def position_to_actual_time(self, wnt_position):
    (tempo_wnt_floor, tempo_element) = self.tempo_mt_map.floor_entry(wnt_position)
    tempo_actual = self.tempo_time_map.reverse_get(tempo_element)

    (ts_wnt_floor, ts_element) = self.ts_mt_map.floor_entry(wnt_position)
    ts_actual = self.ts_time_map.reverse_get(ts_element)

    start_wnt = max(tempo_wnt_floor, ts_wnt_floor)
    start_actual = max(tempo_actual, ts_actual)
    # at this point, we have:
    #   start_wnt: a whole time to start from
    #   start_actual: the actual time to start from
    #   tempo_element: the current Tempo
    #   ts_element: the current TimeSignature
    delta_wnt = min(position, self.max_position) - start_wnt
    translated_tempo = tempo_element.effective_tempo(ts_element.beat_duration)
```

```
# time = wnt_time / (beat_duration * tempo)
delta_actual = (delta_wnt.duration / (ts_element.beat_duration.duration *
        translated_tempo) if delta_wnt > 0 else 0) * 60 * 1000
return start_actual + delta_actual
```

In the following example, we convert a whole time position to real time, and then back again.

```
from timemodel.time_conversion import TimeConversion
from structure.tempo import Tempo
from structure.time_signature import TimeSignature

tempo_line = EventSequence([TempoEvent(Tempo(60), Position(0)),
                            TempoEvent(Tempo(20), Position(4, 4))])
ts_line = EventSequence([TimeSignatureEvent(TimeSignature(3, Duration(1, 4)), Posi-
tion(0)),
                            TimeSignatureEvent(TimeSignature(2, Duration(1, 8)), Posi-
tion(5, 4))])
conversion = TimeConversion(tempo_line, ts_line, Position(2, 1))
actual_time = conversion.position_to_actual_time(Position(6, 4))
print(actual_time)
# 4 quarter notes @ 60 with 1/4 beat = 4000
# 1 quarter note @ 20 with 1/4 beat  = 3000
# 2 eighth notes @ 20 (effective 40) with 1/8 beat  = 3000

position = conversion.actual_time_to_position(10000)
print(position)
```
```
10000.0
```

5.7   Exercises

5.7.1 Design BeatPosition so that like Position and Duration, it also has arithmetic operations. What is the key complication in doing this that is not an issue with Position and Duration?

5.7.2 For Position, Duration, and OrderedMap, focus on the overridden methods, discuss why the overrides are (or are not) necessary, and what problems they solve.

5.7.3 Develop a music timeline having 3 time signatures and 3 tempos changes. Compute the position and actual times for each beat using the TimeConversion class. Compare these results with hand calculations.

5.7.4 Develop methods in TimeConversion that convert actual time to/from beat time.

5.7.5 The code base introduces the class Offset, another Fraction based class. It represents something of a type neutral value used to modify a Position and Duration and comes in handy when a Position or Duration needs alteration with other than a Duration or Position. In that sense it is a neutral value type. Extend the composition matrix of *Fig. 5.3* to include the Offset type.

6 The Note and Note Aggregates

This chapter introduces the concept of the musical note, perhaps the most fundamental concept in music. This seemingly unusually late introduction of such a fundamental topic in this text is due to laying the preceding groundwork of supportive foundations, including pitch, duration, and position. These concepts factor into note's defining structure and its richness.

Along with introducing the definition of note, we also consider several structural concepts that support and organize notes such as beams and tuplets. These aggregative or grouping structures may, at first blush, seem to pertain mainly to notation or scoring needs. While there is truth to that, these structures are at the same time powerful compositional semantic structures that are useful towards organizing or encapsulating melodic, rhythmic, or even harmonic elements, by aggregating common durations, e.g., 1/4, 1/2, 1/8, etc., and creating non-standard durations. It is in that spirit that we pursue note aggregative structures.

This chapter provides an introduction and explanation of these musical concepts. It also dives into the software representation behind them. We see that these simple concepts provide a rich software structure managed through an overarching object-oriented design along with various constraints. A discussion follows on algorithms behind both the manipulation and maintenance of these structures.

6.1 Notes and Their Aggregative Partners

The following sections introduce the concept of note, as well as the supportive aggregative structures, beam and tuplet. The introduction is given from a music theory viewpoint to provide an introduction and basic understanding of these concepts.

6.1.1 The Note

At its most fundamental level, a note is a combination of duration and pitch. Duration values are often given in units of whole note time, fractions of a whole note, and usually in powers of 1/2. The most common durations symbolically are:

These are respectively whole note, half note, quarter note, eighth note, and sixteenth note, with durations 1, ½, ¼, 1/8, 1/16 respectively. The duration of any of these notes is called the note's ***base duration*** in this text.

D. P. Pazel, *Music Representation and Transformation in Software*, https://doi.org/10.1007/978-3-030-97472-5_6

Fig. 6.1 B:4 Note

Each note is assigned a pitch. In the context of a staff, one easily recognizes the pitch to which a note is assigned. For example, Fig. 6.1 shows a G clef staff with the whole note assigned to B:4, B on the fourth octave. A discussion of staffs is getting ahead of ourselves just now and is only mentioned to provide a common usage and visual context.

A note's duration value can be modified in two ways. One way is to indicate duration extension visually by adding a number of 'dots' just after the note. Each dot indicates an additive extension by combinative 1/2 factors. For example, a dotted quarter note's duration is, $1/4 + 1/8 = 3/8$. A double dotted quarter note's duration is $1/4 + 1/8 + 1/16 = 7/16$, and so on. The number of dots following a note is an attribute of note, indicating that a note has an additional durational value besides its base duration. Its *full duration* is the total duration of the note including the extension based on the number of dots applied to the base duration.

We point out that a rest is also a note, but is a note without an assigned pitch.

Another way to achieve the effect of modifying a note's duration is to *tie* it to predecessor or successor notes. For two or more tied notes, we have:

- That the notes follow sequentially.

- That the notes have the same pitch.

- That the total duration is the sum of the full durations of the notes.

Fig. 6.2 Tied Notes

Fig. 6.2 shows two notes tied at the same pitch. In the context of the tied notes, there is a combined total duration, consisting of the sum of the notes' full durations. The combined duration of the tied notes here is:

$(1/4 + 1/8) + (1/8 + 1/16) = 9/16$.

It should be pointed out however that unlike dotted notes, tied notes do not change the full duration of any individual note involved in the tie.

Finally, although it rarely arises explicitly in music discussion, notes also carry positional information of various kinds. In Fig. 6.2, the two notes are:

- Positioned sequentially relative to each other.

- In absolute position, presumably, to some beginning of the music score.

Position at this level of detail does not arise much in music theory but is important in software representation. This is mentioned now to prepare for its deeper discussion later.

6.1.2   Beams

Beams provide a way to group notes of similar short durations, usually to a combined duration of a beat, or to a melodic or rhythmic unit. In that sense they are aggregative note structures. Consider the following examples:

The examples above show in order:

- An 1/8th followed by two 1/16ths.

- A dotted 1/8th followed by a 1/16th.

- Four 1/16th notes.

- Two 1/8th notes.

Beams facilitate score reading, with beams grouping or consolidating sequential notes with similar numbers of stems into meaningful musical groups or blocks. Visually they provide a way for performers to immediately see common note duration values in blocks or groups, and finer duration value note groups in sub-blocks. This helps instruct a performer to anticipate how to play groups of notes, especially if a group of notes fall on a beat. Beams provide a compactification of what would otherwise be a possibly illegible and confusing assortment of notes.

Beams induce an implicit 'halving' factor on the durations of notes attached to the beams. That is, notes underneath a single beam are 1/8th notes; 2 beams, 1/16th notes; 3 beams, 1/32nd notes, and so forth. A closer look at beaming semantics will be discussed later in the text. However, the world of note duration consists of more than durations of powers of 1/2, and this is solved with tuplets.

6.1.3   Tuplets

A tuplet is also an aggregative note structure that, like the beam, functions in note grouping. However, unlike beams, tuplets allow the durations of contained notes to take values other than powers of ½, but to specific determinative rules. Examples include:

These examples, in order, are interpreted to mean:

- Three quarter notes to be played over a 2-quarter note duration.

- Three 1/8th notes played over 2-1/8th note duration.

- Much like the first but illustrates that rests are allowed.

The "3 for 2" factoring described is only an example of what can be done with tuplets. In fact, tuplets provide a generalization in that, for a given note duration value, the full tuplet duration is determined by two parameters 'M:N'. This means perform M notes in the time of N notes of the given note duration, with the M notes in equal duration.

Consider Fig. 6.3. This is an example of a 6:4 tuplet. This indicates that 6 notes are to be performed in a duration of 4 quarter notes. To do this, the durations of the 6 quarter notes need to be shortened equally so that six of them can occupy 4 quarter note duration.

Fig. 6.3 6:4 Tuplet Example

While that sounds difficult to gauge for performance, it really is not. Usually these situations occur on beats, and all one needs to do is fit some number of notes into a number of beats. However, in software this needs to be precisely defined, and each note in this case would be assigned a whole time duration value of 1/6.

Beams and tuplets can be combined seamlessly into a set of nested aggregative structures. The combination of beams and tuplet notation is powerful, compact, and highly useful to instruct complex note structures and timings. Take for example Fig. 6.4:

Fig. 6.4 Complex beaming

The example shows an eighth note, followed by 3 $1/16^{th}$ notes played in the time of 2 $1/16^{th}$ notes, followed by 2 eighth notes. In the following sections we look closer at nesting from a software representation view, and how to compute the beam and tuplet effects on individual note durations.

6.2   Representation

In this section, we take the music concepts just introduced and recast them as explicit software model objects, that is, Python class structures. It is seen that going from conceptual to explicit models requires a good amount of attention to detail and intuitive foresight, and in fact some easily glossed over aspects about beams and tuples have intricacies that factor into devising detailed definitions.

We start with devising a software model that encompasses note, beam, and tuplet, the latter two being nesting aggregative structures. We formulate a class inheritance structure to accommodate notes, beams and tuplets, and introduce a new aggregative structure Line. The semantics of the different class structures are described and followed by discussing subtleties and clarifications of the representation.

6.2.1   The Note Inheritance Hierarchy

When designing a software model that includes note, beam, and tuplet, we consider several aspects. First, identify the entities that hold separate and cohesive identities, that is, that have unique characteristics. Clearly, note, beam and tuplet come to mind as concrete examples. Second, identify common characteristics amongst entities that indicate common sub-structure that can be factored into a new but abstract class of its own which can be commonly inherited. For example, position as well as duration, is common to all three cited class candidates. This kind of class factoring reduces design and therefore implementation redundancy. Third, identify relationships that exist outside of inheritance, e.g., containment, and decide upon the best way to implement those relationships. Finally, determine the constraints that hold our model together, that are required to maintain consistency of state. These become critical factors to designing algorithms.

We begin our analysis with the following observations:

- Beams and tuplets are containers of other beams, tuplets, and notes. This relationship builds a structural hierarchy, i.e., a tree, with notes at the leaves.

- Beam, tuple, and note all have parent references to the structure that immediately contains them. Further parents are unique, i.e., a structure cannot have multiple immediate parents.

- Beam, tuplet and note each have a positional attribute that indicates its position within its immediate parent structure. These are relative positional measurements of child to parent.

- Beams and tuplets impose various multiplicative factors on the durations of other elements. For example, a tuplet significantly affects the duration and positional values of any child note in the tuplet. Further, these factors propagate downward multiplicatively through the structure hierarchy.

These pieces of information inform us that there are common characteristics indicating class factoring. For example, beams and tuples, but not note, have collection characteristics. All elements possess a parent reference and positional characteristics. And so forth.

Typically, at this stage design proceeds with white boarding several possible class structure designs, that through some trial and error and much discussion reveal something of a final optimal design considering many alternative designs and examples. For the sake of discussion, we will forgo that process and consider a specific class inheritance model that incorporates many these considerations. Possibly not the best model, but one sufficiently accessible for illustration. A diagram detailing the model is shown in Fig. 6.5, and shows the key model classes, and the lines indicate inheritance relations, super-class (top) and subclass (bottom). The following sections describe this model in detail, including the rationale behind this inheritance structure, along with the types of issues for maintaining its integrity.

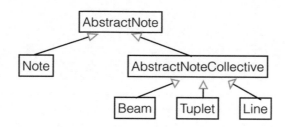

Fig. 6.5 Note Inheritance Hierarchy Design

Observe the new primitive class, Line, that appears in the diagram and had not been discussed earlier. Line is unique to this text and is a simple aggregative class that allows one to add to it any of Note, Beam, Tuplet, and Line. It is similar to but not to be confused with the concept of voice and is described later.

The above discussion is rather abstract. In the interests of better understanding, to make the discussion clearer and more concrete, the reader may jump ahead to Fig. 6.7 in section 6.2.2. It shows a music example recast into class instances (objects) of many of the classes referenced in our class design. The tree on the right of that diagram is an illustration of the aggregative nature of many of these classes, and how beams and tuplets nest[28].

---

[28] In Fig. 6.7, L, B, T, N denote instances of Line, Beam, Tuplet, and Note respectively.

AbstractNote

AbstractNote is the root class of the hierarchy, meaning that all other classes in the hierarchy are either directly or indirectly subclasses of it. AbstractNote has class properties that have common usage with all the derived classes. Those properties include:

- *parent* – A reference to the immediate parent, typically a subclass instance of Abstract-NoteCollective.

- *relative_position* – A whole time valued relative offset to its immediate parent.

- *contextual_reduction_factor* – A multiplicative factor imposed by the instance to downward instance durations, e.g., ½ for beam.

In the code below, we see the three properties and their defaults. All three are defined as Python properties with both getter and setters. Those for the property "parent" are shown.

```python
class AbstractNote(object):
    def __init__(self):
        self.__parent = None
        self.__relative_position = Offset(0)
        self.__contextual_reduction_factor = Fraction(1)
    @property
    def parent(self):
        return self.__parent
    @parent.setter
    def parent(self, parent):
        self.__parent = parent
    @property
    def duration(self):
        raise NotImplementedError(
                'define duration in subclass to use this base class')
```

Regarding the property relative_position, we are not concerned so much with an absolute position here, so much as a position relative to the immediate parent. This simplifies algorithms, and absolute position is easily computed by summing the relevant relative_position's in a containment hierarchy. Note also that relative_position has type Offset. Offset is like Position and Duration in that it holds a whole time value as a Fraction. Semantically however it is different and has something of a neutral meaning, more as a value that 'adjusts' duration or position. Look at the operator overrides in the class Offset for further clarification.

One might question why beams and tuplets are considered 'notes', even if abstract. This is mainly due to the parent and relative_position attributes they share and found in the definition of AbstractNote class. All classes have a duration attribute but implement it in different ways. So 'duration' is given as an abstract property in AbstractNote, in that each subclass must define its own implementation of the duration property lest a NotImplementedError is thrown at runtime.

Finally, beams and tuplets impose dilation factors on duration and position, that apply equally through the other class instances. The contextual_reduction_factor attribute is the multiplicative factor an aggregative structure contributes to the hierarchy. For example, for beams it is 1/2. For Note it is simply 1. For Tuplets, duration is a bit more complicated. More on this is discussed later.

Note

Note is the central class of the model. As mentioned earlier, it is characterized with having a pitch, duration, and position. So, Note has the following attributes:

- *diatonic_pitch* – A reference to a DiatonicPitch instance specifying the Note's pitch. When the value is None, the note is treated as a rest.

- *base_duration* – The specified duration, e.g., ¼, ½, etc. The value is a Duration instance. The STANDARD_NOTES static specification of note type to duration can be used to simplify specification, e.g., use STANDARD_NOTES.Q for Duration(1, 4).

- *num_dots* – The number of 'dots' applied to the note's base duration. Recall that dots extend the note duration additively, using multiple factors of ½ on the base duration.

- *duration* – The full note duration, accounting for base_duration and the number of dots.

Note picks up the attribute relative_position from AbstractNote and specifies relative offset to an immediate container note when it is contained.

Note's constructor takes diatonic pitch, base duration, and the number of dots as parameters. The number of dots is optionally specified but defaults to 0, since in many cases notes are not dotted. Again, it is worth observing that there are many common base durations, typically whole, half, quarter durations, and so forth. Using STANDARD_NOTES static information, symbolic references to these standard durations can be specified in the base duration parameter of Note construction. Alternatively, an arbitrary positive duration value can be specified as well. The simplified code below shows elements of the constructor. Note that the duration extension calculation due to dots on the base duration is achieved through a method found in the class Duration.

```
class Note(AbstractNote):
    def __init__(self, diatonic_pitch, base_duration, num_dots=0):
        AbstractNote.__init__(self)
        self.__diatonic_pitch = diatonic_pitch
        self.__num_dots = num_dots
        self.__base_duration = base_duration
        self.__duration = base_duration.apply_dots(num_dots)
```

A few examples follow:

```
# Quarter note at C:4
note = Note(DiatonicPitch(4, 'c'), Duration(1, 4))
print('{0} duration={1}'.format(note.diatonic_pitch, note.duration))
# Double dotted quarter not at F#:5
note = Note(DiatonicPitch(5, 'f#'), 'Q', 2)
print('{0} duration={1}'.format(note.diatonic_pitch, note.duration))
C:4 duration=1/4
F#:5 duration=7/16
```

A subtle but very important implementation aspect of Note is how it records ties to a successor note or from a predecessor note. This implementation can be achieved in several ways, from a simple Boolean indicating 'tied to successor', to a separate catalogue/dictionary recording ties. In this representation, we choose the simple technique of recording Note references to both the successor and predecessor Note instances directly in Note. This approach is convenient for algorithm implementations. Thus, the attribute tied_to is a reference to the successor note to which a note is tied, while tied_from references the predecessor note from which a note is tied. The reader should weigh the pros and cons of different representations for ties as an exercise.

AbstractNoteCollective

AbstractNoteCollective is a subclass of AbstractNote that encapsulates the behavior of note containers such as Beam and Tuplet and Line. Observe that hierarchically, Tuplets and Beams contain other Tuplets, Beams, and Notes. The data attribute sub_notes, a list, enables that collective capability. For simplification, we make an implicit assumption that the elements in the list follow in strict sequence, and that there are not, for example, overlaps of position/duration with the objects in sub_notes.

AbstractNoteCollective is also a subclass of Observer and Observable, which are part of the code base. These are classes that allow notifications to pass upward through a hierarchy of classes instances based on AbstractNoteCollective. We see these in action in discussions about algorithms that maintain the integrity of the hierarchy in the face of modification, e.g., adding notes to the hierarchy. For an explanation of notification and the observer pattern, see Appendix C.

```
class AbstractNoteCollective(AbstractNote, Observer, Observable):
    def __init__(self):
        AbstractNote.__init__(self)
        Observable.__init__(self)
        Observer.__init__(self)
        self.sub_notes = []
```

For now, we leave this discussion with two thoughts to keep in mind about AbstractNoteCollective. Reference Fig. 6.6 .

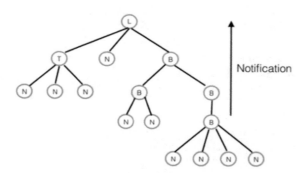

Fig. 6.6 *AbstractNoteCollective tree and notification and its direction*

Consider the following aspects of AbstractNoteCollective:

- When realized as objects, in practice, AbstractNoteCollective's are structured as trees that can be traversed using the parent and sub_notes properties. All the leaves of the tree should be Note's.

- AbstractNoteCollective is both an Observer and an Observable, with parents observing the elements of sub_notes. With that relationship, parents react to changes occurring in lower elements of the tree. An example is when notes are added to beams. By adding to the lower structure in the tree, the upper elements adapt by adjusting positions and durations.

Beam

A beam is an aggregative or grouping model class, and as such it is a subclass of AbstractNoteCollective. Its sub_notes list contains any of notes, tuplets, or other beams. Beams contribute an implicit reduction factor of 1/2, in that each beam contributes a 1/2 reduction factor to contained notes. For example, if you have a beamed 1/8 note, and place that beam as a child of the lower of two nested beams, the 1/8th note becomes a 1/8 * 1/2 * 1/2 = 1/32nd note.

The semantics of beams however can be a little tricky to model, especially when beams and tuplets interlace over a note container hierarchy. Precise details are spell out in the algorithms section.

```
from structure.beam import Beam
# Creating a beam with 1/8, 3/8, and 1/16 notes
note0 = Note(DiatonicPitch(4, 'c'), Duration(1, 8))
note1 = Note(DiatonicPitch(4, 'd'), Duration(1, 8), 1)
note2 = Note(DiatonicPitch(4, 'e'), Duration(1, 16))
beam = Beam([note0, note1, note2])
print(beam)

Beam(Dur(3/8)Off(0)f=1)[
    [C:4<1/8>-(1/8)] off=0 f=1
    [D:4<1/8@>-(3/16)] off=1/8 f=1
    [E:4<1/16>-(1/16)] off=5/16 f=1
```

A subtle point about adding notes to a single Beam, is that a note's duration before added has the same duration value after added to that single beam. Adding notes at twice their duration value with an understanding that a Beam factor of ½ applies would be an awkward policy for usability. So, in the above example, the three notes in the beam are 1/8th, 3/16ths, and 1/16, just as they were created before adding to the beam. Take note also of the relative offsets (off) to the beginning of the beam. A better appreciation of beam's ½ factor is seen when adding a beam to a beam.

Tuplet

A tuplet, like a beam, is a container of other note structures and a subclass of AbstractNoteCollective. However, it uses a dilation factor to modify the durations of the contained notes to a fixed total duration value. That fixed duration is calculated using two factors. One factor is a ***unit_duration*** which is a duration value representing some whole note time functioning as a duration unit within the tuplet. For example, a tuple may comprise 1/8th notes so the unit_duration is 1/8. The other factor is ***unit_duration_factor***, which is the number of unit_duration's that equate to the full duration of the tuple. That is, the total duration of the tuplet is:

$$unit\_duration\_value * unit\_duration \qquad (6.1)$$

which is held constant for the tuplet, no matter its contents.

This imposes a dilation factor based on the fixed total duration and the sum of the actual note durations in the tuplet. This duration value is applied uniformly over the notes in sub_notes, to enforce that total duration. Assuming the notes under the tuplet have durations d0, d1, ..., the dilation factor that holds the whole tuplet structure to the total fixed duration is:

$$dilation = \frac{(unit\_factor * unit\_duration)}{\sum d_i} \qquad (6.2)$$

This way of specifying tuple dilation is slightly at variance with music theory. Music theory generally specifies a pair of numbers a:b [20] where a is the number of unit notes to fit into the tuplet, and b is the number of unit notes constituting the fixed duration of the tuplet. In that case the unit value (or unit_duration) must be inferred from time signature or other. Tuplet notation sometimes allows the specification of the unit explicitly, making it closer to the above specification. However, the tuplet class does not need that 'a' factor, as we assume a pre-reduced duration total based on the sum of the durations in sub_notes.

```
from structure.tuplet import Tuplet
# Create tuplet of 3 1/8 notes with for duration 1/4 note
note1 = Note(DiatonicPitch(4, 'c'), Duration(1, 8))
note2 = Note(DiatonicPitch(4, 'd'), Duration(1, 8))
note3 = Note(DiatonicPitch(4, 'e'), Duration(1, 8))
tuplet = Tuplet(Duration(1, 8), 2, [note1, note2, note3])
AbstractNote.print_structure(tuplet)

Tuplet dur 1/4 off 0 f=2/3
    Note [C:4<1/12>-(1/12)] off=0 f=2/3 off 0 f=2/3
    Note [D:4<1/12>-(1/12)] off=1/12 f=2/3 off 1/12 f=2/3
    Note [E:4<1/12>-(1/12)] off=1/6 f=2/3 off 1/6 f=2/3
```

Line

A Line is a note aggregation class, a subclass of AbstractNoteCollective, whose sub-notes are instances of Note, Beam, Tuplet, or other Lines. It is different from Tuplet and Beam in several ways.

First, it can contain any of the other major AbstractNote classes, namely Note, Beam, Tuple, and Line, whereas Beam and Tuplet are limited to Note, Beam, and Tuplet. This means that it is less a partner in nested aggregation, than a means for 'gluing' together bits and pieces comprised of the other note types.

Secondly, it supports the concept of pinning, meaning for example, that an abstract note can be positioned precisely within a Line without requiring other elements to fill in the gaps before it, which are treated as implicit rests. It's the kind of structure one can use to stitch together musical voices, melodies, and accompaniment.

Line will be used more extensively later in the text. It is mentioned here for completion in the context of nesting semantics of Beams and Tuplets.

```
from structure.line import Line
vnote0 = Note(DiatonicPitch(4, 'a'), Duration(1, 8))
vnote1 = Note(DiatonicPitch(4, 'b'), Duration(1, 8))
vnote2 = Note(DiatonicPitch(4, 'c'), Duration(1, 4))
vnote3 = Note(DiatonicPitch(4, 'd'), Duration(1, 2))
line = Line([vnote0, vnote1, vnote2, vnote3])
AbstractNote.print_structure(line)

Line dur 1 off 0 f=1
    Note [A:4<1/8>-(1/8)] off=0 f=1 off 0 f=1
    Note [B:4<1/8>-(1/8)] off=1/8 f=1 off 1/8 f=1
```

```
Note [C:4<1/4>-(1/4)] off=1/4 f=1 off 1/4 f=1
Note [D:4<1/2>-(1/2)] off=1/2 f=1 off 1/2 f=1
```

6.2.2   Semantic Clarifications

The inheritance scheme presented provides a powerful representation for both note and note aggregations. In particular, the aggregation concepts provide a means to represent complex music structures. In this section we look closely at details underlying this inheritance scheme that effect common changes to these elements, and the constraints needed to maintain and uphold structural integrity.

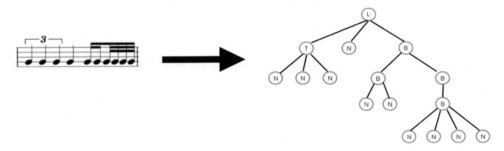

Fig. 6.7 Simple melody converted to note structures.

Fig. 6.7 shows a modestly complex music structure and its decomposition into a tree composed of Line, Note, Tuplet, and Beam nodes. We refer to this kind of tree as an ***abstract note tree*** or simply ***note tree***. Verifying that the resulting tree represents the given music input is easy and clear. However, we are concerned here with operational issues related to constructing the tree one element at a time, e.g., inserting beams, tuplets and notes. These operations are the sources for algorithms for building and maintaining this model.

We begin with looking at several important semantic issues regarding these entities, that at first blush may not be readily apparent. These clarifications help us to understand and devise important algorithms.

We begin with a Beam and the semantic issues involved in adding notes or other structures. There are two rules about this:

1. It is not allowed to add a note whose duration is greater or equal to a quarter note. This says nothing about the duration of the beam, only about the duration of notes to be added to the beam. Those notes retain their duration value under the beam.

2. Adding a beam under a beam reduces element durations under the added beam by a factor of ½.

Operationally there appears to be a conflict in uniformity of duration scaling. Adding a note under a beam does not incur a halving factor, while adding a beam does. We could resolve this by adding notes whose durations are less than a half note duration, and make the halving apply to anything added to a beam. That approach is certainly awkward in usability. Alternatively, we can add notes to beams as semantically dictated by (1) which is more intuitive. We take this latter position for our API.

Adding to this discussion, the operation of adding elements to a beam can be seen either in context of only that beam, or of the beam and all its parents. In the latter case, we could add, for example, 1/16th notes to a double nested beam, or 1/32nd notes to a triple nested beam, and so forth. In such a case, the user must be aware of context unfortunately. Consequently, we choose to keep the context simple and to add notes to beams as dictated by (1) with the focus on one beam irrespective of nesting and automate the existing tree structure to apply appropriate dilation factors dictated by the elements that comprise the nesting. That means, for example, adding a 1/16th note to a beam with a parent beam, effectively make it a 1/32nd note through calculation.

Another example of the semantic subtleties in dealing with note collectives can be seen in a case involving tuplets. Consider the two tuplets in Fig. 6.8.

Fig. 6.8 Beamed and unbeamed tuplet

Visually the difference is that one triplet is not beamed and the other is, and that semantically they seem to be otherwise identical, namely 3 1/8th notes over a quarter note span. The subtlety we aim to point out is that these cannot be substituted wholesale into different contexts and expect the same results. Consider Fig. 6.9:

Fig. 6.9 Tuplet substitution example

On the surface one sees the two triplets of Fig. 6.8 inserted into a musical figure which surround the triplets by two eighth notes. However, in each the results are entirely different. In the first, the 3 inner 1/8-th notes combine to a quarter note duration; in the second, the full duration is 3/8. In other words, the beam on the tuplet (right example) has the same semantic effect as described in the beaming section, applying a 1/2 factor to the child notes of the tuplet. The two common tuplet representations are in fact semantically different.

This example is mentioned to help avoid semantic problems later. The above observation points out that one needs to be careful and very precise when working with software representations. For clarification, the tree models for the embedded examples above respectively are shown in Fig. 6.10. Recall that B, T, N stand for Beam, Tuplet, and Note respectively.

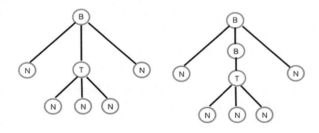

Fig. 6.10 Tree representations for Fig. 6.9

As an additional consideration, there is a question regarding the right node tree as to whether the beam/tuplet nodes in the center of the tree should be in interchanged. As shown, this is the more common circumstance showing a close binding between tuplet and its child nodes in terms of dilation. The beam is simply a holder of the tuplet and that contributes a ½ dilation factor, and at that level renders 1/8th full duration for the inner structure. If the beam and tuplet nodes were reversed, the tuplet arguments enforces a full duration of ¼ to the inner structure, which is not the same as we just described. However, if in this scenario the tuplet full duration is given as 1/8th, it would be the same. The scenario of a single structure under a tuplet is somewhat unusual. The first scenario, as given conforms more to common practice.

The given model provides a powerful representation for note grouping. Certainly, one can construct tree structures that might rarely be see in music scores. However, restriction to only common practice is not the intention of this text, but rather we aim at times to attempt a wider and less restrictive set of rules. As well, dilation specification is far less restrictive than in common music theory. A tuplet, in particular, by way of its 2 parameters can provide a wide range of note duration values.

This leads us back to the rationale behind contextual_reduction_factor data member of the Abstract-Note class. As mentioned, normally this is set to 1 as in the case of Note. However, reading down a note tree representation, beams or tuplets contribute dilation factors, which multiplied out at each level yielding the full dilation factor for each level. That is the contextual_reduction_factor value.

Finally, relative_position is the whole note time position of an element relative to its parent. We retain this instead of absolute time to maintain independence from other parts of the tree, so that for example, if notes are added to an earlier (leftmost) part of the tree, we would not need to recompute element positions across the full tree. Regarding computing the absolute position of any part of the tree, it is a simple matter of following the parent pointers and summing through their relative_positions. It a small trade-off that gives flexibility to the tree structure over expediency of absolute position access.

6.3   Algorithms

In this section we look at several algorithms that are generally useful or otherwise helpful in maintaining the integrity of the grouping structures described earlier. The algorithms examined here concern accessing the leaf Note's of a tree based on the Note hierarchy and adding Note's to the tree. The former algorithm is important for quickly acquiring all individual notes within a grouping scheme composed of beams and tuplets. The latter is the foundational API for building a tree incrementally with beams and tuplets. Other operations such as removing tree substructures or changing note durations or tuplet dilation values in the context of a tree are deferred as exercises.

We finish the chapter with a novelty: an algorithm for reversing a melody. This algorithm reverses the notes in a Line, and with that, the nodes in a note tree.

6.3.1   Accessing Notes

We start with the algorithm of accessing all the Note's in a note tree. More precisely, given a tree based on the note hierarchy, the objective is to access all the individual Note's (the leaves of the tree) into a list. The objective is achieved though simple recursion.

```
@abstractmethod
AbstractNote.get_all_notes(self):
    raise NotImplementedError('users must define get_all_notes to use this base class')


AbstractNoteCollective.get_all_notes(self):
    notes = []
    for abstract_note in self.sub_notes:
```

```
        notes.extend(abstract_note.get_all_notes())
    return notes
Note.get_all_notes(self):
    return [self]
```

While AbstractNote declares get_all_notes() for the entire hierarchy, the work occurs in the method overrides in AbstractNoteCollective and Note.

AbstractNoteCollective provides a simple recursive descent through the tree, while Note overrides with providing itself as part of the result. Bear in mind that the note provides its duration in the context of the note tree, so Note.duration() returns the duration as modified by the note tree. The same applies to relative_position. However absolute position is computed in AbstractNote using a simple upward parent traversal to the root, adding relative positions along the way. Refer to AbstractNote.get_absolute_position().

This is a highly practical method, avoiding the user's traversing complex note trees. However, the user should bear in mind that the result consists of the actual Note instances in the tree, not replicas. That means the elements in the returned list should be treated as immutable.

6.3.2   Adding a Note

The key to designing operations on a note tree, like adding a note, is to observe that note tree consistency is based on a set of constraints that dictate to the leaf notes and the intermediate nodes both precise durations and relative positions. Tuplets and beams dictate dilation factors on durations and positions, with multipliers that accumulate throughout the vertical depth of the tree. Thus, changes to the note tree resulting from adding or removing notes and nodes, require a re-calculation of positions and durations. Operationally, maintaining these constraints is a kind of algorithmic layout problem. In this section, we look at what is necessary to recalculate position and duration when a note is inserted into a note tree, and how to do the recalculation. Other operational activities would require similar.

Fig. 6.11 Adding a note into a note tree hierarchy.

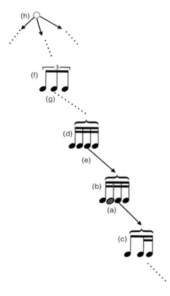

Setting context with *Fig. 6.11*, suppose we add the note at (a) to the beam node (b). The note to its immediate right is not a single note but is the beam referenced from the arrow to (c) - similar visual notation is used in other parts of the diagram. Because of the note addition, all notes to the right of the (a) need new relative position calculations. That also applies to all descendants of those notes, including all the members of (c) and their descendants.

Since beam (b) is actually (e) in beam (d), the resize of (b) forces a new relative position for the successors of (e), i.e., they are being pushed to the right. This same happens for any other parent beams from (d) up to the root node as long as these are beam nodes. However, if we have a tuple (f) whose node (g) is a parent to the chain of beam nodes wherein the note addition is made, then we observe that since (g)'s duration has changed, the tuplet needs to be recomputed in that all children of (f) require re-calculation of durations as well as relative positions. Also, that computation must equally percolate down the tree, resetting durations and relative positions. So, finally, this scenario of adding to a beam involves a downward, upward, then downward tree calculation.

The constraints to observe in adding a note to a note-based substructure, e.g., Beam or Tuplet, are:

- If adding the note results in the immediate structure changing its total size, then all notes logically following that inserted note should recalculate their relative positions. This typically applies to Beams. Because the structure size changes, this change accounts for why there is both a downward and upward/downward path to do the relative position recalculations.

- If adding the note does not result in the immediate structure changing its total size, then all contained notes durations are changed as well as their relative positions, which in turn results in changing durations and relative positions of all descendant notes and note structures from that structure. This applies to Tuplets. Because Tuplet durations do not change, changes only advance underneath the Tuplet in the algorithm.

The logic for this is relatively straight forward but found and detailed in AbstractNoteCollective.upward_forward_reloc_layout. This method is called by Beam when a note is inserted. So, its primary function is to reset the relative_position of nodes that come after the insertion. It recurses up the tree until either the parent is None or the parent is a Tuplet. In the latter case, it calls upon the tuple to rescale itself.

```
AbstractNoteCollective.upward_forward_reloc_layout(self, abstract_note):
    index = self.sub_notes.index(abstract_note)
    current_position = Offset(0) if index == 0 else
        self.sub_notes[index - 1].relative_position + self.sub_notes[index - 1].dura-
tion
    for i in range(index, len(self.sub_notes)):
        self.sub_notes[i].relative_position = current_position
        current_position += self.sub_notes[i].duration

    # Once size no longer changes, no need to propagate
    if self.parent is not None and not isinstance(self.parent, Tuplet):
        self.parent.upward_forward_reloc_layout(self)

    if self.parent is not None and isinstance(self.parent, Tuplet):
        self.parent.rescale()
```

Adding a note to a tuplet has some detailed considerations that will not be focused upon here. Critically, however the durations of the sub-notes of the tuplet change due to the increase in the number of sub-notes, while the tuplet's dilation itself is unchanged. Because the duration of each note in the tuplet has a changed dilation factor, this change is consequently passed appropriately down the tree and structures resized and repositioned accordingly.

Before presenting the Tuplet method rescale(), we note that recursing through all the children of the tuplet, and their children, recomputing new dilation factors is not terribly efficient, but there is a better way, implemented in the rescale() method shown later. The idea is based on computing one multiplicative factor to pass downward to apply to each node. Let's look at how to compute the new dilation factor due to note insertion in a tuplet.

Consider the tuplet in Fig. 6.12:

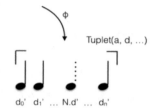

Fig. 6.12   Tuplet with added note N

- Let d = the tuplet's unit note duration.

- Let a = the number of unit notes represented by the tuplet.

- Let $d_i, 0 \leq i < n$, represent the unmodified durations of the notes in the tuple

- Let $f = \frac{a*d}{\sum d_i}$ be the original contextual reduction factor for the tuplet.

- Let Φ = the contributing dilation factor from the tuplet's ancestors.

- Let $F = f\Phi$ the full contextual reduction factor of the tuplet in the context of the tree.

- Let $d'_i = F * d_i$ be the reduced duration based on F.

Suppose a note N is inserted somewhere into the tree, with duration N.d. We first compute the new contextual reduction factor f' for the tuplet with the note N added:

$$full\_d = \sum d_i + n.d$$

$$f' = \frac{a * d}{full\_d}$$

With this, we find the revised full dilation factor F' that includes the added note.

$$F' = f' * \Phi = \left(\frac{f'}{f}\right) * F = \left(\frac{f'*\Phi}{F}\right) * F = I * F \quad \text{where } I = \frac{f'*\Phi}{F}.$$

The above math uncovers two important things. First, it reveals the process for re-computing the dilation factors, both for the tuplet alone, f', as well as the total dilation factor in the note tree context F'. Secondly, the term rearrangements in the final equations serve an important function. The factor I is a multiplicative value needed to convert F to F'. So, all we need to do is multiply all the child node durations and relative positions by I to properly reset the tuplet dilations due to adding of the note. This also applies recursively downwards and facilitates the durational and positional reset for all the nodes under the tuplet.

```
Tuplet.rescale(self):
    original_full_duration = self.duration.duration / self.contextual_reduction_factor
    new_factor = self.unit_duration.duration * self.unit_duration_factor /
                                                    original_full_duration


    #  get the contextual reduction factor contribution the parent give to self.
    contrib = self.parent.contextual_reduction_factor if self.parent else 1
    orig_f = self.contextual_reduction_factor / contrib
    # self.contextual_reduction_factor
    incremental_contextual_factor = new_factor / orig_f


    self.downward_refactor_layout(incremental_contextual_factor)

AbstractNoteCollective.downward_refactor_layout(self, incremental_factor):
    self.contextual_reduction_factor *= incremental_factor
    relpos = Offset(0)
    for n in self.sub_notes:
        if isinstance(n, Note):
            n.apply_factor(incremental_factor)
        else:
            n.downward_refactor_layout(incremental_factor)
        n.relative_position = relpos
        relpos += n.duration
```

The logic for correcting durations and relative positions from the topmost tuplet, as given in the preceding argument, is shown. The logic in downward_refactor_layout() is simply a depth first recursion on the tree, applying the incremental factor to both duration (apply_factor()), and dilating the relative position.

6.3.3   Reversing a Melody

As an example of dynamics considerations that go along with this note and note container representation, we look at the logic for reversing a melodic line. More than simply an algorithmic curiosity, reversing a melody has practical value in creating and contributing related melodic material to a composition.

For our purposes there are three aspects to this algorithm. One is to reverse the order of the notes, as well as the elements in the note tree. Another is to re-compute the relative positions of the structure elements at each level, the durations remain the same. And finally, there is the issue of reversing the note ties. The algorithm is as follows:

```
AbstractNoteCollective.reverse(self):
  # reverse recursively
  self.sub_notes.reverse()
  for n in self.sub_notes:
      n.reverse()


  # recompute the relative locations
  current_position = Offset(0)
```

```
    for n in self.sub_notes:
        n.relative_position = current_position
        current_position += n.duration


    # if we are at the top, parent == None, get all notes and reverse ties
    if self.parent is None:
        notes = self.get_all_notes()
        # see discussion why we cannot march forward nor backwards
        # and just untie and tie.
        notes_to_tie = []
        for n in notes:
            if n.is_tied_to:
                notes_to_tie.append(n.tied_to)
                n.untie()
        for n in notes_to_tie:
            n.tie()
```

This reverse() method is an abstract method in AbstractNote, but the main logic given above is located in AbstractNoteCollective as the main logic applies to the note collection class, reversing the notes and dealing with the ties. It starts with the recursion part of the algorithm so that each tree node's node has the notes reversed. The leaf notes, when called simply return themselves. Additionally, with the reversal of the note is the straightforward recompute of the relative positions.

The reversal of ties can only occur at the top level, but after all the reversal has been done. The logic involves building a list of all notes tied to, from the notes already tied, and untying them along the way. Then using that list, those notes are tied in the proper order. Observe that in performing the tie, Note looks for its note successor by traversing the note tree, see Note.tie() and Note.next_note().

6.4   Exercises

6.4.1 Build Lines for several of your favorite melodies. Print out the note durations and positions to verify the Line's structure matches your intentions.

6.4.2 Design and develop both depth first and breadth first iterators over the inheritance tree. Design and develop a leaf-only node iterator, including reverse iteration.

6.4.3 Develop a visitor design pattern [10] implementation for the note inheritance tree. For what purposes would you use this?

6.4.4 In the reverse melody code, the technique in reforming the ties is based on collecting all notes to tie, while undoing the ties, then loop over that collection to do the ties. Why could we not just do a forward loop and untie the tied notes and tie the former 'tied_from' forward? Would it make a difference if that process was done in reverse order? [Hint: explore what happens in a—>b—>c tie patterns.]

6.4.5 Explain the logic in Note.next_note().

6.4.6 Assume you have a Line with an associated time signature, and that the line starts on the first beat. Modify the model so that each group of beamed notes at the line level must necessarily sum to one beat duration and on beat. Then change this so that each group of beamed notes sums to a multiple of beat duration value.

6.4.7 Develop n algorithm to invert a melody line. Try using the inversions of consecutive intervals.

7 Chords

This chapter introduces and discusses chords, which serve as a starting point on harmony. The topic of chords is extensive, and we do not describe the entire range of chord types here. We nonetheless discuss a broad family of chords with which most musicians are familiar. These include including tertian, 7-chords, secundal, quartal, and secondary. To help the reader understand the many of the chords discussed, appendix D provides examples of tertian, secundal, and quartal chords.

We begin with a short music theoretic introduction to chords and define and explore the categories and classes of chords for which we produce software representations. We move to a discussion of a class hierarchy for chordal software representation. We show how this class hierarchy provides the foundation for representing each specific *chord category*, namely tertian, secundal, quartal, and secondary. We further introduce a means for describing chords using a semantically precise textual representation, and how to parse these textual representations into chord definitions, and eventually into chord instances.

Of particular note in these discussions are secondary chords. Harmonically these are important in that they suspend a current tonality for another, providing a means to transition to a different tonality. Additionally, they provide a unique kind definitional dependence in using the current tonality as a parameter to the chord definition.

For academic references to chord construction and theory, refer to [21] and [22].

7.1 A Brief Introduction to Chords

Chords are comprised of 3 or more tones, frequently sounded together or in positional proximity. Chords are used typically to define a harmonic foundation for music contemporaneous to the chord's tones in melody. With that, the topic of chords is a relatively deep topic in music theory. Musicians and theorists have spent a long time precisely defining them and exploring their usage.

A *chord type* defines a process for building a chord which, no matter on which tone it is constructed, sounds the homologous, or informally "much the same". Examples include major chords, minor chords, diminished seventh chords, and the many chord types that are explored here. Chord construction uses of two ingredients:

- A *root* or base tone that is formally the first tone of the chord.

- A *set of intervals* which when applied to the root tone or iteratively there from, provide all the other tones of the chord.

D. P. Pazel, *Music Representation and Transformation in Software*, https://doi.org/10.1007/978-3-030-97472-5_7

A chord type is an abstraction wherein the root tone is presumed but unspecified, and the type is principally defined by the interval set. In other words, chords are derived from chord types and specified roots.

A simple and common example is the major chord type, which is defined by the interval set {P1, M3, P5}. For a given tone, say A, we get the A major chord with {A, C#, E} as the tone set. For now, we avoid the use of pitches in this discussion. Usually, the chord tones occur as pitches over a wide range of registers, and generally the root tone is treated as the lowest pitch of the set.

Many times, composers want other than the first tone to serve as the lowest pitch. When a different chord tone of the tone set is specified to be the first, the chord type is said to be an ***inversion***. The root remains the same, but the first tone of the chord is not the root. Tone for tone, the inverted chord has the same tone set as the non-inverted one. This is another way of saying that the definitional set of intervals is relative to the root and not the first tone.

We have two ways to specify the root tone for chord construction. The first way, as we have seen already, is to specify the root tone explicitly, e.g., BbSus4, F#Min, etc. Another often used way is to assume a tonality and indicate the tone through a relative scale degree. So, assuming a C major tonality, we could specify a chord like IVMaj to be the F major chord, VIMin specifies the A minor chord, and so on. Specifying just VI would be interpreted to mean, use A as the root and infer the chord type from the scale's native intervals in scale 3rd 's – in this case, AMin. It is often a rule in music theory to distinguish chord type based on the letter case given. For example, "vi" should specify AMin. For our purposes we will not make such distinctions and use upper or lower case indiscriminately for scale degree with the appropriate inference of type by a provided tonality[29].

7.1.1   Tertian Chord Types

Tertian chords are generally composed of incremental thirds. For example, a C major triad is C, E, G, with E a major third above C, and G a minor third above E. However, our preference is to describe tertian chords with root relative intervals. In this case, C is a perfect unison, E is a major third above C, and G is a perfect fifth above C. This convention works best for tertian chord types as some chord types, e.g., MajVI, reference tones by interval number based on the root.

Clearly, by expanding tertian triad chord types using intervals extending further in thirds, tertian chord types may also include compound intervals. It may include odd intervals, like 9ths, 11ths, and 13ths, which otherwise might be considered even intervals of 2nds, 4ths, and 6ths. These are called ***tensions***. All tertian triads extended with a 7th interval are called 7-chords which also belong to the tertian class.

However, several outlier chords are introduced into the chordal lexicon, that are best described as tertian for our discussions. For example, the CMaj6 chord is C, E, G, A. For the most part this chord is tertian with the A being a 6th. Also, CSus4 is C, F, G. Again, this is close to being formally tertian, however the chord includes a 4th. There are many other interesting chords, such as those based on the augmented 6th, namely the Italian, French, and German that we also consider tertian.

The constituents of the tertian class include chord types that are varied and rich in texture. These chords can be found in classical, jazz, and popular music.

7.1.2   Secundal Chord Types

Secundal chords are built on incremental major or minor seconds. Whereas tertian chords are primarily based on combinations of various root-based intervals, secundal chord intervals are 'grown' from a

---

[29] In music scores, tonality is rarely, if ever, directly specified especially for minor modalities, but inferred from context. We are breaking away somewhat from convention as we are leading to precise software-based definitions for chord type and chord.

root tone incrementally using a list of major or minor seconds. In that sense these chords are more simply specified than tertian chords. Secundal chords bear similarity to cluster chords found in modern music compositions.

As an example, the GMajMaj chord is a triad comprised of {G, A, B}, with A, a major third above G, and B, a major third above A. Appendix D provides more examples.

7.1.3   Quartal Chord Types

Quartal chords are built on incremental perfect or augmented fourths. Like secundal, the intervals are built incrementally using fourths as opposed to an aggregated list of intervals. These may be found in modern classical and jazz.

EPerPer, for example, consists of {E, A, D} with A, a perfect fourth above E, and D, a perfect fourth above A. See appendix D for more examples.

7.1.4   Secondary Chord Types

Secondary chords may be the most useful and dynamic of all chords in the chord families. They are typically used to set up transitions from a tonality to a different tonality. It does this by indicating an immediate suspension of the current tonality for another, followed by a cadential resolution in the new key. When done without resolution to a new key, the suspension provides an interesting musical tease or question mark on the harmonic direction of the music.

Secondary chords have the form X/Y where X and Y are scale degrees. For our purposes, X is called the *primary chord*, and Y the *secondary triad*. A secondary chord is the lead component in the typical chord sequence:

X/Y Y

This is a cadential sequence in the spirit of a "V, I" cadential form, for example, but using a foreign tonality.

The scale degree Y indicates two items. First, it indicates a secondary triad that is the native triad on scale degree Y in the current tonality. Second, it indicates a secondary tonality based on Y and a modality commensurate with the secondary triad being a I chord. For example, if Y = VI in the key of C, the secondary triad is A minor. The secondary tonality then is A minor, usually melodic minor by default.

X is usually restricted to dominant chords like V, V7, or VII. So, continuing with the example, V/VI would be an E major chord, the V chord in A minor. In that sense, secondary chords are strictly *secondary dominants*. While limiting secondary chords in this way is also not a hard and fast rule, it is nonetheless nearly universal. Our example resolves to:

V/VI VI == EMaj AMin

To make this notation work, the secondary triad must be either major or minor to establish the secondary tonality. For a major tonality, only ii, iii, IV, V, vi are allowed for Y. VII, being diminished, not only is considered unstable but further does not represent a cogent tonality.

In some texts, the Y component is indicated by major and minor roman numbers as indicated by case, e.g., ii, iii, IV, V. The idea being that lower case is for minor secondary triads, and upper case for major. However, there are variances in practice, and so this is not a set rule.

7.2   Chord Template and Chord Representation

In this section, our goal is to design a software representation for chords general enough to accommodate the four categories of chords just discussed, tertian, secundal, quartal, and secondary. Each chord type belongs to precisely one category. Further, as seen in a later section, a chord can be specified textually, e.g., CMaj7, and parsed, which in turn can be converted to class instances for a software representation.

The software representation concerns representing both chord types and chords as classes. We bear in mind the following:

- A chord type is typically defined by either root-based intervals or incremental intervals. Details vary with chord type. Different chords have different constructive details. We call this definitional object a ***chord template***.

- The actual ***chord*** is defined by a set of tones which are derived during construction using the corresponding chord template. There are other general chord properties such as the root tone, as well as chord type specific properties.

As an example, consider the EMaj7 chord. The chord template is based the tertian chord category with defining intervals P1, M3, P5, M7, and in root inversion (that is, no inversion). From the template information, the chord tones generated are E, G#, B, D#.

Note that our approach defines chords as comprising tones, not pitches nor notes. We are only interested in uncovering the chord's tones. The assignment of a tone to a register (pitch) or additionally to a note, is beyond our scope currently. The assignment of chord tones to pitches is part of larger discussions.

With this in mind, we look at chord construction as a two-part process. One is to build a chord template instance which contains semantic information on how to construct the chord, and the other is to build the chord itself which contains the chord's actual tones. The process looks like this:

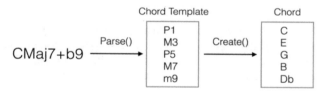

Fig. 7.1 Chord construction: parse to template, create chord

One could ask if it is necessary to require two different class structures like this. Could we not have one chord class per chord type that does the function of both and holds combined information. Design wise, that is possible, in fact it is easy to do. The separation however provides us with reusable chord definition objects (chord templates), that can be used to generate chords of a particular type many times.

This arrangement may be of less value for a chord like CMaj7 which is ***static*** in as much as the tones depend only on the chord definitional information and given root C. However, it does make a difference for ***relative*** chords like VMaj7, or better yet, VMaj7/II, wherein the chord tones depend on a given tonality. We look closer at these later, but the point is that relative chords are a function not only of the template, but of a contextual tonality, i.e., they are parameterized by a contextual tonality. In that sense, their reusability makes for higher value. Design wise it is better to have one consistent way to process all chord types, i.e., template and chord, than making a special case for either static chords or relative chords.

7.2.1   Template and Chord Class Design

Based on the previous discussion, the class design for templates and chords is based on two different but parallel class hierarchies. The ChordTemplate class serves as the common subclass to tertian, secundal, quartal, and secondary template classes. Each subclass holds information specific to its chord types represented by the class. For example, a tertian chord template would hold the basis tone, inversion, tension intervals, etc. The Chord class is the root subclass to tertian, secundal, quartal, and secondary chord classes. Each Chord subclass holds information regarding the chord tones, and the means (methods) for constructing the chord from the corresponding template. This hierarchy is shown in Fig. 7.2.

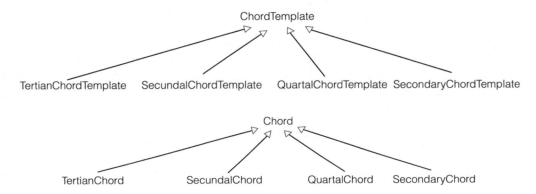

Fig. 7.2 Class Hierarchy for Chord Construction.

While this design raises flags about maintaining parallel structure for each new chord category, one should consider that these are broad chord categories that cover large chord definitional territories. When looking across the template classes, note that each has unique characteristics and implementation details, particularly in the case of secondary chords. New categories of chords if needed would likely be based on different core musical ideas, and likely have completely different definitions and implementations from the above, and so rightfully would deserve their own class types in the chord category hierarchy. The same applies to the respective chord subclasses. So given that there are not many categories, and that each has unique implementations, the parallel structuring is not so burdensome.

7.2.2   Chord Construction

The process outlined above shows that the chord template maintains sufficient information about a chord type so that the chord itself can be constructed. Those tones and other information are held in an instance of the Chord class. This design provides a separation of chord semantics from specific instance of it, a practical separation, e.g., maintain a chord definition instance to create chord instances in different tonal contexts.

Towards that end, the class ChordTemplate provides two methods, one to help create the correct chord template using a textual specification, and one to help create the chord:

```
# From ChordTemplate
@staticmethod
@abstractmethod
def parse(chord_string):
    raise NotImplementedError('users must define parse to use this base class')
```

```
@abstractmethod
def create_chord(self, diatonic_tonality=None):
    raise NotImplementedError('Users must define create_chord to use this base class.')
```

The method create_chord() is the constructive link between template and chord instance. This method is called to create the chord itself, providing a tonality that in some cases is essential and other cases not, as discussed earlier.

Consider the following example which creates a CMaj9 instance of a TertianChordTemplate following by using that template to create the chord itself:

```
# Create a template for CMajM9, with the M9 as root
template = TertianChordTemplate.parse('CMaj+9@(9)')
if template:
    chord = template.create_chord()
    print(chord)
```
```
TCMajM:9@(M:9)  [D, C, E, G]
```

The parse method makes template access immensely easy and so, learning the chordal syntax (presented later) is well worth the effort. For example, the following accomplishes the same without the direct parse:

```
template = TertianChordTemplate(DiatonicToneCache.get_cache().get_tone('C'),
                                None,
                                TertianChordType.to_type('Maj'),
                                [Interval(9, IntervalType.Major)],
                                None,
                                Interval(9, IntervalType.Major))
chord = template.create_chord()
```

It was mentioned that in some cases the template instance can be reused, changing only the underlying tonality. The following is an example of this reuse:

```
template = TertianChordTemplate.parse('IVMin')
diatonic_tonality = Tonality.create(ModalityType.Major, DiatonicTone("Db"))
chord = template.create_chord(diatonic_tonality)     # IVMin [Gb, Bbb, Db]

diatonic_tonality = Tonality.create(ModalityType.Major, DiatonicTone("F"))
chord = template.create_chord(diatonic_tonality)     # IVMin [Bb, Db, F]

diatonic_tonality = Tonality.create(ModalityType.HarmonicMinor, DiatonicTone("C"))
chord = template.create_chord(diatonic_tonality)     # IVMin [F, Ab, C]
```

The kinds of information that a chord template maintains is relatively clear. It retains the chord intervals, including any others explicitly added by the user. The root tone if specified is kept, and the scale degree if specified, as well as chord type. The reader can look through the various chord template classes and review the chord specific information. Although it varies by chord type, in general, it is quite similar.

For chord construction, the principal computation produces the constituent tones. For the chords specified in this chapter, there are two kinds of calculation, namely, one where the root-to-tone intervals are specified (e.g., tertian), and one where incremental intervals are specified (e.g. secundal, quartal). The implementation differences are noted below:

```
TertianChord.__create_chord_on_diatonic(self, diatonic_tone):
    self.chord_basis = []
    for interval in self.chord_template.base_intervals:
        tone = interval.get_end_tone(diatonic_tone)
        self.__tones.append((tone, interval))
        self.chord_basis.append(interval)
    ...


SecundalChord.__create_chord_on_diatonic(self, diatonic_tone):
    self.chord_basis = []
    current_tone = diatonic_tone
    for interval in self.chord_template.base_intervals:
        tone = interval.get_end_tone(current_tone)
        self.__tones.append((tone, interval))
        self.chord_basis.append(interval)
```

These are two simple variations on the same generative process, the first using a given first tone as the base over all intervals, and the second with incremental intervals using the prior generated tone to compute the following tone.

The question arises as to whether the incremental intervals in the second approach (secundal) could simply be additively aggregated to root-to-tone intervals, allowing tone computation to be achieved with the first approach alone. The issue with this concerns the lack of closure on interval arithmetic. Consider the case of combining 3 minor 2nd intervals from root tone C. The first give Db, a minor 2nd . The second give D, a diminished 3rd. However, adding a minor 2nd interval to a diminished 3rd is not allowed in interval arithmetic.

7.3   Chord Categories: Syntax and Examples

Given the design for this chordal system, we look closer at each category of chord. Each chord type within a category can be specified textually, with a category dependent parser doing the heavy work in detailing the intervals used to construct the chord. With this in mind, we look in finer detail at the syntax behind each category, give both syntactical and code-based examples, and cover additional details as necessary.

Before diving into each category separately, we offer a small clarification on invoking the different parsers. Each chord template Python class has a parse() method, as we have seen. So, you can find implementations for parse() within TertianChordTemplate, SecundalChordTemplate, QuartalChordTemplate, and SecondaryChordTemplate, with each class having its own chord category syntax.

To bring some level of unity and simplicity to this, the class ChordTemplate has a generic_chord_template_parse() method that tries each of the four mentioned class parsers and returns the first that works. That is, it returns the appropriate template. This is a great convenience, and to get the chord instance, simply call create_chord() using the returned template, without a need to test for template type as follows:

```
template = ChordTemplate.generic_chord_template_parse(chord_txt)
if template:
    chord = template.create_chord()
```

The remaining caveat is that to reduce any chance of an incorrect template being returned, the syntax for tertian, secundal and quartal chords allow optional single letter prefixes that fail outside of the intended parser. Without this feature, you could parse for say, "vi", and get a tertian template instead of secundal template.

For tertian, start the text with T or t, e.g., "TSus4", to ensure a tertian chord template. For secundal, start with S or s, e.g., "SCMajMaj". For quartal, start with Q or q, e.g., "QCPerPer". There is no lead letter for secondary chords which are parsed first in generic_chord_template_parse(), and which should fail even without the prefixes for the other three categories.

7.3.1 Tertian Chords

Tertian chords form the largest category of chords that we cover. It includes not just the standard diatonic triads, but 7-chords, and a host of less common but well-known chords such as the Neopolitan, French, Italian, German, and so forth. It also allows the addition of multiple tensions, or additional notes.

The syntax can be broadly thought of in the following syntactic chunks, constructing text from left to right. The first indicates whether the chord is based on a chordal root tone, or a relative tone to a given tonality (to be specified in code):

CHORD_BASE = DIATONIC_NOTE | SCALE_DEGREE

This is followed by the chord type name:

CHORD_NAME = 'Maj7Sus4|Maj7Sus2|Maj7Sus|Maj7|MajSus4|MajSus2|MajSus|Maj6|Maj|Min7|

MinMaj7|Min6|Min|DimMaj7/Dom7Flat5|Dim7|Dim|AugMaj7|Aug7|

Aug|Dom7Sus4|Dom7Sus2|

Dom7Sus|Dom7|HalfDim7|Fr|Ger|It|N6'

Tensions may be added with '+' following by the interval number with an optional tonal augmentation, e.g., +b9 for flat ninth:

TENSION = '+' AUGMENTATION? INTEGER

Finally, the inversion is specified with an @ symbol followed by either an integer (origin 1) indicating which tone in the generated tone sequence should be the bass tone, or by an interval qualification, indicating the tone from the interval to use, e.g. @3, @(b9):

INVERSION = '@' (INTEGER | '(' AUGMENTATION? INTEGER ')')

Finally, the full syntax for the tertian chord template is:

TERTIAN = (t|T)? CHORD_BASE CHORD_NAME? TENSIONS? INVERSION?

The tertian syntax provides a nice way to cover many of the common chords found in the literature, from basic triads to 7-chords, to elegant classical chords like the French or Neapolitan, to jazz chords with added tensions. Jazz notation is somewhat different, and the reader is invited to formulate a syntax more adherent to that genre.

Examples include: EbMaj7 C#Dom7+b9+bb11 IIDom7Sus4@3 VAugMaj7+#11@4

When the chord base is a diatonic tone followed by a chord qualifier, the chord is fully qualified and constructible. No further information is necessary to generate the tones. However, when the chord base is a scale degree, a tonality must be supplied to generate the chord from the template. The point of bringing this to attention here, is to indicate that under some conditions, templates can be viewed as functions that take a tonality argument to produce chords.

Also, there are cases where no chord name is specified, e.g., "C", "IV" In the first case, we use the I triad defined by the specified root as a major tonality. In the second case, we use the scale degree of a specified tonality in code.

Also note the optional requirement for beginning with a T or t. This syntax forces a tertian interpretation of the string. This syntax comes in handy for distinguishing tertian chord types from other types.

The following examples illustrate various combinations of tertian syntax:

```
template = TertianChordTemplate.parse('CN6')
chord = template.create_chord()     # CN6 [Ab, Db, F]


diatonic_tonality = Tonality.create(ModalityType.Major, DiatonicTone("F"))
template = TertianChordTemplate.parse('IVDom7@2')
chord = template.create_chord(diatonic_tonality)  # IVDom7@2 [D, Bb, F, Ab] on F Major


template = TertianChordTemplate.parse('EbDimMaj7+9')
chord = template.create_chord()     # EbDimMaj7M:9 [Eb, Gb, Bbb, D, F]


template = TertianChordTemplate.parse('EbDimMaj7+9@(9)')
chord = template.create_chord()     # EbDimMaj7M:9@(M:9) [F, Eb, Gb, Bbb, D]


template = TertianChordTemplate.parse('C')
chord = template.create_chord()     # C [C, E, G]


template = TertianChordTemplate.parse('VI')
chord = template.create_chord(diatonic_tonality)     # VI [D, F, A] on F Major
```

7.3.2   Secundal Chords

As mentioned, secundal chords are based on a stack of major 2nd and minor 2nd intervals, applied incrementally to a root tone. Like the syntax for tertian chords, the following syntax applies to secundal:

CHORD_NAMES = 'MinMin|MinMaj|MajMin|MajMaj'

CHORD = (CHORD_NAMES | (M|m)+)

INVERSION = '@' INTEGER

SECUNDAL = CHORD_BASE? CHORD? INVERSION

Compared to the tertian syntax, this syntax is much simpler:

- The root is determined by CHORD_BASE, and is either a specified tone, or a scale degree from a given tonality.

- Chord names like MinMaj interpret as iterative successive tone generation. In this case, for a given root, the next tone is a minor 2nd above it, and the next tone is a major 2nd above the prior tone.

- Instead of specifying chord names, combinations of "M" and "m" can be specified for incremental major and minor 2^{nd}s.

- Optionally, inversion is specified only by an index (origin 1) over the generated tones.

Note that secundal syntax may require an S or s prefix. This is for syntax disambiguation amongst chord types, as otherwise a chord like 'II' could be any of tertian, secundal, or quartal with no deciding indication which.

The following examples illustrate various combinations of secundal syntax:

```
template = SecundalChordTemplate.parse('CMinMaj')
chord = template.create_chord()        # CMinMaj [C, Db, Eb]

diatonic_tonality = Tonality.create(ModalityType.Major, DiatonicTone("G"))
template = SecundalChordTemplate.parse('IIMajMaj@2')
chord = template.create_chord(diatonic_tonality)        # IIMajMaj@2 [B, A, C#]

template = SecundalChordTemplate.parse('GMMmmM')
chord = template.create_chord()        # GMMmmM [G, A, B, C, Db, Eb]

template = SecundalChordTemplate.parse('IIMMmmM@3')
chord = template.create_chord(diatonic_tonality)        #  SIIMMmmM@3 [C#, A, B, D, Eb,
F]

template = SecundalChordTemplate.parse('C')
chord = template.create_chord()        # C [C, D, E]    default is MajMaj

template = SecundalChordTemplate.parse('III')
```

7.3.3   Quartal Chords

Quartal chords are based on combinations of perfect and augmented 4^{th}s. The syntactic form is identical to that of secundal:

CHORD_NAMES = 'PerPer|PerAug|AugPer'

CHORD = (CHORD_NAMES | (P|A)+)

INVERSION = '@' INTEGER

QUARTAL = CHORD_BASE? CHORD? INVERSION

Like the secundal type, quartal chords are described as incremental combinations of intervals. Quartal applies inversion using an index specification over the generated tones.

Note that quartal syntax may require an Q or q prefix. This is for syntax disambiguation amongst chord types, as otherwise a chord like 'II' could be any of tertian, secundal, or quartal with no deciding indication which.

The following examples demonstrate various syntactic combinations:

```
template = QuartalChordTemplate.parse('GPerAug')
chord = template.create_chord()      # GPerAug [G, C, F#]

diatonic_tonality = Tonality.create(ModalityType.Major, DiatonicTone("Bb"))
template = QuartalChordTemplate.parse('IIPerPer@2')
chord = template.create_chord(diatonic_tonality)      # IIPerPer@2 [F, C, Bb]

template = QuartalChordTemplate.parse('GPPAAPP')
chord = template.create_chord()      # GPPAAPP [G, C, F, B, E#, A#, D#]

template = QuartalChordTemplate.parse('IIIPAPAA@3')
chord = template.create_chord(diatonic_tonality)      # IIIPAPAA@3 [C#, D, G, F#, B#,
E##]

template = QuartalChordTemplate.parse('C')
chord = template.create_chord()      # C [C, F, Bb]   defaults to PerPer

template = QuartalChordTemplate.parse('IV')
# Follow 4ths but stay in the tonality
chord = template.create_chord(diatonic_tonality)  # QIV [Eb, Ab, Db]
```

7.3.4   Secondary Chords

An earlier discussion indicated that secondary chords are musically effective for key transitions or temporary suspension of one key for another. Recall that secondary chords have the form X/Y where X and Y are scale degrees, with X being the primary chord, and Y the secondary triad. It was indicated that secondary chords are generally restricted to dominants, and further have limits on the secondary triad specification. We will broaden the definition of secondary chords, allowing more possibilities in specification as reflected in the following syntax. The result will be a flexible definition for defining chords over various modality preferences. The syntax is as follows:

PRIMARY_CHORD = TERTIAN_CHORD | SECUNDAL_CHORD | QUARTAL_CHORD

SECONDARY_TONALITY = SCALE_DEGREE ('[' DIATONIC_MODALITY ']')?

DIATONIC_MODALITY = Major|NaturalMinor|MelodicMinor|HarmonicMinor|Ionian|...

SECONDARY_CHORD = PRIMARY_CHORD '/' SECONDARY_TONALITY

There are several key aspects about this definition that makes it stand out in distinction to the classical secondary chord specification.

- The secondary modality must be a diatonic modality but can also include modal keys as well as the standard major and minor variants.

- The secondary modality can be explicitly specified. This means we can construct V/II [Aeolian], where II [Aeolian] means using the current tonality, 2nd note, and make the secondary tonality the Aeolian key with that note as root.

- When the secondary modality is not explicit, we revert to the traditional convention for compatibility. That is, the secondary triad based on the current tonality and secondary scale degree infers the secondary tonality, e.g., V/II in C Major context has a D minor chord based on II, and so D minor (melodic minor) is the secondary tonality, upon which the primary chord (V = A major) is determined.

- The upper/lower case of the roman numerals are not semantic indicators of anything except scale degree.

- The primary chord can be any of tertian, secundal, or quartal.

- The primary chord can be based on scale degree relative to the secondary tonality, or can be specified by diatonic tone, e.g., CMaj7/V.

The combination of chord syntax, chord template and chord make for a very useful software combination for chord generation, especially for secondary chords. Following are some examples.

```
diatonic_tonality = Tonality.create(ModalityType.Major, DiatonicTone("A"))
template = SecondaryChordTemplate.parse('V/V')
chord = template.create_chord(diatonic_tonality)      # V/V(Major) [B, D#, F#]


template = SecondaryChordTemplate.parse('III/II')
#  II is b and default to melodic minor.
chord = template.create_chord(diatonic_tonality)      # TIII/II(MelodicMinor) [D, F#,
A#]


template = SecondaryChordTemplate.parse('CMaj7/II')
# Here the secondary key is irrelevant
chord = template.create_chord(diatonic_tonality)      # TCMaj7/II(MelodicMinor) [C, E,
G, B]


template = SecondaryChordTemplate.parse('V/V[NaturalMinor]')
# V[NaturalMinor] is E Natural Minor.
chord = template.create_chord(diatonic_tonality)      # V/V(NaturalMinor) [B, D, F#]


template = SecondaryChordTemplate.parse('V/V[Phrygian]')
chord = template.create_chord(diatonic_tonality)      # TV/V(Phrygian) [B, D, F]


template = SecondaryChordTemplate.parse('QVIPPAP@2/V')   # Secondary quartal chord!!!
chord = template.create_chord(diatonic_tonality)      # QVIPPAP@2/V(Major)
                                                      # [F#, C#, B, E#, A#]
```

7.4 Exercises

7.4.1 Secundal and quartal chords are based on incremental intervals while Tertian uses root intervals to compute tones. The secundal and quartal implementation approaches are essentially identical. Redesign the template and chord hierarchy to subsume the incremental interval approach to one class, with secundal and quartal being subclasses of it.

7.4.2 Write a program to compute for two diatonic tonalities, their common triads.

7.4.3 As a variant to the above, build a map/dict that for each diatonic tonality and any of its triads, finds all diatonic tonalities that have that triad. Give a space estimate for this map.

7.4.4 As a student project, study the Bartok Axis System, and write functions to provide substitute chords for tonic, dominant, and subdominant across all keys.

7.4.5 Augment the secundal chord syntax to add extra tones based on arbitrary intervals, and wherein an inversion is specified by an interval that is not necessarily the additive result of the secundal intervals used to form the chord.

7.4.6 As a student project, study the class ChordClassifier which attempts to find all chords that match a given set of tones. Run test cases and consider strategies to improve on performance.

8 Instruments

The prior discussions on notes and chords were abstract in the sense that they were without context to actual identifiable sound as we know it. Musical instruments provide a context for realizing notes not just as sound, but with a means for expressiveness along with timbral nuances that make music emotionally accessible.

The topic of instruments is a complex and expansive one. It is not the intention in this chapter to expound on instruments in any great depth. Instead, the focus is on a somewhat simplified instrument genealogy and classification with sufficient detail to give the reader an appreciation for the topic, and the ability to associate instruments to musical artifacts described later. We establish instrument classes families and associate with them properties that are important for later discussion.

Many readers may already be aware of the large number of virtual digital instruments (sometimes called sound samples) on the market. Many composers or performers attach these to midi-based applications, during or after composing music. These digital instruments are typically concrete examples of well-known instrument types, for example, violins, trumpets, and keyboards.

To be clear in setting the stage for discussion, this chapter is about a genealogy underlying these digital examples, which indicate where they fit into the family tree of instruments, and qualities expected from their genre. From general instrument information, we extract information that influences how we compose using notes in the context of specific instrument types, e.g., how notes can be performed, the articulations, the nuances, and the pitch ranges. While a specific digital instrument may override and add to some of these qualities, the genealogy and related information described here provide information to proceed before selecting a specific virtual instrument for a track of music.

After describing a genealogical model for instruments, we look at how to represent this genealogy as Python classes. The collection of actual data for the genealogy forms a data catalog, which we can opt to save and retrieve when needed. We discuss how to represent this data in XML so it can be easily stored and retrieved with persistence. Examples are given on how to navigate and retrieve instrument specific information from the instrument catalog.

8.1 A Simple Genealogical Model for Instruments

We introduce a classification model for musical instruments that while far from fully inclusive, is broad enough to encompass many commonly known instruments, especially those usually affiliated with an orchestra or professional soloists.

D. P. Pazel, *Music Representation and Transformation in Software*, https://doi.org/10.1007/978-3-030-97472-5_8

Fig. 8.1 Instrument Hierarchy

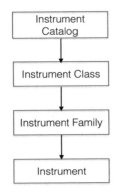

In this text, this classification is called the **Instrument Catalog**. *Fig. 8.1* shows the principal elements of the instrument catalog. The arrows indicate a containment relationship as in "has a set of". The instrument catalog consists of five broad categories, or **Instrument Classes**:

- Strings, e.g., violin

- Woodwinds, e.g., clarinet

- Brass, e.g., trombone

- Percussion (pitched), e.g., Timpani

- Keyboard, e.g., piano

While some instruments might fall directly to a class, some common instruments like clarinets further separate into differences typically based on instrument key, for example, clarinet in Bb, or clarinet in Eb. To accommodate differences in similar instruments based on key or other, we introduce the notion of **Instrument Family**. To clarify, in the case cited, under the woodwinds instrument class, there is a clarinet instrument family, with various key-based clarinets falling into that family. Specific instruments and their properties are **Instrument** objects within their appropriate Instrument Family.

As represented above, this schema covers a basic set of instrument classes. For example, percussion here is limited to pitched percussion for instruments like timpani, chimes, or xylophone. Further elaboration could include an instrument class for unpitched instruments like drum kits, bongos and maracas. An electronics class could add synthesizer and theremin.

In some implementations, parallel instrument catalogs could be established distinguishing, for example, solo from ensemble instruments. For the most part, both catalogs refer to the same types of instruments but in this new catalog for ensembles or orchestra sections indicating the number of players of a kind of instrument, e.g., 10 violins. In some cases, specific mixtures of, say, different string instruments could be recognized as an instrument. Our focus here is limited to solo instruments.

Instruments have several properties of interest. Most important is an instrument's pitch range, the pitch range being the lowest and highest pitches the instrument can audibly play, and assuming all pitches in between. For example, the piano has the sound range [A:0, C:8]. Later we will see that the pitch range can be used to constrain notes we place into a score, or otherwise flag a warning.

As noted, an instrument range is written as an interval defined by a pair of pitches. This indicates the instrument can sound all pitches between and including the pitch pair. However, key based instruments have a range specified to the tuning of the instrument, which is a transpose of instrument range as described. We refer to the key-based range as the **written range**, while its transposition to the key of C is the **sound range**. Many instruments are based on the key of C, and so the written and sound ranges are identical. However, instruments in keys other than C have a transpose interval, which can be used to shift the written range to the sound range accordingly (or visa-versa). Consequently, outside of instrument name, the main instrument attributes are:

- Key – The key of the instrument.

- Transpose interval – The interval from instrument key to the key of C

- Transpose direction – Indicates the interval transposes to higher or lower pitches.

- Written range – The pitch range of the instrument in the instrument's key.

- Sound range – The actual pitch range of the instrument as heard in the key of C.

Another characteristic is articulation. ***Articulations*** are performance directions on how a note should be performed for an instrument, many times in conjunction with transitions to succeeding notes but not strictly so. Many instruments share articulations, such as legato, staccato, or tenuto. Some are more specific to an instrument class or instrument, such as ***tonguing*** is for wind instruments. So, with the model at hand, articulations are characteristics found in instrument class, family, and the instrument itself. When we ask for the articulations of an instrument, we want the articulations of the instrument itself, and those in the family of the instrument, and those in the class owning the family.

As a point of reference, a table of instruments and their pitch ranges can be found at [23]. A reference on instrument articulations is found at [24].

8.2   A Software Model for an Instrument Catalog

We introduce the software class model for the instrument catalog described above. We follow with details on modelling articulations. Further, we add to the design details for implementing fast access to instrument data within the model, and by step the hierarchical complexities of the model.

8.3   The Instrument Catalog Class Model

Following the above discussion, we design a software version of the instrument catalog using five distinct Python classes as shown in Fig. 8.2:

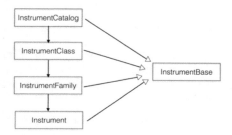

Fig. 8.2 Instrument Catalog class hierarchy

We have the following classes:

- InstrumentCatalog – Root node to catalog.

- InstrumentClass – One per class of instruments.

- InstrumentFamily – One per similar instruments in class.

- Instrument – One per instrument.

- InstrumentBase – Common information across model.

We assume that InstrumentCatalog is the root of this structure, and like the schema described above, we have a tree-like structure. In a full object instantiation, we observe a hierarchical structure as in Fig. 8.3:

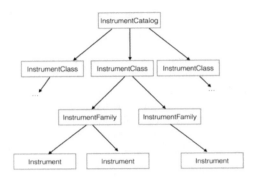

Fig. 8.3 Instrument Catalog Instantiation

We observe the following on instantiation:

- One InstrumentCatalog instance serving as the root of the tree.

- A layer of InstrumentClass objects directly beneath the InstrumentCatalog.

- Per InstrumentClass instance, a layer/list of InstrumentFamily class objects.

- Per InstrumentFamily instance, a layer/list of Instrument class objects.

We have seen this kind of tree structure earlier, and it simply means that the class objects form a straight-forward tree. We observe from this that all the objects, except Instrument, hold a list of children of some class, and for convenience [as seen later], each class has a parent reference to the object that holds it in their list. The combination of list and parent reference provide a means for navigating upwards or downwards in the tree. An example of this kind of instantiation is shown in Fig. 8.3.

Details common to all classes are held in a separate base class to all these classes. The class InstrumentBase, a superclass to all the other classes, holds for example name and parent references. We exclude putting lists in InstrumentBase since Instrument, the more populous of these classes, does not break down into further sub-categories.

On an issue the reader may have observed, many instrument families have only one instrument. For example, most string instruments belong each to one family, e.g., violin. With that, allocating an InstrumentFamily that has only one instrument seems wasteful. In the scheme of things for instrument data, begin relatively small in size, it does not make much of a difference. For the purists, a different structural arrangement may be called for (reference exercises for this section). For our part, we retain this somewhat pure solution which opts for a stable and predictable structure. Besides should a family become non-singular, the addition of a new instrument is a readily available option, e.g., adding electric violin to the Violin instrument family.

8.3.1   Articulations

An articulation list is included in InstrumentBase, that in conjunction with the parent reference, provides an easy way to accumulate the full set of articulations for an instrument. Just take the instrument's articulations, follow the parent reference to the instrument family, and add the articulations found there, follow that pointer to the instrument class, and so on. The implementation and technique are demonstrated below as found in the class InstrumentBase.

```python
class InstrumentBase(object):
    def __init__(self, name, parent=None):
        self.__name = name
        self.__parent = parent
        self.__articulations = []


    def get_native_articulations(self):
        return list(self.__articulations) # The list is mutable but
                                          # each articulation is not.


    def get_articulations(self):
        art_list = self.get_native_articulations()
        parent = self.parent
        while parent is not None:
            art_list.extend(parent.get_native_articulations())
            parent = parent.parent
        return art_list
```

8.3.2   Accessing Instrument Data

For usability, easy access to instrument data is very important. While the hierarchical nature of the given class model fits well with an abstract instrument genealogy, it is awkward for a user to traverse a structure like this to gain access to information, say, about piano, or violin, or A-flat clarinet. It is desirable to have in our design API, methods to access this information by name, e.g., getInstrument("Piano") or getInstrument("piano"), and forego the details of hierarchy navigation, and for that matter, text case issues in calling for that information by instrument name.

Similarly, it should be equally easy to get all the instruments' data of a class family, say all clarinets in the clarinet family, e.g., getInstruments("Clarinet") returns a list of Instrument objects for A-Flat Clarinet, E-Flat Clarinet, etc.

This is easily accomplished with a couple of Python dictionaries, mapping upper case strings to either family instrument lists, or to the instrument itself. The logic for building these is as follows:

```python
def build_maps(self):
    self.instrument_map = {}
    self.instrument_family_map = {}


    for inst_class in self.inst_classes:
        families = inst_class.families
        for family in families:
            instruments = family.instruments
            self.instrument_family_map[family.name.upper()] = instruments
```

```
                for instrument in instruments:
                    self.instrument_map[instrument.name.upper()] = instrument

def get_instrument(self, name):
    return self.instrument_map[name.upper()] if name.upper() in self.instrument_map
else None

def get_instruments(self, name):
    return self.instrument_family_map[name.upper()]
                    if name.upper() in self.instrument_map
                    else None
```

The method build_maps() is called at completion of populating the catalog or if incremental changes are made to it. In usage, user instrument access looks like this:

```
instf = c.get_instruments("Clarinet")
inst = c.get_instrument("vIOlin")
```

As for the instrument data itself, the Instrument class offers a host of properties representing critical details, including:

- *name* - The name of the instrument, as string.
- *key* - The key of the instrument if given, as string.
- *written_low* - The low pitch on range, stored as DiatonicPitch.
- *written_high* - The high pitch on range, stored as DiatonicPitch.
- *transpose_interval* - If there is transposition, the Interval to shift the written range to the sound range, and stored as Interval
- *transpose_up* - If there is transposition, Boolean indicator if up (True) or down (False).

We add to these two computed attributes:

- *sound_low* - DiatonicPitch of low-sounding pitch.
- *sound_high* - DiatonicPitch of high-sounding pitch.

The sound range is very important, as it is used to check if notes are in instrument range, when notes are added to a score. Not being in range is cause for raising an error flag.

The conversion of written range to sound range is easy using either Interval.get_lower_pitch() or Interval.get_upper_pitch(), depending on whether the shift is up or down.

```
from instruments.instrument_catalog import InstrumentCatalog, InstrumentClass,
                                            InstrumentFamily, Instrument

c = InstrumentCatalog.instance()
inst = c.get_instrument("vIOlin")
print(inst)

instf = c.get_instruments("Clarinet")
```

```
print('[{0}]'.format(', '.join(str(inst) for inst in instf)))
```

```
[Clarinet [E:3-C:7] down M:2 [D:3-Bb:6], Clarinet [E:3-C:7] down m:3 [C#:3-A:6],
 Clarinet [E:3-C:7] up M:2 [F#:3-D:7], Clarinet [E:3-C:7] up m:3 [G:3-Eb:7],
 Bass Clarinet [Eb:3-G:6] down M:9 [Db:2-F:5]]
```

8.3.3   The Instrument Catalog as Persistent Data

While a class model for an instrument catalog as described serves as a basis for our representation, populating the model with actual instrument objects is quite another issue. Typically a catalog like this would be constructed and made accessible at application initialization. There are several approaches to constructing an instrument catalog. One is to hard code the data in code. This approach is impractical, inflexible, and about as bad a choice possible. Although adding, modifying, or remediating instrument data would happen seldomly, changing code every time the model needs updating is not good software practice.

Another approach is to insert the instrument catalog data into a database. This solution is not bad and may be useful in distributed applications. However, the amount of data here is relatively small, so a database is overkill in effort and need. Also, adding the cost of database transactions when all access operations can be done easily and faster in computer memory makes having the catalog instantiated into application memory the strongest preference.

The easiest and most expedient approach is to retain the instrument data in a readable, shareable data file. Changing, adding, or deleting data items in the catalog then is simply a case of editing or updating a text file. To guard against many common text input errors, it is important that the data be well organized and structured, so that:

- Visually reading or parsing the data in the file is non-problematic.

- Adding and/or changing data in the file can be done easily.

With that in mind, we turn to a data representation and organizing methodology called XML. Unfamiliar readers can reference Appendix E on XML for a brief introduction. With XML one can organize complex data using a universally accepted syntax. The resulting formatted data provides an orderly structured organization of the data. Furthermore, the data is machine readable using well known XML libraries. In that way, the instrument catalog can be wholly read into and accessed through memory.

An example XML file for an instrument catalog is found in the code base. Reference instrument/data/instruments.xml. This file provides a starting point for expanding your own instrument catalog.

An outline on how the data is structured in XML is:

```
<InstrumentCatalog>
    <InstrumentClass>
        <InstrumentFamily>
            <Instrument>
            </Instrument>
        </InstrumentFamily>
    </InstrumentClass>
</InstrumentCatalog>
```

In the above, we have a nested set of XML tags that corresponds to the nesting structure of the model classes defined for instruments. The details on attributes are not shown, but more on that later. For now, we have structured input data, and our goal is simply to add or change details as we learn more about instruments. The file is read using well-established XML api's, and with that and a little extra effort, comes a direct transition from structured file data to the class objects hierarchically structured as discussed earlier.

To illustrate data entry for instrument details, we consider data entry for the clarinet instrument family. The XML below shows a segment of XML starting at the instrument family level.

```xml
<InstrumentFamily name="Clarinet">
  <Instrument name="Clarinet" key="Bb">
    <Range>
      <Low>e:3</Low>
      <High>c:7</High>
    </Range>
    <Transpose direction="down" interval="M:2"/> </Instrument>
  <Instrument name="Clarinet" key="A">
    <Range>
      <Low>e:3</Low>
      <High>c:7</High>
    </Range>
    <Transpose direction="down" interval="m:3"/> </Instrument>
</InstrumentFamily>
```

This XML defines two different clarinets in the clarinet family, for keys Bb and A. The principal data are the range given as high and low pitches, the transposition interval, and its direction. The range is given for the "written" range, not the sounding range. There are several ways the attributes could have been specified here. In this case, we break range out as a sub-structure '<Range>'. Alternatively, we could specify the range pitches as xml attributes, e.g., reference 'direction' in Transpose. These are design choices that depend on input convenience, clarity, or level of data complexity.

So far, the class structure and XML structure are in lock step, which provides many conveniences for reading the file at load time. However, that is not always convenient from the file editing viewpoint. For example, the XML structure insists on an InstrumentFamily tag even for instruments that effectively have no family, i.e., single instruments. Adding the InstrumentFamily to the XML for single instruments makes the text verbose, and further confuses manual input editing. However, changes can be made to the XML structure as long as structural changes do not cause incompatibilities with the machine reading process.

Towards that end, we make the following changes to how InstrumentClass is structured in XML:

- We introduce tags that form a sub-segment of data under InstrumentClass called Instrument-Group.

- In InstrumentGroup we input a mixture of Instruments and InstrumentFamilys appropriate to the class.

An example for Woodwinds Instrument class is shown below. Note how Piccolo stands as an instrument by itself, followed by the InstrumentFamily for Flute. Also, an Articulations sub-segment is included that includes 'double tonguing' as an articulation common to the class.

To make a clean separation of instrument data from articulations for the InstrumentClass, the instruments are encapsulated within the InstrumentGroup tags, and the articulation particulars within the Articulations tags. Basically, the InstrumentGroup tags serve as an instrument list demarcation from the Articulations.

```
<InstrumentClass name="Woodwinds">
   <InstrumentGroup>
      <Instrument name="Piccolo">
         <Range>
            <Low>d:4</Low>
            <High>c:7</High>
         </Range>
         <Transpose direction="up" interval="P:8" </Instrument>
      <InstrumentFamily name="Flute">
         ...
      </InstrumentFamily>
   </InstrumentGroup>
   <Articulations>
      <Articulation name="double tonguing"/>
      ...
   </Articulations>
</Articulations>
```

8.3.4   Instrument Catalog Initialization

The class InstrumentCatalog is the user facing class for the instrument catalog. There are two ways to go about constructing InstrumentCatalog's content. In one approach the entire catalog is constructed manually by the user using the classes of the InstrumentCatalog. In the other way, the InstrumentCatalog itself constructs all instances of the other classes in the catalog by reading the catalog XML file. In that case, all the user needs to do is construct the InstrumentCatalog specifying the XML file.

For example, the following code is an example of building the instrument catalog manually and piece-meal using the InstrumentCatalog classes:

```
catalog = InstrumentCatalog(xml_file='')
inst_class = InstrumentClass("Strings")
catalog.add_instrument_class(inst_class)

inst_family = InstrumentFamily("Violins")
inst_class.add_family(inst_family)

instrument = Instrument("My Violin", 'C', 'C:3', 'C:7', None, None)
inst_family.add_instrument(instrument)
```

Note in this instance that one specifies xml_file='' to InstrumentCatalog which builds an empty catalog which is then populated incrementally.

If the catalog is based on an existing instrument catalog XML file, one just specifies it as follows:

```
catalog = InstrumentCatalog(xml_file='/Users/music/muse_project/my_instruments.xml')
```

If the argument xml_file is the value None, the instrument catalog is constructed based on the default XML file in the source code mentioned earlier. This is the default behavior when xml_file is unspecified in the constructor.

In applications, it is convenient to have the InstrumentCatalog to behave as a singleton, so that it is only created once, and to have a single point of access to the catalog. Generally, applications should have a single unique repository reference for information that is global in nature. Duplication only serves for confusion in an application. Having a unique reference to the instrument catalog is the best way to ensure the information is definitive, unchanging, or if changed, uniformly accessible.

We accomplish this by having InstrumentCatalog inherit from the Singleton class. An excellent discussion upon which this approach is based can be found in [25].

```python
class Singleton(object):
    _instances = {}

    @classmethod
    def instance(cls, *args, **kwargs):
        if cls not in cls._instances:
            cls._instances[cls] = cls(*args, **kwargs)
        return cls._instances[cls]
```

The singleton nature of InstrumentCatalog is achieved by sub-classing to the class Singleton, as seen in InstrumentCatalog. The Singleton class achieves a singleton nature by overriding the "instance(cls)" class method and using a static map of class to instance. When called for some class, if the class is not a key in the map, the instance is built and the map from class to instance is entered into the map, and the instance is returned. If the class key exists in the map, the method simply returns the mapped instance as seen above. That way, the instance is only created once, but returned by repeated calls to instance(), as seen in the following user code.

```python
catalog = InstrumentCatalog.instance(xml_file=xml_location)
...
# catalog == cat
cat = InstrumentCatalog.instance()
```

The use of generalized arguments (*args and **kwargs) allows the user to pass arguments, both unnamed and named to the constructor. For any class using this singleton technique, ensure the constructor can recognize generalized arguments.

Readers may recognize that this approach is not thread safe, and we leave making this code thread safe as an exercise for the user.

Another aspect of InstrumentCatalog instance initialization are the details for reading the xml instrument file and converting it to an instantiation of instances of the instrument catalog class hierarchy. The details of this are found in InstrumentCatalog._parse_structure(). We will not labor through the details of that aspect of initialization here. What is important is that the xml internal tree is acquired through calling ET.parse(), and that the XML root node is accessed by calling tree.getroot().

Once the XML root is acquired, the XML tree can be traversed node to node, and depending on the type of node, the appropriate class instances are created with transfer of attribute settings from the xml node to the class instance.

8.4   Exercises

8.4.1 XSD (ref. [26]) is a way to formalize an XML schema. It basically is an XML description of how XML data should be structured, making it easier to avoid mistakes when editing the InstrumentCatalog file, enforcing compliance to the schema. Write an XSD schema for the instrument catalog XML and demonstrate how to check for errors in the instrument catalog XML.

8.4.2 Create an api at the InstrumentCatalog level that queries instrument by family name and instrument name. Can you devise one map that can quickly find the answer?

8.4.3 Make the method Singleton.instance() thread safe.

8.4.4 Explore replacing XML with JSON (ref. [27]). What are the plusses and minuses of XML versus JSON?

8.4.5 Address the issue concerning InstrumentFamily instances containing only one Instrument. What modifications in structure or logic can facilitate a solution? Provide an estimate on the relative amount of storage saved on a typical catalog through different approaches to this issue.

9 Score Representation

In the prior chapters many basic music elements were introduced in isolation from each other. Amongst these elements are pitches, notes and note structures, time signatures, chords, and instruments. All together, these can be used to create music. The goal of this chapter is to construct a unified structure for these elements, which we call a *score*, that can be used to construct music.

The intention is to construct a broad model for score that can be utilized many ways. For example, one might want a score that scales to a multi-instrument ensemble. Or for example, one might want to simply focus on a melodic line or limit the score to a single instance of some specific instrument. For our purposes, we model score so that it could apply to a wide range of instruments with multiple voices that can play together, making it general enough for simple and modestly complex arrangements, but simple enough to avoid specifying of the nuances and subtleties in composition, such as phrasing, slurs, etc. which are beyond the scope of this text.

An underlying concept to this score model is the line introduced in Chapter 6. Line embodies a generalization of 'melodic line' or 'base line'. Using Lines promotes focus on the musical interactions or inter-leaving of musical ideas, and how they can support each other.

The chapter starts with a conceptual introduction of a score and its basic elements. We then examine a Python class model for implementing these concepts, and how they relate to each other. Amongst concepts modelled are the line, voice, and tempo and time signature events. We also look at an implementation for time-based search on a score using the interval tree data structure. Specifically, we explore a technique to locate notes that sound or start to sound within some time interval.

In the next chapter, we look at how to convert a score to MIDI, allowing the user to listen to the results of a score that in a way wraps up the representation section of this book.

We pointed out early, especially for the reader who has glanced at the second part of this book, that we later introduce the notion of LiteScore which strips away much of the heavier software machinery behind Score, and with that, a reduction in functionality. The purpose of LiteScore is to facilitate discussion and demonstration on transformations only and should not be considered a replacement for the larger Score design considered here.

Finally, it should be emphasized that our score software model is not intended for complex applications such as composition notation applications. The presentation here is intended as a learning experience about building a music composition model from foundational elements in software. A full application requires designing and implementing a user interface for scoring. That is a highly difficult task that requires graphics skills and further demands an attention to detail that would distract this discussion from focusing simply on core ideas in music representation.

© The Author(s), under exclusive license to Springer Nature Switzerland AG 2022
D. P. Pazel, *Music Representation and Transformation in Software*, https://doi.org/10.1007/978-3-030-97472-5_9

9.1 What is a Musical Score?

We can think of a score as information about a piece a music that details the performance instruments and the notes each instrument must perform, in a unified context of time and tempo. One may think of 'song' or 'symphonic movement' as an embodiment of score. Multiple related instances of these can be modeled as a set of score movements for, say, a symphony or ensemble.

An exemplar fragment of a score can be seen in Fig. 9.1, which was composed by this author. In this score there are three instruments, namely piano, violin, and violincello. Each instrument has one or two staffs with the notes to be performed by them, along with articulation markings. The combination of an instrument with its music is called a *voice*. Each staff is read horizontally in time. The figure shows a part of this combination of elements including all involved instruments, and is called a *system*, and the actual composition consists of many systems per page, over many pages.

Fig. 9.1 *Example of Score fragment*

As an initial consideration, global aspects of score include:

- The set of instruments as voices associated with the score.

- The voices containing aggregations of notes each voice is to perform.

- A common tempo and time signature over all voices uniting the performance over time.

A score is often united over time by common tempo and time signature across all the voices. Often a score is similarly united over key signature. More will be discussed about key signature later in this chapter.

All voices are synchronized to the same timeline which for us is measured in whole time, section 5.2. Independent of voice, tempo markings and time signatures are positioned along that timeline as events indicating tempo or time signature changes. In other words, these are events global to the score which signify changes affecting all voices uniformly and their real-time performances. We call these collections of tempo and time signature change events, *event sequences*, and define them more fully later.

To gain a better understanding of how these elements fit together in a score, let's consider a conceptual break-down of a score based these components. Fig. 9.2 depicts a score and its elements and their relationships. The score has a set of tempo elements, each event etched onto a whole note time-based timeline (as a set of x's). The same is shown for time signature, with time signature elements spread over time. These timelines indicate the occurrence of a tempo or time signature specification or change. The combination of an element with a position is called an **event**. Thus, these elements are not pure tempo and time signatures specifications as we discussed earlier, but combinations of these specifications with a time position. The two timelines indicate sets of tempo events and time signature events respectively.

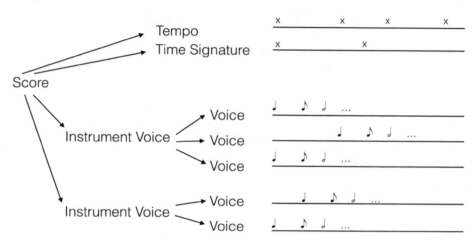

Fig. 9.2 A conceptual example of a score

Several instruments participate in the score. Each instrument involved in the score typically has one or more staffs, or voices, indicating a multiplicity of that instrument, each with one voice. For example, there may be two clarinets, four French horns, or even one piano taking 2 staffs. So, there is a one-to-many relationship[30] between each instrument type and the voices in which it participates. Clarifying the example of two clarinets, there is 1 instrument type (clarinet) for the 2 clarinets, meaning there are two voices, one for each clarinet, and so forth.

Definitionally, our model accommodates this complexity with the introduction of the concept *instrument voice*, which references some instrument type, but also has a set of voices each of which is played by an instrument of the specifically named instrument type. Normally we would expect each instrument voice to be unique by instrument type across the score, but not necessarily. That is, we can allow, say, two trumpet instrument voices, each with voices played by trumpets. That may sound redundant but an option dependent on compositional needs.

In practice, there is flexibility in instrument to voice assignment. Within the context of one instrument voice, there may be multiple instances of the instrument, each playing a different voice as we have discussed. Better yet, in some cases, there may be more than one instrument of a particular type playing a voice. For our purposes this will not matter much. A detailed breakdown of voice/instrument-instance falls to the user and is not enforced by the overall score conceptual model.

9.2   Score as a Class Model

With the score elements described and detailed above, the translation from conceptual model to Python class model is relatively direct. Fig. 9.3 below identifies and describes the classes and their inter-relationships.

---

[30] In a one-to-many relationship between entities in sets X and Y, any $x \in X$ is related to or linked to some set of y in Y, i.e., $\{y\} \subset Y$. However, each $y \in Y$ is linked by at most one $x \in X$. [There can exist a y not linked from any x.]

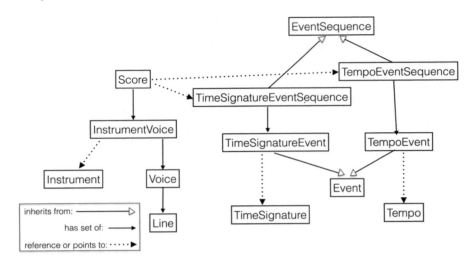

Fig. 9.3 Score Class Model

The main classes include InstrumentVoice, Voice, EventSequence, etc. as counterparts to elements of the conceptual model presented earlier. Dashed lines indicate referential or pointer relationships, while solid arrows indicate one-to-many relationships, and as discussed earlier, the white-headed arrow indicates inheritance. The figure broadly is in two parts, one concerning the organization of instrument and voice, and the other in managing tempo and time signature events. Despite appearances, the former has more complications. The latter has more to do with several simple inheritances and event collections management for two event sequences that affect the score globally. We look closer at these classes and their implementations, and examples on building a score, in the following sections.

9.2.1 Voices and Lines

The concept of voice is central to the scoring model. It holds the basic musical content, that is, notes, as well as information regarding note interpretation, i.e., dynamics and articulations. Architecturally, voice is based on the concept of Line making Line its core musical concept. In that way, melody or bass lines, or melodic fragments thereof become the foundation of a piece of music and take on a useful identity within the score. This approach offers many advantages over simply adding note content to a voice. For one, it offers a way to designate musical ideas, and to relocate or replicate them easily. It also provides a way to instantiate multiple musical ideas and weave them together.

As a simple example of multiple lines, consider the following:

Fig. 9.4 Two lines as two musical ideas within a voice.

In this case, we have two musical ideas, one in black and one in red. The design allows for the representation of these two ideas as two lines collocated at the same time position within a voice.

To explore these ideas in detail, consider the voice design shown in Fig. 9.5. Voice does not behave like a simple note collection class. In fact, it only collects lines. We make a restriction that a voice can only consist of other lines 'pinned' to locations at the Voice level. This makes Voice a kind of meta structure for Line or a palette upon which one can "paint" musical ideas as Lines. As mentioned earlier, a Line may consist of other Lines, Beams, or Notes. In that sense, we construct a hierarch of musical structures, starting with Voice having a set of Lines, and Lines having Lines, Beams, Tuples, Notes, etc., and on downward[31].

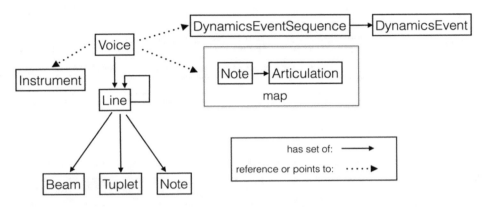

Fig. 9.5 Voice design

Voice has a several other interesting attributes. We mention here but explore in detail later that Voice tracks musical dynamics. By dynamics we mean the volume level, e.g., p, pp, f, fz, ff. Dynamics settings are stored as DynamicEvent's on a DynamicsEventSequence that Voice references. DynamicsEventSequence is a subclass of EventSequence and is discussed more fully a little later. Suffice to say for now that EventSequence is a kind of list structure for time-tagged elements. Secondly, Voice tracks note articulations, e.g., staccato, legato, tenuto, marcato. It does this via a map, mapping each Note [any of which are in the Voice's aggregate note content] to its respective articulation value.

A design argument could be made that articulation setting should be a property of the note itself. The short answer is yes but be mindful that note articulations are also a function of the instrument to which the note is assigned, i.e., that articulation must be valid for the instrument. If, say, a line of notes has articulations, then the line should relate to a voice and voice's instrument that supports those articulations. The design approach here looks at articulations as contextual, specifically to the Voice and Instrument involved. Note articulation changes or instrument changes are easier to deal with, using a single map, than running through a tree of Lines and Notes to accommodate changes. That's why keeping articulations as part of the Voice/Instrument context is preferred in order to keep data management simple[32].

The idea behind using Line as a scoring fundamental (say as opposed to Note in itself), is to provide a focus on linear or time-based musical structures. An example is given in Fig. 9.6. The Voice shows

---

[31] The self-referencing set pointer on Line in Fig. 9.5 indicates a hierarchical or tree structure based on Line. The hierarchy's leaves are always Notes.

[32] The reader may be confused on how Voice and Instrument are used in this argument relative to the class InstrumentVoice. InstrumentVoice is a class that manages the Voices using that instrument. Voice itself however also references Instrument, and in that sense, it is appropriate to retain the articulation map in Voice for its content as opposed to all the content across all voices that use the same instrument.

two Lines pinned to it. By *pin*, we mean the Line starts at a relative whole-time position to Voice. One line is a bass line, essentially a rhythmic beat line. The other is a composite line that has two melodic lines pinned to it. The combination of pinning to location along with the nested nature of line, allows one to build sophisticated melodic ideas[33]. Line's "pinning" capability allows these constructs to be moved either individually, or as a group.

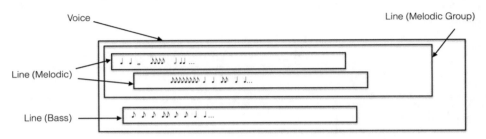

Fig. 9.6 Nested lines in a voice.

In user code, here is an example of how to construct a nested line sequence much as in Fig. 9.6.

```
voice_line = Line()
melody_line = Line()

# Construct music content
melody_1 = Line([Note(DiatonicPitch(4, y), Duration(1, 8)) for y in 'aceg'])
melody_2 = Line([Note(DiatonicPitch(4, y), Duration(1, 8)) for y in 'cadg'])
base_line = Line([Note(DiatonicPitch(4, y), Duration(1, 4)) for y in 'dddddddd'])

melody_line.pin(melody_1, Offset(1, 8))   # Pin melody_1 1/8 note into melody_line
melody_line.pin(melody_2, Offset(1, 4))   # Pin melody_2 1/4 note into melody_line
voice_line.pin(melody_line)    # Pin melody at start of voice_line, Offset(0)
voice_line.pin(base_line)      # Pin base at start of voice_line, Offset(0)

print(voice_line)
-------------------------------------------------------------------------------
Line(Dur(2)Off(0)f=1) [
   Line(Dur(3/4)Off(0)f=1) [
     Line(Dur(1/2)Off(1/8)f=1) [
        [A:4<1/8>-(1/8)] off=0 f=1
        [C:4<1/8>-(1/8)] off=1/8 f=1
        [E:4<1/8>-(1/8)] off=1/4 f=1
        [G:4<1/8>-(1/8)] off=3/8 f=1
     ]
     Line(Dur(1/2)Off(1/4)f=1) [
        [C:4<1/8>-(1/8)] off=0 f=1
        [A:4<1/8>-(1/8)] off=1/8 f=1
        [D:4<1/8>-(1/8)] off=1/4 f=1
```

---

[33] Additional structural support using motifs, phrases, and forms can be found in the transformation part of this book.

```
       [G:4<1/8>-(1/8)] off=3/8 f=1
    ]
 ]
 Line(Dur(2)Off(0)f=1)[
    [D:4<1/4>-(1/4)] off=0 f=1
    [D:4<1/4>-(1/4)] off=1/4 f=1
    [D:4<1/4>-(1/4)] off=1/2 f=1
    [D:4<1/4>-(1/4)] off=3/4 f=1
    [D:4<1/4>-(1/4)] off=1 f=1
    [D:4<1/4>-(1/4)] off=5/4 f=1
    [D:4<1/4>-(1/4)] off=3/2 f=1
    [D:4<1/4>-(1/4)] off=7/4 f=1
    ]
]
```

Having dived deeply into voices and lines in this discussion, we have a sense of how music content is managed. However, there is much more in the modeling details for score to discuss. We now look at the details behind the score model specifically related to event sequences for tempo and time signature.

9.2.2   Event Sequences for Tempo, Time Signature, and Dynamics

We discussed earlier that the Score class design included references to tempo and time signature event sequences. These event sequences are timelines, measured in whole note time, and each sequence contains events for specific times, thus providing a time-based map of tempo and beat throughout the music contained in all the score's voices.

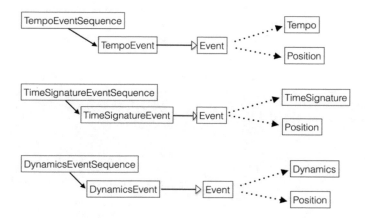

Fig. 9.7 Event design. Event holds the references.

The event sequence with its constituent events is a frequently referenced paradigm, and so with a little bit of generalization, we make these sequences generic. Generally, an event is little more than an association of some/any class instance to a time value. As such, the Event class is little more than a reference to an object and time value. Given that, a TempoEvent is a subclass of Event that references a Tempo object and has a Position in whole time. Also, TimeSignatureEvent is also an Event subclass referencing a TimeSignature object and having a Position in whole time. Similarly for Dynamics. Reference Fig. 9.7.

An implementation of the class EventSequence is simply based on a list of events provided the events are maintained in time order which is easy enough to do. When deciding on an implementation however, one needs to consider how that information would be accessed. Just using an ordered list for the sequence and given an arbitrary position or time, locating the prior Tempo or TimeSignature would be O(n) when n is the number of events in the event sequence. We speed the access time considerably using the OrderedMap introduced earlier through the floor() method. That improves the access time to O(log(n)). With that, EventSequence uses OrderedMap for tracking events.

Another implementation decision is deciding whether EventSequence should be a subclass to Ordered-Map or if EventSequence should reference an instance of OrderedMap. The former case is convenient if all the methods in OrderedMap should be exposed in EventSequence. However, that's not quite the case for EventSequence. But even if it were, we would choose not to subclass. The main reason is a reluctance to use a utility class as a base class to a specialized class. EventSequence is not a utility class but is more aligned with time models and other specializations. Put another way, EventSequence is less a kind of OrderedMap, than a time-based event model in its own right.

We implement EventSequence as a class that references and maintains an OrderedMap instance. The OrderedMap maps an event's time to the event itself. Note that EventSequence only checks if an object to add to the map is an Event. If one wants finer specificity, say that only TempoEvent can be added, one can simply subclass to EventSequence and add that kind of specialization check.

Further, Event has neither successor nor predecessor reference. The OrderedMap in EventSequence is the only ordering entity. For that reason, EventSequence maintains successor and predecessor maps mapping each event to successor and predecessor respectively. This allows the user to run through an ordered list of the contained events.

Using the OrderedMap's floor() function, for any specified time, an event is returned i.e., the event whose time is closest less than or equal to the given time. [Note that the event's successor event's time is greater than the given time.] It is worth noting, that time can be specified as Position, or int, or any rational number. That capability does not come for free. The value type for time in this case, like Position, requires an implementation of __hash__() and __eq__() in order for floor() to work. The reader should review a Python reference on identity and equality to ensure an adequate understanding of why this is the case.

Examples for creating and populating the three kinds of EventSequence's are shown below.

```
seq = TempoEventSequence()
seq.add(TempoEvent(Tempo(TempoType.Grave), Position(0)))
seq.add(TempoEvent(Tempo(TempoType.Moderato), Position(10)))


seq = TimeSignatureEventSequence()
seq.add(TimeSignatureEvent(TimeSignature(3, TSBeatType(TSBeatType.Quarter)), Posi-
tion(0)))
seq.add(TimeSignatureEvent(TimeSignature(2, TSBeatType(TSBeatType.Half)), Posi-
tion(10)))


seq = DynamicsEventSequence(events)
seq.add(DynamicsFunctionEvent(Dynamics.P, Position(0)))
seq.add(DynamicsFunctionEvent(Dynamics.F, Position(1, 2)))
```

9.2.3   What Happened to Key Signature?

With all the attention on tempo, time signature, and dynamics, it would seem that key signature would be an event sequence as well, and likely positioned at the global level much like tempo and time signature. However, to this point in the text, key signature has not arisen in our discussions on music concepts.

Functionally, key signature is generally useful in two ways:

- To indicate a major or minor key.

- To help eliminate a multitude of sharps or flats in writing music at the note level. Specific pitches are altered by the inherited sharps and flats in the key signature definition.

The first point is generally useful when reading a score, however, it is not fail-proof and often ambiguous. Often major/minor key transitions happen during a single key signature timeline with no explicit marking. Key transitions are often transitory so that sharps and flats are introduced or neutralized with naturals over very short temporal ranges.

Later, we introduce a harmonic annotation that provides a very precise tonality (key) for every temporal stretch of music, and significantly specifies a harmony (chord) as well. So, the first point on key signature is at best a weaker form of what is introduced later.

The second point is the most useful aspect of key signatures, that they remedy the need for writing explicit sharps/flats when writing for a specific key. This speaks to a remedy for visual notational issues. In this text, notes are added to note aggregate structures to build up larger note-related entities. Notes are meant to be independent from contextual influences, like key signatures, that could result in implicit changes to pitch. Key signature has more to do with note display in a notation system, lessening the visual load of a score. As mentioned earlier, this book is not about building a notation system. Building independent note structures sufficient to play, transfer, or transform is at the core of what this book is about, and less about how notes are visually represented.

With that, key signature would only serve to increase the complexity of an already complex topic and would contribute only to areas that are not the focus of this text.

9.2.4   Putting It All Together

We show how to create a somewhat simple score and how to put the all the pieces together for a short musical segment.

```
from instruments.instrument_catalog import InstrumentCatalog
from structure.score import Score
from structure.instrument_voice import InstrumentVoice
from timemodel.time_signature_event import TimeSignatureEvent
from structure.time_signature import TimeSignature
from timemodel.tempo_event import TempoEvent
from structure.tempo import Tempo


score = Score()


# set up 3 instrument voices: 2 violins, 1 trumpet, 1 clarinet
catalogue = InstrumentCatalog.instance()
score.add_instrument_voice(InstrumentVoice(catalogue.get_instrument("violin"), 2))
score.add_instrument_voice(InstrumentVoice(catalogue.get_instrument("trumpet")))
```

```
score.add_instrument_voice(InstrumentVoice(catalogue.get_instrument("clarinet")))

#  1 beat == 1 sec, 3/4 TS + 60 beats per minute,
score.tempo_sequence.add(TempoEvent(Tempo(60), Position(0)))
score.time_signature_sequence.add(TimeSignatureEvent(TimeSignature(3, Duration(1, 4)),
                                                    Position(0)))


# set up notes in the two violins
violin_voice = score.get_instrument_voice("violin")[0]
violin_voice.voice(0).pin(Line([Note(DiatonicPitch(4, y), Duration(1, 8))
                                            for y in 'afdecd']))
violin_voice.voice(0).pin(Line([Note(DiatonicPitch(4, y), Duration(1, 4))
                                            for y in 'cdc']))
. . .
```

To clarify, there is one violin instrument voice, which has 2 violin voices. To each, a Line of notes is pinned at position 0. An initial tempo marking of 60 (beats per minute) is added to the score's tempo_sequence, at position 0. Similarly, a ¾ time signature is added to the score's time_signature_sequence at position 0.

9.3   Time-Based Note Search

The following sections focus on augmenting score design with a capability to quickly determine, for a given whole time interval, all notes in all the voices that are either sounding or alternatively starting to sound in the interval. Why is this important? In some score processes, it is reasonable to read the score's notes in sequential increments over time. As one important example, in processing notes to audio in a streaming process, one might want to determine the starting notes in each voice, incrementally, per some time increment, as the basis for a sequential set of midi-to-audio processing events. Another reason is simply for anomaly detection, such as verifying all notes in a score identified to a time-based interval are valid, e.g., all notes at measure 77, beats 3 and 4 are sounding.

This search feature is achieved effectively using interval trees which are based on red-black trees (RB trees). Our discussion takes a close look at how RB trees are the foundation for the search feature. The discussion on this is non-trivial. However, to simplify the discussion, some aspects of RB trees are described but not in detail. In succeeding sections, we look at what it takes to properly maintain this design considering dynamic changes to voices, specifically in terms of adding/removing notes.

The point of this discussion is in part to show that music scoring is a complex topic, and that a comprehensive design often begins with finding the proper software fundamentals to utilize. We are not saying that the score design here is complete, but how one begins on a path towards a successful completion. Part of software design is not simply class modelling but looking for and integrating appropriate algorithms into the design to make desired outcomes practical and efficient.

Before jumping into this topic, we advise the readers to familiarize themselves with one of most basic search techniques, binary search. Appendix F is a brief chapter covering this ground.

9.3.1   Red-Black Trees

A red-black tree[34] (RB-tree) is a sophisticated search mechanism and algorithm, commonly used in applications that require rapid search. A few comments about RB-trees however are useful to understand why/how they fit into of music note search. An RB-tree is a kind of binary search tree, as described in Appendix F. The distinction is that RB-trees are ***self-balancing***. This means that with node insertions and deletions, the paths in the tree are approximately the same optimal size, $O(log_2(n))$ where n is the number of nodes in the tree. In fact, per node, its longest path to a leaf is at most twice that of the shortest path to a leaf [28].

The technical details of red-black trees are not described in this book as that discussion is beyond the scope of this text. Indeed, node insertion and deletion are more complex than in a binary tree and would require a lengthy distracting discussion. However, there are many excellent descriptions of these tree operations online and in [28]. What is important to keep in mind is that RB-tree nodes are essentially like binary tree nodes regarding keys and values. The difference is that RB-tree nodes carry a little extra information to help ensure node balancing.

9.3.2   Notes and Intervals

The foundation upon which the search capability goals of this chapter build, is that notes have a starting position and a duration. The beginning and ending position of that note defines an interval, that is, a numerical interval, not to be confused with musical interval. For our purposes, an interval consists of three characteristics:

- A starting numeric.

- An ending numeric.

- A ***boundary policy*** defining the interval boundary in terms of:
    - Open: Excludes begin and end values, written (a, b).
    - Closed: Includes begin and end values, written [a, b].
    - LO_Open: Excludes begin value, includes end value, written (a, b].
    - HI_Open: Includes begin value, excludes end value, written [a, b).

The default boundary policy used is HI_Open, which reflects for example, that a note begins at a precise time, but ends before an adjacent note begins. Of the methods in Interval, the most important are Interval.contains() that determines if a given interval includes a specific value, and Interval.intersection() which computes the intersection of two intervals. Note in these methods, the complexity is mainly in determining the result to the interval's boundary policy. Some simple illustrations clarify these concepts.

```
from misc.interval import Interval, BoundaryPolicy

# Default is HI_Open
f_interval = Interval(Fraction(1, 4), Fraction(3, 5))
print(f_interval)      #    [1/4, 3/5)
assert f_interval.contains(Fraction(1, 4))
assert not f_interval.contains(Fraction(3, 5))
```

---

[34] The qualifier red-black is based on the tree nodes being designated red or black during the tree construction. The designation assists the construction process in maintaining balance.

```
# Intervals can be constructed with integer ranges. Note the resulting boundary pol-
icy.
interval = Interval(1, 5, BoundaryPolicy.Closed).intersection(Interval(4, 6,
                                                        BoundaryPolicy.Open))
assert interval.policy == BoundaryPolicy.LO_Open
print(interval)      #    (4, 5]
```

As mentioned, Note naturally defines an interval based on its position and duration. Computing the interval for a note is trivially:

```
interval = Interval(note.get_absolute_position(), note.get_absolute_position() +
                                                        note.duration)
```

using the default boundary policy HI_Open.

We return to this subject again later when we add notes to an interval tree.

9.3.3   Interval Search Trees

Given RB-trees and their improved search capability, we return our original search problems, i.e., finding all notes that sound or start sounding within a given time interval. Given that a note is associated with an interval and an interval tree behaves as a map, we can imagine an RB tree for search with nodes having:

- Key values derived from intervals from all the notes.

- Mapped values being the note associated with the respective intervals/keys.

However, that alone does not tell us how the nodes in the tree are ordered. With a few simple modifications, the RB-tree approach to note search becomes viable.

Use the interval's low value as the key.

This modification effectively sorts the intervals by the left endpoint.

Add a covering interval, called a span, to each tree node.

The span is a covering interval that contains all intervals below the node in the tree and contains the node's interval itself. The purpose of the span is that in a search based on a given interval, we can quickly tell if there are result candidates at or below that node, guiding us to paths in the tree where there might be results, and avoiding those where there are none.

We consider an example of an RB-Tree based on intervals. The RB-tree in Fig. 9.8 is based on the following intervals in order: [15, 30), [16, 30), [18, 25), [20, 40), [23, 50), [5, 10). The intervals are shown in boxed nodes. Clearly this is a binary tree ordered by the low value of each interval. Next to each node is an indication of the span the node covers. It is derived from the minimum of left values of intervals at or under each node, and the maximum of right values of intervals at or under the node. Note also how nicely balanced the tree is, which is a major benefit of using RB-trees. This means that all searches, in theory, will follow paths of near equal size, in this case $\log_2(n)$, where n is the number of nodes in the tree.

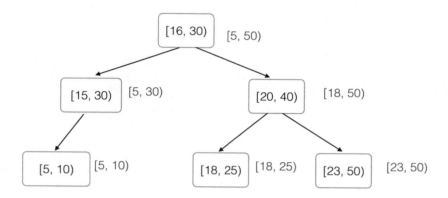

Fig. 9.8 Interval Tree example based on RB-Tree.

Given this, we will assume each node has the following information per note the node represents:

- Interval: The (whole note time-based) interval of the note.
- Key: The low value of the interval.
- Note: The note itself as the value associated with the key.
- Span: The minimal interval that "covers" all intervals at or below the node.

The following interval tree code[35] illustrates how to construct the interval tree in Fig. 9.8:

```
from misc.interval_tree import IntervalTree
from misc.interval import Interval

tree = IntervalTree()
tree.put(Interval(15, 30), MyObject(1))    # My object is some user-defined object
tree.put(Interval(16, 30), MyObject(3))
tree.put(Interval(18, 25), MyObject(5))
tree.put(Interval(20, 40), MyObject(4))

tree.put(Interval(23, 50), MyObject(6))
tree.put(Interval(5, 10), MyObject(2))
```

Further information on interval trees can be found in [28].

In the next sections, we explore several algorithms for note search by interval and see how they work with this tree.

9.3.4   Finding all Notes Sounding in an Interval

Given an whole time interval I, the goal is to find all notes that are active or sounding or beginning to sound in I. The summarized core logic is found in the class RBNode as follows:

---

[35] The class IntervalTree is general purpose regarding intervals, is a general interval map, and does not depend on Note. Score, Voice, and InstrumentVoice use IntervalTree purposed to Notes and their naturally defined sounding intervals.

```
RBNode: query_interval(seek_interval, answer):
  if seek_interval.intersects(self.interval):
     answer.append(node.interval, node.value)
  if self.left and seek_interval.intersects(self.left.span):
     self.left.get_sounding_notes(seek_interval, answer)
  if self.right and seek_interval.intersects(self.right.span):
     self.right.get_sounding_nodes(seek_interval, answer)
```

The algorithm is a basic recursive descent through the tree as long as the span interval intersects the given search interval. While at each node there is no guarantee that the node's interval intersects the search interval, the path is short, and all intersecting nodes are found. The downside is that multiple tree paths will be explored as long as the span interval and search interval intersect.

While the above algorithm concerns how to scan the interval tree for results, its invocation is preceded by several method calls through Score, InstrumentVoice, and Voice. The front-end method is:

```
from structure.score import Score
result = score.get_notes_by_wnt_interval(interval)
```

where interval is the interval over which the query is made for all notes sounding in that interval. The query result is a nested map. It maps each InstrumentVoice to a map which maps each voice in the InstrumentVoice to a list of notes meeting the criteria in that voice. This gives a full accounting not only of the notes but where they are logically located in the score. Diagrammatically:

InstrumentVoice → { Voice → [Notes] }

Here is an example, complete with output [score construction is omitted]:

```
# search for notes sounding in [1/4, 3/4]
voice_note_map = score.get_notes_by_wnt_interval(Interval(Position(1, 4), Position(3,
4)))
for (k, v) in voice_note_map.items():
    print('InstrumentVoice {0}:'.format(k))
    for (k1, v1) in v.items():
        print('    {0} --> [{1}]'.format(k1.instrument,
                                  ', '.join(str(n) for n in v1)))


    # Sample Output:
    InstrumentVoice IV[Violin [G:3-A:7], 1]:
         Violin [G:3-A:7] --> [[C:4<1/8>-(1/8)] off=1/4 f=1,
                               [D:4<1/8>-(1/8)] off=3/8 f=1,
                               [E:4<1/8>-(1/8)] off=1/2 f=1,
                               [F:4<1/8>-(1/8)] off=5/8 f=1]]
    InstrumentVoice IV[Clarinet [E:3-C:7] down m:3 [C#:3-A:6], 1]:
         Clarinet [E:3-C:7] down m:3 [C#:3-A:6] --> [[B:5<1/4>-(1/4)] off=1/4 f=1,
                                         [C:5<1/4>-(1/4)] off=1/2 f=1]]
```

9.3.5   Finding All Notes Starting in an Interval

Searching for all notes that start in a given interval is very similar to finding all notes that sound in the interval, except for the check, which is simply ensuring the note actually starts in the interval:

```
RBNode: query_interval_start(seek_interval, answer):
    if seek_interval.contains(self.interval.lower):
        answer.append(node.interval, node.value)
    if self.left and seek_interval.intersects(self.left.span):
        self.left.get_sounding_notes(seek_interval, answer)
    if self.right and seek_interval.intersects(self.right.span):
        self.right.get_sounding_notes(seek_interval, answer)
```

Again, while the above algorithm concerns how to scan the interval tree for results, its invocation is preceded by several method calls through Score, InstrumentVoice, and Voice. The front-end method is:

```
from structure.score import Score
result = Score.get_notes_starting_in_wnt_interval(interval)
```

Here is an example, complete with output [score construction is omitted]:

```
# search for notes starting in [3/8, 3/4)
voice_note_map = score.get_notes_starting_in_wnt_interval(Interval(Position(3, 8),
                                                                    Position(3, 4)))
for (k, v) in voice_note_map.items():
    print('InstrumentVoice {0}:'.format(k))
    for (k1, v1) in v.items():
        print('    {0} --> [{1}]'.format(k1.instrument,
                                    ', '.join(str(n) for n in v1)))


# Sample Output
InstrumentVoice IV[Violin [G:3-A:7], 1]:
    Violin [G:3-A:7] --> [[D:4<1/8>-(1/8)] off=3/8 f=1, [E:4<1/8>-(1/8)] off=1/2 f=1,
                          [F:4<1/8>-(1/8)] off=5/8 f=1]
InstrumentVoice IV[Clarinet [E:3-C:7] down m:3 [C#:3-A:6], 1]:
    Clarinet [E:3-C:7] down m:3 [C#:3-A:6] --> [[C:5<1/4>-(1/4)] off=1/2 f=1]
```

The class RBNode has other interesting algorithms, including gathering all intervals in the interval tree, and so on. These are left to the readers to peruse on their own.

The runtime for search in an interval tree is $O(log_2(n) + k)$, where k is the number of solution intervals found. Note that in the worst case where for example the search interval contains the root span, $O(log_2(n) + n) > O(n)$.

9.3.6   Adding Note Search to Score

In the score design discussion, note search was not included to properly develop interval trees as a separate discussion topic. Note search properly resides in the Voice class, allowing at this low level the ability to acquire notes based on whole note time search. Therefore, an interval tree is constructed in the Voice class synchronized to the notes in the voice. Each Voice has an interval tree.

As was alluded to in the prior sections, the call sequence for these searches starts at Score and pass through InstrumentVoice and finally Voice, ultimately returning the two-layer dictionary described earlier for results.

Score class includes other methods using real time and beat time and the time conversion methods introduced earlier in this text to invoke search with whole time arguments. Covering all these cases provides leverage in searching notes in a score. For example, suppose one has an application that cannot process all the notes in a score at once, and needs to access notes using real time intervals. These apis allow one to acquire the notes piecemeal, say over 1000ms time segments, to process in the application. Again, the reader should look through the code at the available apis.

9.4   Score Management

The score design as it stands provides a start for creating and managing a score. One problematic data management area of concern is adding or deleting notes from a voice and how the voice's interval tree is appropriately updated. Without addressing that issue, it is easy for the interval tree and the voice data to get out of sync.

The focus of this section is on adding notes to a score. Removing notes is left as an exercise. Notes are added to a score through modifications of note structures already in the score, or by pinning a Line to Voice. In fact, we have already demonstrated the latter approach in an example in section 9.2.4.

Of course, there are good and bad designs for our problem in interval tree update due to adding notes. One design is to build into the Line interface a reference to the interval tree so that when the line (or other sub-structures) is updated, the interval tree is updated as well. This is problematic as well for a variety of important reasons:

- Line and IntervalTree are conceptually and functionally orthogonal. That is, outside of this solution design, there is no reason for Line to manage an IntervalTree.

- Suppose other design artifacts require updating due to Line updates. Adding those artifacts to Line management overloads the Line class with further orthogonal functionality.

- The relationship between Line and IntervalTree would then be one way. If the interval tree was changed, e.g., cleared, should Line react to that change?

- Line has a relatively simple interface, and one tries to maintain that simplicity.

The solution we explore involves capitalizing on the observer pattern, which we have already seen and is explain in more detail in Appendix C. This approach simplifies the update relationship between Line and IntervalTree and allows further extension, i.e., updates to other artifacts like IntervalTree, as needed.

9.4.1   Interval Tree Update using the Observer Pattern

We discuss the use of the observer pattern to solve the problem of maintaining or updating the interval tree when the score is changed. As stated earlier, the interval tree is a field in Voice. The concern is that adding or deleting notes to any note-based structure such as Beam, Tuplet, Line should result in the interval tree in Voice being updated regarding that note, e.g., adding or deleting that node and its interval. Line, Beam, Tuplet can be deeply nested, and getting a notification or message that one of these structures has changed could take a complicated call path to Voice to inform Voice to update the interval tree. Reference Fig. 9.9.

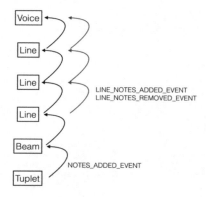

LINE_NOTES_ADDED_EVENT
LINE_NOTES_REMOVED_EVENT

NOTES_ADDED_EVENT

Fig. 9.9   Event notification for adding notes.

When a note is added to the tuplet at the bottom of the diagram, it generates a NOTES_ADDED_EVENT which must reach Voice in order for it to update the interval tree. Line modification behaves somewhat differently from BEAM or TUPLET modification and generates a different but similar message[36] which again cascades to Voice through all the intermediate structures.

In terms of the observer pattern, each parent is an observer to its child observable. That is, Voice observes its child Lines, each Line observes its children, etc. The pattern as depicted in the diagram is clear.

Building this kind of message system can take a lot of coding effort with a lot of code duplication. Implementing the observer pattern at each level helps, but still is repetitious. However, the score design provides us with extra help that makes implementing this kind of message passing structure particularly easy.

Line, Beam, and Tuplet are subclasses to AbstractNoteCollective. Attaching the observer/observable relationship to the parent child relationships can therefore be implemented within this one class. The design diagram below details how to organize the classes and how the implementation is done. AbstractNoteCollective subclasses to Observer and Observable, making it both an Observer and an Observable. We take advantage of this whenever the parent property is set. In that time, we register the parent as an observer of the child observable. Secondly, and very importantly, when AbstractNoteCollective receives a notification, we issue self.update() transferring the message to its parent observer. These two simple changes, result in the cascading notifications depicted in the Fig. 9.9.

Because the observer pattern is in the common subclass to Line, Beam, and Tuplet, the notification cascading occurs seamlessly. Also, the event reaches Voice even though it is not an AbstractNoteCollective since Voice is also made an observer of Line [note that Voice is a subclass of Observer].

---

[36] The difference is due to the packaging of the added notes into the event message. A line is passed for Line; a list for other Note structures. This may not have been necessary, but if at a later point in development, Line needs to react to sub-line changes, the identity of that sub-line could be useful. Just contingency planning.

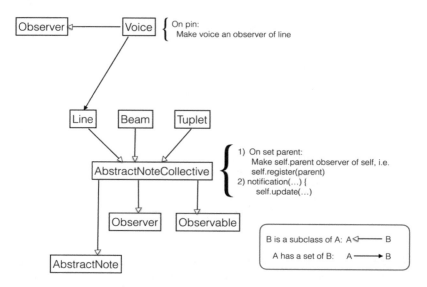

Fig. 9.10 Notification Architecture

In a closer look, the event/observer code in key classes AbstractNoteCollection and Voice show the simplicity of update mechanics:

```
AbstractNoteCollective.notes_added(self, note_list):
    self.update(AbstractNote.NOTES_ADDED_EVENT, None, note_list)


AbstractNoteCollective.notification(self, observable, message_type, message=None,
data=None):
    if message_type == AbstractNote.NOTES_ADDED_EVENT:
        self.update(AbstractNote.NOTES_ADDED_EVENT, None, data)
    elif message_type == Line.LINE_NOTES_ADDED_EVENT:
        self.update(Line.LINE_NOTES_ADDED_EVENT, None, data)


Voice.notification(self, observable, message_type, message=None, data=None):
    from structure.abstract_note import AbstractNote
    if isinstance(observable, Line):
        if message_type == Line.LINE_NOTES_ADDED_EVENT:
            self._add_notes_to_tree(Voice._extract_all_notes(data))
        elif message_type == Line.LINE_NOTES_REMOVED_EVENT:
            self._remove_notes_from_tree(Voice._extract_all_notes(data))
        elif message_type == AbstractNote.NOTES_ADDED_EVENT:
            self._add_notes_to_tree(Voice._extract_all_notes(data))
```

As you study this logic, recall that parent nodes are Observers. So, when an action like adding notes to beams or tuplets happen, the update for NOTES_ADDED_EVENT is sent, and when intercepted in passing the event upward, they are further passed to their parents. Eventually, Voice.notification() receives the event(s) and takes action on updating the interval tree, e.g., self._add_notes_to_tree().

For Voice, not only are the notes added/removed from the interval tree, but in the case of adding notes, the notes are checked to ensure they are legitimate for the voice's instrument. That is, the code ensures that the note's pitch lies within the sounding range of the instrument.

It's worth noting that AbstractNote is a super class to AbstractNoteCollection, and that the same observer pattern changes could have been made there. Placing the notification relationships in Abstract-NoteCollective is a semantic choice. AbstractNoteCollective is concerned with sets of notes, and we are interested in changes to sets of notes. That is not the case with AbstractNote. So semantically, the observer pattern implementation rightfully belongs in AbstractNoteCollective. This is an example of the kind of detail and attention that if not followed rigorously, eventually can cause problems later, as projects evolve.

9.5   Final Remarks

As we draw this chapter on the score to a close, there are several important points to be made, mainly for the computer science audience.

One of the intentions in developing this chapter is to convey a sense of how difficult it is to model a musical score. There are a surprising number of elements that coalesce in the design – everything from time signatures, and tempo markings, to all the varieties of note durations, along with articulations, and instruments and their relationship to voices. The identities and relationships among these artifacts are captured and shown in the design figures. As mentioned earlier, depending on the level of usage one has in mind for the software, this is where the effort begins, and it must be thought out clearly at the early stages. During development iterations, this is only bound to get more complex.

The latter sections on search and update illustrate the kind the complexity to be expected on further development. Search introduced the use of an interval tree into the design. Updating a score as an effect of updating any of the score's artifacts, in this case adding or deleting notes, involves cascading through the score to see that all score elements align properly. We focused on how this drives the interval tree update in particular. In more thorough designs, this kind of update would be seen frequently.

A reader interested in constructing a user interface using this score model faces significant challenges in reflecting all the score artifacts on screen. This involves screen layout issues, especially graphics layout at the note level including scrolling. As well, the screen presentation has to react to and reflect any changes to the score the user may make and has to be executed quickly with minimal disruption to the end-user. User interface efforts can be very difficult and require a special kind of expertise on presentation above and beyond the minute details of managing on-screen artifacts.

So, the main point to take away from this is that the score model presented in this chapter is something of a sketch or outline for beginning work in this area. What is present is of use and value in the context of this book, especially in the remaining sections of this part of the book wherein the score can be converted to MIDI, and with the expansion of dynamics behaviors. Expansion to ever greater musical coverage, e.g., different instrument support, etc., requires much more work and is a significant effort.

9.6   Exercises

9.6.1 Given an RB-tree where each node represents an interval sorted by interval.lower, write a recursive method to compute the span interval for each node.

9.6.2 The text shows a method in IntervalTree wherein for a given interval, it finds all objects whose interval.lower lies within the interval. Add a method for interval. upper. Same for both.

9.6.3 Redesign score so that articulation is attributed to note. How would you deal with conflicts wherein the articulation does not belong to the instrument type? Can you design an 'articulation override' policy at the voice level, in reference to the instrument?

9.6.4 Is the interval tree structure unique to the order of interval input?

9.6.5 An interesting RBTree interactive visualization can be found online [29]. Play with it to gain an understanding of how the algorithm reorders nodes.

9.6.6 Study RBNode.delete_node() and prepare a presentation for the different cases to be considered, and the kinds of changes that need to be made. For reference, refer to [28].

9.6.7 Examine how the RB-tree node span is computed and functions in search. Discuss different score characteristics that can affect the efficiency of search relative to the spans produced during construction, i.e., short versus long notes, note overlaps within and outside of a single voice, etc.

9.6.8 What are the issues with building the interval tree for note search at higher levels of the design, i.e., Score or InstrumentVoice?

9.6.9 The code shown for AbstractNoteCollective.notification() could have been significantly simplified with a single call to self.update(). Is there an advantage to calling out each event type with its own logic, as shown? Weight default behavior of the method versus behaviors of yet to be defined events. Does this apply as well to Voice.notification()?

9.6.10 As a project, starting with the current implementation of Score and its related artifacts:

- Develop a set of a few new features to implement.
- Develop a set of current bugs to address.
- Develop a plan to develop these new features and fix existing bugs.

9.6.11 Using Score along with a potential graphical user interface for it as an example, discuss the tradeoffs between model development (backend) and UI design (frontend), if we imagine two developer groups, one for each. When does UI design drive model development, and when does model development drive UI design? What kind of issues drive conflict between the two groups?

10 Rendering Score to MIDI

To this point, the focus has been on co-developing music theory along with software design analysis for a music model, the latter attending to objectifying both music concepts and algorithms into Python code. The software design discussions towards development of music in terms of voices, lines, and notes, and ultimately in their integration as a score are intellectually interesting and the core of this book. However, at some point, one wants to be able to hear results - to take music from the abstract to the concrete, from notes to sound. The aim of this chapter is to build towards that critical step.

We start this chapter with an introduction to MIDI, a kind of low-level programming language for making sound on a computer. As an introduction, only the most essential features are discussed that are relevant to this book. It is important that the reader becomes familiar with MIDI terminology, and in particular with a few MIDI messages that are frequently used.

The goal of this chapter is to design software to convert a score, as discussed earlier, into a MIDI file. This involves understanding the comparative structures of Score and MIDI files and developing algorithms for the structured conversion of one to the other.

Once a MIDI file has been produced, the reader can play it on a computer using applications supporting MIDI playback.

10.1 An Introduction to MIDI

MIDI is an acronym for Musical Instrument Digital Interface. MIDI is a technical standard, adopted by the MIDI Manufacturer's Association (MMA), for a protocol for sending and receiving music information to/from varieties of MIDI compatible devices. There are many configurations for linking and configuring MIDI devices. Fig. 10.1shows a MIDI keyboard controller which generates MIDI messages. These messages are sent to a set of daisy chained sound modules. The messages can alternatively be sent to a computer and converted to sound. Also, the computer could simply collect the messages and send them to the sound modules. The extend of configurations is enormous and is not a topic we delve into in any length.

MIDI messages typically concerns the starting and stopping of pitch sound instructions for an instrument. For example, on a MIDI keyboard controller, pressing a key sends a "note-on event" or message, indicating a pitch and velocity (a term affiliated with volume). Releasing the key, sends a "note off event" or message. There are other message types for instrument articulations, for example. MIDI messages are short in terms of number of bytes. This makes MIDI a terse but versatile protocol for sending relatively large pieces of music from small sized files.

For clarification and contrast, MIDI is not the same of digital audio which concerns the representation and/or transmission of audio wave formats, e.g., MP4, WAV, which is closer to a recording of an audio

D. P. Pazel, *Music Representation and Transformation in Software*, https://doi.org/10.1007/978-3-030-97472-5_10

event. MIDI is a very terse music representation wherein MIDI messages received from/by attached devices or similar are expected to reproduce sound based on the instructions during playback, e.g., which note to play.

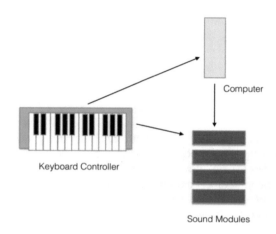

Fig. 10.1 Possible MIDI Configurations.

MIDI messages can be collected into a file. This file can be used to re-create the messages and process them to sound on MIDI supported hardware/software. Our focus is on this approach. While we will not use a keyboard for input, we will manufacture MIDI events from Score or Line, and store them in file format to be played later.

To be clear, A MIDI file is a collection of a MIDI message playback history. There are cases wherein a file is not necessary, for example a MIDI performance may in fact be the real time rendering of a performance based on MIDI instruments and MIDI synthesizers. The point is that MIDI messages are generated and rendered into sound in some manner, be it in real-time or originating from a file.

Standard MIDI is an extensive topic. This introduction only serves to provide the reader familiarity with terminology and the most basic conceptual information about MIDI. The reader is encouraged to delved deeper into MIDI topics on her/his own. There are many outstanding references such as [30], and online [31].

10.1.1 Tracks, Channels, and Messages

We are interested in understanding the structural concepts behind MIDI entities. Towards that, we begin with analyzing Fig. 10.2 which introduces MIDI channels, tracks, and messages.

The main elements are:

- Message – A MIDI message is a command related to producing sound, e.g., turn on/off the sounding of a pitch at some velocity.

- Channel – A channel can be considered as a route to/from a MIDI device. Roughly speaking, channels can be thought of as instruments.

- Track – A track is a sequential collection of MIDI messages, usually all of which are associated with some channel, but not necessarily one channel. Track is typically affiliated with MIDI files only but can be of conceptual use outside that context.

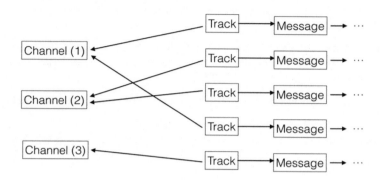

Fig. 10.2 MIDI as channel, track, message structure.

A MIDI channel comes closest to the concept of instrument, with the instrument being the device attached to that channel. The device could be a software synth, say a VST®[37] sound sample package, or otherwise virtual instrument, wherein the channel interacts with the device. MIDI is limited to 16 channels, numbered 1 to 16. Sending messages to a channel is called sequencing. Typically channel 10 is reserved for drum instruments. In programming MIDI, we often use origin 0. So the 16 channels are numbered 0 to 15.

On the other hand, there can be any number of tracks. Think of tracks as a convenient way to organize messages by the instruments/devices to which they should be sent. For example, we may have some instrument, say Trombone, and we want all trombone messages to be collected into some one track in time-based order.

The relationship between channel and track is orthogonal. In practice though, an organizationally beneficial relationship can be defined. Fig. 10.2 shows a mapping of tracks to channels, i.e., a track sends messages to only one channel, which generally works out well for organizing MIDI messages. Reversing the map, the diagram virtually assigns a channel to one or more tracks in a one-to-many mapping, but no track sends messages to multiple channels. This is only in as much as the messages in each track are assigned to some same channel. It should be noted as well that track 0 is typically reserved for non-note information such as MIDI tempo setting, time signatures, and so forth.

The tracks and midi messages can be consolidated into a file having a standardized MIDI file format. We will not describe that format in any great detail here, except to say that there are three types of MIDI file formats:

- Type 0 – The file contains a single multi-channel track.

- Type 1 – The file contains one or more simultaneous tracks.

- Type 2 – The file contains one or more sequentially independent single tracks.

---

[37] VST - Virtual Sound Technology, ref. [47]. VST is a registered trademark of Steinberg Media Technologies GMbH.

Type 2 is generally rare. For the purposes of this text, we only use type 1.

10.1.2   Time Representation in MIDI

MIDI has its own representation of time, measured in a unit called a ***tick***. Briefly, a tick is a sub-division of a quarter note, and tempo ties a tick to a real-time duration value. So, tick is not a uniform measure in real time. More precisely,

- Tick – a unit measured in PPQN (pulses per quarter note) or simply PPQ, is a whole note time measurement. It is based on breaking a quarter note to a smaller unit division. 480 pulses/ticks per quarter note is an example of a PPQN.

- Tempo - MIDI tempo is a music rendering value based on microseconds per quarter note.

Suppose we are given a MIDI tempo as τ, and the PPQN value is μ, e.g., 480 ticks per quarter note. Let t be some given number of ticks. The formula for T, the real-time (in μs) for t ticks is

$$T = \frac{t}{\mu} * \tau \qquad (10.1)$$

We note that all MIDI messages are associated with a timestamp in terms of ticks. What's more, a message's timestamp value is relative to the previous event in the track. So, for example, given a track, the first event is at tick 0, the next 240 ticks after, so the timestamp is 240, and the next 200 after that, so 200, and so on! The message timestamp is specified in ticks relative to the previous event in the track. Note that the timestamp is not part of the message itself, but part of the track to which the message is added. It is set when a message is added to a track.

10.1.3   MIDI Messages

MIDI has a rich message system for defining and controlling music and synchronizing sound. MIDI messages are broken into 4 categories:

- Channel Voice Messages – e.g., note-on, note-off.

- Channel Mode Messages – e.g., all notes on, off.

- System Common Messages – SysEx, e.g., ticks per quarter frame

- Meta Messages – e.g., tempo, time signature.

For our purposes the only messages we consider in depth are the note-on and note-off messages. The interested reader can study other messages in more depth.

The note-on message includes the following information:

- An identifying code that this is a note-on event, the value 9.

- The channel identifier, 0-15.

- The identity of the sounding pitch, an integer with 60 corresponding to middle C, and unit increments representing ½ step frequency increments/decrements.

- A velocity or volume number for the note, an integer between 0 and 127.

The MIDI message format squeezes all this information into 3 bytes, mainly by combining the code and channel together into one byte.

The 3-byte binary template for the note-on event is:

```
Note-on: 1001nnnn 0ppppppp 0vvvvvvv
    nnnn is the channel number (origin 0),
    ppppppp is the pitch value,
    vvvvvvv is the velocity value.
```

As an example, consider the note-on event for channel 3, for pitch MIDI C:5, with a volume level of 110. The binary template is 10010010 01001000 001101110 == [92 48 6E] in hexadecimal.

Note that in the framework discussed earlier, C:4 is 48 while in MIDI it is 60. So, in conversion to MIDI, MIDI pitches as 12 units higher than pitches in the framework.

The content of the note-off message is like note-on, except the MIDI code is 8.

```
Note-off: 1000nnnn 0ppppppp 0vvvvvvv
    nnnn is the channel number (origin 0),
    ppppppp is the pitch value,
    vvvvvvv is the velocity value.
```

To turn off the note in the prior example, we have 10000010 01001000 001101110 == [82 48 6E] in hexadecimal. In some implementations, you many simply set the velocity parameter to 0.

Another MIDI event of interest is tempo change:

```
Tempo-change: FF 51 03 tt tt tt
    tttttt: 24-bit value for the number of microseconds per quarter note.
```

Another is the time signature event:

```
Time-Signature-change: FF 58 04 nn dd cc bb
    nn: numerator of time signature
    dd: denominator of the time signature, as power of 2.
    cc: Number of MIDI clocks in a metronome click
    bb: number of notated 32nd notes in a MIDI quarter note (24 MIDI clocks).
```

This event depends on the MIDI concept of MIDI clocks. This differs from MIDI timestamps (ticks) described earlier. MIDI clock events are used for MIDI device synchronization. For our purposes, it is enough to know its event rate is 24 pulses per quarter note.

As an example, consider the event for a 6/8 time-signature. Then nn=6 and dd=3. Taking MIDI quarter note identical to a notated quarter note, bb=8 (8 32nd notes is a quarter note). Assume a metronome click every 3 eighth notes, cc=$\frac{24}{2} * 3 = 36$. So, in hexadecimal, the time signature event is [FF 58 04 06 03 24 08].

The final event we consider controls the volume level of a channel. Each channel provides a control of its overall volume independently of the volume specified on each note. Think of this specification as a mixing volume relative to the other channels. This event comes from the class of *control change events*. The reader should read about these events in a MIDI reference to gain a better understanding of this class of events.

```
Channel Volume Change: 1011cccc 00000111 0vvvvvvv
    cccc: channel number (origin 0)
    vvvvvvv: volume specification 0-127
```

So, for channel 3 setting volume to 100, we have in hexadecimal [B2 07 64].

Finally, MIDI has a very rich set of events with which the user can be very creative. In some ways, it is an assembler language for sound generation. For our part, we are interested in these few events just described that may surface as we translate score (a kind of higher-level language for music) into sound.

10.2 Mapping a Score to a MIDI File

The goal of this chapter is to devise an algorithm to convert a score to a MIDI file. With a MIDI file, one can use any DAW[38] or other MIDI applications to play the music on a computer[39].

Converting a score to MIDI involves analyzing how the components of a score map into the concepts of MIDI or MIDI file. Consider the following with reference Fig. 10.3:

- How to map voices to tracks?

- How to map instruments to channels?

- How to convert notes to MIDI messages?

- Subordinate to the above, how to add note velocity to the MIDI messages?

Later, we will deal with tempo, and how to convert score tempo to MIDI tempo.

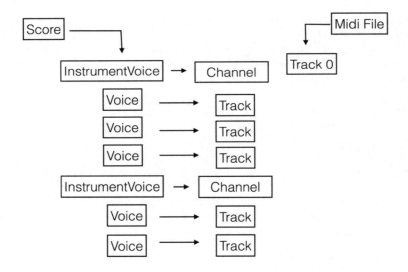

Fig. 10.3 Score-to-MIDI conversion details.

The first two issues concern the allocation of MIDI channels to instrument voices and the allocation of MIDI tracks to voices. The solution is visually illustrated on the left of Fig. 10.3. The idea is to map each score's instrument voice to a channel, which conceptually corresponds to an instrument.

Recall that an instrument voice is a collection of voices, all to the same instrument. Conceptually then for each voice of an instrument voice, there is a unique MIDI track associated with the channel of the instrument voice. This allocation scheme keeps the number of channels to a minimum, which is good

---

[38] DAW, Digital Audio Workstation.

[39] For example, GarageBand®, GarageBand® is a trademark owned by Apple Corporation.

since we have only 16 of those. With this, the stage is set to convert each voice's notes to MIDI messages.

That conversion is not difficult. The process involves, per voice of an instrument voice, acquiring all the notes in the voice, sorting them by starting positions, and then converting them to midi messages for the tracks associated with each voice.

10.3 Time Conversions

As discussed earlier, MIDI uses a tempo independent measurement for time in units of ticks. A MIDI file has a whole note time conversion factor, called 'ticks_per_beat', which is a constant indicating the number of ticks per quarter note, a typical value is 480. Recall also that MIDI tempo is measured as microseconds per quarter note. MIDI assumes a quarter note beat in both critical values.

The first conversion of interest is whole note time to MIDI ticks. Because MIDI ticks is tempo independent, the conversion is quite straight forward. Assume a quarter note beat,

t = a whole note time quantity,

T = equivalent to t but in ticks.

tpb = ticks per beat, typically 480.

$$T = {}^{t}\!/_{\frac{1}{4}} * tpb = 4 * t * tpb \qquad (10.2)$$

For our second conversion, we convert score tempo to MIDI tempo which is a bit more involved. Assume

β = The score tempo, or some whole time for a beat.

τ = The MIDI tempo equivalent to β.

We have:

$$\tau = ms\_per\_score\_tempo\_beat * num\_score\_tempo\_beat\_per\_quarter\_note \qquad (10.3)$$

Given:

BPM = Score tempo in beats per minute.

β = Score beat in whole note time.

$$\tau = \left(60 * 10^6 \middle/ BPM\right) * \left(\frac{1}{4}\middle/\beta\right) = \frac{15 * 10^6}{BPM * \beta} \qquad (10.4)$$

As an example, given a tempo of 90 beats per minute, a beat measured as an eighth note, we have $BPM = 90$, $\beta = \frac{1}{8}$. Then, $\tau = 1333333$.

Recall that a time signature has its own beat definition in whole note time. The time signature setting has no influence on the prior calculation, only tempo and its beat. In many cases the time signature beat duration and tempo beat duration are identical, and equation (10.4) works just fine. The problem in using the time signature beat is that it is often not the same as the tempo beat. We could use it if we knew the time signature's BPM, or TS_BPM. The relationship we need is:

$$TS\_BPM = T\_BPM * \frac{\beta}{d} \qquad (10.5)$$

Where T_BPM is the same as BPM in equation (10.4) and d is the time signature beat (whole time). The MIDI tempo calculation relative to the time signature beat should be the same as the MIDI tempo calculation for the tempo beat. This calculation shows that is the case:

$$\tau\,(rel\;tsig\;beat) = \left(\frac{15*10^6}{TS\_BPM}\right) * \left(\frac{1}{d}\right) = \left(\frac{15*10^6}{T\_BPM*\left(\frac{\beta}{d}\right)}\right) * \left(\frac{1}{d}\right) = \frac{15*10^6}{BPM*\beta} = \qquad (10.6)$$

$$\tau(rel\;tempo\;beat)$$

10.4 Score to MIDI Conversion Algorithms

The basis of score to MIDI file conversion should now be clear. There are two parts to the process. The first is to translate per instrument voice, per voice, all the notes in the voice to MIDI events within a MIDI track. The track is built for and from the voice, and the track is also affiliated to a channel associated to instrument voice. The second is to translate all score tempo changes into MIDI tempo change events.

Regarding the first part and using Fig. 10.3 as an architectural map, recall that each instrument voice consists of a set of voices. Each voice comprises a set of notes. The translation algorithm is straight forward. For each voice, loop over its notes. For each note, create a MIDI 'note_on' and a MIDI 'note_off' event. The MIDI tick position of each is easily computed from the note's whole-note position and duration. The process is outlined as follows:

```
ScoreToMIDIConverter._add_notes(self, inst_voice, channel):
  voice_note_map = inst_voice.get_all_notes()
  for voice, notes in voice_note_map.items():
      track = MidiTrack()
      self.mid.tracks.append(track)
      msgs = []
      for n in notes:
          ticks = self._wnt_to_ticks(n.get_absolute_position())
          msg = NoteMessage('note_on', channel, n.diatonic_pitch.chromatic_distance +
                                    12, ticks,
                            voice.get_velocity(n.get_absolute_position()))
          msgs.append(msg)
          end_ticks = self._wnt_to_ticks(n.get_absolute_position() + n.duration)
          msg = NoteMessage('note_off', channel, n.diatonic_pitch.chromatic_distance +
                                    12, end_ticks)
          msgs.append(msg)
      msgs = sorted(msgs, key=cmp_to_key(lambda x, y: ScoreToMidiConverter.
                                    compare_note_msgs(x, y)))
      prior_tick = 0
      for m in msgs:
          logging.info('{0}'.format(m))
          ticks_value = int(m.abs_tick_time - prior_tick)
          track.append(m.to_midi_message(ticks_value))
          prior_tick = m.abs_tick_time
```

Several aspects of the code snippet to call out include:

- It builds a MIDI track for each Voice.

- It constructs a MIDI note-on event using the note's position (converted to ticks), the note's pitch (using offset 12 to convert to equivalent MIDI pitch), and the note's nearest velocity articulation.

- It constructs a MIDI note-off event using the note's position and duration (converted to ticks).

- The MIDI messages are directed to the channel indicated by the input argument.

- The set of messages is sorted by MIDI tick position.

- In order, an event's tick time based on differences with successor event, is calculated as the message is appended to the track.

The conversion from note position to ticks is based on equation (10.2) given earlier. This process is modified in the next chapter on variable dynamics and tempo.

The second part of MIDI conversion as mentioned earlier involves setting all tempo change MIDI events. The algorithm again is straight forward as the given below. The calculation of MIDI tempo is based on Equation (10.4) given earlier. Usually, the first track allocated in the MIDI file, track 0, is used to contain this and other meta-type events, e.g., Tempo, TimeSignature. Track 0 is typically devoid of note_on/note_off events.

```
ScoreToMIDIConverter.generate_tempo(track, tempo_sequence):
    prior_tick = 0
    for tempo_event in tempo_sequence:
        midi_tempo = self.calc_midi_tempo(tempo_event.tempo)
        current_tick = self.to_ticks(tempo_event.time)
        delta = current_tick - prior_tick track.add(MetaEvent('set_tempo', midi_tempo,
                                                             delta))

        prior_tick = current_tick
```

This simple example shows how to use the score to MIDI converter with trace output showing the resulting interlacing of note on and note off events. The last argument on ScoreToMidiConverter.create() is a Boolean which when True turns on console tracing. The default is False.

```
def test_score_MIDI_conversion_example(self):
    score = Score()
    catalogue = InstrumentCatalog.instance()
    score.add_instrument_voice(InstrumentVoice(catalogue.get_instrument("violin")))

    score.tempo_sequence.add(TempoEvent(Tempo(60), Position(0)))
    score.time_signature_sequence.add(TimeSignatureEvent(TimeSignature(4,
                                                         Duration(1, 4)),
                                      Position(0)))

    violin_voice = score.get_instrument_voice("violin")[0]
    note_1 = Note(DiatonicPitch(4, 'A'), Duration(1, 4))
    note_2 = Note(DiatonicPitch(5, 'C'), Duration(1, 8))
    note_3 = Note(DiatonicPitch(5, 'B'), Duration(1, 8))
    note_4 = Note(DiatonicPitch(5, 'D'), Duration(1, 4))
    note_5 = Note(DiatonicPitch(5, 'E'), Duration(1, 8))
```

```
    note_6 = Note(DiatonicPitch(5, 'D'), Duration(1, 8))
    note_7 = Note(DiatonicPitch(4, 'G'), Duration(1, 4))
    note_8 = Note(DiatonicPitch(4, 'C'), Duration(1, 4))


    line = Line([note_1, note_2, note_3, note_4, note_5, note_6, note_7, note_8])
    violin_voice.voice(0).pin(line)


    smc = ScoreToMidiConverter(score)
    smc.create('book_example_midi_file.mid', True)


=========================================== Trace =====================
0/0 note_on[2]:pv=(69, 64)
480/480 note_off[2]:pv=(69, 64)
0/480 note_on[2]:pv=(72, 64)
240/720 note_off[2]:pv=(72, 64)
0/720 note_on[2]:pv=(83, 64)
240/960 note_off[2]:pv=(83, 64)
0/960 note_on[2]:pv=(74, 64)
480/1440 note_off[2]:pv=(74, 64)
0/1440 note_on[2]:pv=(76, 64)
240/1680 note_off[2]:pv=(76, 64)
0/1680 note_on[2]:pv=(74, 64)
240/1920 note_off[2]:pv=(74, 64)
0/1920 note_on[2]:pv=(67, 64)
480/2400 note_off[2]:pv=(67, 64)
0/2400 note_on[2]:pv=(60, 64)
480/2880 note_off[2]:pv=(60, 64)
```

The output format shows delta tick time, absolute tick time, MIDI message type, channel (bracketed), pitch and velocity values ("pv" as noted in output).

10.5 Converting a Line to a MIDI File

The Score class represents a relatively complete attempt to build a multi-instrument, multi-voice score allowing changes in time signature and tempo. While this moderate degree of completeness is of utility value, it is at the same time somewhat onerous to work with. There are many cases wherein all we require is to produce the MIDI for a simple Line of notes, maybe for piano, with a 4/4-time signature and a moderate tempo. The focus is to render the Line, to hear results, and not be distracted by too much detail.

The ScoreToMidiConverter class provides the static method convert_line() to address this need, allowing in-memory music Lines to be easily converted to a MIDI file. The parameters for convert_line() are:

- Line: Line to convert.

- Filename: The filename of the MIDI output file.

- Tempo: The Tempo object to set the starting tempo. The default is 60 quarter note BPM.

- TimeSignature: The TimeSignature object to set at the starting time signature. The default is 4/4.

- Instrument_name: The name of an instrument assigned to the Line. The default is 'piano'.

The implementation is quite unsurprisingly simple. With these few arguments, a score is constructed with tempo and time signature events inserted at position 0. The score then is converted into a MIDI file, basically leveraging the conversion logic already discussed.

This method is very useful for 'trying out' musical ideas without going through the overhead of building an actual score. Here is an example:

```
note_1 = Note(DiatonicPitch(4, 'A'), Duration(1, 4))
note_2 = Note(DiatonicPitch(5, 'C'), Duration(1, 8))
note_3 = Note(DiatonicPitch(5, 'B'), Duration(1, 8))
note_4 = Note(DiatonicPitch(5, 'D'), Duration(1, 4))
note_5 = Note(DiatonicPitch(5, 'E'), Duration(1, 8))
note_6 = Note(DiatonicPitch(5, 'D'), Duration(1, 8))
note_7 = Note(DiatonicPitch(4, 'G'), Duration(1, 4))
note_8 = Note(DiatonicPitch(4, 'C'), Duration(1, 4))


line = Line([note_1, note_2, note_3, note_4, note_5, note_6, note_7, note_8])

ScoreToMidiConverter.convert_line(line, 'line_example_midi_file.mid',
                                  instrument_name='violin')
```

Presently the way to generate a line is awkward and verbose at best. Later on, we introduce a far more expedient and convenient means to produce a line using textual specification. Interested readers may want to look ahead to learn about it (ref. section 12.2).

10.6   Exercises

10.6.1 Write a simple Python program (using MIDO [32]) to read a MIDI program and format the output to your liking.

10.6.2 Write a Score with at least two instrument voices, with one instrument voice having several voices. Check the generated MIDI, both using the supplied trace option and by reading the MIDI file contents. Note also track 0 and how the Tempo and TimeSignature events are translated as MIDI.

10.6.3 Read about MIDI program change events and what they do. Discuss their utility, if any, in the conversion software or the design of Score.

10.6.4 Suppose a score's tempo is 90 beats per minute with a 3/8 beat duration. If the time signature is 3/2 what is the BPM based on the time signature's beat duration?

10.6.5 Modify convert_line() to take a list of lines, with optionally each line associated with a different instrument for conversion to MIDI. There are several ways to package the arguments, weigh the price of generality versus ease-of-use. Also recall that your limit on channels is 16, actually 15 since track 0 is dedicated to meta-events. By the way, add an option for tracing like create().

10.6.6 (Advanced) Articulations in MIDI are triggered with MIDI CC messages, depending of course if your virtual instrument supports them. They provide a wide range of useful sound changes, such as legato, soft pedal, and other useful qualities such as panning and channel volume (as we have seen in the text). Consider design considerations that must be made to add articulations to score MIDI conversion?

10.6.7 (Advanced) Given a MIDI player of choice, add to the conversion logic an option to play the MIDI file immediately, if possible.

11 Variable Dynamics and Tempo

In the discussion on score's software design and modelling, we introduced event sequences as a collection mechanism for dynamics and tempo events. In both cases, an event sequence represents a set of tempo or dynamic events, each event positioned at a specific whole note time. The interpreted behavior of these events is **static** in that each event sets either a dynamics or tempo value that continues forward in the timeline until either the next event or to the end of the score. Also, as a point of clarification, each voice has a dynamics event sequence, but the score has one tempo event sequence which acts globally and uniformly over all voices.

In this chapter we generalize both event types to allow, per event, their respective values to vary over whole time. Not only does this allow the familiar musical notions of crescendo, diminuendo, accelerando, and ritardando, but also provides a generalized foundation for far more interesting time-based variations of value for these kinds of events.

The goal of this chapter is to define this generalization and provide a software design for its implementation. This design impacts the score design previously discussed, but not in a significant manner. It also has an impact on the MIDI conversion utility design as well.

11.1 What are Variable Dynamics and Tempo?

In this section we first describe what variable dynamics and tempo are, from the traditional music viewpoint. This is what every music student first learns when studying scores. These artifacts are performance markings, that is, markings that indicate details on how the performer should perform the notes. In this way, details about volume (dynamics[40]) and speed (tempo) are indicated. The discussions that follow then changes the descriptive perspective on these concepts to a more analytical and software oriented one, bearing more precision on which we elaborate. This latter perspective provides the foundation for this chapter.

11.1.1 An Introduction to Variable Dynamics and Tempo

The score markings for dynamics and tempo we considered so far are static in nature, in as much as say, setting a voice's volume to 'ff', and that voice stays at that volume until the next dynamic marking or the end of the score. We've seen similar behavior for tempo settings in the score.

---

[40] In current usage, the term dynamics strictly refers to volume changes. This can be confusing as one might misconstrue dynamics as meaning generalized changes, be it to tempo or volume as well.

© The Author(s), under exclusive license to Springer Nature Switzerland AG 2022
D. P. Pazel, *Music Representation and Transformation in Software*, https://doi.org/10.1007/978-3-030-97472-5_11

We are familiar with the hairpin music notation for crescendo and decrescendo shown in Fig. 11.1. In this simple example, the performance volume instruction is initially set to piano or soft, and over the course of the first measure the notes gradually become louder until forte at the beginning the second measure. The volume then gradually decreases note to note in the second measure until the end at mezzo forte. This notation is very common in music scores. The rate of increase/decrease of volume is generally assumed to have a real time linear, gradual, and smooth quality that is left as a matter of performance interpretation.

Fig. 11.1 Crescendo/Decrescendo

A similar indication of continuous variability of a musical quality, this time for tempo, is shown in Fig. 11.2

Fig. 11.2 Accelerando/Ritardando

In this case, an accelerando over the first measure indicates increasing the tempo gradually up to the tempo indicated in the second measure. The second measure holds onto this last tempo for its duration. A ritardando on the third measure indicates gradually slowing the tempo over the third measure. No tempo markings are shown in Fig. 11.2 at the beginning and end in this example, but we presume an earlier and later tempo marking is given that provides more precise referential information regarding variable tempo change.

Fig. 11.1 and Fig. 11.2 are examples of variable dynamics and tempo respectively. These kinds of changes are common throughout music scores. They both share the common theme that over time, some value or measure (dynamics or tempo) changes in some way, either increasing or decreasing. This theme of value change over time leads to an interesting and powerful generalization, and that is as functional artifacts of time versus value.

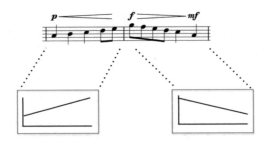

Fig. 11.3 Dynamics as graphs.

Fig. 11.3 illustrates this perspective for the crescendo/diminuendo example from Fig. 11.1. In that perspective, each measure can is seen as a graph of time, that is, whole note time, versus volume or velocity value. In the case of the crescendo the upward gradient illustrates a gradual and smooth volume increase. Similarly, the downward graph line for the second measure illustrates a gradual and smooth volume decrease.

Similarly, one can "graph" the tempo behavior of accelerando/ritardando as in Fig. 11.4.

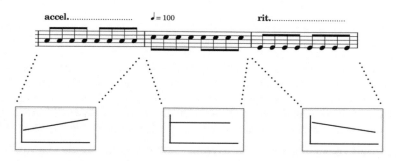

Fig. 11.4 Tempo change as graphs.

The three projected graphs map whole note time (horizontally) versus beats per minute (vertically), and the meaning of the graphs should be very clear. Note the middle graph shows a constant value, being the indicated assigned tempo which is equal to the last tempo value of the prior measure.

The point of displaying dynamic behavior graphically on these common musical artifacts is to indicate a generalization. If flat or diagonal lines indicate common musical qualities, why not allow other types of graphs, e.g., curves or perhaps a sequence of step ups and step downs in value? Our goal is to get a handle on representing these possibilities, and ultimately describing how to incorporate tempos or velocities defined by graphs into music itself.

The following sections explore the idea of generalizing changing volume and tempo specification as graphs or functions. Before proceeding however bear in mind that we will be using this generalization to provide precise tempo and volume values over performance time. As mentioned earlier, conventional music dynamic markings are approximate and guided by performance context and performance interpretation. This is generally good for music as it provides performance variability over multiple performances of the same piece of music. While such imprecise variability will not be the case in what follows, one will be able to change the functions to get a similar interpretive effect. However, in the end, each graph nonetheless provides precise settings for volume or tempo over time.

11.2 Functions and Graphs

In the prior section we informally introduced graphs to broaden our view of varying volume and tempo. More precisely though, each graph is an example of a function. A *function*, or *map*[41], describes a relationship between a set of input values, call a *domain*, and a set of output values, called a *range*. Each domain input must map to exactly one range output. Notationally, this is written as in equation (11.1):

$$f : D \rightarrow R \qquad\qquad (11.1)$$

---

[41] One should not confuse the mathematical term map with the same term used in computer science. In the latter, map or dict (in Python) refers to an associative container. In mathematics, it relates to functional qualities as explained. Proper meaning of the term should be inferred by context.

where f is the function, D is the domain, and R is the range. There is no implicit guarantee that every element in R has an element in D that maps to it. Examples include:

$$f(x) = 2x + 3$$

$$f(x, y) = x^2 + y$$

$$f(x, y, z) = (x^2 + y^2 + z^2)^{1/2}$$

These are examples of functions that map real numbers to real numbers for their domains and ranges. In some cases, like the first function, the domain is given by one value. We say that f has one **parameter**, namely x, in f(x). The other two functions take 2 and 3 parameters respectively. The number of values used to express the domain is call the **dimension** of the domain. We call functions having a one-dimensional domain, **univariate functions**. Otherwise, the function is called **multivariate**.

A function's range also has a dimension. For example, if the range is a single real value, then the range is 1 dimensional. If two values, the range is a 2-dimensional system, and so forth. It is worth noting that for a multidimensional range of a function expressed in Python, the function's result would generally be expressed as a n-dimensional tuple, where n is the range's dimension.

In the function examples above, we focus generally on mapping numerical values to numerical values, and in general we discuss these kinds of functions in the coming sections. The reader should be aware that the definition of function is far broader than that, in that it maps 'things' to 'things' just as long as any one thing in the domain maps to exactly one some other thing in the range.

In the following sections we focus on univariate functions on a real number domain that map to a real number range. These are very useful in the context of charting variable dynamics and tempo. We start with a description of two specific types of univariate functions, the piecewise linear function, and the stepwise linear function. We then proceed to more generalized functional forms.

11.2.1 The Piecewise Linear Function

The piecewise linear function is likely the most commonplace and intuitive of univariate functions. Generally speaking, it is the basis of most common graphs, consisting of connected straight line segments. We find it for example in charts of time to temperature, and in displaying stock market behavior, but at a coarse level, say over days or months in order to generalize fine-grained behavior into broader strokes. Fig. 11.5 shows an example:

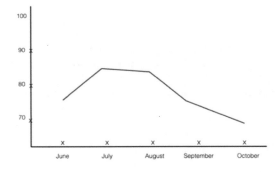

Fig. 11.5 Piecewise Linear Function Example.

The figure shows an example of a simple monthly temperature graph. It consists of a set of connected straight lines that seamlessly connect over the course of June through October. The X axis or domain consists of a monthly timeline, and the Y axis or range consists of temperature values. As a piecewise linear function, it has the following characteristics:

- The chart's X axis references 5 points, one per month, arranged consecutively.

- The chart line itself is composed of 4 straight line segments.

- The chart is seamless, that is, from June through October, the line has no gaps. Note that the end of one line connects to the start of the next. That is, the line endpoints connect, leaving no vertical gaps. It also means the function is continuous.

These are characteristics of a univariate piecewise linear function.

To be more precise, we define a simpler concept upon which to build. A ***univariate linear function*** is a function of the form:

$$y = f(x) = ax + b, where \ x, y, a, b \in Reals \qquad (11.2)$$

In equation (11.2), a and b are fixed[42]. The graph of this function is a straight line. If a=0, the line is horizontal running through b on the y axis. If b=0, the line runs through the origin (0, 0) at some angle.

Given two graph coordinates (r, s) and (t, u) where r and t are domain elements, and s and u are range elements, we can define a linear function y = ax + b with:

$$a = \frac{(u - s)}{(t - r)}, \quad b = s - ar \qquad (11.3)$$

This function charts a ***linear segment*** from (r, s) to (t, u) on the X-axis interval [r, t]. There is an exceptional case where t = r, which can be interpreted as a vertical line through t. We assume this will never be the case for our purposes. We call the function the segment's ***linear form***.

We define a piecewise linear function as follows:

Let {P_i} be a set of N>1 points in the real plane, where $P_i = (x_i, y_i)$ and $x_1 < x_2 < \cdots < x_N$.

*Let {L_i} be the set of N-1 linear segments where L_i is the linear segment from P_i to P_{i+1} over the X axis segment [x_i, x_{i+1}], with respective linear form l_i: [x_i, x_{i+1}] → R. The **piecewise linear function** f: [x_1, x_N] → R is defined for x ∈ [x_1, x_N] as*

$$f(x) = l_i(x) \ for \ x \in [x_i, x_{i+1}]. \qquad (11.4)$$

Note that by the definitions of {P_i} and {L_i}, we have $l_i(x_{i+1}) = l_{i+1}(x_{i+1}) \ for \ 1 \leq i \leq N - 2$. Intuitively speaking, the piecewise linear function defines a 'curve' built with line segments defined by consecutive pairs of graph points that abut seamlessly to each other from beginning to end[43].

---

[42] In some texts, a linear function is simply y=ab, and an affine function is y=ax+b. We take the liberty of using either for the more general affine form.

[43] More formally, this is a continuous piecewise linear function. In some discussions, the line segments may not abut as described.

Piecewise linear functions are very useful functions for several reasons. One is that the defining domain points can be used to define target states, with linear transitions from state to state. Secondly it is easy to define, and easy to implement, ref. function/piecewise_linear_function.py in the code base.

An example of typical usage in Python follows:

```
from function.piecewise_linear_function import PiecewiseLinearFunction
array = [(5, 1), (7, 3), (10, 6), (12, 8)]
f = PiecewiseLinearFunction(array)

assert f.eval(5)  == 1
assert f.eval(6)  == 2
assert f.eval(7)  == 3
assert f.eval(8)  == 4
assert f.eval(9)  == 5
assert f.eval(10) == 6
assert f.eval(11) == 7
assert f.eval(11.5) == 7.5
assert f.eval(12) == 8
```

Note that definition (11.4) above leaves the evaluation for x not in any of [x_i, x_{i+1}] undefined. That behavior is a choice for the user. However, one intuitive extension is to use:

$$f(x) = l_1(x_1) \ for \ x \leq x_1, and \ f(x) = l_{N-1}(x_N) \ for \ x \geq x_N. \qquad (11.5)$$

11.2.2   The Stepwise Function

The simplest way to describe a stepwise function is that it strictly charts time-based segments to constant values. This is very much like tempo or dynamics being held constant over time ranges, and in this sense the stepwise function is very useful. Consider Fig. 11.6:

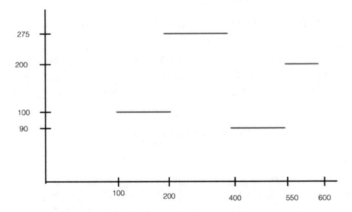

Fig. 11.6 Stepwise Function Example

This function maps the range [100, 200) to 100, [200, 400) to 275, [400, 550) to 90, and [550, 600) as 200. Recall that [a, b) is a half open interval meaning $\{x \in R | a \leq x < b\}$. Outside the range [100, 600), the function is undefined. Note in this example how the consistent usage of half open intervals, makes the function well-defined at the boundaries, e.g., $f(200) = 275$ whereas $f(200 - \varepsilon) =$

100 *for small ε*. It should be clear, for example, how statically fixed tempo over time could be modelled in this fashion.

The definition for a stepwise function is very similar to that of piecewise except for the behavior of the linear form:

> Let *{Pᵢ}* be a set of N>1 points in the real plane, where $P_i = (x_i, y_i)$ and $x_1 < x_2 < \cdots < x_N$.

> Let *{Lᵢ}* be the set of N-1 linear segments where Lᵢ is the linear segment from Pᵢ to Pᵢ₊₁ over the X axis segment [xᵢ, xᵢ₊₁), with respective linear form $l_i: [x_i, x_{i+1}) \to R$, and $l_i(x) = y_i$. The **stepwise function** $f: [x_1, x_N) \to R$ is defined for $x \in [x_1, x_N)$ as

$$f(x) = l_i(x) \; for \; x \in [x_i, x_{i+1}).$$
(11.6)

As with piecewise functions, the definition also leaves the evaluation for x not in $[x_1, x_N)$ undefined. However, an intuitive extension is:

$$f(x) = l_1(x_1) \; for \; x \leq x_1, and \; f(x) = l_{N-1}(x_{N-1}) \; for \; x \geq x_N.$$
(11.7)

Implementation is easy and can be found at function/stepwise_function.py.

Typical usage is as follows:

```
from function.stepwise_function import StepwiseFunction
array = [(5, 1), (7, 2), (10, 1.5), (12, 38)]
f = StepwiseFunction(array)

assert f.eval(0) == 1
assert f.eval(2) == 1
assert f.eval(5) == 1
assert f.eval(6) == 1
assert f.eval(7) == 2
assert f.eval(8) == 2
assert f.eval(9) == 2
assert f.eval(10) == 1.5
```

11.2.3 The Constant Function

The constant function is trivially the stepwise function limited to one segment. Domain extension over the entire real line is obvious. Refer to function/constant_univariate_function.py for implementation details.

11.2.4 Generic Univariate Function

Clearly piecewise and stepwise functions constitute an important subset of all possible functions over a single parameter. However, many times there is a need to use any manner of function, including smooth (differentiable) univariate functions such as:

$$y = 3x^2 - 5x$$

$$y = \frac{3}{2}\sin\left(\frac{5x}{3}\right)$$

An important aspect illustrated by these examples is that a well-defined evaluation exists over a single input parameter x, presumably over a defined real-valued domain with start and end points.

We introduce the class UnivariateFunction to provide that level of generalization for use in our framework. It is a template, or rather abstract class, for all functions of a single variable. It provides three methods eval(), domain_start(), and domain_end(). It is a simple coding exercise to subclass UnivariateFunction to provide adequate semantics for any univariate function. In fact, PiecewiseLinearFunction, StepwiseLinearFunction and ConstantFunction are subclasses to it. See Fig. 11.7.

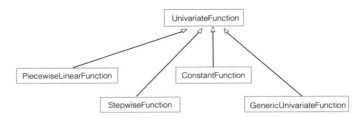

Fig. 11.7 Function Inheritance scheme.

There are times when a univariate function is defined and constructed in code and easily accessible, but to subclass it from UnivariateFunction is undesirable or even impossible (especially if the function is part of third-party software). For those situations, a 'shell' class is provided through GenericUnivariateFunction, that accepts the function as an argument, and allows the user to define the domain start and end values as arguments, and access the function through eval(). Here is an example:

```python
from function.generic_univariate_function import GenericUnivariateFunction


def square(x):
    return x * x


f = GenericUnivariateFunction(square, -1, 5)

assert f.eval(-1) == 1
assert f.eval(0) == 0
assert f.eval(1) == 1
assert f.eval(2) == 4
assert f.eval(3) == 9
assert f.eval(4) == 16
assert f.eval(5) == 25
assert f.eval(6) == 36
```

With this kind of preparation, for the purposes of the provided code base, any suitable function could be used for tempo or dynamics valuation.

To summarize, the class hierarchy that unifies this discussion is shown in Fig. 11.7. All the previously discussed functions are subclasses of UnivariateFunction, and as mentioned GenericUnivarateFunction is a shell subclass that parameterizes user defined functions. Of course, one can create specialized versions of UnivariateFunction for other computational needs.

11.2.5 Domain Reset with Affine Transformations

We return to linear or affine functions and utilize function composition to enable a simple transformation that proves useful for functions describing variable dynamics or tempo. As will be seen, composition provides flexibility in extending the transformation over alternatively defined domains.

We begin with a brief review of function composition. Function composition is an operation that feeds the output of one function as input to another, assuming the output range of the first is compatible with the input domain of the second. This effectively defines a new function from the first's domain to the second's range. For example for functions $f: X \to Y$, $g: Y \to Z$, we define a new function $gf: X \to Z$:

$$gf(x) = g\big(f(x)\big) \, for \, all \, x \in X, and \, gf: X \to Z. \qquad (11.8)$$

The point of interest we are calling out is that function composition provides a way for the function g to change its domain from Y to X.

Unlike many discussions on function composition, we call this out ability to reset the domain for the case wherein a function is defined on some linear segment, say [c, d], but one may want it to be defined on the linear segment [a, b]. This is a very useful technique to understand and be able to apply effectively.

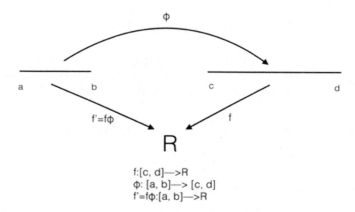

f:[c, d]—>R
Φ: [a, b]—> [c, d]
f'=fΦ:[a, b]—>R

Fig. 11.8 Resetting f's domain.

In Fig. 11.8, we have a function $f: [c, d] \to R$, that we want to redefine over the domain [a, b]. We need a mapping $\Phi: [a, b] \to [c, d]$, from the first segment to the second, so that in composition with f, we get a function $f' = f\Phi: [a, b] \to R$.

This argument does not quite solve our domain reset problem. One could contrive all manner of functions for Φ, and the more irregular Φ is, generally, the more irregular f Φ behaves. In that sense, we lose the behavior of f through its composition with Φ.

To deal with this irregularity, we define Φ as an affine transform that linearly stretches [a, b] to [c, d]. With that kind of well-behaved quality, using a combination of stretching and offsetting, Φf will remain much more like f, by "evening out" f's behavior over the new domain segment [a, b].

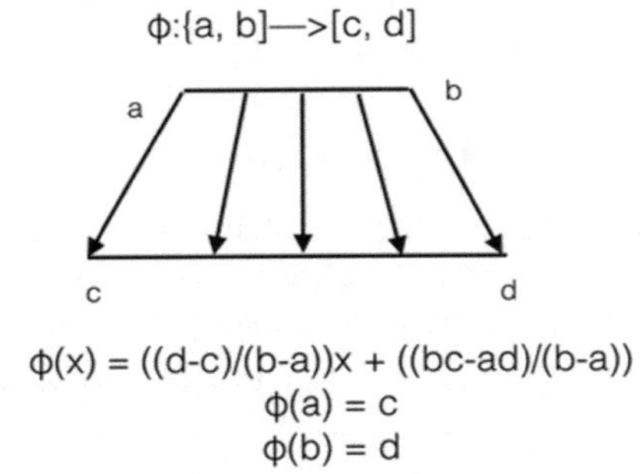

$$\phi:[a, b] \longrightarrow [c, d]$$

$$\phi(x) = ((d\text{-}c)/(b\text{-}a))x + ((bc\text{-}ad)/(b\text{-}a))$$
$$\phi(a) = c$$
$$\phi(b) = d$$

Fig. 11.9 Affine Transformation.

Towards that end, we construct the affine transform from [a, b] to [c, d] shown in Fig. 11.9. The arrows demonstrate that the transform maps the first to second segment in a kind of even-handed manner. The function for the affine transform is:

$$\Phi(x) = \left(\frac{d-c}{b-a}\right)x + \left(\frac{bc-ad}{b-a}\right) \qquad (11.9)$$

And of course, from this we get:

$$f': [a, b] \to R \ where \ f' = f\Phi(x) = f(\Phi(x)) \qquad (11.10)$$

Note that f' is in a sense 'proportionate', that is, that a point on [a, b] maps to a point on [c, d] retaining proportionally where each point is located on their respective segment. The ostensible effect is that f's domain has been moved to a different segment while retaining f's behavior in a relatively admissible manner!

A more transparent way to formulate equation (11.9) is to express $x = a + o$, then we have:

$$\Phi(a + o) = c + \left(\frac{d-c}{b-a}\right)o = c + o' \qquad (11.11)$$

Meaning $o \sim o'$, the delta distances are truly proportional.

This compositional technique provides a way to rewrite functions to one standard domain, say [0, 1], and use the same function otherwise defined on an arbitrary real domain segment. In this way, we get function reusability and extensibility through a combination of standardization on domain using an appropriate affine function to transform from the standardized domain to the function's domain.

11.3 Using Functions for Variable Tempo

In Chapter 9, we introduced EventSequence as a means for collecting either tempo setting events or voice dynamics setting events over time in a score. In Chapter 10, we used those sequences in MIDI conversion. In both cases, the settings were static, in the sense that an event in each case provides a fixed setting that remains in effect in the music until either the next event or the end of the music.

In this section we expand the tempo event sequence to include variable tempo events, as in accelerando and ritardando, based on functions. Notice that we address tempo over dynamics first. It is important to address variable tempo first, as variable dynamics has a dependency on variable tempo regarding time conversions.

11.3.1   Tempo Functions and the TempoEventSequence

Fig. 11.10 shows the relevant classes for our discussion and how they relate to each other. We introduce variable tempo with the class TempoFunctionEvent. TempoFunctionEvent, like TempoEvent, is a subclass of Event, and either can be included within TempoEventSequence which inherits from EventSequence. TempoFunctionEvent is not designed as a TempoEvent subclass, due to complexities involving tempo beat and its need for specification of next event position to determine domain extents. More on this later. However, because of these issues, it is easier to construct a separate class instead of subclassing from TempoEvent.

TempoFunctionEvent references a TempoFunction object, which in turn references a UnivariateFunction. The typical case is for TempoFunction to reference any of a variety of univariate function passed to it as a constructor argument.

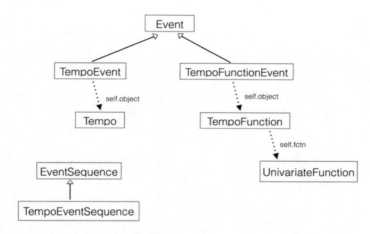

Fig. 11.10 Dynamic Tempo Design class diagram.

For convenience, TempoFunction may also be passed a Tempo object or rational number as tempo setting. These are converted to constant functions. The domains of these functions span from the sequence position (whole note time) of the TempoFunctionEvent to the sequence position of the following event. The defined univariate function's time domain is independent of that but is evaluated scaled to the domain defined by the duration between this event's position and the next event position. Reference discussion on affine transformation Section 11.2.5 to understand how this scaling is achieved.

As mentioned TempoEventSequence is a specialized EventSequence. This is to deal with the complexities described above. Additionally TempoEventSequence provides a convenient tempo() method to determine tempo at any given position directly from the sequence.

To understand these object dynamics better, consider the example tempo event sequence construction found in Fig. 11.11.

This shows a 7-event tempo sequence. The first three are simple fixed tempo events, just setting a fixed tempo until the next event. The same for events at time 45 and 65. However we have tempo function events at 32 and 50. The first is a strict accelerando from allegro to vivace. The second is a kind of meandering tempo fluctuation from vivace ending at adagio. Each of these tempo function events are built with univariate functions. The first is a simple piecewise linear function, and the second is a generic function represented by a specialized curve.

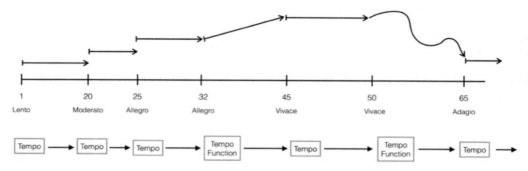

| 1 | 20 | 25 | 32 | 45 | 50 | 65 |
| Lento | Moderato | Allegro | Allegro | Vivace | Vivace | Adagio |

Fig. 11.11 Example Tempo Event Sequence.

The following code shows how to set up a tempo sequence, including tempo functions:

```
score = Score()

score.tempo_sequence.add(TempoEvent(Tempo(60, Duration(1, 4)), Position(0)))

t_low = 60
t_hi = 120
array = [(Position(0), t_low),
         (Position(1), t_hi),
         (Position(2), t_hi),
         (Position(3), t_low)
         ]
f = PiecewiseLinearFunction(array)
event1 = TempoFunctionEvent(f, Position(1))
score.tempo_sequence.add(event1)

score.tempo_sequence.add(TempoEvent(Tempo(t_low, Duration(1, 4)), Position(4)))
```

There are three events. First a 60 quarter-note beats per minute tempo event at whole time 0. The second is a piecewise linear function starting at 60 bpm, then 120 bpm, then back to 60 bpm, starting at whole time 1. Finally, at position 4, a tempo of 60 bpm. Conveniently these are positionally place end to end so that the function has domain of length 3 as defined. The user should try other durations by placing the final event at a different position.

Several points should be made:

First, a TempoEvent sets a fixed tempo within its effective domain, i.e., from the event's start position to the next event's start position. Its value is constant within that domain. However, a tempo function event is not only positionally dependent, i.e., the tempo function requires the position, but is also dependent on the position of the next event! However, the univariate function's domain is defined independently of the event's effective domain. It is in the interest of facile construction to do just that and develop the tempo function to a domain best suited only of the function, e.g., [0, 1]. We deal with this independence in the TempoFunction by applying an affine function to convert from the event's effective tempo domain to the function's actual domain. The only caveat is computing the event's effective domain, which means knowing the position of the next event. All this plays out in the code base (reference TempoEventSequence) which the reader can read to understand in detail.

Secondly, the development of a tempo function must be done with some care in two respects. The range of the function must have realistic values, that is, the values cannot be negative, and certainly not 0, but also not say above 300, but meaningful as tempo beats per minute. Another point is the importance that the tempo settings are not incongruent to the surrounding events. As shown in Fig. 11.11, the curves make seamless transitions from the prior and to the next event. There can be jumps of course like those seen using TempoEvents, but only as it makes musical sense.

With this elaboration on tempo design, let's move forward and see how tempo event functions within a score figure into MIDI event generation and time conversion operations.

11.3.2 Tempo Functions, MIDI Generation and Time Conversion

In Chapter 10 we examined how to convert a score to MIDI. In that discussion the score used discrete tempo events to specify the tempo. Tempo functions provide a challenge as over their domain, tempo varies continually over time as determined by an arbitrary user function. The question considered here is how to generate MIDI tempo change events for tempo functions?

A similar situation arises regarding time conversion, Section 5. The conversion algorithms discussed use event sequences as input, specifically sequences for time signature event and tempo event types. Tempo function events were not used in the algorithm.

Time varying tempo poses difficulties for MIDI event generation as well as time conversion. The tempo cannot be counted on to remain fixed for any whole note time interval. However, we take an approach wherein we 'discretize' the function, and in doing so, break the function into small pieces which approximate accurate tempos but over small durations, and so refine the tempo event sequence with static tempo events in place of tempo functions. In general, this general approach is commonly found in similar computational situations with arbitrary functions, say in numerical integration.

The objective of this section is to show how to sample a tempo function at regular discrete real times, and substitute those sampled tempo events for the tempo function event in an event sequence. We highlight that the sampling is done in discrete real-time. This means:

- We are using real-time as opposed to whole note time for sampling.

- We sample using a small real-time interval across the whole note time domain of the tempo function.

The incremental sample real time Δt should be small enough that the resulting tempo sample value changes should be perceived as seamless and matching to the tempo function's behavior. The idea is that changing tempo at regular small intervals should provide an experience of continuous change of the tempo. The reader might start with $\Delta t = 50$ milliseconds, and refine that value as needed.

Fig. 11.12 illustrates the essentials of tempo function sampling. We assume as before that we sample in real time Δt increments. Assume we sample at whole note time τ, $f(\tau)$ is the tempo value (BPM). Retaining that tempo for Δt in real time corresponds to some $\Delta \tau$ increment in whole note time.

The required calculation is to compute $\Delta \tau$ using Δt and $f(\tau)$. That calculation is:

$$\Delta \tau = \frac{f(\tau) * \Delta t * beat\_duration}{60 * 1000} \qquad (11.12)$$

With that, we proceed to generate the tempo event across $\Delta \tau$,

TempoEvent($f(\tau), \tau$).

Proceeding with the next sampling iteration, we sample at $\tau + \Delta \tau$, and so forth, until we get to b, the end of the tempo function's domain.

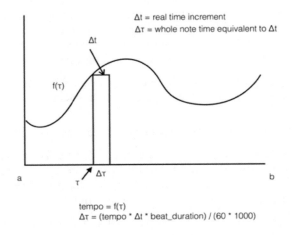

Fig. 11.12 Tempo Function Sampling

A sketch of the logic for this sampling process is shown below. It is a simple iterative process for computing successive tempo events and adding the events to the tempo sequence. The reader should review the code to understand the larger context of the code, in this case, in the conversion of a score to MIDI.

```
def sample_tempo(tempo_function_event, delta_ms, beat_duration, tempo_sequence):
    a = tempo_function_event.domain_start
    b = tempo_function_event.domain_end
    while a < b:
        tempo = tempo_function_event.eval(a)
        delta_wnt = (tempo * delta_ms * beat_duration) / (60 * 1000)
        tempo_sequence.add(TempoEvent(tempo, a))
        a += delta_wnt
```

Given a tempo sequence consisting of TempoEvents and TempoFunctionEvents, we can build an event sequence entirely out of tempo events with no tempo function events. We use that event sequence to build a TimeConversion object to use in other parts of the code where needed. And of course, static incremental tempo events are used to generate the MIDI set_tempo events much as we had done earlier, ref. Section 10.4.

11.4 Using Variable Dynamics Functions

The approach to rendering variable dynamics to MIDI proceeds much like that of variable tempo. The only significant difference to our earlier discussion on dynamics is in the generation of velocity events that we require the TimeConversion instance based on the new tempo event sequence constructed by discretizing the tempo event functions, described in the prior section.

11.4.1 Details on Variable Dynamics Functions

Like tempo sequence, a dynamic event sequence for dynamics can look like Fig. 11.13.

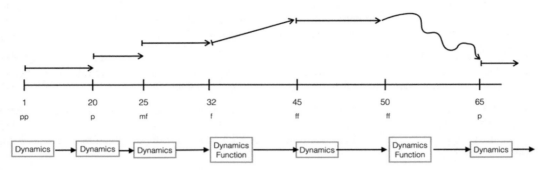

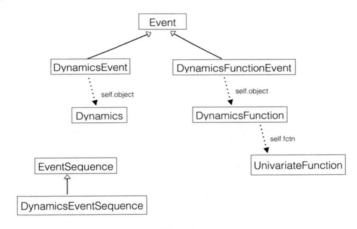

Fig. 11.13 Example of event sequence with static and dynamic velocity events.

The graph's domain is in whole note time versus the range as dynamics value. And like before, we assume a range of [0, 127] for dynamics, which corresponds to the MIDI velocity range. We introduced the concept of dynamics function event which is the functional counterpart of the dynamics event.

The object schema for dynamics is a replication of that for tempo. The key difference is in the value being held and that the functions involved concern dynamics as opposed to tempo. The schema for dynamics/velocity is shown in Fig. 11.14.

Fig. 11.14 Dynamics/Velocity Class Schema

The semantics of each class along with the details should be self-evident. Note the caveats made about tempo also apply:

- The event domain is different from the function domain, allowing independence of a function's defined domain from domain of the function event's domain, its location and distance to the next event.

- Care must be taken for the function to maintain staying in a realistic velocity range.

We now look at how the dynamics events are generated for dynamics function events.

11.4.2   Computing MIDI Velocity Events

The approach to generating MIDI messages for variable dynamics is like the approach for variable tempo just discussed. The dynamics function is discretized on real time-based increments, and MIDI channel volume change events are generated based on the function's value in each increment, the main point being that we want the dynamics changes realized over real time and not whole time. For sufficiently fine increment values, the produced volume changes over time should be perceived as seamless.

However, there is a difference between the two approaches in as much as the tempo may change over the dynamics function domain, which means that the real time to whole note time ratio changes over the course of producing incremental-based volume change midi events.

The process is to fix some real time increment, Δt, mark off the dynamics function event's function domain in successive Δt increments, and to sample the velocity function on these real time intervals from start to end. The issue is, of course, that the event's function domain is defined in whole note time, not real time.

Thanks to the work of the preceding sections on tempo, we have a tempo event sequence to adequately address tempo events in the presence of dynamic tempos. So, it is a simply the case of converting the dynamics function domain to real time using a TimeConversion instance defined by our new tempo event sequence.

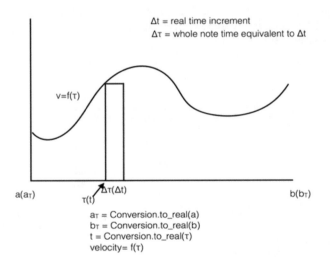

Fig. 11.15 Dynamics Function Sampling.

The remainder of the algorithm is straight forward. We loop over the function domain as real time, using Δt. Along the way we convert the time values to whole note time values to compute the current velocity and generate the MIDI control change event for each position.

The process proceeds until we have covered the extent of the event's velocity function's domain as real time values. Keep in mind there is an extra step wherein an affine transformation converts the event's domain to the velocity function's domain before velocity valuation, like what was done for tempo in the last sections.

A sketch of the MIDI event generation logic is shown below. The reader should use Fig. 11.15 as a reference point. Of course, this is only the code fragment for processing velocity events in the context of score to MIDI conversion. The reader is encouraged to study the full score conversion code to understand the context.

```
def sample_velocity(dyn_function_event, delta_ms):
    midi_msgs = []
    aT = Conversion.to_real(dyn_function_event.domain_start)
    bT = Conversion.to_real(dyn_function_event.domain_end)
    while aT < bT:
        a_WNT = Conversion.to_wnt(aT)
        velocity = tempo_function_event.eval(a_WNT)
        midi_msgs.add(ChannelChangeEvent(velocity, to_ticks(a_WNT)))
        aT += delta_ms
    return midi_msgs
```

As an alternative to the above, using whole-time values of the dynamics function for the loop control is left as an exercise for the reader to work out.

11.5 Exercises

11.5.1 Derive the affine equation (11.9). Provide an example and demonstrate equation (11.11).

11.5.2 Construct examples of imaginative and interesting tempo and dynamics event functions. Build test cases to demonstrate their expected behaviors.

11.5.3 What are the issues for using real time for the dynamics function time axis? Does it make sense for either tempo or velocity?

11.5.4 Can you devise a velocity function parameterized by whole-time and tempo? Consider design alterations to make that possible. Can articulations also serve as a parameter? Give examples.

11.5.5 As in the last question, can articulations be assigned using a whole-time based function, or of say a function of tempo and/or velocity.

12 Further Representations

As we conclude the representation section, we introduce a few further concepts and their representations that are essential or useful to the transformation part of this text. In a way these concepts span both parts of the book in that they are interesting if only considering music representational issues, yet they are extremely useful in furthering music transformation research and technology.

We consider here three concepts:

- An explicit way to express music harmony and make it part of representational practice.

- A way to textually represent music to produce "lines" as introduced earlier. This greatly facilitates writing terse code to produce lines, as well as facilitates production of more complex examples of music based on the representation introduced so far.

- A simpler representation of score that allows one to rapidly manufacture them for test purposes. The tradeoff is in limiting the number of voices to one. Additionally, this representation incorporates the concept of harmony.

It is unfortunate that the second concept is introduced this late. However, its dependence on the first concept made for an awkward earlier introduction.

12.1 Harmonic Context

We consider a means for expressing the intended harmony underlying an extent of music. The idea of using a representation for musical harmony can be found in [2] [1], and as in these references we call such a representation a "harmonic context". A harmonic context serves many uses, including:

- An additional music annotation for the intended harmony in a musical piece.

- A constraint artifact intended to flag errors when/if the music is not composed to the harmony represented.

- An enforcement artifact used to trigger transformational processes on music to meet the harmony represented.

In this section we only consider the first item, namely introducing harmony into the representation. In the second part of this book, harmonic representation takes on the role of an enforcing artifact in music transformations.

© The Author(s), under exclusive license to Springer Nature Switzerland AG 2022
D. P. Pazel, *Music Representation and Transformation in Software*, https://doi.org/10.1007/978-3-030-97472-5_12

12.1.1   HarmonicContext and HarmonicContextTrack Representations

We develop harmony based on two fundamental music concepts: key (or tonality), and chord, very much in line with how classical harmony is developed. We call the pairing of tonality and chord over a temporal extent a ***harmonic context***, abbreviated ***hc***. In classical terms, one often has large temporal extents over the same tonality, but with variation in chords compatible with the tonality. For jazz, one might have large temporal extents over a chord using a variety of compatible tonalities.

It is often the case, that a tonality-chord pair are related in as much as all or most of the chord's tones can be found in the tonality. While one finds that very often, it is by far not a rule. It is difficult to define a rule regarding chord tone membership in an accompanying tonality. Even what might be seen as extreme cases, such as a Gb-Major chord over C major, cannot be ruled out of possibility in the vast world of music composition. To summarize, we will neither propose nor apply any rule regarding the relationship of chord to tonality, except for very clearly marked association, e.g., VDom7 from Bb-NaturalMinor (the V indicates use of tonality to help derive chord tones).

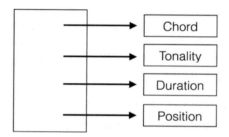

Fig. 12.1 A representation of HarmonicContext

From a design viewpoint, a harmonic context is represented by the class HarmonicContent with a Tonality property and a Chord property. In discussion, we usually cite a harmonic context textually by "Chord/Tonality", e.g. A-Major7/E-Major.

In the broader scheme of design however, a harmonic context stands for a harmony over a whole-time temporal extent of music, be it within a Line or a Score. In the latter case, the harmony cuts across a temporal extent of music, and importantly across all voices. The expectation is that all voices adhere to the same harmony, as defined by harmonic contexts, each for a given (whole-time) extent. With that, the Duration and Position properties stand for the whole-time temporal extent of the hc as well as its whole-time starting position.

To represent harmony in a score, we have a list of distinct harmonic contexts, in temporal sections, which in total define the harmony across the full whole-time extent of the music. Fig. 12.2 shows an example of a piece of music along with its harmony. We call this list of harmonic contexts, a ***harmonic context track***, abbreviated ***hct***.

Fig. 12.2 A harmonic context track defining the harmony for a piece of music.

Fig. 12.2 shows a staff over three harmonic contexts, each under one measure of the music, the first a C-Major chord over C major, then a G-Major chord over C, and finally an A-Minor chord over A melodic minor. The last could be seen as A-Minor over C, a six-chord. We intentionally placed this somewhat awkward harmonic context at the end only to illustrate the flexibility the user has in formulating harmonic contexts, and that an extent of music can harmonically match to more than one harmonic definition.

Representationally, the hct is little more than an OrderedMap, as a map ordered by position. The class HarmonicContextTrack has an OrderedMap member holding all the hc's, along with a set of methods for properly inserting/removing hc's. As a point of interest, hct regulates the OrderedMap's state so that all contained hc's are non-overlapping and abut to each other from the start to end over time. This enforcement on the hc's happens on all critical operations, e.g., inserting, removing, etc. Users should keep this in mind or check the state of the hct before undertaking hct modifying operations in any case.

An example of setting up a simple hct is as follows:

```
diatonic_tonality = Tonality.create(ModalityType.Major, DiatonicTone("C"))
chord_t = TertianChordTemplate.parse('tIV')
chord1 = chord_t.create_chord(diatonic_tonality)
chord_t = TertianChordTemplate.parse('tV')
chord2 = chord_t.create_chord(diatonic_tonality)
chord_t = TertianChordTemplate.parse('tVI')
chord3 = chord_t.create_chord(diatonic_tonality)

hc_track = HarmonicContextTrack()
hc_track.append(HarmonicContext(diatonic_tonality, chord1, Duration(1, 2)))
hc_track.append(HarmonicContext(diatonic_tonality, chord2, Duration(1, 4)))
hc_track.append(HarmonicContext(diatonic_tonality, chord3, Duration(1, 3)))

print(hc_track)
```

```
[0] h.c.[C-Major, TIV [F, A, C], 1/2]
[1] h.c.[C-Major, TV [G, B, D], 1/4]
[2] h.c.[C-Major, TVI [A, C, E], 1/3]
```

12.2   A Syntax for Constructing Music Structures

Given the music structures and representation introduced to this point, the process for quickly creating music structures like Line or HarmonicContextTrack is tedious and error prone. Even creating a simple melody and harmony requires many individual coding steps such as the creation of individual notes, beam and tuplet formations, lines, harmonic contexts, to name a few. Filling in all necessary object properties and assembling structures can result in tedious coding during which it is easy to make errors, and complex to replicate for alternative examples. This is an obstacle to moving forward on even the simplest of testing or example creation.

To help circumvent this issue, we introduce a textual syntax to specify a melodic line and harmony, that is, the notes, tonalities, and chords one finds in a melody and harmony, and a parser that converts that information into Line and HarmonicContextTrack structures. With that, specification of melody is much easier, and quicker to change. As a result, both testing and recreational use of the code base becomes more accessible and far simpler.

In the following, we describe a syntax for melody and harmony specification, and then look at the process for converting that information into a Line and HarmonicContextTrack.

12.2.1 The Music Parser

The Antlr4 grammar for our music syntax is found in the source code at resources/LineGrammar.g4. Antlr [33] is a parser generator. The grammar specified in the above-mentioned file, LineGrammar.g4, is input to Antlr4, which generates Python code for that grammar which is used to build the parser based on the grammar syntax input. The complete process involved in building and using this parser is showing in Fig. 12.3, and breaks into the following parts and steps:

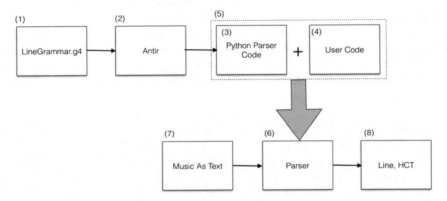

Fig. 12.3 Parser build and usage.

- The grammar for our music language (1) is passed to the Antlr parser (2).

- Antlr (2) produces Python parser code (3) specific to this input grammar.

- That Python parser code (3) and related user Python code (4) [e.g., to formalize input and output parameters] are combined (5) to produce the parser (6).

- A user writes music as text (Python string) (7) based on the music grammar and passes that text to the parser (6).

- The output, barring errors, are two python objects. One is a Line, and the other is the HarmonicContextTrack for that line.

For now, details on building the parser are less important for the reader. The focus here is on using the parser (6) for meaningful work.

12.2.2 A Music Syntax

In this section we describe the textual syntax for music specification. Instead of beginning with a top-down look at the grammar, we start by diving directly into the following simple example:

```
'{<C-Major: I> iC:4 C qD E <:IV> iF G hA <:V> ig b qf g <:VI> ie e qd ic d <:I>
```

This is a very simple melody line. Looking through it one immediately identifies familiar elements. For example, one observes a reference to C-Major, a tonality. There are also references to I, IV and VI chords. There are notes C:4, D, and so forth. Something less obvious is the use of the characters i, q, h, and h@ which look like they have something to do with note durations. So, from the start, this input is already starting to make sense. This input is based on the music in Fig. 12.4.

Examining the realization of this grammar example, we now see that i stands for eighth note, q means quarter, and h means half, and finally h@ means dotted half wherein the @ symbol represents a dot

The chords listed on top are meaningful and comprise the contents of a harmonic context track. The chordal notes in the base (Fig. 12.4) were entered by the author and are not part of the generated line.

Fig. 12.4 Corresponding music to input music text.

This example alone provides a large percentage of what the reader should know about using the grammar. The following sub-sections provide deeper details.

Text Structure

Braces, { }, contains the music content as text. Within the braces the text is a mixture of tonality and chord notations intermixed with note notations, interpreted left to right.

Harmonic Notation

The syntax for harmony is

```
<tonality: chord>
```

which specifies a tonality and chord. As an example, <Db-Major: ii> indicates the tonality Db-Major and ii for the relative chord in that tonality. Chords can be specified either by relative numeral or explicitly such as Eb-Dom7, e.g., <Ab-Major, Eb-Dom7>.

The default tonality is C-Major when no tonality is specified in the text. Once a tonality is specified, that tonality is "in effect" until re-specified following to it. With that understanding, the tonality does not need to be further explicitly specified and a shorthand for harmonic notation simply becomes <:chord>. For example, <:V> is the relative fifth chord based on the prior tonality specified (or default tonality if no tonality was prior specified).

Note Notation

Notes are specified as a combination of four qualities:

```
(duration)(letter)(alteration):(register)
where for duration: W,w-Whole; H,h-Half; Q,q-Quarter; I,i-Eighth; S,s-Sixteenth;
                    T,t-Thirtysecond; X,x-Sixtyfourth;
```

For example, hEb:5 is Eb in the 5th register as a half note, and iA:6 is an eighth note with pitch A:6. Alterations include the usual symbols #, b, ##, bb.

Similar to how harmony behaves with tonality, once a duration is specified on a note, that duration becomes the default for succeeding notes until specified explicitly again. For example, "iE:4 B:4" indicates two eighth notes. The same behavior holds for register specification, making the prior example "iE:4 B". Both conventions promote speed and brevity in specification.

Note that tonality specification does not provide default pitch alteration as you would find in a score. For example, if the current key if G-Major, the note F is not converted to F#. All alterations must be explicitly stated in the music text.

Dotted duration notation is based on the @ symbol. So, q@A specifies a dotted quarter note. Multiple dotted notes can be specified, e.g., "q@@A" for double dotted quarter note A.

Beams and Tuplets

Beamed notes are specified with brackets, [ ], containing the notes within the beam. Beams may be nested with the expected effect. For example [… […]] results in something like .

A simple set of beamed eighth notes can be seen in this example:

{qC:5 D [G:4 A [C:5 D E D]]} which in score notation is:

and comprises quarter notes C:5 and D:5 followed by a beam of eighth notes G:4, A:4, followed by sixteenth notes C:5, D:5, E:5, D:5. Note that beaming applies an implicit ½ duration factor to the contents' durations.

The following example clarifies register inheritance as well:

{C:4 [E:5 F [G:4 A B A] B]} which in score notation is:

is comprised of quarter note C:4, followed by eight notes E:5 F:5, then sixteenth notes G:4, A:4, B:4, A:4, followed by eight note B:5. Notice that the inherited register specification nests in that the final B is B:5, not B:4!

The beaming system also allows for tuplets to be defined. They are considered beamed tructures and can be nested. The syntax for tuplets is:

```
(duration_unit, #)[ ... ]
```

The notes in the tuplet are specified within the brackets []. The duration signature is (duration_unit, #). The concept is that tuplet duration is usually specified as some number of unit durations, e.g., 2 eighths, etc. The duration_unit and # correspond to those specifications. For example:

{qC:4 D:4 ((1:8), 2)[E:4 F G]} in score notation is:

The 2 eighth notes, or quarter note is the full duration of the contents of the tuplet. When parsed, the E:4, F:4, G:4 each have a duration of 1/12th notes, which is what we usually have in practice for the typical stand-alone triplet seen in music scores.

User-Defined Modalities

A user defines a modality, "MyModality" say, with the following:

```
modality_type = ModalityType('MyModality')
incremental_interval_strs = ['P:1', 'm:2', 'M:3', 'm:2', 'm:2', 'M:2', 'A:2' ]
modality_spec = ModalitySpec(modality_type, incremental_interval_strs)
ModalityFactory.register_modality(modality_type, modality_spec)
```

With that, the user is free to reference that modality in the syntax.

```
'{<C-!MyModality: I> F#:4 A D}
```

Note the use of "!" to indicate that the referenced modality is user-defined.

12.2.3 Invoking the Parser in Code

The parser is invoked in the following manner:

```
from structure.LineGrammar.core.line_grammar_executor import LineGrammarExecutor
l = LineGrammarExecutor()
syntax_line = '.........'
line, hct = l.parse(syntax_line)
```

There is little more to this process than creating a LineGrammarExecutor object and calling the parser with the specified syntax as a string. It returns two items: the Line object representing the input notes, and the HarmonicContextTrack also for that input.

12.3 LiteScore

Score introduced in Chapter 9, is a relatively complex class. It tracks multiple voices, associated metadata such as time signatures, tempo markings, and so on. In the transformation part of this book, Score is more complex than we need to demonstrate transformational algorithms. Besides, Score takes some effort to set up simply and cleanly.

For that reason, we introduce LiteScore as an easier-to-use substitute for Score, and will be used extensively in the second part of this book. The main simplification is that LiteScore takes only one Line and uses that as its voice. Its key quality is that it provides a harmonic context track, which will be used substantially in transformations.

The constructor arguments for LiteScore are:

- Line: To be used as its single voice.

- HarmonicContextTrack: Optionally, the hct for harmony associated with Line.

- Instrument: Optionally, the instrument to be used with the single voice (Line).

- TempoEventSequence: Optionally a tempo sequence for the score.

- TimeSignatureEventSequence: Optionally a time signature sequence for the score.

With these arguments, there is little to setting up a LiteScore, especially when combined with using the music syntax introduced in the prior section.

```
from structure.lite_score import LiteScore
from structure.LineGrammar.core.line_grammar_executor import LineGrammarExecutor
```

```
from instruments.instrument_catalog import InstrumentCatalog

line, hct = LineGrammarExecutor().parse('{<C-Major:I> C:4 [E:5 F [G:4 A B A] B]}')
lite_score = LiteScore(line, hct, InstrumentCatalog.instance().get_instrument("vio-
lin"))

print(lite_score.line)
=========================================================
   Line(Dur(7/8)Off(0)f=1) [
     [C:4<1/4>-(1/4)] off=0 f=1
     Beam(Dur(5/8)Off(1/4)f=1) [
       [E:5<1/8>-(1/8)] off=0 f=1
       [F:5<1/8>-(1/8)] off=1/8 f=1
       Beam(Dur(1/4)Off(1/4)f=1/2) [
         [G:4<1/16>-(1/16)] off=0 f=1/2
         [A:4<1/16>-(1/16)] off=1/16 f=1/2
         [B:4<1/16>-(1/16)] off=1/8 f=1/2
         [A:4<1/16>-(1/16)] off=3/16 f=1/2
       ]
       [B:5<1/8>-(1/8)] off=1/2 f=1
     ]
   ]
```

LiteScore has several methods primarily related to accessing its core content.

12.4 Exercises

12.4.1 Devise a harmonic context track with relatively complex harmonies. Write the code for explicitly building the hct. Then use the music syntax to produce the same hct.

12.4.2 Develop a lite score using a line and harmony based off a major composer, e.g., Mozart, Beethoven.

12.4.3 Build a LiteScore to MIDI converter – start with midi/score_to_midi_converter.py. Hint: build a LiteScore to Score converter first!

Part 2: Music Transformations

The representation section demonstrates that music's conceptual model is structurally complex, that from detailed through large scale organization and everywhere in-between, many musical facets are necessary and coordinated that lead to constructing a coherent piece of music. The representation tackles the complexity to bring about a high level of order and completeness to the many details of music theory and composition in software. While there are many other aspects that were not covered, for the purposes of this exposition and context, what has been described provides an adequate foundation to proceed to further advanced topics.

With this foundational effort behind us, this book now takes on the task of applying that foundation to the topic of "music transformations". To which one asks, "What are music transformations anyway?". Before formally undertaking a somewhat rigorous definition of the title meaning, we introduce it through intuitive notions of its meaning. For example, on a rudimentary level one can think of "changing the key" of a section of music as executing a transformation on the music. Typically, in those terms, this means retaining the modality and changing the root or key tone. This transform amounts to raising or lowering pitches by an interval. This is among the more fundamental of music transformations and is typically found in many if not all notation software systems.

More complex music transformations are further imaginable. Changing modality on a piece of music is the kind of transformation that is much more complex. For example, a major to minor key change involves decisions on which minor key to use, or if we switch minor modalities based on ascending versus descending melodic lines. Issues arising from modality changes wherein the cardinality, i.e., number of modality tones, of the modality changes (such as in major to pentatonic) are even more difficult to address, whether for accounting for pitches that no longer exist, or for taking into account new pitch options that may work better in a musical context.

Other types of music transformations may include harmonic changes. For example, one may want to change a chord (within the same key/modality) on a section of melody. In this case, there may be issues maintaining chordal melodic notes, possibly retaining melodic shape, as well as ensuring melodic resolutions to surrounding notes. This kind of transformation can impact whether the melody can retain its character in the face of the harmonic change.

These examples are but a few of the types of music transformations that can be imagined. For our purposes, our focus is on a *localized* meaning for transformation, that is, transformation isolated to say within a measure or over a handful of measures. Transformations at a more *global* level, that affect large sections of music, are far more challenging. Considerations involving key/modality changes, along with melodic variation constitute a complexity that is difficult to encapsulate into a single transformational definition. While these transformations are not excluded from possibility, they are not the focus of the discussions here.

In that sense, we distinguish global from localized transformation, and focus only on localized or basic music transformations in this text. To be clear, we use the term music transformation to implicitly mean localized music transformation.

13 An Introduction to Music Transformations

We now dig deeper into the topic of music transformations, what they are, and what topics are discussed further in this part of the book.

13.1 What is a Music Transformation?

The above discussion brings intuitive clarity to our meaning of 'music transformation'. We could continue, but in the end, its definition will still have some lingering degree of "fuzziness" to account for the fact that music correctness regarding the result of a transformation is in many ways a subjective judgment. However, by defining a few terms we can bring a little more concreteness to defining what a music transformation is, while at the same time couching our discussion in familiar territory defined in the first part of this book.

For our purposes, we define *music fragment* as a combination of some number (typically small) of music measures for some voice, along with their corresponding harmonic contexts. In terms of our software representation, think of a music fragment being provided by a Line and its harmony defined by a HarmonicContextTrack composed of HamonicContexts. A music fragment can be qualified with a temporal extent, i.e., given by beginning and ending whole times, that defines the precise portion of a line and harmony track to which a music transformation could be applied.

The term *music feature* refers to some significant aspect of a music fragment, such as the notes in the melody - their pitch values, durations, and offsets, more precisely. It also refers to the key and tempo of the music. And it refers to the chords, their chord types, roots, and inversions, and durations.

By *musical cohesion* we mean that for a given music fragment, its music features conform to some music practice that in some way, even subjectively, makes musical sense. In common vernacular, "the music sounds right" or "as the composer intended". Music cohesion can implicitly imply an understood music style or genre, or other criteria that are considered 'proper' for the music under consideration as source and/or target of a transformation.

A music transformation or *music transform* maps a music fragment into another in such a way that some music features are preserved while others are changed to meet user provided criteria, while at the same time preserving musical cohesion. See Fig. 13.1. While this definition grounds further what we mean by music transform, there is still much open to interpretation. Suppose for example, we want 'melodic preservation' in using a transform. The meaning would vary over circumstances. In one interpretation, 'melodic preservation" might mean 'the melodic notes remain the same, identical in pitch, duration, and offset'. That kind of identity transform is generally too restrictive to be meaningful.

© The Author(s), under exclusive license to Springer Nature Switzerland AG 2022
D. P. Pazel, *Music Representation and Transformation in Software*, https://doi.org/10.1007/978-3-030-97472-5_13

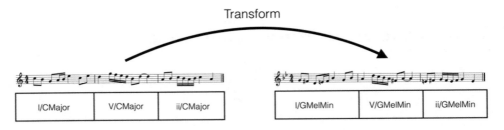

Fig. 13.1 Music transformation

However, in a key shift in the same modality, the notes' pitches are changed, but otherwise the melodies are isomorphic (identical) regarding durations, relative note offsets, pitch, and overall shape. If the modality is changed though and possibly as well as tonal root, we want the melodic shape or contour to be less isomorphic but rather homeomorphically[44] preserved even though the resulting pitches may vary significantly in pitch from the original. So, we are not speaking of a strict isomorphic relationship here. This is illustrated in Fig. 13.1 in the transform from C Major to G Melodic Minor.

These differences in required interpretation of transformation are fine, as long as they are consistent with the meaning of "musical cohesion" imposed on the transform under consideration. In Fig. 13.1 the interpretation of transform derives from the change in harmony, and an acknowledgement that the musical cohesion remains intact.

The general idea of transformation is so defined with much latitude on intention. Clearly, due to variety of circumstances and contexts, a transform must be defined individually to include all required nuances. However, when musical coherence is sufficiently subjective that its objective rules cannot be easily specified, the transform is approximate at best and may produce a set of proposed solutions which only then can be judged and ranked later.

13.2 Outline on Transformations

The music transforms presented in this section mainly focus on adaptive pitch adjustment on a given music fragment subject to harmonic change and/or varieties of constraint specification. That is, there is no focus on rhythmic or otherwise substantive note changes[45] of the melody itself. Nor is there any focus on generative or constructive music. This approach constitutes no meaningful restriction on discussing music transformations. Music transformation is a deep and rich topic, and the purpose of this book is to introduce the topic in a meaningful somewhat introductory manner.

With that, we begin with introducing a constraint engine that enforces constraints on how pitches relate to each other. The engine itself constitutes a simple heuristic enumerative approach to searching what can be a relatively large search space. The focus of the engine's search is to satisfy all the pitch constraints related to transform changes to a given melodic fragment. Constraint engines constitute a complex and rich research topic. It is not the intention of the author to provide a comprehensive, efficient state-of-the-art constraint engine technology, but rather an engine sufficient to demonstrate the music transformations presented, which is the focus of this book This constraint engine, besides offering a kind of music transformation utility in itself, is used several times in transformations presented later in the text.

---

[44] By homeomorphically we mean that the two melodic shapes move up and down in tandem even if the successive note's pitch distances in each are not the same.

[45] Note changes excluded include the addition or deletion or notes, or changes in the durations of existing notes.

The first transforms presented either relate directly to music theory or composition, or are of general interest in shaping melody:

- Shift – This transform involves changes in tonality. This entails either change in root tone or change in modality, or both. This transform also addresses change in mode.

- Reflection – This transform addresses a common compositional technique to find new melodic material by reflecting a melody across a horizontal axis. This can be done in two different ways, either tonally or chromatically as is described in detail.

- Reshape – This transform addresses adjusting the pitches in an existing melody to approximate lie on a given pitch-based curve. There are several ways to achieve this, adhering to tonality-based or chromatic pitches.

- Dilation – This transform applying a numerical factor to note durations, effectively stretching, or shrinking a melody.

- Step Shift – This transform shifts a melody a few tonal steps while preserving harmony. This transform is useful for developing sequences.

Other transforms are more advanced, and require the constraint engine:

- Harmonic Transcription - This transform involves the full replacement of a harmonic context for another. Harmonic transcription addresses melodic transformations over chord changes.

- Retrograde – This transform involves melody reversal. There are complexities involving refitting the reversed melody into the existing measure and harmonic structure, as well as whether to reverse the associated original harmony.

- Melodic Search and Pattern Substitution - This transform involves a technique for finding a melody or variations on the melody over a score, and for each found instance to substitute another based on a generic specification that can adapt to varieties on harmony.

Each chapter defines the issue, a solution, and a description of the algorithm as implemented in Python. There are examples of each transform with some analysis of the positives and negatives of the transformation.

13.3   A Word on Machine Learning

The reader may ask as to how machine learning techniques fit into this discuss, or if not at all. The short answer is that it does not, at least not in this text.

At the time of this writing, an enormous effort in research and work in machine learning is ongoing involving many institutions. In some cases, machine learning research is actively being applied to music [34] either for generative capability or in other related senses, creatively.

The point of this book is to retain the perspective of working with music theory and compositional structures as foundation, and to present algorithmic solutions that arise more from techniques a professional composer would use, more as an assist than an alternative, and certainly not fully generative. Some criticisms of machine learning include its "black box" approach wherein interesting or good solutions arise from a massive infusion of data but lack explanation on how those solutions are derived [35]. Avoiding this situation, this book is focused on algorithms based in music theory and logic that lead to solutions, even as or if some things are missed along the way.

13.4 Moving Forward

The exposition in this part of the book is different from the first part. In the first part, care was taken in laying out basic music concepts and tying music concepts to Python objects. Care on presentation was given towards defining the methods and properties of each object, and detailing algorithms related to music concepts.

While at times there will be a similar kind of exposition, this section is developed at a broader level. That is, the discussion focuses primarily on algorithms and techniques behind the topics of discussion, and less so on detailed discussion of representation, or even tangential details related to the algorithms. The intention is to cover material with a focus on the intent and means of the transformations, and the processes with which they are involved. Ancillary details can be viewed as exercises, class discussions, or homework.

As we move forward, several topics are introduced that may not appear at first to address music transformation, but as the topics develop, their relevance is shown. The initial discussion on constraint solutions is one of these topics and will be borne out to be important in later transforms. This is an interesting discussion in and of itself and can be seen in importance beyond it use here, potentially for example in generative music. Melodic search is yet another discussion that does not seem related to music transforms but will be shown to play a key role leading to pattern substitution.

The topics presented may at times seem dense, and indeed in detail need to address the complexity of music, as seen in the representation section. However, bear in mind that these discussions on transforms are but the tip of an iceberg on the topic, that music transforms comprise a deep academic topic. They could provide powerful techniques for music composition tools, and a foundation for even more powerful transforms at the same or broader applicability.

A final note to be made about this material. The following topics should not be considered as definitive final words on their subject. These are all research topics that should be further studied and upon which further research could proceed.

14 A Constraint Engine for Pitch Assignment

We begin our study of music transforms with introducing a technology that will prove useful for other transforms presented later. This technical approach uses constraint specifications as a foundation. That is, a problem is specified by a set of conditions over a set of parameters, or variables. Generally, a constraint approach to problem solving does not provide succinct efficient algorithmic solutions tailored to a problem domain. Rather, it is a generalized approach that attempts to extract from the problem parameters an exhaustive set of potential solution values. With that, it searches over all those parameter values to find combinations which succeed as a solution. In this approach, the solution search space can be large and the corresponding search times can be long. The main benefit of this approach is that the user describes a problem succinctly as a set of desired conditions on problem parameters without needing to provide domain-specific algorithms for solution.

We begin with describing generally what constraints are and how they are used in a constraint programming environment. We limit the discussion to a music constraint system (constraints and engine) that focuses on note pitch assignment for a melody. The constraints formulate conditions about the notes and their pitches. We describe how constraints are specified, how the output is captured, and finally the workings of the music constraint engine, with a particular focus on optimizations (See Appendix G).

The reader should understand that the music constraint engine described here is prototypical and strictly for educational purposes to provide a means for solutions. Other designs to provide more efficient heuristics and domain-specific optimizations are left to study and research. The design presented here is educational in value and provides a launching point for the topic of constraint engines on music systems.

14.1 Constraint Programming

Constraint programming is a form of programming in which a problem is formally described in terms of:

- A set of *variables* that take on values from various value domains, e.g., integer, strings, etc.

- A set of *constraints* or relationships amongst the variables that describe a state to be satisfied.

A *constraint solver/engine* is a software tool that takes as input a set of variables and a set of constraints about a problem, and produces solutions, i.e., a set of variable value assignments, that satisfy those constraints. The process is shown in Fig. 14.1.

© The Author(s), under exclusive license to Springer Nature Switzerland AG 2022

D. P. Pazel, *Music Representation and Transformation in Software*, https://doi.org/10.1007/978-3-030-97472-5_14

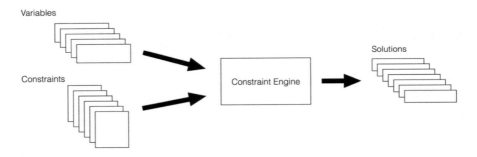

Fig. 14.1 Problem specification as variables and constraints and solutions.

Constraint programming, or similarly constraint logic programming, rose to prominence in the 1980's, and was popularized in the Prolog [36] programming language. Details related to constraint engines are more properly found in [37] and [38]. SWI-Prolog can be found at [39]. Other options include Gecode [40] or OptaPlanner [41] or python-constraint [42].

As an example, consider the following constraint problem:

```
Variables: I ε Integers; S ε Strings
Conditions:
    S.starts_with("abc")
    S[3] ε {'1', '2', '3'}
    len(S) == 4
    I == len(S) + as_integer(S[3])
```

The problem solutions comprise assignments of integers to I and strings to S that solve the conditions. Solutions for (S, I) assignment include (('abc1', 5), ('abc2', 6), ('abc3', 7)}.

Unlike Python programming as we described in the representation part of this book for formulating processes or algorithms to calculate a solution, constraint programming focuses on problem description as a first order of business. That problem description is based on defining a set of variables and the domains from which they are assigned values, and a set of conditions or constraints to which solution variable values must adhere.

On how solutions are calculated is not part of the problem specification nor part of any other input from the user. The solution is produced by a constraint engine, a software program that processes the problem variables and constraints to one or more solutions. The inner workings of that engine can be very general and complex, and not in the user's purview.

The topic of constraint programming is deep and rich. As to the workings and algorithms within a constraint engine that calculate solutions, these are deep topics, which could occupy a book itself. It is not the intention of this book to probe deeply into this technical area. We take a somewhat simplified approach that provides an introductory education to this topic and use it as an approach to finding solutions to music related problems that are described later. In the end, the content on constraint programming presented here should provide a nice dropping-off point for further exploration and optimization by readers.

14.2 Music Constraints and Solution Spaces

With the above introduction to constraint programming, we now set out to discuss the music domain problem space in which we are interested. We describe the types of problems we are trying to solve.

and address why constraint programming is a good approach to use for solutions. At the same time, we acknowledge that constraint programming is not always the best approach and discuss when or if it is possible to avoid it, in particular, for the problem space presented here.

Recall from our introduction to music transformation, that the transform involves mapping a music fragment to a new music fragment, that holds to some desired set of conditions. Those conditions mainly involve altering the pitches of the original fragment. We start with a source fragment which consists of a set of notes, and based on that source, a target harmony track, and specified constraints, we want one or more solution music fragments based on the source that satisfy those constraints. The target harmony track is a significant input, as it informs tonality (key) and harmonic (chordal) structure for the transformed output.

Because our transforms focus on music fragment remapping, the source notes of the input music fragment are in some sense 'place holders' for new notes wherein their attributes are changed, i.e., in this case pitch. Following this line of thought, for our discussion in the context of constraints, these source notes, which we call ***actors***, constitute the set of variables for our constraint problem. We build constraints, which we also sometimes call ***policies***, around actor variables to inform the kinds of values the actors take and relationships among actors.

To make this discussion more concrete, we provide an example. Suppose we have an input music fragment with four notes that comprise the set of actors {N1, N2, N3, N4}. Think of each actor as a note with pitch, duration and offset. We may insist that:

1. N1 and N3 should have the same pitch

2. N1 and N2 should not have the same pitch

3. N3 should be assigned 'C:4'

4. N2, N4 should be assigned consecutive scale notes

Fig. 14.2 illustrates this problem, its specification, and one solution. Note that there can be many solutions based on the constraint specification, e.g., N2 and N4 can have many valid assignments. In instances such as that, either adding further constraints or quantifying/scoring solutions based on an objective ranking criterion can serve towards picking a solution out of many solutions[46].

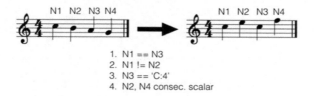

Fig. 14.2 Constraint solution example.

These are a few from a wide variety of constraints that could be imagined and applied as conditions that will inform our solutions. Notice here that the original pitch values serve no value; they will be changed for the sake of given constraints which deal with pitch value properties and note pitch relationships. Also note that each actor's duration and offset values remain the same.

For the discussion in this chapter, the focus is on constraints concerning pitch, as in this example. That means our constraints, also as shown, focus on pitch value, and pitch value relationships amongst notes.

---

[46] This example focuses only on clarifying what constraints are and can be. We intentionally avoided overcomplicating the example with a target harmony track.

Addressing other note properties could be similarly addressed, but not in the context of this presentation.

That being the case, each actor could potentially take on many values. Developing a specialized efficient heuristic that can address an arbitrary policy with multiple actors optimally is difficult, and beyond the scope of this text. That is why we use a general heuristic search approach through pitch value settings over all actors as the means for solving our problem. While that kind of search is sub-optimal, time being roughly multiplicative over actor value sets, the exhaustive search can cull obvious and non-obvious solutions at least on shorter music fragments reasonably. Larger fragments many times means longer search times, making a constraint engine less desirable to develop problem-specific algorithms should they exist. However, for the small input music fragments used in this text, it is reasonable to consider using a constraint engine as the solution means over this problem space.

14.3 Music Constraint Programming Elements

This section introduces elements of the music constraint engine exposed to the end-user. It introduces the class PMap, which defines and describes solutions, and the class AbstractConstraint upon which all constraints are defined. A selection of constraints packaged with the constraint engine package are also discussed. We also look at how the constraint solver is invoked and how results are packaged and read, before proceeding to examples.

14.3.1 PMaps

In setting context for discussion, we begin with a melody comprised of a set of notes, and a set of constraints related to pitches of these notes, much like those mentioned earlier. We also specify a target hct to which solutions must conform. The goal is to find solutions, each of which has pitch reassignments to the original notes that satisfy all the user provided constraints. These solutions are discovered through a search over possible pitch assignments to the notes in a way that is described later (Appendix G). Each solution represents for the original notes, replacement notes which satisfy the constraints and the target hct. There may be multiple solutions.

Fig. 14.3 PMap example.

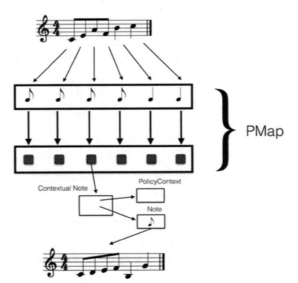

This representation we introduce expresses either a full or partial solution to the pitch assignment problem. More than representing a solution set, it also provides a partial or in-process result representation to use during the search process. For our discussion, we call that representative class PMap or "parameter map". See *Fig. 14.3*. A PMap contains a map from the source note actors to new notes whose pitches are determined by constraint solutions. To be clear, the source note actors are not changed by the engine. New notes to which the source actors map in PMap mirror the source actors in all aspects except for pitch. The new notes inherit position, duration, and offset from the input source actors by default.

Fig. 14.3 depicts the structure of PMap. Reading top to bottom, some music is the input. Each of its notes is an actor in the PMap. The PMap maps the actor notes to a set of 'to be filled-in' structures called ***contextual notes.*** Contextual notes are undefined notes that are filled in by the constraint engine in satisfying the constraints. Each contextual note holds a PolicyContext containing useful information to compute a replacement note. For example, it holds a HarmonicContext providing the key and chord for the note. This comes from the target hct. The PolicyContext also hold the pitch range for the note, as derived from, say, the music's instrument. The pitch range is also in input parameter for PMap construction.

Finally, the contextual note references a newly computed note that is the result of the constraint engine search using the constraints. For our limited purposes, the only change from the corresponding input note is the pitch, as we hold onto the original note's duration and position. When/if the PMap finds a replacement note for each input note, the new resulting melody can be constructed from the PMap, as shown in *Fig. 14.3*.

A few items about the input are worth mentioning. First, we observe that the input notes comprising the source of the PMap seem inconsequential, in that other simpler representations, for example, consecutive integers could have worked as well. That is, assuming the integers correspond to the input notes consistently for representation purposes. To a great degree that is true. However, having access to the original notes provides information about the original context that could prove to be useful information, for example in enforcing policies. Also, all PMaps use the same actors, and in fact, as will be seen, all constraints are based on this same set of actors. In that sense, then, the input notes provide a common reference across PMaps and policies that is important for the constraint engine design.

In addition to the input music fragment, we assume an input harmonic context track defining the harmony (keys and chords) for the output. That is how the harmonic context is provided to each policy context of the earlier discussion. Manual PMap construction can be somewhat onerous. However, PMap provides a construction method to facilitate its creation. PMap.create() uses text syntax for creating lines and hcts, as described in section 12.2. In one case, the user codes the target harmonies into the text (even though presumably the melody does not match to those harmonies). In the other, the user specifies a list of harmonic contexts and durations for the target hct. In all cases, a pitch range is specified defining the range of pitches over which the constraint engine search. Both techniques are illustrated below:

```
ln = '{<Ab-Major:I> qC:4 D E F <Db-Major:IV> iDb:4 Eb F Gb <C-Major:IV> qE:4 F G A }'
pr = PitchRange.create('Ab:3', 'C:5')
pm = PMap.create(ln, pr)     # Uses the harmony in variable ln!
--- or ---
target_harmonic_list = [('A-Melodic:iv', 1),
                        ('A-Natural:i', Duration(1, 4)),
                        ('A-Melodic:V', 1)]
pm = PMap.create(ln, pr, target_harmonic_list)    # Uses the harmony in
                                                  # target_harmony_list
```

PMaps are used as solution output to constraint problems. Therefore, one needs to know how to read them to use the new solution note output. The following example shows how to extract the source actor notes, and the notes to which they map, sorted in whole-time.

```
pmap = …
source_notes = [k for k in pmap.keys()]   # Turn the keys into a list
source_notes = sorted(source_notes, key=lambda sn: sn.get_absolute_position())
target_notes = [pmap[key].note for key in source_notes]
```

14.3.2 Constraints

The basis for constraints involves defining, for a given set of input notes (actors), a set of relationships amongst them, or alternatively individual properties about them. As an example of the first, we many want the interval defined by the 4th and 8th note to be an augmented fifth. As for defining properties, we may want the 10th note's pitch to be chordal relative to its harmonic context, or perhaps the 8th note fixed to pitch "G:4".

Constraints define qualifications on a set of actors. Many kinds of constraints for relationships and properties on the actors can be defined. We consider the definition of constraints and the precise information that constraints should provide for constraint processing, and how the constraint processor accesses that information.

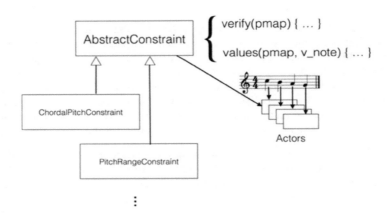

Fig. 14.4 AbstractConstraint.

For designing a constraint, we establish the abstract class AbstractConstraint, Fig. 14.4. All other constraints derive directly from it (subclass from it). AbstractConstraint defines three central components

- Actors – These represent the notes to which pitch values are to be assigned. Typically, they represent the notes of a given melody. As a constructor argument, these are pass as a list of Notes.

- verify(pmap) - For a given potential solution (pmap), this method verifies that the constraint's actors map to values and that those values meet the qualifications of the constraint. The method returns true if the constraint is met.

- values(pmap, actor) - For a potential solution (pmap), this method determines values the given constraint actor can take, even for partial solutions. The method returns a set of possible values (a set of Notes).

The verify() method serves a rather obvious need. At various times in constraint processing, the process needs to know if a proposed solution satisfies a constraint. The values() method returns possible values for a specified actor that the constraint process should checked. Early in solution processing, the number of actor values can be large. For example, we may want the pitch value to be scalar to the key defined in the policy context, over the range of an instrument, say a piano. This range is noted in the policy context. That set of pitches can be a large, and the larger the set, the more effort in terms of constraint processing, possibly resulting in excessive processing time. It's good to keep this in mind when developing constraints.

One finds that as partial solutions have actors assigned values, the value sets on unassigned actors narrows quickly. As an example, suppose two actors are constrained to an interval, when the first actor is assigned a pitch, the second actor's pitch is immediately calculated and so it has one value solution. Similarly, if the second actor is assigned first, the first actor's pitch value follows immediately. While such circumstances depend on the constraints used in the problem, this behavior is relatively frequent, which helps in shortening the constraint engine's processing, and lessening the number of partial solutions to further process. These calculations occur in the values () method.

We emphasize that value computation is solely in the context of each constraint relative to a pmap. Inter-constraint coordination is not the responsibility of any constraint itself. While one might think that knowing, for example, that constraining an actor to be chordal would greatly cut down on the value space in a way that would be in the interest of other constraints to incorporate into their logic, that is not the case. Constraints do not communicate amongst themselves. Constraints are developed in isolation and independent of others and rule out the possibility of inter-constraint dependencies. The constraint engine itself is fully capable of culling value spaces over multiple constraints. In a way, it can be said that the perceived inter-constraint dependence is taken care of by the constraint engine.

With constraint system users likely wanting to define their own constraints, it is useful to present the constraint base class and make critical behaviors (methods) exposed and formal. So, we define the class AbstractConstraint, which highlights the actor parameters as well as the verify() and values() methods, which must be defined in each and every constraint.

```
class AbstractConstraint(object):

    def __init__(self, actors):
        self.__actors = list(actors)

    @property
    def actors(self):
        return list(self.__actors)

    @abstractmethod
    def clone(self, new_actors=None):
        """
        Clone the constraint to a different set of actors.
        """

    @abstractmethod
    def verify(self, pmap):
        """
        Verify that the actor map parameters are consistent with constraint.
        :params pmap:  map of actors to ContextualNotes.
        :return: Boolean, True if verification holds.
```

```
        May throw Exception dependent on implementation.
        """


    @abstractmethod
    def values(self, pmap, actor):
        """
        Method to generate all possible note values for actor v_note's target.
        The method returns a set of values for v_note.
        :param pmap: map of actors to ContextualNotes.
```

14.3.3 Types of Constraints

We now discuss some constraints found in the code base. In presentation we show what can be specified as a constraint, and thereby making the topic of constraints less abstract for the reader.

To facilitate presentation, we can classify the constraints around one actor (unary), two actors (binary), or multiple actors (multi-actor).

Unary Constraints

`FixedToneConstraint(actor, diatonic_tone):`
> Specifies the actor and tone, but not the octave/register, to which the actor must be held.

`FixedPitchConstraint(actor, diatonic_pitch):`
> Specifies the actor and pitch to which the actor must be held.

`ChordalPitchConstraint(actor):`
> The actor's pitch must be held to a pitch within a specified chord. The chord is not an argument to the constraint but is specified by the input harmonic contexts.

`ScalarPitchConstraint(actor, tone_index_list=list()):`
> The actor's pitch's tone must be from a specified tonality. The tonality is found in the input harmonic contexts. An optional constraint parameter specifies by indices (origin 0), a subset of the tonality's tone set to which the tone selection is restricted.

Binary Constraints

`ComparativePitchConstraint(actor1, actor_2, comparative):`
> In this constraint, two actors, actor1 and actor2 are specified, along with a required pitch comparative relationship. The pitches assigned actor1 and actor2 must match the relationship, being one of less than, less or equal, equal, greater or equal, greater than.

`RelativeScalarStepConstraint(actor1, actor2, below_steps, above_steps):`
> Constraint to ensure actor2's pitch is within an interval of actor1's pitch bounded by a range of diatonic steps, below/above.

Mulit-Actor Constraints

`EqualPitchConstraint(actor_list):`
> For a given list of actors, ensure those pitches are equal in assignment.

`NotEqualPitchConstraint(actor_list):`
> For a given list of actors, ensure those pitches are not equal in assignment pairwise.

`StepSequenceConstraint(actor_list, variance_list):`

Given an ordered list of actors, and a list of integers representing incremental numbers of diatonic steps, the result ensures a set of actor pitch assignments whose diatonic step distances matches in sequence the variance list.

14.3.4   Invoking the Pitch Constraint Solver

Constraint problems are solved with the pitch constraint solver. The constructor takes a set of constraints. The solve() method takes a PMap derived from initial conditions, and optionally an integer limiting the number of full solutions found, and optionally, a Boolean flag as to whether or not to return partial results (the default is False). The method solve() return two lists. The first is a list of full solutions, each solution being expressed as a PMap. The second is similar but for partial solutions. More precisely:

```
from melody.solver.pitch_constraint_solver import PitchConstraintSolver
from melody.solver.p_map import PMap


pmap = …
solver = PitchConstraintSolver(policies)
full_results, partial_results = solver.solve(p_map)
```

14.4   Examples

We present a couple of examples[47]using the pitch constraint engine on defined constraints over simple melodies. For the first example, consider the following melody:

C-Major/IV

This is a simple melody in C major based on the IV chord. The goal is to rewrite this melody to a V chord in G major. The code below begins with setting up the melody and initial PMap. Several constraints are defined related to the shape of the melody and actor chordal roles. We have 10 actors in order, indexed 0 to 9. We define 12 constraints. The first 6 constraints aim to preserve stepwise descent and ascent on the 8th notes:

```
# Setup - Build melody line, initial p_map, and get the actors.
source_instance_expression = '{<C-Major:IV> [sC:5 B:4 A G] qF:4 [sA:4 B C:5 D] qD:5}'
pitch_range = PitchRange.create('C:2', 'C:8')
p_map = PMap.create(source_instance_expression, pitch_range, [('G-Major:V', 1)])
actors = p_map.actors
policies = set()

policies.add(PitchStepConstraint(actors[0], actors[1], 1, PitchStepConstraint.Down))
policies.add(PitchStepConstraint(actors[1], actors[2], 1, PitchStepConstraint.Down))
policies.add(PitchStepConstraint(actors[2], actors[3], 1, PitchStepConstraint.Down))
```

---

[47] The results of these examples came by way of the book's source code at the time of this book's writing. The reader should understand that over time the code may have changed. With that the results may not conform to the presentation here.

```
policies.add(PitchStepConstraint(actors[5], actors[6], 1, PitchStepConstraint.UP))
policies.add(PitchStepConstraint(actors[6], actors[7], 1, PitchStepConstraint.UP))
policies.add(PitchStepConstraint(actors[7], actors[8], 1, PitchStepConstraint.UP))
```

We then want to make the 3rd and 4th (origin 0) notes equal in pitch, as well as the 8th and 9th.

```
policies.add(EqualPitchConstraint([actors[3], actors[4]]))
policies.add(EqualPitchConstraint([actors[8], actors[9]]))
```

To stabilize the variances in octave ranges, we want to ensure the 5th note is either equal to the 4th or within a major 3rd. Similarly, we want the 8th note to be within a perfect 5th of the 3rd note.

```
policies.add(RelativeDiatonicConstraint(actors[4], actors[5],
         Interval(3, IntervalType.Major), Interval(1, IntervalType.Perfect)))
policies.add(RelativeDiatonicConstraint(actors[3], actors[8],
         Interval(5, IntervalType.Perfect), Interval(1, IntervalType.Perfect)))
```

Finally, we want the 4th and 9th notes to be chordal, in this case the V in G major. After that, the solver is created and called.

```
policies.add(ChordalPitchConstraint(actors[4]))
policies.add(ChordalPitchConstraint(actors[9]))

solver = PitchConstraintSolver(policies)
full_results, _ = solver.solve(p_map)
```

We run the constraint engine with these constraints and find 11 results. The result list is built with results as they are found, and the order does not reflect any kind of relative quality, i.e., that the first is note "better" than the second in any defined sense of the word. There are basically 2 results written in different octaves of our specified range:

The first solution is quite acceptable. The second is less so with the repetitions of the A's.

We note that generally the input melody, outside of note duration, position, and harmony provides little valuable input. To make input easier, we assign the same pitch to each input note. With that our second example is:

Our goal here is to reshape the melody, especially the 16th notes, declare some notes chordal, and enforce some of equal pitch. Additionally, our reshaped melody will be in G Major with the measures taking a I and IV chord respectively.

The Python setup is nearly identical to the first example except for the input music text and the output harmonies. The constraints are given as:

```
policies = OrderedSet()
policies.add(StepSequenceConstraint([actors[0], actors[1], actors[2], actors[3]],
                                    [1, 1, 1]))
policies.add(ChordalPitchConstraint(actors[0]))
policies.add(ChordalPitchConstraint(actors[4]))
policies.add(ChordalPitchConstraint(actors[8]))
policies.add(StepSequenceConstraint([actors[8], actors[9], actors[10], actors[11]],
                                    [1, -1, -1]))
policies.add(EqualPitchConstraint([actors[0], actors[12]]))
policies.add(EqualPitchConstraint([actors[4], actors[7]]))
policies.add(RelativeDiatonicConstraint(actors[4], actors[5],
                Interval(3, IntervalType.Major), Interval(1, IntervalType.Perfect)))
policies.add(StepSequenceConstraint([actors[5], actors[6]], [-1]))
```

In summary:

- Notes 0,1,2,3 stepwise ascend.

- Notes 0, 4, and 8 are chordal.

- Notes 8,9 stepwise ascend while 9,10,11 stepwise descend.

- Notes 0 and 12 have equal pitch, as do notes 4 and 7.

- Notes 4 and 5 are at most a major third distant.

- Notes 5,6 descend stepwise.

The search finds 714 matches on these constraints over a somewhat limited two octave pitch range of C:4 to C:6. Again the order of solutions is not based on any qualification. We discuss three of these solutions. We note in the first two solutions several issues. These plus the high number of results, indicates a lack of constraints generally. In that sense, the constraint engine, while providing many answers for us to explore, at the same time and by virtue of the many answers, is teaching us what may be missing in framing our melodic shaping as constraints.

The first output above looks generally pretty good, but there are a few issues. First, in measure one the repeated B:4 is a bit awkward. That could be fixed with a NotEqualPitchConstraint. Alternatively, the two B:4's could be tied. Secondly the B:4 on the first beat of measure two clashes with the IV chord. That can be fixed with a ChordalPitchConstraint on that note, while being mindful that that note is in an EqualPitchConstraint with the 5th note in measure 1!

The second solution above fares a little better. However, it may not be to the user's liking to have the major 7th downward jump between the C:5 and D:4 in measure one. One suggestion is to provide a RelativeDiatonicConstraint on those notes. Also, the D:4 on the beat of measure 2 clashes with the chord, again asking for a ChordalPitchConstraint for that note.

Finally, the third output considered for this example has an acceptable melodic line. In this example, we include the ChordalPitchConstraint for the first note in measure 2. Since it must equal the pitch of the note on the second beat of measure 1, and which is also chordal, the only tone it can be is G, the only common tone between the two chords.

G-Major/I   G-Major/IV

Overall, the constraints on both examples worked as expected. As a bonus, user analysis of output can indicate needed constraint specification. When the number of successful outputs is high, or processing time excessive, these are indications that you likely need to add further constraints.

In both examples, we had no filters on the output results, and selected a few solutions, and not necessarily the best, to analyze. While automating a filtering process can be a good way to isolate the better solutions for one's purposes, one must further ask if the filtering process itself, that is the objective function used to evaluate fitness, is in fact based on constraints missing in the problem specification.

14.5 Final Thoughts

Using constraints to invent or modify existing music content is an interesting technical approach. Optimistically, as it computes through all legal pitch assignments, one can be quite sure that:

- If there are outputs, you get all of them.

- If there is no output, you have likely over-constrained the input.

- If the compute time takes too long, you have likely under-constrained the input.

As seen in our examples, the constraint engine provides a heuristic exploration of pitch assignments and from the output, the user can search for 'best fit' solutions. At the same time, one can try to understand how to fix issues present in the solutions by adjusting the constraints, for example.

Perhaps, the biggest problem with this approach concerns a potentially lengthy algorithmic runtime. Depending on the constraint specifications, the algorithm can take abnormal amounts of compute time to generate outputs. Enhancements to implementation, such as implementing 'cut off compute times' discussed previously, may help reduce that burden.

The astute reader may observe that the constraint engine presented here only reshapes at best a purely rhythmic note sequence using pitch assignments. There are no provisions/constraints for adding or deleting notes to the input melody, nor modifying onsets and durations. Adding these kinds of capabilities is a topic for further interesting research.

One further area of research concerns diagnostics which infer from the output, remediation or suggestions on the constraints to help improve the output and/or lessen compute time. Heuristics to evaluate outputs is an interesting research topic, regarding ranking output against some set of melodic quality criteria, which for whatever reason may not be relatable to constraint specification.

There are many opportunities to improve on the presented algorithm, as well as the constraints, which are left to further discussion for now.

15 Shift: A Transform for Key Change

The first transform we discuss aligns with the most found in music tools, namely, to shift a melody to a different tonality and/or mode. One typically finds variations of this transform in notation editors and in some midi-based players. The concept involves taking a selection of music, perhaps a score or simply a midi source, and raising or lowering the root tone of the same modality, e.g., say from G-Major to E Major. In some cases, this transform also involve changing the modality, usually with the same root tone, e.g., E-Major to E-Minor. Of course, there are cases for doing both root tone and modality change.

In this chapter, the "shift" transform performs similar operations, but it also optionally incorporates not only change of key root and/or modality, but also a change in modal index. So, for example, one could consider a shift from F-Major to G-MelodicMinor Dorian (F#).

The music segment on which the operation takes effect is represented by a Line and its associated HarmonicContextTrack as introduced in the representation sections. Readers are encouraged to review these concepts before moving forward on this chapter.

Along the way, we introduce a host of representational mapping structures with which the reader can work outside the shift transform context to create or enhance their own novel types of operations. The chapter concludes with some examples and final thoughts.

15.1 An Overview of the Shift Transform

We begin by looking at the shift transform as an operation that transforms a piece of music (instantiated as Line and hct using the representation discussed earlier) into similarly represented music, with the intention of changing any of key, modality, and modal index. Additionally, we apply the representation over some temporal extent of the input music. A summary diagram of the shift operation is shown in Fig. 15.1.

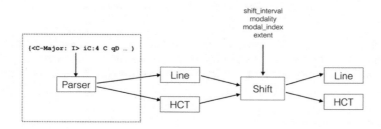

Fig. 15.1 Shift operator.

© The Author(s), under exclusive license to Springer Nature Switzerland AG 2022

D. P. Pazel, *Music Representation and Transformation in Software*, https://doi.org/10.1007/978-3-030-97472-5_15

The music is represented by a Line and a HarmonicContextTrack (hct), which serve as input to the shift transform. These optionally can be more conveniently and directly represented by a string formatted in the music grammar described earlier, which is parsed into a Line and hct.

The remaining parameters that can be specified on input determine how the output music should be shifted. These parameters consist of:

- shift_interval: The interval between the root tone of the input key and the new root key tone.
- modality: The modality of the output key.
- modal_index: An integer representing which tone in the new tonality serves as the key root.
- extent: the temporal range of the input music to transform.

The extent parameter is given as a temporal interval[48], indicating the temporal section of the input to be transformed in whole note time.

The transform's output is a Line and hct, based on the input, transformed to the shift specification. These are identical in duration to the input with the portions outside the temporal extent not transformed.

For clarification, shift's transformed tonality is derived from the original tonality, shift interval, specified modality, and modal index, and is computed as follows. Recall that a tonality has a basis tone, strictly based to a modality (without regard to modal index). There is also a root tone based on the modal index which indexes into the tone set of that tonality with basis tone. For example, D-Dorian is based on C-Major. C is the basis tone, D is the root tone, and the modal index is 1 or "C-Major D(1)"

The shift interval is applied to the root tone, giving a new root tone for the new tonality. That tone corresponds to the modal index on some tonality based on the input modality parameter. Using the new modality tone set, the derivation of the basis tone is achieved by "counting backwards" from the new root tone to a new basis tone by the specified modal index.

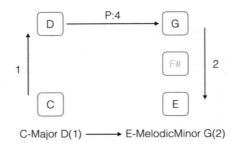

C-Major D(1) ⟶ E-MelodicMinor G(2)

Fig. 15.2 Shift calculation P:4, modal index 2

To clarify this somewhat convoluted explanation, consider Fig. 15.2. Assume the current tonality is 'C-Major D(1)' that is, modal index 1 on a C-Major scale, or simply D-Dorian. Suppose we shift the root a perfect 4th and to a melodic minor tonality with a modal index 2. The root D then shifts to the

---

[48] The class Interval here (found in misc.interval) must not be confused with the musical Interval defined earlier. In this context, Interval is defined by a start and end position. This is an unfortunate coincidence of named meanings.

root G (perfect fourth). But G is the third scalar tone (Phrygian) to E melodic minor. Thus, this shift operation is given by:

C-Major D(1) —> E-MelodicMinor G(2)

Returning to Fig. 15.1, the shift transform returns the transformed line, and a transformed hct as well, that is, an hct reflecting constituent HarmonicContext changes. Naturally, the key shift will be reflected in each new harmonic context. And as well, the key change results in chord changes, and the new chord is also noted in the transformed harmonic contexts.

We will not consider shift transforms that result in a change in modality cardinality. That is, we will not consider transforms, say, from diatonic to pentatonic nor vice versa.

15.2   Structural Design of the Shift Transform

In simplified versions of key shifting operations not involving modality chage, it is a case of computing tone to tone changes, with some extra calculations regarding shifts across octave boundary for pitches. However, when modality changes, say from major to minor modalities, a simplified version of shift might only lower (flatten) the 3rd tone, and ignore the distinctions among melodic, natural, and harmonic minor occurring in the 6th and 7th tones. So, ignoring that consideration, these kinds of changes are simple calculations, and the overall effects are less than ideal.

The goal here is a bit more ambitious by accounting for a larger family of modalities and including modal index changes. There is also the issue of how to map non-tonal pitches. As is often the case, for music in a specific tonality and harmony, an occasional non-tonal note is incurred.

The approach taken here in designing a shift transform is to first generate a tone-to-tone map from the input tonality to output tonality and follow that with a pitch-to-pitch map. The latter map is applied to the individual notes of a source line at a following stage of the transform. Harmonic contexts also change in the process, potentially requiring their own pitch-to-pitch maps (secondary chords for example). The advantage of this approach is that it isolates the tonal and pitch mapping logic to a map generation phase as opposed to developing it into a separate complicated pitch change logic. By doing this, complex issues such as octave changes, and non-tonal pitch mapping are developed in an isolated context wherein all pitch map construction issues are considered, away from the note pitch conversion logic which presumable would then be rather straight forward.

In terms of space, pitch maps do not occupy a large memory footprint. After all, there are only 88 distinct pitches which is small, and dealing with enharmonic pitches is not so large an addition. Another feature is that once the tonal and pitch maps are constructed, they can be re-used by caching them.

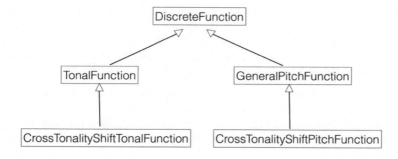

Fig. 15.3 Tonal/Pitch function object design.

The class inheritance structure upon which the tonal and pitch maps are defined is shown in Fig. 15.3.

At the root, DiscreteFunction defines a mapping between two discrete sets of objects. TonalFunction is a discrete function that maps tones to tones based on two given tonalities. The GeneralPitchFunction is like the TonalFunction but maps pitches to pitches.

The remaining shift functions capitalize on their base classes' mapping capabilities allowing them to focus on specifics of shifting operations on tonalities. The CrossTonalityShiftPitchFunction maps pitches to pitches and is the primary map used in transforming notes and harmonic contexts. Further details are provided in the following sections.

15.3   Tonal and Pitch Functions

The mapping structures given above are richer that one might have expected in a Shift transformation. In fact, the structure reveals something of a forward anticipation of needs or functionality outside of the shift function, and some of that structure will be reused in a later transform.

We will not look deeply at DiscreteFunction, as it is essentially a cover class for an internal object map, with access to domain keys and range values. Its utility is in providing an object level base for the other function objects. For the remainder of this section, we look more deeply at each of the other functions and how they work.

To reduce duplication of explanation in the following, the reader will note that these functions often cite *primary maps* and *extension maps*. Primary maps concern mapping tones/pitches that are strictly in the domain and range tonalities of these maps. Extension maps concern mapping tones/pitches that are outside of the domain and range tonalities of these maps.

15.3.1   Tonal Functions

A tonal function maps the tones of the domain tonality to the tones of the range tonality. The construction parameters include:

- domain_tonality: The map's domain tonality.

- range_tonality: The map's range tonality.

- primary_map: Optional map of domain tonality tones to range tonality tones, map entries can be specified as diatonic tones or strings.

- extension_map: Optional map of tones outside the domain tonality to those outside the range tonality, with entries specified as diatonic tones or strings.

Clearly, if only domain and range tonalities are specified, and if they have the same cardinality, the default primary map is a straightforward 1-1 map of tones in order by default. The value of having the primary and extension map arguments is to override default behavior in favor of user specified mappings. For example, one might want to build a permutation of tones on a tonality (domain and range tonalities having the same tone set), or simply build a tone-to-tone map between the input tonalities in some user specified manner (primary), and/or outside the tones of the tonalities (extension).

The point of the having an extension map is clear. Looking forward to the shift operation, it is often the case in melodic construction to use tones outside the current key. Extension maps allow the specification of how those tones should be mapped. Later, we will look at how an extension mapping can be built in a default manner, but for now, in the context of TonalFunction, this is an explicit parameter and there is no default construction.

Keeping to the general nature of TonalFunction, we note that when the domain and range tonalities have different cardinalities, with the domain's cardinality larger than the range's, the default primary mapping uses a cycling assignment technique over the range's tones, allowing every domain tone to map to a range tone. This is a feature of TonalFunction. Other functions mentioned here do not allow this, and the tonality cardinalities of source and target must be the same, see for example CrossTonalityShiftTonalFunction.

An example construcing a TonalFunction is shown below. Notice the convenient indexing notation of the tonal function f in the mapping, e.g., f['E'].

```
t_domain = Tonality.create(ModalityType.Major, DiatonicTone('C'))
t_range = Tonality.create(ModalityType.Major, DiatonicTone('A'))

# default map between 2 tonalities of same cardinality.
f = TonalFunction(t_domain, t_range)

assert DiatonicToneCache.get_tone('A') == f['C']
assert DiatonicToneCache.get_tone('B') == f['D']
assert DiatonicToneCache.get_tone('C#') == f['E']
assert DiatonicToneCache.get_tone('D') == f['F']
```

Additionally, TonalFunction introduces the TonalFunctionTemplate class. This is simply a convenience class to generate one TonalFunction from another, when the new tonality parameters have the same cardinality as the old. TonalFunction provides the method create_adapted_function() that does this. Note in the following how a tonal function using similar tonalities to a prior tonal function is derived directly from the original.

```
t_domain = Tonality.create(ModalityType.Major, DiatonicTone('F'))
t_range = Tonality.create(ModalityType.MelodicMinor, DiatonicTone('G'))

f = TonalFunction(t_domain, t_range)

nt_domain = Tonality.create(ModalityType.Major, DiatonicTone('Ab'))
nt_range = Tonality.create(ModalityType.MelodicMinor, DiatonicTone('e'))

pf = f.create_adapted_function(nt_domain, nt_range)

assert DiatonicToneCache.get_tone('E') == pf['Ab']
assert DiatonicToneCache.get_tone('F#') == pf['Bb']
```

The reader is left to explore the logic behind mapping different modalities in TonalFunction and consider improvements.

15.3.2 CrossTonalityShiftTonalFunction

TonalFunction is meant to provide flexibility in specifying how the tones of the domain tonality map to the tones of the range tonality. The user provided extension map is used to account for tones outside the domain tonality. The CrossTonalityShiftTonalFunction, a subclass of TonalFunction, adds a default computational means for extending the map on tones not in the domain tonality. A restriction however is that the domain and range tonality cardinalities must match.

The extension on non-domain tonality tones is important. Even when key and chord are specific in music, it is often the case that non-key tones are added to enhance musical color. TonalFunction only uses a user provided extension map to make that capability. In CrossTonalityShiftTonalFunction, a computational model is provided to extend the map over non-domain tonality tones. As mentioned, this may optionally be overridden with a user provided extension map.

A couple of computational techniques are used to calculate non-tonal pitch mappings. For simple chromatic augmentations of the domain tonality tones, the map extends to similarly augmented mapped tones.

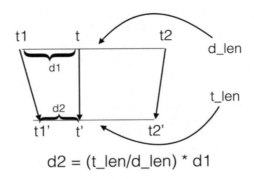

$$d2 = (t\_len/d\_len) * d1$$

Fig. 15.4 Tonal interpolation.

For tones outside of this, for example tones found outside a pentatonic scale, the technique used is a form of tonal interpolation, similar to affine transformations introduced in section 11.2.5 and illustrated in Fig. 15.4. Given tone t outside the domain tonality, t1 and t2 are the closest neighboring domain tones to t, which had already been determined to map to t1' and t2' in the range tonality. d_len is the chromatic distance between t1 and t2, and t_len is the chromatic distance between t1' and t2'. d1 is the chromatic distance between t1 and t. The counterpart range chromatic distance is given through the simple interpolation:

$$d2 = \left(\frac{t\_len}{d\_len}\right) * d1 \tag{15.1}$$

Equation (15.1) computes the chromatic distance d2 which when added to t1' gives the chromatic value of t'. The actual tone t' is then determined[49].

As an example of using CrossTonalityShiftTonalFunction, consider the map between C-MajorPentatonic(0) and E-MajorPentatonic(2). The former's tone set is {C, D, E, G, A}, and the latter is {G#, B, C#, E, F#} (since G# is the third tone (index 2) in the E-MajorPentatonic scale). The result of the mapping is shown in this example:

```
from transformation.functions.tonalfunctions.cross_tonality_shift_tonal_function
    import CrossTonalityShiftTonalFunction
t_domain = Tonality.create(ModalityType.MajorPentatonic, Diatonic-
ToneCache.get_tone('C'))

f = CrossTonalityShiftTonalFunction(t_domain, "G#", 2)
# C, D, E, G. A ==> G#, B, C#, E, F#
```

---

[49] At the time of this writing, t' is determined from a combination of d2 and the diatonic distance of t from t1. Suggestion: let t' = diatonically (letter) nearest tone to t1' with chromatic distance d2.

```
assert 'G#' == f['C'].diatonic_symbol
assert 'B' == f['D'].diatonic_symbol
assert 'C#' == f['E'].diatonic_symbol
assert 'E' == f['G'].diatonic_symbol
assert 'F#' == f['A'].diatonic_symbol

# For the for non-augmented non-domain tones we have:
assert 'G' == f['B'].diatonic_symbol
assert 'D' == f['F'].diatonic_symbol
```

The non-domain tones shown seem to map chromatically well in the example. Of course, there are many other tones to examine for the extension of this map.

Finally, it should be emphasized that the algorithmic extension on the tonality maps just discussed may not produce desired musical results. Algorithmic extension is meant as a service to "fill in gaps by default". However, a hand curated map for non-domain tonality tones can always be specified and may be a better fit for desired musical effects or styles.

15.3.3   GeneralPitchFunction

The development of tonality functions is in many ways a topic to itself. The shift transform, the topic of this chapter, is primarily concerned with pitch mapping. The discussion on tonal functions serves as an essential prerequisite to pitch functions.

The general pitch function is a primary subclass in the development of pitch functions. It represents, for our purposes, the broadest definition of pitch mapping. It provides a means to map any pitch to any pitch, without regard to tonality nor completeness across all pitches.

In that regard, the GeneralPitchFunction is simply and formally a subclass of DiscreteFunction that takes as input a preset map of pitches to pitches, checks that the input represents pitches, and embodies that mapping more formally as a discrete function.

While that may seem of limited use, it has foundational value as will be seen. Aside from that, embodying pitch to pitch functions can be very useful for interesting applications, such as permuted pitch maps and the like.

```
from transformation.functions.pitchfunctions.general_pitch_function import General-
PitchFunction

pitch_map = {'A:7': 'Ab:7', 'Bb:6': 'B:6', 'Db:5': None}

gpf = GeneralPitchFunction(pitch_map)

assert DiatonicPitch.parse('Ab:7') == gpf['A:7']
assert DiatonicPitch.parse('B:6') == gpf['Bb:6']
assert gpf['Db:5'] is None
```

15.3.4   CrossTonalityShiftPitchFunction

The CrossTonalityShiftPitchFunction is a subclass of GeneralPitchFunction, and in many ways looks like the CrossTonalityShiftTonalFunction. In fact, it makes use of the latter in its construction. It has a similar constructor to its tonal cousin, identifying a domain tonality, along with sufficient parameters to construct the range tonality. Additionally, it provides a PitchRange argument that identifies the lowest and highest pitches between which all domain pitches must fall.

The primary task in construction is to build a pitch map (dict), which is passed to its superclass GeneralPitchFunction constructor. The construction of the pitch map, though complex, is based on running through the PitchRange registers, creating domain pitches, and using the CrossTonalityShiftTonalFunction to construct the pitches to which they map. The tedious aspect of this construction is tracking both the domain and range registers and making appropriate register 'bumps' when the scalar "C" boundary is crossed. We defer to the readers to tease out the details.

Consider this example of a map from C-Major to G-Major:

```
from transformation.functions.pitchfunctions.cross_tonality_shift_pitch_function \
                import CrossTonalityShiftPitchFunction

t_domain = Tonality.create(ModalityType.Major, DiatonicTone('C'))
interval = Interval(5, IntervalType.Perfect)
r = PitchRange.create('E:3', 'E:7')

f = CrossTonalityShiftPitchFunction(t_domain, r, interval)
```

A portion of the diatonic pitch mapping and some further examples of non-tonal pitch mappings below:

```
C:4 --> G:4
D:4 --> A:4
E:4 --> B:4
F:4 --> C:5
G:4 --> D:5
A:4 --> E:5
B:4 --> F#:5


Cb:4 --> Gb:4 Db:4 --> Ab:4 Eb:4 --> Bb:4 Fb:4 --> Cb:5 Gb:4 --> Db:5 Ab:4 --> Eb:5
Bb:4 --> F:5
C#:4 --> G#:4 D#:4 --> A#:4 E#:4 --> B#:4 F#:4 --> C#:5 G#:4 --> D#:5 A#:4 --> E#:5
B#:4 --> F##:5
```

Of course, the tone mapping repeats across register assignments.

15.4 The Shift Transform

Having presented the foundations of tonal and pitch functions, we now turn to the shift transform itself. We begin by considering the problem space that the shift transform solves, along with the input parameters to the constructor and the apply() method. After that, we look at the algorithm's internals, and finish with looking at details surrounding chord mapping and how secondary chords are handled by the shift transform.

15.4.1 Problem Context and Interface

Assume we are given a piece of music represented as a line instance and a corresponding hct. We know from this pair the temporal extent of each harmonic context, and with that the tonality and harmony for each note of music in the line. The problem we solve with the shift transform is to change for any temporal extent (to simplify discussion, assume the extent covers one or more contiguous harmonic contexts), the tonality and chord in a way that can be attributed to an intervallic shift and/or modality change (of the same modality cardinality) and/or a mode change, and then change each notes pitch accordingly.

The shift transformation comes in two parts, one a constructor which identifies the key input parameters, and an apply() method which identifies a temporal extent and possible overrides to the constructor. The idea is to specify the general kind of shift to be done in the constructor, and to apply the shift over temporal extents of the input, but with the option to change shift parameters depending on the extent.

The constructor has as input:

- **source_line:** the musical Line being transformed.
- **source_hct:** the HarmonicContextTrack for the line.
- **default_root_shift_interval:** shift interval from old to new tonality.
- **default_range_modality_type:** the modality type for the new tonality.
- **default_modal_index:** modal index identifying the new tonality's root tone.

The action of the transform occurs on the apply() method, not the constructor. The apply() method has these parameters:

- **temporal_extent:** a time range on the music, in whole note time, to apply shift.
- **root_shift_interval:** the interval from old to new tonality, or if none default_root_shift_interval.
- **modal_index:** modal index for the new tonality, or if none default_root_index.
- **range_modality_type:** modality type for the new tonality, or if none default_range_modality_type
- **as_copy:** change the source Line and hct or return a copy of them with changes and leave the originals unchanged. The default is to return as copy, True.

The method apply() returns a pair of values consisting of line and hct. The original line and hct are changed or left unchanged as directed by as_copy. In the latter case, a copy of each with the effects of the transform is returned.

Note that the music source line and hct could have been specified as parameters in apply(), or that the shift interval, modal index, and/or range modality could have been set only in the constructor. This decision depends on the context of how this transform is intended to be used. The reader is welcome to change these parameterizations as needed in a local copy.

15.4.2   The Main Loop

The shift transform shifts pitches from a domain key to corresponding pitches in a range key. For some given input music, the domain key is specified in each HarmonicContext found in the harmonic context track. So, for each HamonicContext covered by the temporal extent of the hct, a new CrossTonalityShiftPitchFunction is created to apply to the notes covered by the corresponding HarmonicContext.

The logic of the main loop is show below. For a given temporal extent, loop over all notes in that temporal extent and build a pitch shift function to change the pitch of each note. However, as long as the harmonic context remains the same, use the same pitch shift function. Note that the shift pitch function is built from the hc identifying the tonality, and the input arguments.

```
last_hc = None
for n in line.get_all_notes():
    if self.temporal_extent.contains(note):
        hc = self.source_hct.get_hc_for_note(note);
        if last_hct != hc:
            f = self.build_shift_function(hc)
            last_hct = hc
        note.diatonic_pitch = f[note.diatonic_pitch]
```

The reader should feel free to rearrange this logic locally if a more efficient coding logic is found. Note that in building the pitch shift function, the harmonic context is found from the note under consideration. The remaining arguments are based on those passed to the constructor or apply().

The construction of the pitch shift function per harmonic context for non-secondary chords is relatively clear. Note that the harmonic context specifies the domain tonality. The shift factors are supplied by the shift transform arguments. As part of each output harmonic context construction, the input harmonic context's chord's tones are remapped, and the chord type of the remapped chord is calculated. The case for harmonic contexts with secondary chords is discussed later.

15.4.3 Clarifying Shifting with Mode Change

With the shift transform a modality change can have unexpected consequences, like the type of a shifted chord changing dramatically, e.g., minor to augmented. The following example in Fig. 15.5 describes the process for such a change.

'{<D-Major(1): I> iE:4 F# G A qE B}'

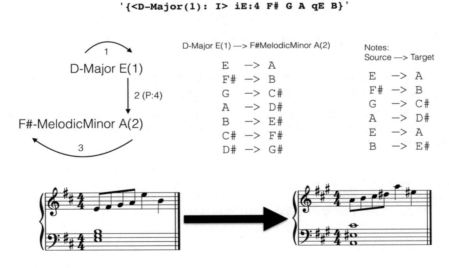

Fig. 15.5 Shift transform details on tonality mode change.

The melody under consideration is shown textually, indicating the tonality is D-Major(1) which is E Dorian. We indicate that tonality with the notation 'D-Major E(1)'. The transform shift interval is P:4. We also indicate a transform to modal index 2 under a new tonality of melodic minor. The code for this kind of shift is:

```
t_shift = TShift.create(source_expression, TonalInterval.parse('P:4'))
target_line, target_hct = t_shift.apply(range_modality_type=ModalityType.MelodicMinor,
                                         modal_index=2)
```

Returning to Fig. 15.5. On the left, we apply P:4 to E giving A. We want A as modal index 2 of a Melodic Minor modality. This means the tonality's basis tone is F#. So the conversion is from 'D-Major E(1)' to 'F#-MelodicMinor A(2)'. The explicit tonal map is shown in the middle, and on the right, each input pitch is remapped giving {A, B, C#, D#, A, E#}. Note that the I chord which originally was the minor chord {E, G, B} is now mapped to {A, C#, E#}, an augmented chord because of the modality and mode change.

15.4.4 Clarifying Shift with Secondary Chords

When the harmonic context specifies a secondary chord, the pitch shift mapping is constructed differently, being based on the secondary chord's temporary tonality specification. We explain by way of an example. Suppose a harmonic context has a C-Major domain tonality with a V/iii secondary chord. The source example and a shift of a major third (M:3) is shown in the following code example:

```
source_expression = '{<C-Major: V/iii> iD#:4 F# G A qD#:5 B:4}'

t_shift = TShift.create(source_expression, TonalInterval.parse('M:3'))
target_line, target_hct = t_shift.apply(range_modality_type=ModalityType.MelodicMinor)
```

Notice here that the apply() asks for a target melodic minor modality. That plus the shift interval of M:3 means an overall shift from C-Major to E-MelodicMinor[50] (E is M:3 above C).

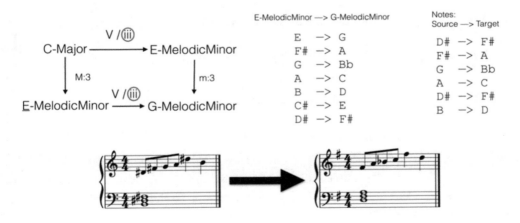

Fig. 15.6 *Shift transform details on secondary chord*

---

[50] This example unfortunately uses E-MelodicMinor in two different ways, one derived from the source by the M:3 shift, and one from the source by way of iii in V/iii. To distinguish these, we refer to the former by E-MelodicMinor.

The process and reasoning behind this example is shown in Fig. 15.6. The chord V/iii in the original harmonic context indicates a temporary tonality of E-MelodicMinor for the original line, and chordal harmony (V/iii) is a B-Major chord in the original as well. So, assuming the source notes are written to E-MelodicMinor, the shifted tonality (E-MelodicMinor) would have an assumed tonality of G-MelodicMinor (from the iii in V/iii). With that, the actual shift map is from E-MelodicMinor to G-MelodicMinor, and not C-Major to E-MelodicMinor! We call this a *secondary remap*.

The figure shows the primary tonal map between E-MelodicMinor and G-MelodicMinor. Note however, that this shift is based on m:3 and not M:3 as given in the shift specification. This is a result of taking the 3rd (iii) secondary root from the major source tonality (C-Major), E, to the 3rd (iii) of the melodic minor target tonality (E-MelodicMinor), G. The left of Fig. 15.6 shows the resulting mapping of the source notes.

Of course, when the harmonic context's chord is secondary, the replacement secondary chord is based on the secondary remap, and the resulting chord is reclassified. Here it is a D-Major chord. The transition on shift is shown at the bottom of Fig. 15.6. (Note: The G-Major key signature is actually an E-Minor signature!)

While the reasoning here should be clear, the logic takes some effort to work out in detail and is trickier when combined with non-zero modal indices.

15.5 Examples

We show a variety of examples of the shift transform in practice, showing before and after results.

15.5.1 Simple Key Shift using Intervals

We have the following simple harmonically annotated melody in C-Major that we use for all our examples.

Fig. 15.7 *Example annotated melody used for transformation.*

Textually, this line and hct is expressed in grammatically as:

```
'{<C-Major: I> iC:4 C qD E <:IV> iF G hA <:V> ig b qf g <:VI> ie e qd ic d <:I> h@c}'
```

This melody is shifted to different keys based on given intervals. To shift a major 3rd (M:3) to E-Major we use the following transform:

```
t_shift = TShift.create(source_expression, TonalInterval.parse('M:3'))
target_line, target_hct = t_shift.apply()
```

This produces the following in E-Major:

Fig. 15.8 Example in Fig. 15.7 shifted upwards a major 3rd to E-Major.

Similarly, a shift downwards a minor 2nd (-m:2) lands us in B-Major:

```
t_shift = TShift.create(source_expression, TonalInterval.parse('-m:2'))
target_line, target_hct = t_shift.apply()
```

With the resulting:

Fig. 15.9 Example in Fig. 15.7 shifted downwards a minor 2nd.

15.5.2 Shift with Modality Change

In these examples, a shift is combined with a modality change and applied to the example in Fig. 15.7. We allow modality change only when the from and to modality have the same number of tones or cardinality, e.g., diatonic major to diatonic minor.

We begin with a P:4 shift to F-MelodicMinor:

```
t_shift = TShift.create(source_expression, TonalInterval.parse('P:4'))
target_line, target_hct = t_shift.apply(range_modality_type=ModalityType.MelodicMinor)
```

The result is in F-MelodicMinor:

Fig. 15.10 Example in Fig. 15.7 shifted upward a perfect 4th plus modality change to melodic minor.

Or to F-NaturalMinor:

```
t_shift = TShift.create(source_expression, TonalInterval.parse('P:4'))
target_line, target_hct = t_shift.apply(range_modality_type=ModalityType.NaturalMinor)
```

Fig. 15.11 Example in Fig. 15.7 shifted upward a perfect 4th plus modality change to natural minor.

15.5.3 Modality and Modal Index Change

We introduce examples of modal index change. Again, we use our initial melodic example, Fig. 15.7. We begin with a modal index change to C-Mixolydian[51].

```
t_shift = TShift.create(source_expression)
target_line, target_hct = t_shift.apply(modal_index=4)
```

Note how this modal index change also changes the tonality as well, even without an explicit shift interval:

Fig. 15.12 Example from Fig. 15.7 shifted to C-Mixolydian.

Combining modality and modal index changes yields interesting color changes, like the following Lydian of melodic minor change to our sample yielding G-MelodicMinor C(3):

```
t_shift = TShift.create(source_expression)
target_line, target_hct = t_shift.apply(range_modality_type=ModalityType.MelodicMinor,
                                         modal_index=3)
```

---

[51] The key is actually F-Major C(4)! The arguments may cause some confusion for the reader. The gist is that we want root tone "C" as if it was modal index 4 (Mixolydian). The basis tonality is therefore F-Major, with root tone "C". That is effectively C-Mixolydian.

Fig. 15.13 Example from Fig. 15.7 shifted to C-Lydian on melodic minor scale.

15.5.4 Modulating Sequence

As a final example we demonstrate the construction of a sequence[52] that modulates one key to another. The example is show below:

Fig. 15.14 Example of modulating sequence.

The first measure comprises the seed for the sequence, and with being in C-Major uses the chord sequence IV, V/ii, ii. This constitutes a modulation to D-Minor. This means that with a M:2 shift upwards, this seed measure could be transformed into appended D-Major measure and qualify as a follow-on to the modulation of the first measure[53]. The same is true when the second measure is shifted upwards a M:2, and so on. So overall the tonality key switches from C to D to E. The result is a continuous sweeping modulating sequence by way of using the shift transform.

The code for constructing this modulating sequence shows the piecemeal steps used to get the desired results.

```
source_expression = '{<C-Major: IV> sf:4 a b C:5 <:V/ii> sa:4 e:5 tc# b:4 sC#:5 ' \
                     '<:ii> sd tc a:4 sb:4 a}'

lge = LineGrammarExecutor()
source_instance_line, source_instance_hct = lge.parse(source_expression)
print_score('\n[0]: ', source_instance_line, source_instance_hct)

t_shift = TShift.create(source_expression)
target_line, target_hct = t_shift.apply(
                               root_shift_interval=TonalInterval.parse('M:2'),
                               range_modality_type=ModalityType.Major)
print_score('\n[1]: ', target_line, target_hct)
```

---

[52] For reader who are unfamiliar with sequences, please refer discussion about them in [19].

[53] The switch from D-Minor to D-Major is not a major violation in switching tonality.

```
t_shift = TShift(target_line, target_hct)
target_line, target_hct = t_shift.apply(
                               root_shift_interval=TonalInterval.parse('M:2'),
                               range_modality_type=ModalityType.Major)
print_score('\n[2]: ', target_line, target_hct)
```

15.6 Final Thoughts

The shift transform is very powerful and useful. It combines the notions of root tone interval shift, with modality change, and adds the optional setting of modal index. Several points for consideration and/or future work could be considered.

One consideration involves the constructor and apply() method parameters, and determining what works best for the end user. For example, the transform as presented here takes the music to transform as a parameter. The benefit is that once constructed, apply() can be executed on portions of the music, with various parameter overrides. Another point of view is having the music as a parameter to the apply() method, best used when the music being transformed is in separate pieces.

More to the core of the transform, however, is the consideration of how the non-tonality notes should map in the CrossTonalityShiftTonalFunction and CrossTonalityShiftPitchFunction. We looked at a default generic technique based on half-tone interpolation. This may not be satisfactory for some uses. Readers can change this around to explore variations, even specialized variations based on specific modalities, to see which may address user needs best.

16 Reflection: A Transform for Melodic Inversion

Reflection is a common compositional technique for constructing melodic variations. In simplistic terms, pitch motion upwards turns downwards, and visa-versa, while generally holding to the same or similar rhythm. Essentially, the shape of the inverted melody is like a horizontal reflection of the original melody over a pitch. For example, consider the melody in Fig. 16.1.

Fig. 16.1 Sample Melody in consideration for reflection.

An example of inverting this melody is shown in Fig. 16.2.

Fig. 16.2 Reflection of melody in Fig. 16.1. Reflection is around C:4

Note the inversion of note direction (ascending/descending) as well as retention of rhythm (note duration and offset values). In fact, this is a scalar reflection around C:5 in that each note is moved above/below C:5 as it was below/above C:5 in the original. Notes at C:5 themselves remain at C:5. This is an example of what we will call diatonic or scalar reflection.

A composer must be quite careful when composing reflected melodies. One concern is that harmonic (chordal) notes remain harmonic after reflection. Another concern involves pitch range, and if adherence to reflected pitch motion takes notes too high or too low, or out of instrument pitch range altogether! And of course, there are considerations as to whether to replicate or redefine the harmony.

In this chapter we look at reflection in detail. We consider two kinds of reflection, diatonic and chromatic. Along the way, we look at some interesting mathematical structures and their application to reflection. We take a close look at architectural and algorithmic considerations and tie off the chapter with some examples.

D. P. Pazel, *Music Representation and Transformation in Software*, https://doi.org/10.1007/978-3-030-97472-5_16

16.1 An Overview of Melodic Reflection

Melodic reflection is based on the idea of a *cue pitch*. A cue pitch is a reference pitch that defines a focal point for reflective pitch mapping. With it, we map concentric pairs of pitches about the cue to each other. Those pitches are, in a sense to be defined, the same "distance" from each side of the cue pitch. We use those concentric pairs to create a reflection mapping to use in a reflection transform.

Reflection is based on how one interprets tonal distance. If distance means "the same number of scalar steps from the cue pitch", we call this form of reflection, *scalar or diatonic reflection*[54]. We saw an example of this in Fig. 16.1 and Fig. 16.2. However, if distance means "the same number of half-steps from the cue pitch", we call this form of reflection *chromatic reflection*.

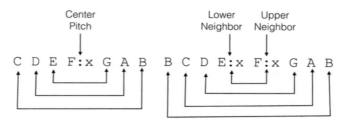

Fig. 16.3 Cue as center, lower, or upper pitch.

In scalar reflection, a cue pitch is a scalar pitch, which by its position, defines a line on a staff about which concentric scalar pitches above and below mapping to each other in order. However, there are two ways pairing occurs with a cue pitch. We illustrate these in Fig. 16.3 showing pitches in place of tones at an anonymous octave, x.

In one way, the cue pitch maps to itself, and the other pitches map in pairs as shown at left in Fig. 16.3. In this case, the cue F:x is called a *center pitch* for this reflection. In the other, the cue is defined as being to the left or right (lower or upper) of its immediate neighbor, and so cue mapping is to its scalar neighbor, with the remaining pitches mapping to each other in concentric pairs. In the right of Fig. 16.3, E is called the *lower* neighbor cue and F is called the *upper* neighbor cue for this reflection. The necessity of this formulation is shown in that diagram wherein E/F map to each other, and there is no scalar tone "between" them to serve as a center pitch cue. Which of center pitch or lower/upper neighbor is used is called the *flip type* of the reflection.

So, in the left side of Fig. 16.3 we have F←→F, E←→G, D←→A, and C←→B. On the right, we have E←→F, D←→G, C←→A, and B←→B. While in this latter case, B is something of a center pitch which does not map to itself pitch wise, which is a happenstance of the diatonic scale.

Fig. 16.4 Chromatic reflect on a diatonic scale.

---

[54] The use of the term "diatonic" is something of a misnomer here. However, much of common practice is around heptatonic scales, in which case the reference reduces to common practice. For our purposes, it implicitly has the broader meaning of 'scalar over tonalities' of different cardinalities, in a way that should become clearer.

Chromatic reflection, in contrast to scalar reflection preserves chromatic distances. For example, a chromatic reflection about cue pitch G is shown in Fig. 16.4. Here chromatic distances from G:x are preserved. For example, E which is 3 half-steps below G, maps to Bb which is 3 half-steps above G. This example resembles a kind of "reverse mapping" between C-Major to the Phrygian of Bb-Major, i.e. C-Major—> Bb-Major D(2).

As a richer example, consider the melody in Fig. 16.1, but this time do a chromatic reflection with center cue pitch C:4, we see in Fig. 16.5. Compare this to the scalar reflection of the same melody shown in Fig. 16.2 and note the differences.

Fig. 16.5 Chromatic reflection about center cue C:4, using Fig. 16.1.

In the above examples, we simply considered scalar tones in order over one register. However, one can easily extend the maps above and below to fill out a complete map across multiple registers! More on that later.

In the following section, we look at the reflection transform in ways somewhat similar to the shift transform. We define class structures followed by investigating issues in defining scalar and chromatic reflection, with appropriate examples. We will also introduce the concept of permutations, a powerful mathematical tool for defining interesting pitch mappings, but in the context of musical pitch reflection.

16.2 Permutations

Much like the shift transform, the reflection transform's foundations rest on tone and pitch mapping functions. Before we discuss the class structures behind these reflection variants of functions, we introduce the notion of permutation, and build it into our discrete function framework. Although this topic is not essential for our purposes, we introduce permutations to provide theoretical and developmental convenience. In themselves, permutations are interesting. Starting with an introduction to permutations provides a substantial benefit to the reader in further research and work in the music transforms generally.

16.2.1 Definition and Permutation Composition

A *permutation* is a map of a set of objects, for our purposes a finite set, to itself, one-to-one and onto. Effectively this defines a re-arrangement of the objects. For our examples, we use the set S = {1, 2, 3, 4, 5}. Let's define an example permutation, f:S—>S, by:

1→2, 2→3, 3→4, 4→5, 5→1

Permutations can be specified by a shorthand notation called *cycles*, wherein we start with some element in S and follow the map iteratively until we return to the starting element. For example, starting with 1, then f(1), f((1)), f(((1)), and so forth, we build the cycle (1 2 3 4 5), noting that with 5→1 we cycle back to the starting object 1. Importantly, all permutations can be expressed as a set of disjoint cycles. Cycles of precisely 2 elements are call *transpositions*. For example, (312)(45) gives:

1→2, 2→3, 3→1, 4→5, 5→4

We can define a product or composition of permutations defined in terms of function composition. Given permutation f and g on the same object set, then

g * f = g(f)

So for example, consider f=(1 3)(2 4) and g=(1 3 2)(4) We have

g * f = (1 2 4) (3).

The reader can work out details. For example, (g*f)(3) = g(f(3)) = g(1) = 3, giving the cycle (3), since 3 maps to itself. Also, g(f(1)) = g(3) = 2, which is the 2 part of (1 2 4), when you work out all the other mappings.

In group theory, the set of all permutations on a set S is called the **symmetric group** on S. Of interest are some of a group's properties:

- The permutation that maps each element identically to itself is called the identity permutation, indicated by id.

- Each permutation f has a unique inverse g such that f*g=g*f=id. For example, if f = (1 3 4 2), the inverse is (3 1 2 4).

Permutations figure largely in scalar reflection. For example, the center cue mapping shown left in Fig. 16.3 could be formulated in tones in the following permutation:

(F)(E G)(D A)(C B)

The reader should review the concepts of permutation as embodied in the Permutation class in the code base, especially to understand how composition and inverse are computed.

Further reading into the topic of permutations can be found in [17] and [18].

16.2.2   Using Permutations

The code base contains an implementation of permutation and can be found in function/permutation.py. Permutation is a subclass of DiscreteFunction. The constructor has two inputs:

- Domain – A complete set of all possible objects the permutation maps. Recall that the domain and the range are identical.

- Cycle – A list of cycles that comprise the permutation.

In Python, permutations are specified as a list of lists, e.g., [[…], […], …]. Each inner list member specifies a cycle, e.g. [a, b, c] meaning a→b→c→a. The user does not need to specify singleton cycles, e.g., [1]. They are found by the constructor using the specified domain.

An example of constructing permutations follows:

```
from function.permutation import Permutation

domain = {1, 2, 3, 4, 5, 6, 7}
cycles = [[1, 3, 4, 2], [6, 5, 7]]
p = Permutation(domain, cycles)
print(p)
#    [[1, 3, 4, 2], [5, 7, 6]]    Note that [6, 5, 7] == [5, 7, 6]!
cycles = [[1, 3], [2, 4], [5, 7]]
q = Permutation(domain, cycles)
print(q)
#     [[1, 3], [2, 4], [5, 7], [6]]   Note that the singleton cycle [6] is shown!
```

Composition of permutations is achieved through the "*" operator:

```
p3 = p * q        # q then p
print('p1 * p2 = {0}'.format(p3))
#     p * q = [[1, 4], [2], [3], [5, 6], [7]]
p3 = q * p        # p then q
print('p2 * p1 = {0}'.format(p3))
#     q * p = [[1], [2, 3], [4], [5], [6, 7]]   Note that P * q != q * p
```

And finally, inversion:

```
i = p.inverse()
print(i)
#     [[1, 2, 4, 3], [5, 6, 7]]

print('p * i = {0}'.format(p * i))
print('i * p = {0}'.format(i * p))


#     p * i = [[1], [2], [3], [4], [5], [6], [7]]
#     i * p = [[1], [2], [3], [4], [5], [6], [7]]
```

16.3   Class Structures for the Reflection Transform

We turn our attention to class structures used to define diatonic and chromatic reflection transforms. This chapter develops along the lines of the prior chapter on the shift transform by defining tonal and pitch maps, as well as tone/pitch extensions. Here, however, the maps are semantically different from those of shift, and are defined in a different manner.

The inheritance diagram for the classes involved in the reflection transform are shown in Fig. 16.6. The inheritance structure can be seen as three trees. The tree on the left shows the class development based on permutations, going from the most general DiscreteFunction to Permutation and eventually making Permutation specific for tones and tonality.

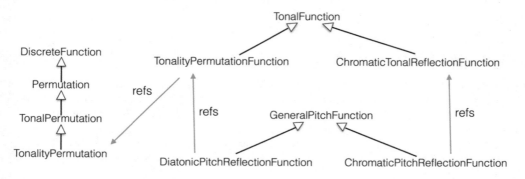

Fig. 16.6 Inheritance tree for reflection transform class structures.

The two inheritance trees on the right involve subclassing from root classes TonalFunction and GeneralPitchFunction, much as we did with the shift transform, but for diatonic and chromatic reflection functions. The details of these classes are the core the reflection transform. To aid in the textual study, reference arrows indicate which classes are used in the development of others, e.g.,

DiatonicPitchReflectionFunction references TonalityPermutationFunction, which references TonalityPermutation, and so on.

While we spend time explaining this inheritance tree, the reader is encouraged to make the effort to explore the associated classes in the code base, and further become hands-on by executing examples and devising their own sample code.

16.4 Scalar Reflection

Scalar or diatonic reflection refers to reflection of pitches of a given tonality across a cue pitch to pitches in the same tonality. The cue pitch is a pitch in that tonality. In this section we explore the classes involved in this form of reflection and how scalar reflection is implemented.

16.4.1 Scalar Reflection Details

We start this discussion by tying up details on permutations and their relationship to tonality. The point behind the class TonalPermutation is to leverage the Permutation class for tone-to-tone mappings. These mappings are specified as cycles composed of tones, as in the earlier discussion, with each tone specified as a DiatonicTone object or a string representation thereof. The cycles and domain set for the permutation are given in the constructor. TonalPermutation is more broadly defined than needed for reflection, and so can be of greater use for other transforms or applications.

To bring clarity to TonalPermutation, the following example shows a simple permutation of tones using cycles. Note that the domain is explicit here. If not specified, the tones in the cycles comprise the domain.

```
from transformation.functions.tonalfunctions.tonal_permutation import TonalPermutation

domain = {'C', 'D', 'Eb', 'F#'}
cycles = [['C', 'D'], ['Eb', 'F#']]
p = TonalPermutation(cycles, domain)   # p maps DiatonicTones or strings to
                                       # DiatonicTones

assert DiatonicToneCache.get_tone('D') == p['C']
assert DiatonicToneCache.get_tone('C') == p['D']
assert DiatonicToneCache.get_tone('Eb') == p['F#']
assert DiatonicToneCache.get_tone('F#') == p['Eb']
```

TonalityPermutation is a subclass of TonalPermutation, and is constructed with a Tonality class object, and tone cycles (as in TonalPermutation). The domain tone set is given by the tonality's tone set. The rationale for TonalityPermutation is that it specializes TonalPermutation to a given tonality.

```
from transformation.functions.tonalfunctions.tonality_permutation import TonalityPermutation

t_domain = Tonality.create(ModalityType.Major, DiatonicTone('E'))
cycles = [['E', 'G#', 'A', 'B'], ('F#', 'G#')]
p = TonalityPermutation(t_domain, cycles)
assert DiatonicToneCache.get_tone('G#') == p['E']
assert DiatonicToneCache.get_tone('A') == p['F#']
assert DiatonicToneCache.get_tone('F#') == p['G#']
```

Scalar reflection is based on the TonalityPermutationFunction class, which by subclassing on TonalFunction, firmly plants TonalityPermutation into the proper class framework for reflection. TonalityPermutationFunction accounts not only for how tonality tones map to other tonality tones, but also includes an extension parameter to specify non-scalar tone mappings.

DiatonicPitchReflectionFunction does all the work in setting up the reflection maps, both for tones and pitches. The creation of permutation cycles based on FlipType and cue is straight forward, and can be found in the source code. Instead, we focus on how the non-scalar reflection tones are mapped by default in reflection.

The problem we want to solve is given a non-scalar tone, *tone*, to what tone, *tone'*, should it map. The problem is depicted in Fig. 16.7. While readers are free to devise their own solutions, we discuss this solution and the problems in determining a solution. The computation we consider involves first determining the closest scalar tone to given *tone*, designated by *cl_scalar*. The tonal mapping, τ, maps *cl_scalar* to $\tau[cl\_scalar]$. The idea here is find some *tone'* near $\tau[cl\_scalar]$ which is chromatically as close to it, as *tone* is to *cl_scalar*, and in the correct scalar direction.

Fig. 16.7 Non-scalar tone mapping.

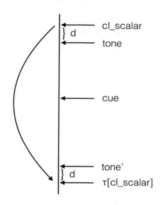

The logic for doing the above task is a little complex, but the summarized logic goes as follows. First to find the closest tone to *tone*, we see if the scale has a tone that matches *tone* in diatonic letter. If so, we use that tone as *cl_scalar*. If not, we search through the scalar tones, to find the scalar tones before and after *tone*, and use the one chromatically closest as *cl_scalar*. After determining the order of *cl_scalar* to *tone*, which requires some octave checking in the comparison technique, we then determine the chromatic distance d between cl_scalar and tone. Then we can adjust the chromatic augmentation of the mapped $\tau[cl\_scalar]$ to determine *tone'*. One more adjustment factor has to be computed, that being the change in diatonic index (letter). For example, *cl_scalar* and *tone* may have a diatonic index adjustment, e.g., C# vs D (difference 1), and that also needs to be accounted for in determining *tone'*, and of course in the correct direction.

Given the complete tonal mapping, the full pitch to pitch mapping is constructed. The main difficulty in construction is in computing through octaves along the full range of pitches, which can change radically over the cue pitch.

16.4.2   TDiatonicReflection

Scalar reflection is achieved by using the TDiatonicReflection class. From the user view it consists of a constructor and an apply(), much as the shift transform, applied to a music selection given as a Line and its hct. The constructor parameters for TDiatonicReflection are:

- source_line: the melodic input as a Line.

- source_hct: the HarmonicContextTrack corresponding to the Line.

- default_cue_pitch: The cue pitch when not overridden in apply().

- default_flip_type: The FlipType to use when not overridden in apply().

The apply() method takes the following parameters:

- temporal_extent: The temporal extent of the Line to be transformed.

- cue_pitch: If specified, the cue pitch to use.

- flip_type: If specified, the FlipType to use.

- as_copy: return a copy of Line, hct or change in place, default is return copy (True).

The class TDiatonicReflection implements the reflection transform for scalar reflection. Its usage is much like that of the shift transform. The constructor takes a Line and its hct, as well as a default cue pitch and default FlipType. The cue and FlipType are given in the apply() so these parameters can be re-specified to a given temporal extent. However, having defaults in the constructor is good in cases where the music does not change tonality very often.

The TDiatonicReflection class builds a DiatonicPitchReflectionFunction for each harmonic context encountered. That function is then applied to each Line note for that harmonic context. One complication occurs when the harmonic context's chord is secondary. For secondary chords, we build a reflection function based on the secondary tonality. The specified cue pitch is used if the cue pitch exists in the secondary tonality. Otherwise, we build a reflection around one of the neighboring scalar pitches as the cue. This is one of the simplest strategies to use in this situation.

Of course, the chords are remapped as well as in the shift transform, by remapping their notes and re-classifying each chord. Note that root position triads now become 6-4 chords because the highest tone (the 5th) now becomes the lowest. For our purposes however, we take the "flipped" chords only as chord suggestions, with more definitive suggestions open to user preference.

16.4.3 Examples of Scalar Reflection

Recall the example phrase from the shift transformation chapter:

Fig. 16.8 Scalar reflection example I.

Our first demonstration is a scalar reflection about F:4, given by the following code:

```
from transformation.reflection.t_diatonic_reflection import TDiatonicReflection
    source_expression = '{<C-Major: I> iC:4 C qD E <:IV> iF G hA <:V> ig b qf g <:VI> ie
e qd ic d <:I> h@c}'
```

```
t_flip = TDiatonicReflection.create(source_expression, DiatonicPitch.parse('F:4'))
target_line, target_hct = t_flip.apply()
```

This resulting music is shown in Fig. 16.9:

Fig. 16.9 Scalar reflection about F:4 of example in Fig. 16.8.

For convenience, we retain the original key, and cite the re-mapped chords relative to that original key. As noted in the discussion, triads are remapped to second inversion. A consideration is that it might be better to declare the key E-Phrygian and, ignoring the inversion, use the chords, I, V, IV, III, I.

Applying an A:4 reflection to the original phrase produces the music in Fig. 16.10. The choice of cue pitch can have a dramatic effect on moving notes higher or lower. However, that can be remedied with a shift to normal pitch range positions. This result might best be analyzed as a B-Locrian key.

Fig. 16.10 Scalar reflection about A:4 of example in Fig. 16.8.

Consider now the following Bb Major melodic line and harmony:

Fig. 16.11 Scalar reflection example II.

We apply a scalar reflection on Eb4:

```
from transformation.reflection.t_diatonic_reflection import TDiatonicReflection
source_expression = '{<Bb-Major: I> sBb:4 A G F qEb D sF g iA i@Bb sF <:IVMaj7> ' \
                    'ir Eb sEb F G A iBb sEb:5 F i@Eb C ' \
                    '<:IIIMin7> sR F:5 Eb D C Bb:4 C:5 D i@Eb sC sr G:4 A G <:I> ' \
                    'sG:5 F Eb D D C Bb:4 A ir q@G}'
```

```
t_flip = TDiatonicReflection.create(source_expression, DiatonicPitch.parse('Eb:4'))

target_line, target_hct = t_flip.apply()
```

Fig. 16.12 *Eb:4 diatonic reflection of example in Fig. 16.11.*

This example highlights one of the main problems with reflection, namely, that even moderately high note pitches can reflect to pitches far too low. A solution is to simply follow the reflection with an upward octave shift:

```
t_shift = TShift(target_line, target_hct, TonalInterval.parse('P:8'))
final_line, final_hct = t_shift.apply()
```

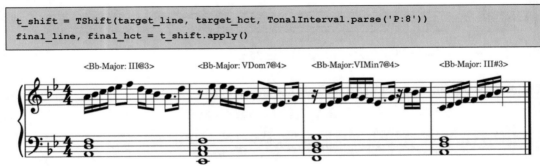

Fig. 16.13 *Eb:4 reflection followed by shift of example in Fig. 16.11.*

The above result is interesting in its reversal of scalar sequence direction, leaving a quite different effect from the original in Fig. 16.11. Scalar reflection can produce many interesting results that a composer can use to reinvigorate the creativity involved in music composition. While the resulting chords may strike many as being of questionable value, they still could provide novel ideas for music creation.

16.5 Chromatic Reflection

Chromatic reflection has FlipType and cue pitch arguments like that found in scalar reflection. However, chromatic reflection tries to preserve chromatic distances across the cue. One consequence of this, as we will see, is that chromatic reflection may not preserve key.

16.5.1 Chromatic Reflection Details

Much like scalar reflection, chromatic reflection uses a tonal function (ChromaticTonalReflectionFunction) to build the basic tone to tone mapping both regarding the input Tonality, as well as the extension to non-tonal tones. That is followed by a pitch-to-pitch mapping (ChromaticPitchReflectionFunction), based on the tonal function, with appropriate octave mapping.

The tonal mapping is very interesting. As mentioned FlipType and cue tone are similarly interpreted as in scalar reflection. However, scalar reflection retains the same tone set, but chromatic reflection generally does not, and so in fact maps to a different key. Visuals for center and neighboring tonal mapping is shown in Fig. 16.14.

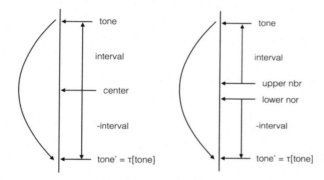

Fig. 16.14 Chromatic tonal mapping.

There are several ways to approach the tonal reflection algorithm, but it basically comes down to the process shown in Fig. 16.14. For center tone reflection, a tone defines an interval with the center cue. That tone should map to the tone below the center cue using the negative of that interval. Also, for non-center tone reflection, using the two neighbors, a tone a given interval above the upper neighbor should map to the tone below the lower neighbor by the same interval. The concept of using an interval to define the mapping preserves both the chromatic and diatonic distances, both of which are crucial in defining the resulting scale.

Examples of tonal chromatic reflection are rather striking, as we will see. For now, focusing on diatonic scale transition, Table 16-1 shows the resulting scale tones on reflecting the C-Major scale using each one as center cue. For each cue it shows the result of chromatic reflective mapping for {C, D, E, F, G, A, B}. The table also identifies the resulting tonality, along with a modal designation based on the tone to which C maps.

Using only the C-Major scale for reflection, the assortment of resulting scales is quite diverse. Interestingly enough, they are all Phrygian (2)! Reader, explain why? Additionally, the reader should explore why/if the map constructed reflecting pitches only higher than the cue is the same as the map constructed reflecting pitches lower than the cue (hint: complementary intervals)!

Cue	Scale Tones	Scale Name
C	C, Db, Eb, F, G, Ab, Bb	Ab-Major C(2)
D	E, F. G, A, B, C, D	C-Major E(2)
E	G#, A, B, C#, D#, E, F#	E-Major G#(2)
F	Bb, Cb, Db, Eb, F, Gb, Ab	Gb-Major Bb(2)
G	D, Eb, F, G, A, Bb, C	Bb-Major D(2)
A	F#, G, A, B, C#, D, E	D-Major F#(2)
B	A#, B, C#, D#, E#, F#, G#	F#-Major A#(2)

Table 16-1 C-Major chromatic reflection about C-Major cue tones.

Regarding filling the map with non-scalar tones, computing that tonal map extension is as simple as using the same intervallic approach used on tonality, as shown in Fig. 16.14. We leave to the reader to explore the code for details.

The construction of the full pitch to pitch mapping found in ChromaticPitchReflectionFunction is again a matter of:

- Using ChromaticTonalReflectionFunction as a starting point.
- Carefully assigning octaves.

The process is straight-forward and a bit tedious. The details are left to the reader in reading the code.

16.5.2 TChromaticReflection

Chromatic reflection is achieved by using the TChromaticReflection class, and in protocol is very much like what we described in TDiatonicReflection. From the user view it consists of a constructor and an apply() method applied to a music selection given as a Line and its hct. The constructor parameters for TDiatonicReflection are:

- source_line: the melodic input as a Line.
- source_hct: the HarmonicContextTrack corresponding to the Line.
- default_cue_pitch: The cue pitch when not overridden in apply().
- default_flip_type: The FlipType to use when not overridden in apply().

The apply() method takes the following parameters:

- temporal_extent: The temporal extent of the Line to be transformed.
- cue_pitch: If specified, the cue pitch to use.
- flip_type: If specified, the FlipType to use.
- as_copy: return a copy of Line, hct or change in place, default is return copy (True).

Much of what was noted of the TDiatonicReflection class applies to this class. We again mention that chords are remapped as well by remapping their notes and re-classifying each chord. Note that root position triads now become 6-4 chords because the highest tone (the 5th) now becomes the lowest. For our purposes however, we take the "flipped" chords only as chord suggestions, with more definitive suggestions open to user preference.

16.5.3   Examples of Chromatic Reflection

The first example of chromatic reflection is based on the example in Bb-Major in the scalar reflection examples in Fig. 16.11. For reference see Fig. 16.15.

Fig. 16.15 Music from Fig. 16.11 for reference.

Let's see how this music transforms as we move through center, upper neighbor, and lower neighbor on cue tone G:4. We follow each except the last with a shift P:8 upwards to center the results.

For G:4 center, we have:

```
from transformation.reflection.t_chromatic_reflection import TChromaticReflection

t_flip = TChromaticReflection.create(source_expression, DiatonicPitch.parse('G:4'))
target_line, target_hct = t_flip.apply()
t_shift = TShift(target_line, target_hct, TonalInterval.parse('P:8'))
final_line, final_hct = t_shift.apply()
```

Fig. 16.16 Fig. 16.15 with chromatic reflection about G:4 and shift upwards P:8.

This result in Fig. 16.16 looks rather like the last scalar reflection example. However, note that the key has moved to C-Major E(2), the Phrygian based on C-Major. The IV, VI, VII, IV chord sequence seems a little odd. However, on closer inspection, we see that this sequence masks a I, III, IV, I chord sequence.

For G:4 upper reflection, we have:

```
t_flip = TChromaticReflection.create(source_expression, DiatonicPitch.parse('G:4'),
                                     FlipType.UpperNeighborOfPair)
target_line, target_hct = t_flip.apply()

t_shift = TShift(target_line, target_hct, TonalInterval.parse('P:8'))
final_line, final_hct = t_shift.apply()
```

Fig. 16.17 Fig. 16.15 with G:4 upper neighbor reflection and upward P:8 shift.

Recall that G:4 and F:4 swap with stepwise chromatic pairing for the remaining scale tones. Surprisingly the transform only incurs a modal change.

However, using G:4 as a lower cue for chromatic reflection changes the key dramatically. See Fig. 16.18.

```
t_flip = TChromaticReflection.create(source_expression, DiatonicPitch.parse('G:4'),
                        FlipType.LowerNeighborOfPair)
target_line, target_hct = t_flip.apply()
```

Fig. 16.18 Fig. 16.15 with G:4 lower neighbor reflection.

All examples shown have been in major scales. The curious reader may want to explore other possibilities using minor scales. As an example, given the C natural minor scale, and using each tone as a center cue, we obtain the reflection scales in Table 16-2.

Cue	Scale Tones	Scale Name
C	C, D, E, F, G, A, Bb	F-Major C(4)
D	E, F#, G#, A, B, C#, D	A-Major E(4)
Eb	Gb, Ab, Bb, Cb, Db, Eb, Fb	Cb-Major Gb(4)
F	Bb, C, D, Eb, F, G, Ab	Eb-Major Bb(4)
G	D, E, F#, G, A, B, C	G-Major D(4)
Ab	Fb, Gb, Ab, Bbb, Cb, Db, Ebb	Bbb-Major Fb(4)
Bb	Ab, Bb, C, Db, Eb, F, Gb	Db-Major Ab(4)

Table 16-2 C-Major chromatic reflection about C-Major cue tones.

It is interesting that natural minor modality reflects into major modality. The odd resultant Bbb-Major scale found in reflecting on Ab is, of course, just an enharmonic renaming of A-Major. While Bbb-Major can be used as such, it is more an anomoly that came about from the formal definition of reflection, an artifact of calculation.

In fact, consider the example in Fig. 16.19:

Fig. 16.19 Example II.

Take the following transformation:

```
source_expression = '{<C-NaturalMinor: I> qC:4 ieb f g ab <:V> Bb ab gc f eb d ' \
                     '<:IV> q@f ig eb d <:VI> q@Eb id eb d <:I> h@c }'

t_flip = TChromaticReflection.create(source_expression, DiatonicPitch.parse('Ab:4'))
target_line, target_hct = t_flip.apply()
```

The result of the Ab:4 reflection follows. The key has been adjusted from Bbb Major to A-Major to improve comprehension.

Fig. 16.20 Fig. 16.19 chromatically reflected over Ab:4.

The reflection of a minor piece of music into a major modality is a somewhat poetic after effect of the transformation.

16.6 Final Thoughts

The two reflection techniques discussed can produce quite interesting results. Reflection has been long noted as a compositional technique that can be used to re-imagine melodies and provide both inventiveness and surprise in composition.

The reflection transform provides a way to explore a wide variety of compositional variation. However reflected chords produced by the transformation should be seen only as suggestions at best and asks the user to consider carefully in choosing the accompanying harmony.

As an offhand observation, one aspect of reflection is that in some ways, reflection results in a reversed scale. More precisely, not only that you may get different scales, but that the result scales seem to have a reversed orientation relative to the original. With that, the reader may want to explore the idea of reversed or mirrored modalities, and if that concept evolves into anything meaningful, especially harmonically.

Finally, the reader is encouraged to examine the usage of permutations as a musical transformative tool, especially in mapping chromatic pitches. The more mathematical reader will understand the representational power of permutations to group theory (ref. Cayley's Theorem [18]) and may play with possibilities of using group theory as a compositional resource for melodic transformation.

17 Reshape: A Transform for Melodic Shaping

In chapter 11, we introduced functions and affine transformations with application to temporal modification of tempo and dynamics. The goal of this chapter is to explore similar approaches to pitch modification across temporal extents. In particular, we discuss using numerical functions to modify a melodic line.

In this chapter we examine melodic lines and explore the visual shapes of the melodies defined by their pitches in a spatial context. We explore how to represent melodic curves, both mathematically and as a software representation. We further examine how to utilize these shapes as an active means to modify or enhance melodies. We define and explore a reshape transform, which leverages all the shaping machinery described toward building and modifying melodies. We complete the chapter with examples.

17.1 Introduction

We motivate the central idea of this chapter by example. Consider the following melody line found in a Mozart piano sonata in D Major in Fig. 17.1.

Fig. 17.1 Example melody from Mozart piano sonata in D Major KV284 (205b).

This melody has a nice curvy and sweeping descending line. It is so smooth that one might be tempted to connect the notes' dots to visualize the shape of the melodic line. If you did, you might get something as shown in Fig. 17.2.

Fig. 17.2 Mozart melody with connecting melodic curve.

The shape is visually captivating. In fact, one could extract the shape of the curve itself and set it in the context of a time versus pitch axes graph as in Fig. 17.3.

D. P. Pazel, *Music Representation and Transformation in Software*, https://doi.org/10.1007/978-3-030-97472-5_17

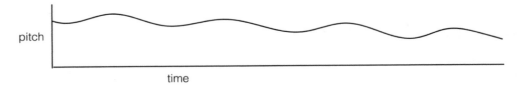

Fig. 17.3 Time versus pitch graph of curve shown in Fig. 17.2.

This extracted shape is very interesting, and intuitively reflects the motion of the melody's sound itself. The reader may look at other pieces of music, and not just in the melody line, but in music bass lines, to find similar visualizations.

Many times, the melodic shape is not so smooth as shown above. In some cases, the music may have more of a choppy character with nasty sharp edges. Consider Fig. 17.4 example from the same sonata:

Fig. 17.4 Another example melody from Mozart piano sonata in D Major KV284 (205b).

In contrast to the prior example, this melody can be characterized as a piecewise curve with many straight edges with many peaks and valleys. The sharp edges of the curve is far away from the smooth and continuous caricature of the prior example[55]. See Fig. 17.5.

Fig. 17.5 Mozart melody with connecting lines.

For clarity, the curve itself as time versus pitch is shown in Fig. 17.6.

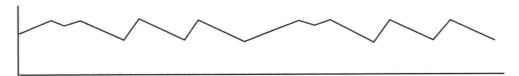

Fig. 17.6 Time versus pitch graph as showing in Fig. 17.5.

The idea of looking at melodic shapes is not new but continues to be alluring and a source of creativity. For example, one can look at the work of Noam Oxman to see how scores can be constructed as fully playable pictures [43] based only on its notes. In contrast, we are not attempting to turn scores into shapes but rather to leverage shapes as a composition tool. The idea behind the reshape transform, the

---

[55] The terms **continuous** and **smooth** have formal mathematical meanings. In short, the former concerns the lack of tears in a curve, and the later the lack of abrupt changes in a curve's direction. We only use these terms in an informal manner. Precise definitions can be found in many calculus textbooks, e.g., [48], or other advanced math textbooks.

central topic of this chapter, is to follow the above process in reverse, that is, to impose a shape on a set of musical notes in order to modify a melody.

In the following discourse, our goal is to define in technical terms what it means to modify a melody with a curve. There are a few technical structures to define to get to that point that concern defining shaping functions and formal means to map time to pitch using them. We touch also on the concept of melodic forms, such as motifs and melodic phrases, and their constraints, which will help us further in breaking down melodic structures. Finally, although not mentioned in the examples above, a given underlying harmony plays a role in melodic reshape as well. The transform must be able to reshape the melodic notes to adhere to the underlying key and harmony while at the same time it attempts to conform the melody to a prescribed shape.

17.2   A Model for Shaping Functions

The reader should review section 11.2 on functions and be familiar with univariate functions and the variants of piecewise linear, stepwise, constant and generic functions.

17.2.1   Shaping Functions

Based on prior discussion in this book, we consider univariate functions of the form $f: X \to Y$, mapping values in some domain X to values of some range Y. The principal rule is that for every x in X, there is exactly one y in Y to which f maps x. Thus, $f(x) = y$. Following along this line, we are interested in a class of univariate functions that include common and interesting curves, with example equations such as:

$y = x^2 + 15x - 32$

$y = \sin (x + 0.3482)$

These are simple real value to real value functions. However, in applying these to the music domain, the data types used for domain and range must be defined with care.

For the remainder of this chapter, we assume the domain of our univariate functions is whole note time, as described in the representation section of this book, ref. chapter 5. That way, a function's domain can include the position of each note in a line or score. [Also recall that whole note time can be obtained from measure/beat or real time with the conversion algorithms also discussed in chapter 5.] We will always assume the range of our functions is the real numbers. For identification purposes, we refer to these functions as *shaping functions*.

A shaping function's range can be any real-valued linear segment, for example [0...1] or [-1...10], of course depending on the curve desired. These functions can be illustrated as graphs with the domain on the X axis and function evaluations along the Y axis. The notion of a graph is very broad, and examples abound. For example, we could have $y = -x^2 + 2x$, a parabola, or a piecewise linear graph built from line segments. See Fig. 17.7.

However, for our purposes, we interpret the X axis values in whole note time. The graph should be a "shape" that we would like to impose on accompanying music notes' pitches, thus the name of the function generating the graph. To do that, we require the range of a shaping function be interpretable as pitch, an issue we discuss in the next section.

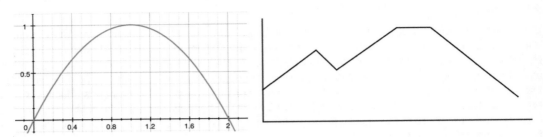

Fig. 17.7 Parabolic curve on left; piecewise linear on right.

17.2.2   The Pitch Range Interpreter

As presented do far, the shaping function range is not based on pitch, but on a real value range based on the definition of the curve itself. We can re-fit the curve so that the range is based on pitch value, using a second function from the shaping function's range (Y axis) to a different axis representing pitch. The benefit of this approach is that, aside from the domain in whole note time, the shaping function's range can be freely defined to a range native to the shaping function itself, unhindered by constraints restricting it to actual pitch range. The mapping of the shaping function's range to pitch is a separate function.

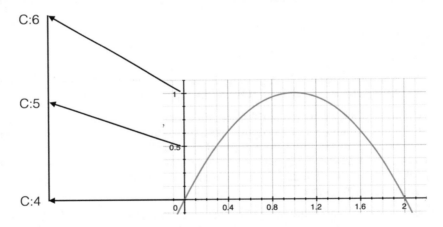

Fig. 17.8 Pitch map from [0 .. 1] to [C:4 .. C:6].

The parabolic shaping function shown in Fig. 17.8 is a continuous mapping from a 2 whole note domain to a range [0..1]. That is, $f:[0..2] \rightarrow [0..1]$ with $f(x) = -x^2 + 2x$. To the left, we have a map from [0..1] to a two octave pitch range [C:4 .. C:8]. For now, we ignore its construction details. Let us call that function p(), i.e., $p:[0..1] \rightarrow [C:4..C:6]$. Composing f with p we have $(p*f):[0..2] - [C:4..C:6]$ defined by:

$$(p*f)(x) = p(f(x)) \tag{17.1}$$

Using this extension, $p*f$, each position on the continuous domain maps to a member of a discret set of pitches. We avoid mapping to fractional pitches by forcing $p(f(x))$ to the nearest pitch, fo example. The function p() from a real domain to a set of pitches, mapping the shaping function's range to pitch is called a ***pitch range interpreter***. For our purposes, the real valued domain of p() is limited to a closed real interval, say $[a .. b]$ $a, b \in Reals, a < b$, and the range is a finite discrete set of pitches. Note that the domain is a continuous real segment, and the range is a discrete set of pitches.

Before moving further, we dig deeper into the pitch range interpreter and clarify further its mechanics and varieties of form. While readers are welcome to develop a pitch range interpreter limited only by their imaginations, there are several features we include for our purposes that help in its simplification and utility. The first is that while the range of a pitch range interpreter is a discrete set of pitches, for conceptual simplicity we prefer to have these pitches imposed on a continuous real value segment, with the pitches laid out evenly. You get this automatically if you use chromatic distance as the pitch measure on a real value segment. In that case, A:0 is 9, and C:8 is 96. So in the range [9..96] you have a continuous real value segment in which all the chromatic pitch distances are evenly spaced units (1 unit per pitch). There is also a map $\tau: \{9,..,96\} \to \{A: 0,..,C: 8\}$, a discrete map of the chromatic distances to a discrete set of pitches. (Of course, with some added effort to account uniquely for enharmonic representations, etc.) From a horizontal perspective, we have the layout in Fig. 17.9.

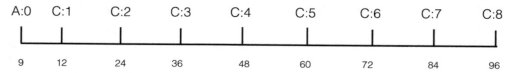

Fig. 17.9 Pitch scale layout to chromatic distance.

Using [0..1] as an example shaping function range, one can build a linear map $\gamma: [0..1] \to [9..96]$. The straight-forward linear map is:

$$\gamma(x) = 87x + 9 \qquad\qquad (17.2)$$

However, one only gets integer values when $x = n/87$ for integers n. Otherwise the result is an "off-pitch" value. To get around that, the most straight-forward method is to round the value to the nearest chromatic integer. So, we redefine γ as follows:

$$\gamma(x) = round(87x + 9) \qquad\qquad (17.3)$$

The combination $p(x) = \tau(\gamma(x)) \epsilon \{A: 0 .. C: 8\}$ maps [0..1] to the pitch set {A:0..C:8}. This is, in fact, an example of a ***chromatic range interpreter***. Underlying that is a rigid constraint relying on the definition of chromatic distance and its map to pitches, namely {9,..,96} maps to {A:0,..,C:8}[56].

A more general approach to defining a chromatic range interpreter consists of establishing a user defined fixed distance between chromatic pitches, and from a single mapping assignment of some value to some pitch, extend the range in both directions. For example, suppose the distance between chromatic pitches is specified to be 2.5, and that we insist that value 0 maps to C:4. That means 2.5 is C#:4, 5.0 is D:4, and so on. As well, -2.5 is B:3, and -5.0 is Bb:3, and so on. This avoids the map to chromatic

---

[56] Alternatively, one could define $\tau: [9..96] \to [A: 0,..,C: 8]$ and subsume the rounding operation into it. Using that with equation 17.3 effectively builds the same chromatic range interpreter as described. There may be benefits in packaging the operations like this and is a decision left to the user.

distance integers used above which is not always convenient for an end user. In this example, the scale then is nicely centered on C:4 and the layout is shown in Fig. 17.10.

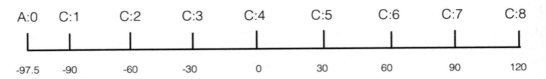

Fig. 17.10 Customized chromatic pitch scale layout, with pitch unit 2.5.

To clarify the context for using this function, suppose a shaping function has a range is [0 .. 120] that covers the range [C:4 .. C:8]. We want 0 to map to C:4 and 120 to C:8. And as we are mapping to chromatic pitches, we specify half-steps being 2.5 apart.

In this approach, the "between distance" value is called the **pitch unit**, the example pitch is called the **anchor pitch**, and the value from which it maps is called the **anchor value**, in this case anchor value 0 maps to anchor pitch C:4. We look closer on how to implement this kind of function later.

Another feature we introduce addresses the case that we are not always interested in the chromatic scale as discussed above. In fact, the above pitch range interpreter is called a chromatic range interpreter. Many times though, we are only concerned with the pitches defined by a tonality, that maps values only to pitches within a tonality. We call this map extension a **scalar range interpreter**.

We reuse the concepts of pitch unit, anchor pitch, and anchor value (assuming anchor pitch is a scalar pitch). Here the units are in scalar pitches with pitch unit being the domain distance corresponding to neighboring scalar pitches between tonal pitches. So, for example, if the tonality is E-Major, pitch unit is 1, anchor pitch is E:4, and anchor value is 0, we get an interpretive range as in Fig. 17.11.

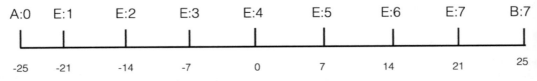

Fig. 17.11 E-Major layout on a scalar range interpreter with pitch unit 1.

In this manner, 0=>E:4, 1=>F#:4, 2=>G#:4, 3=>A, and the remainder of the mapping can be extrapolated backwards and forwards until the full set of scalar pitches in {A:0,..,B:7} are mapped. The range now constitutes a linear scale based on the E-Major tonality scale. As in the chromatic case, resolution for values mapped to non-units can resolve to the nearest scalar pitch. The map always returns a scalar pitch for a range value.

The chromatic and scalar range interpreters are but two types of pitch interpreters and are included in the code base. However, the reader many want to develop these differently, for example by not making the range behave linearly, or allowing for non-scalar pitches within scalar ranges.

17.3 A Representation for Shaping Functions and Pitch Interpreters

As indicated by the above discussion, the combination of shaping function and pitch range interpreter is a natural structure for melodic reshaping, allowing a seamless mapping of note position to pitch. Turning to implementation, one way to achieve this combination is through combining the classes shown in the class diagram in Fig. 17.12.

The left side of Fig. 17.12 relates to shaping functions, and the right for pitch range interpreters. UnivariateFunction is the base class for all univariate functions, and we show two specializations. The GenericUnivariateFunction allows us to define general functions, e.g. sin(), and Piecewise LinearFunction is used to define functions made from line segments. Both classes were introduced in section 11.2 with examples.

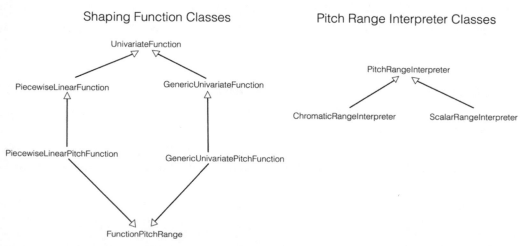

Fig. 17.12 Class Diagram for shaping function and pitch range interpreters.

FunctionPitchRange is the key base class for our design that provides means to combine univariate shaping functions and pitch range interpreters. Its constructor takes a univariate function, and a pitch range interpreter as follows:

```
class FunctionPitchRange(object):
        def __init__(self, univariate_function,
                     pitch_range_interpreter=ChromaticRangeInterpreter()):
```

The primary classes in this diagram are GenericUnivariatePitchFunction and PiecewiseLinearPitchFunction and are the main classes for shaping melodies. Each inherits from multiple classes. GenericUnivariatePitchFunction inherits from both GenericUnivariateFunction and FunctionPitchRange. In implementation, its constructor takes a univariate function and a pitch range interpreter. Similarly, for PiecewiseLinearPitchFunction, but takes arguments related to defining a PiecewiseLinearPitchFunction (transition points).

The simple inheritance tree based on PitchRangeInterpreter is shown to the right in Fig. 17.12 and provides the foundations for chromatic and scalar pitch interpreters. In the following sections we show how to construct PitchRangeInterpreters followed by examples for PiecewiseLinearPitchFunctions and GenericUnivariatePitchFunctions.

17.3.1 The Pitch Range Interpreters, Description and Examples

The class PitchRangeInterpreter is abstract and defines several methods that any derivative of it could or should implement. These methods are basically variations of function evaluation and include:

- eval_as_nearest_pitch(v): Given a numeric v, return the nearest pitch.

- eval_as_pitch(v): Like the above, but in cases where v does not match to an exact pitch, return a list of nearest pitches. Always returns results as a list.

- eval_as_accurate_chromatic_distance(v): Return an approximate chromatic distance of pitch to which v maps. If v maps between pitches, estimate chromatic distance between the two.

- value_for(pitch): return the value which maps to the pitch.

The first interpreter we look at is the ChromaticRangeInterpreter. The constructor takes the following arguments:

- anchor_pitch: A pitch to which the anchor value maps.

- anchor_value: A numeric that maps to the anchor pitch.

- pitch_unit: A numeric that represents a uniform domain distance whose end points map to neighboring chromatic values.

In terms of enharmonic representation, for example which of {C#, B##, Db} to use in representing a tone in a pitch, that representation is left undefined, although, the current implementation favors the sharp augmentation as default.

The following example of the ChromaticPitchInterpreter demonstrates PitchRangeInterpreter methods:

```
from function.chromatic_range_interpreter import ChromaticRangeInterpreter

interpreter = ChromaticRangeInterpreter(DiatonicPitch.parse('C:4'), 0, Fraction(5, 2))

for i in range(0, 13):
    p = interpreter.eval_as_nearest_pitch(Fraction(5 * i, 2))
    print('[{0}] {1}'.format(i, p))
```
```
[0] C:4
[1] C#:4
[2] D:4
[3] D#:4
[4] E:4
[5] F:4
[6] F#:4
...
```
```
assert interpreter.value_for("Eb:4") == Fraction(5 * 3, 2)

pitches = interpreter.eval_as_pitch(3)
print("[{0}]".format(', '.join(map(str, pitches))))
```
```
[C#:4, D:4]
```
```
assert pitches[0] == DiatonicPitch.parse('c#:4')
assert pitches[1] == DiatonicPitch.parse('d:4')
assert 50 == interpreter.eval_as_accurate_chromatic_distance(5)    # 50 for D:4
```

The ScalarRangeInterpreter has the following constructor arguments:

- tonality: A tonality which is being mapped to.

- anchor_pitch: A scalar pitch to which the anchor value maps.

- anchor_value: A numeric that maps to the anchor pitch.

- pitch_unit: A numeric that represents a uniform domain distance whose end points map to neighboring scalar values.

The following is an example using a unit distance between scalar notes:

```
from function.scalar_range_interpreter import ScalarRangeInterpreter

tonality = Tonality.create(ModalityType.Major, 'E', 0)
interpreter = ScalarRangeInterpreter(tonality, DiatonicPitch.parse('E:4'), 0, 1)

for i in range(0, 8):
    p = interpreter.eval_as_nearest_pitch(i)
    print('[{0}] {1}'.format(i, p))
```
```
[0] E:4
[1] F#:4
[2] G#:4
[3] A:4
[4] B:4
[5] C#:5
[6] D#:5
[7] E:5
```
```
gs_value = interpreter.value_for("G#:4")
assert gs_value == 2
gs_value = interpreter.value_for("G:4")
assert gs_value == None

pitches = interpreter.eval_as_pitch(5.2)
print("[{0}]".format(', '.join(map(str, pitches))))
```
```
[C#:5, D#:5]
```
```
assert pitches[0] == DiatonicPitch.parse('c#:5')
assert pitches[1] == DiatonicPitch.parse('d#:5')

assert 66 == interpreter.eval_as_accurate_chromatic_distance(8)   # 66 for F#:5
```

17.3.2   Shaping Classes, Description and Examples

The class FunctionPitchRange is abstract and defines several methods that any subclass of it could or should implement. As a base class for shaping classes, it provides a means for combining a univariate function with a pitch range interpreter. The shaping subclasses of FunctionPitchRange also are subclasses of some specialization of UnivariateFunction. Here GenericUnivariatePitchFunction derives from UnivariatePitchFunction and FunctionPitchRange. Also, PiecewiseLinearPitchFunction derives from PiecewiseLinearFunction and FunctionPitchRange. We will explore each in some detail.

Regarding FunctionPitchRange, besides a constructor and a couple of accessor properties, its methods are basically variations of function evaluation in the spirit of PitchRangeInterpreter and include:

- eval_as_nearest_pitch(v): Given a numeric v, return the nearest pitch.

- eval_as_pitch(v): Like the above, but in cases where v does not match to an exact pitch, return a list of nearest pitches. Always returns as a list.

- eval_as_accurate_chromatic_distance(v): Return an approximate chromatic distance of pitch to which v maps. If v maps between pitches, estimate chromatic distance between the two.

- eval(v): evaluate the univariate function at v.

The GenericUnivariatePitchFunction is a shaping class that allows the specification of a univariate function as well as a FunctionPitchRange. In that sense, it is the more broadly defined shaping function of the two presented here. Its construction arguments are:

- f: User supplied function that evaluates to a value meaningful to a PitchRangeInterpreter.

- domain_start: Numeric value for start of domain.

- domain_end: Numeric value for end of domain.

- restrict_domain: True means adhere strictly to domain specification.

- interpreter: A PitchRangeInterpreter that maps f 's range values to pitches. If None, ChromaticRangeInterpreter is used.

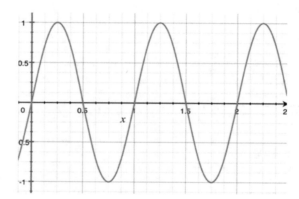

Fig. 17.13 $y = sin\ (2\pi x)$

Fig. 17.13 shows the graph of a simple GenericUnivariatePitchFunction. The graph is that of a sine curve given by $y = sin\ (2\pi x)$ over a real domain given as [0..2]. Note that every 0.5 on the x-axis marks off a half of a complete sinusoidal cycle. There are two sinusoidal cycles shown over that range.

Our example uses a chromatic pitch range interpreter that maps 0 to C:4 and 1 to C:5. To accomplish that the pitch unit specified is 1/12.

The following code provide details on how to set up this configuration.

```
from function.generic_univariate_pitch_function import GenericUnivariatePitchFunction
from function.chromatic_range_interpreter import ChromaticRangeInterpreter

def local_sin(v):
    return math.sin(2 * math.pi * v)
# Interpreter 0->C:4 and each step of 1/12 maps to new chromatic
interpreter = ChromaticRangeInterpreter(DiatonicPitch.parse('C:4'), 0,
                    Fraction(1, 12))
```

```
# local_sin maps 0->0 .25->1 .5->0 .75->-1 1->0 and so on.
f = GenericUnivariatePitchFunction(local_sin, Position(0), Position(2), False,
                                   interpreter)

for i in range(0, 9):
    p = f.eval_as_nearest_pitch(i * 0.25)
    print('[{0}] {1}'.format((i * 0.25), str(p)))
```
```
[0.0]   C:4
[0.25]  C:5
[0.5]   C:4
[0.75]  C:3
[1.0]   C:4
[1.25]  C:5
[1.5]   C:4
[1.75]  C:3
[2.0]   C:4
```

All results give the tone C across octaves 3, 4, and 5, as expected.

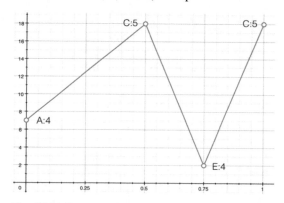

Fig. 17.14 PiecewiseLinearPitchFunction example

Given a piecewise linear curve, as described in section 11.2.1, as a shaping curve, it simply can be handed to GenericPitchRangeFunction, and the user could also provide any kind of pitch range interpreter for it. However, the PiecewiseLinearPitchFunction shown in the class diagram Fig. 17.12 is a specialized form of FunctionPitchRange formulated for ease of use. The class PiecewiseLinearPitchFunction in this case specializes so that transition points are specified as pitches. The class therefore, underneath, uses chromatic distances as shaping ranges and interpreter domains. It uses a ChromaticPitchRangeInterpreter by default. In that way, this class is a specialized case for building piecewise linear functions to pitches provided by the end user.

The example in Fig. 17.14 is an example of a piecewise linear shaping function. The transition points are the pitches A:4, C:5, E:4, and C:5. By default, a ChromaticPitchRangeInterpreter is assigned to interpret values along the shape as pitches. So, the reader should expect pitches on the curve to be interpolated values between neighboring transitions points.

The following provides further details of the above example:

```
from function.piecewise_linear_pitch_function import PiecewiseLinearPitchFunction

array = [(0, 'A:4'), (Fraction(1, 2), 'C:5'), (Position(3, 4), 'e:4'), (1, 'C:5')]
f = PiecewiseLinearPitchFunction(array)

assert 'A:4' == str(f.eval_as_nearest_pitch(0))
assert 'C:5' == str(f.eval_as_nearest_pitch(0.5))
assert 'E:4' == str(f.eval_as_nearest_pitch(0.75))
assert 'C:5' == str(f.eval_as_nearest_pitch(1))

# Recall f is also an instance of PiecewiseLinearFunction, so eval should work
assert DiatonicPitch.parse('A:4').chromatic_distance == f.eval(0)
assert DiatonicPitch.parse('C:5').chromatic_distance == f.eval(0.5)
assert DiatonicPitch.parse('E:4').chromatic_distance == f.eval(Fraction(3, 4))
assert DiatonicPitch.parse('C:5').chromatic_distance == f.eval(Position(1))

# 0.25 has two tones that are considered close between A:4 and C:5
print('[{0}]'.format(','.join(str(p) for p in f.eval_as_pitch(0.25))))

# 0.625 between C:5 and E:4 comes to G#:4
print('[{0}]'.format(','.join(str(p) for p in f.eval_as_pitch(Fraction(5,8)))))
```
```
[A#:4,B:4]
[G#:4]
```

17.4 Melodic Forms and Constraints

Music compositions usually introduce themes expressed as short melodic ideas that recur throughout the music, including across key and harmony changes, as well as through similar sounding variations. Sometimes these are known as **leitmotifs** that express personifications or allegorical references. They are sometimes called **idée fixe** if the themes are strongly emphasized or dominant in the music. While these two examples are artistic expressions used effectively in compositional structure, at a more basic level, they are examples of motifs. Our focus on motifs is to explore how melodies or melodic fragments can be structurally built and/or analyzed.

We introduce the notion of motif in this chapter, because although our discourse concerns adhering notes to a given shape, motifs are less pliable to this kind of shaping. Afterall, if a composer wants motific melodic figures to be a corner stone of a composition, the last thing the composer wants is to see them disappear by blending them seamlessly into an imposed shaping curve.

By way of introduction, consider the simple C-Minor melody in Fig. 17.15

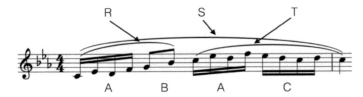

Fig. 17.15 Example motif and its structure.

Measure one is broken into four parts:

- The C-Eb-D-F labelled A.

- The G-Bb labelled B.

- The C-Eb-D-F labelled A since it is structurally like the first instance of A encountered.

- The Eb-D-C-D labelled C.

Also, phrases R, S, T are clearly shown.

Many melodies can be broken down in this fashion. A, B, and C are examples of basic structures in the melody, discussed earlier, known as motifs. A *motif* is typically a pattern of sequential notes of a particular shape and structure that, as a unit, are often repeated, often with some minor structural differences, or are shifted in pitch unilaterally. In the example, A is a repeated motif. However, as the piece progresses, B or C may be repeated and incorporated into other melodic sections of the music. The concept of a motif is a relatively open-ended concept in music, but usually is based on shape.

R, S, T are called phrases. A *phrase* consists of a set of sequential notes which may contain motifs and other phrases, that collectively form a meaningful element of the music. Phrases can account for more complexity in the music for which motifs alone cannot fill. For example, the final C:4 is part of the T phrase which also contains motifs A and C. It is also the end note to the S phrase. However, the final C:4 is not a motif itself, nor is intended to be one.

We emphasize again that if one reshapes a melody to some curve, the fine structures of motifs and phrases can be distorted at best if not destroyed. The introduction of these concepts identifies the kind of structures we may want to preserve even in the face of a reshape transform, and as will be seen, the key element that helps us preserve motifs over reshaping are constraints as introduced in chapter 14.

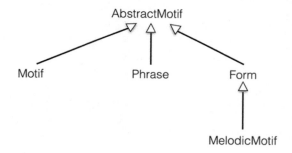

Fig. 17.16 Motif class structure.

The class structure surrounding these concepts is shown in Fig. 17.16. It consists at root with Abstract-Motif from which Motif, Phrase, and Form derive, and from Form, the concept of MelodicMotif is derived. In essence, as will be seen, many of these classes are quite similar, but differ mainly in how each aggregates structure.

At the root, AbstractMotif holds a set of actors (Notes) and constraints which only apply to those actors. Motif is constructed from a richer set of Note structures such as AbstractNoteCollectives and Notes. It also provides a method of reproducing itself to other notes similarly structured, along with cloning constraints using different actors. This is how a motif can be reused throughout a piece of music. A Form is built from other Motifs and Forms. If one had motifs A, B, for example, one can imagine a form like the concatenation AB or ABAB. A Phrase is essentially a less rigidly defined Motif, consisting of a set of notes. It may involve Notes not involved in any Motif and may extend over a partial Motif. Finally, a MelodicMotif is a Form consisting of other Motifs and Forms and Phrases.

The Motif hierarchy described is an aid to structure a melody, and the constraints are a way to enforce note relationships amongst its notes. For example, some notes may be designated as chordal. Some pairs of notes may have pitch relationships such as 'higher than' or 'equal' or have intervallic relationships. Phrases and Forms provide a means for specifying constraints across motifs and to non-motif structures. Be mindful that analysis of a melody into these components is not always exact. You may find that parts of a melody fit these patterns and other parts do not. That is in the creative nature of music. With these classes, one should be able to create essential melodic structures with desired constraints.

The following code example of Motif shows how to create and copy a motif. Note that the constraints are copied with correct actor note substitutions into the new motif.

```python
from melody.structure.motif import Motif

s = Beam()
s.append(Note(DiatonicPitch.parse('C:4'), Duration(1, 8)))
s.append(Note(DiatonicPitch.parse('D:4'), Duration(1, 8)))
s.append(Note(DiatonicPitch.parse('C:4'), Duration(1, 8)))
s.append(Note(DiatonicPitch.parse('F#:4'), Duration(1, 8)))
notes = s.get_all_notes()

c = [
    EqualPitchConstraint([notes[0], notes[2]]),
    NotEqualPitchConstraint([notes[1], notes[3]])
]

m = Motif(s, c, 'A')
cs = Beam()

cs.append(Note(DiatonicPitch.parse('C:5'), Duration(1, 8)))
cs.append(Note(DiatonicPitch.parse('D:5'), Duration(1, 8)))
cs.append(Note(DiatonicPitch.parse('C:5'), Duration(1, 8)))
cs.append(Note(DiatonicPitch.parse('F#:5'), Duration(1, 8)))

c_motif = m.copy_to(cs.get_all_notes()[0])   # Build motif with cs based on motif m

assert 'A' == c_motif.name
assert len(c_motif.actors) == len(notes)
assert len(c_motif.constraints) == len(c)

assert isinstance(c_motif.constraints[0], EqualPitchConstraint)
assert c_motif.constraints[0].actors[0] == c_motif.actors[0]
assert c_motif.constraints[0].actors[1] == c_motif.actors[2]

assert isinstance(c_motif.constraints[1], NotEqualPitchConstraint)
assert c_motif.constraints[1].actors[0] == c_motif.actors[1]
assert c_motif.constraints[1].actors[1] == c_motif.actors[3]
```

The following example illustrates how to piece together a MelodicForm comprised of motifs and a phrase, along with an extra constraint for the melodic form itself.

```
from melody.structure.melodic_form import MelodicForm
from melody.structure.motif import Motif
from melody.structure.phrase import Phrase

line_str = '{<C-Major: I> iC:4 D C F F A G A iC:5 D C F f A G A}'

lge = LineGrammarExecutor()
target_line, _ = lge.parse(line_str)
notes = target_line.get_all_notes()

ca = [
    EqualPitchConstraint([notes[0], notes[2]]),
    NotEqualPitchConstraint([notes[1], notes[3]])
]

cb = [
    NotEqualPitchConstraint([notes[4], notes[5]]),
    EqualPitchConstraint([notes[5], notes[7]])
]

a = Motif([notes[0], notes[1], notes[2], notes[3]], ca, 'A')
b = Motif([notes[4], notes[5], notes[6], notes[7]], cb, 'B')

phrase_constraints = [
    EqualPitchConstraint([notes[3], notes[4]]),
]
phrase = Phrase([notes[2], notes[3], notes[4], notes[5]], phrase_constraints, 'P')

mf_constraints = [
    EqualPitchConstraint([notes[2], notes[5]]),
]

mf = MelodicForm([a, b], [phrase], mf_constraints, 'MF1')
print('[{0}]'.format(','.join([str(n.diatonic_pitch) for n in mf.actors])))
mf_dup = mf.copy_to(notes[8])
print('[{0}]'.format(','.join([str(n.diatonic_pitch) for n in mf_dup.actors])))
[C:4,D:4,C:4,F:4,F:4,A:4,G:4,A:4]
[C:5,D:5,C:5,F:5,F:5,A:5,G:5,A:5]
```

Reference the motif formations in Fig. 17.17.

Note that the melodic motif covers all of the first 8 notes of the input melody given at the beginning of the code. As an exercise the reader should invoke copy_to() on the 9th note in notes to duplicate the melodic form "mf", and make various checks that it is a duplicate with different actors and that the duplicated constraints are consistent with the actors of the duplicate.

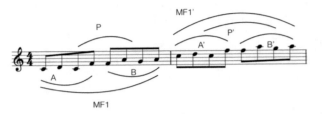

Fig. 17.17 Motif Example from code above.

17.5 The Reshape Transform

The problem at hand is to alter the pitches of an existing melody to fit to a given curve, except for specified motific substructures. We examine a solution that makes use of constraints and the constraint engine. However, even with that, it is possible to attempt optimizations and shortcuts. So, while the intent is to show a viable solution, the reader should look at the reshape transform as research in progress and look for additional approaches.

Instead of presenting a low-level approach, we show a high-level one that speaks to the concepts and data flow within the reshape transformation. A process chart for reshape is given in Fig. 17.18. It begins with gleaning constraints from any given melodic forms. Recall that the melodic form embeds constraints for retaining a likeness of shape/form for motifs and their derivatives.

Fig. 17.18 Process chart for reshape transform.

We note that there may also be constraints on the beat structure which force notes to strong or weak beats. This topic is not covered in this text, but the reader can delve into this topic as found in the code base. Each of those solutions is passed to the pitch constraint solver to generate yet a newer set of solutions, but only for notes/actors that are members of constraints. (If there are no beat constraints, the pitch constraint solve is called with the input melody line.) For each of these solutions, the notes/actors not involved in the constraints have their pitches fit to the curve, using the interpreter technology discussed earlier. Finally, each constraint solution is extended with the curve fitted actors. With that the solutions are returned.

The returned results can be further analyzed, sorted, and filtered. The code package includes a Min CurveFitFilter class, which when given the results of the reshape transform, sorts the solutions using a means square technique on how well each solution fits to the curve. The idea here is that the filter could weed out solutions where motifs are too irregularly shaped relative to the curve.

The code for reshape also has an optimize switch, which is basically an experimental method wherein new curve fit constraints are built for the actors in the melodic form constraints that try to keep certain actors pitch-wise close to what would be a curve fit.

As a side note, although the logic as presented is relatively simple, the code is complex due to the translation of solutions between phases with maps from one solution's actors to another. Perhaps the clever student and find an easy way around this issue, or a nice way to encapsulate a solution.

17.5.1   The TReshape Transform API

This chapter expends considerable effort in setting up software "machinery" to achieve formulating and developing the reshaping transform just described. At the transform's foundation there are shaping classes based on UnivariateFunction and FunctionPitchRange, and interpreters based on PitchRange-Interpreter. We also introduced a somewhat generic software model for Motif whose essential shape and structure in part is based on constraints introduced in chapter 14.

With that we are now able to introduce the TReshape transform API. Like many of the transforms described, it consists of a constructor and an apply() method.

The constructor takes the following arguments:

- score: This is an instance of LiteScore.

- pitch_function: A shaping function based on UnivariatePitchFunction and Func-tionPitchRange,

- time_range: The range of the domain (in whole note time) on which the transform acts.

- melodic_form: An instance of MelodicForm based on score's line.

- optimize: Attempt of add restrictive pitch constraints on first notes of constraints, based on reshape function. This is a Boolean value whose default is True.

Of these arguments, please note that the argument optimize is somewhat experimental. The idea is based on a premise that the first note of each Motif constraints should be close to the curve. So further constraints based on limiting the note's pitch solution set to proximity to the curve are added to limit the search for the note's pitch solution values.

The apply() method takes no arguments. It returns a list of LiteScores representing successful application of the TReshape transform to the input arguments.

17.6   Examples

We take for a first example curve fitting to a simple sinusoidal curve:

$$y = \sin\left(\frac{2\pi x}{3}\right) \qquad (17.4)$$

or in Python, simply:

```
import math

def three_sin(v):
    """

    Maps v to a chromatic distance.
    [0..3] -->[0..2*PI]-->C:4 + [0, 1/19, …, 1] with origin C:4==0, and steps in
    1/19 units
    """

    return math.sin(2 * math.pi * v/3)
```

This function maps [0..3] to a complete sine curve as show in Fig. 17.19. In whole note time, the intention is to have a domain of 3 measures in 4/4 time. In addition we use a chromatic pitch interpreter to map the usual [-1..1] range of sine to the chromatic range [G:2..G:5].

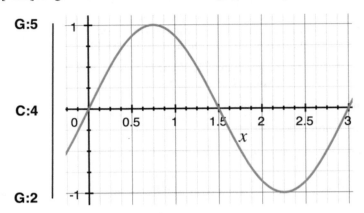

Fig. 17.19 Sine curve mapped to [G:2..G:5] pitch range.

That is what we get from an appropriately constructed ChromaticPitchRangeInterpreter. Using this function in an application of the reshape function, imagine a simple melodic line as input. As we saw in some prior transform examples, since the reshape is destructive across the input melody, each note can initially be at some neutral pitch, say E:4. This is a good technique to use with reshape as it allows one to focus on rhythm and let the shape take form almost purely from a shape function, in this case the shape function in equation 17.4.

In our example, we start with the flattened melody including the harmony in Fig. 17.20:

Fig. 17.20 Flattened melody along with harmony for reshape transform input.

The first application of the reshape transform uses the sinusoidal function defined above over the three full measures. We create the score, the chromatic interpreter, and pitch function as follows:

```
line_str = '{<C-Major: I> iE:4 E E E E E E E <:IV> qE ie e <:V> qe ie e <:VI>   qE E iE
E E E}'
score = create_score(line_str, 'violin', (3, 4, 'sww'))

all_notes = score.line.get_all_notes()

# 19 scalar notes from C:4 (0) to G:5 (1) with pitch unit 1/19
interpreter = ChromaticRangeInterpreter(DiatonicPitch.parse('C:4'), 0,
```

```
                                    Fraction(1, 19))

pitch_function = GenericUnivariatePitchFunction(three_sin, Position(0), Position(3),
                                      interp=interpreter)

# The first note should have one of 3 values, C:4, E:4, G:4
constraints = {
    ChordalPitchConstraint(all_notes[0]),
    ChordalPitchConstraint(all_notes[8]),
    ChordalPitchConstraint(all_notes[11]),
    ChordalPitchConstraint(all_notes[14]),
    PitchRangeConstraint([all_notes[0]], PitchRange.create('C:4', 'E:4')),
}

motif = Motif([all_notes[0], all_notes[8], all_notes[11], all_notes[14]], constraints,
'A')
melodic_form = MelodicForm([motif])
t_reshape = TReshape(score, pitch_function, Range(0, 3), melodic_form, True)

results = t_reshape.apply()
```

One result is the revision of the input melody shown in Fig. 17.21.

Fig. 17.21 three_sin() with chromatic interpretation.

Note that the chordal constraints ensure chordal notes on the first beat of each chord. The PitchRangeConstraint simply limits the choices of the first note and was done more for optimization of the constraint engine run. Outside of constraints, the melodic motif serves limited value for this example. More on the poor chord match later.

For this example, apply() returns a list of LiteScore results. The shown result is the top result from using the MinCurveFilter class:

```
from transformation.reshape.min_curve_fit_filter import MinCurveFitFilter

filter = MinCurveFitFilter(pitch_function, results)
print('{0} filtered results'.format(len(filter.scored_results)))

for index in range(0, min(3, len(filter.scored_results))):
    result = filter.scored_results[index]
    print('[{0}] {1} ({2})'.format(index, str_line(result[0].line), result[1]))
```

```
16 filtered results
[0] iC:4 F A D:5 E F# G F# qF iA:4 F qB:3 iD B:2 qA:3 F:2 iG B D:3 G
(184.79155791961475)
[1] iC:4 F A D:5 E F# G F# qF iA:4 F qD iD:3 B:2 qA:3 F:2 iG B D:3 G
(187.79155791961475)
[2] iE:4 F A D:5 E F# G F# qF iA:4 F qB:3 iD B:2 qA:3 F:2 iG B D:3 G
(200.79155791961475)
[3] iE:4 F A D:5 E F# G F# qF iA:4 F qD iD:3 B:2 qA:3 F:2 iG B D:3 G
(203.79155791961475)
```

The returned filter.scored_results is a list of ordered pairs, each of which reference a LiteScore and its score respectively. The score is based on least square distances from of the LiteScore notes from the curve. Filter.scored_results is sorted by low score.

Prior to applying the reshape transform, each note held some statically assigned pitch, marking a basic rhythm. After application, we obtain a melody whose pitches approximates the $\sin\left(\frac{2\pi x}{3}\right)$ curve. Most of the notes come from the C tonality, save for the F#. Chromatic interpretation should behave that way, especially on non-chordal tones to provide closer adherence to the curve. As a further note, after applying a reshape, especially in the absence of constraints, the user should feel free to adjust the harmony to make better sense with the melodic changes. That is, transforms are not so 'hard and fast' providing complete solutions but meant to be an assist to the composer.

If we change the pitch interpreter to scalar, which preserves tonality, and retaining the same constraints, we obtain a result as shown in Fig. 17.22.

Fig. 17.22 three_sin() with scalar interpreter.

The F# goes away and in fact we get three G's which elide into a dotted quarter note. The change of pitch interpreter is achieved in the following manner:

```
# 11 scalar notes to C:4 (0) to G:5 (11) with pitch unit 1/11
interpreter = ScalarRangeInterpreter(tonality, DiatonicPitch.parse('C:4'), 0,
                                     Fraction(1, 11))
```

Note that unlike the chromatic interpreter, we have scalar 12 tones between C:4 and G:5 with a spacing of 1/11 so that G:5 has a valuation of 1 as a range.

It is also noteworthy, as alluded to earlier, that the original harmonies may not be the best match. For example, the above melody is more suited to a F-Major (IV) chord or D-Minor (IMin7). Taking the second note, F:4, for example, a close review of the curve fitting algorithm shows that E:4 and F:4 are candidate choices but F:4 is a closer fit to the curve. The algorithm has no preference for the given chord except when dictated by constraints. Otherwise, it picks the closest tone to the curve. The user may choose to either add more chordal note constraints or manually produce alternative harmonies for chord choice for the curve.

The next example considers a shaping function based on the piecewise linear curve in Fig. 17.23:

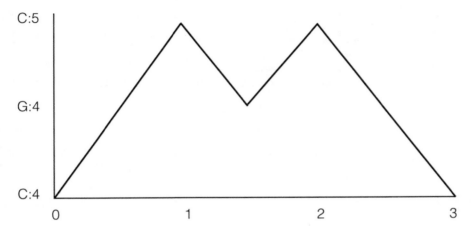

Fig. 17.23 Piecewise linear curve over 3 whole note measures in range [C:4 .. G:5].

Piecewise linear curves are great for passages with long linear sequences of notes. The above graph is composed of four lines indicating linear progressions of notes. The graph is plotted to four line segments covering the whole note range [0..3] or 3 4/4 beat measures, with segment points mapping:

$(0, 0) \longrightarrow (1, 8) \longrightarrow (1.5, 4) \longrightarrow (3, 0)$

In code this is:

```
plf = PiecewiseLinearFunction([(0, 0), (1, 8), (Fraction(3, 2), 4), (2, 8), (3, 0)])
```

The range of this function is [0..8] which in scalar terms is C:4 to C:5 with the value 4 matching to G:4. What we are trying to achieve in this example is build scalar passages along the straight lines. The code for this example is:

```
line_str = '{<C-Major: I> iE:4 E E E E E E E E E E E E E E E E E E E E E E E wE}'
score = create_score(line_str, 'violin', (4, 4, 'swww'))

tonality = score.hct.get_hc_by_position(0).tonality
all_notes = score.line.get_all_notes()

plf = PiecewiseLinearFunction([(0, 0), (1, 8), (Fraction(3, 2), 4), (2, 8), (3, 0)])
time_range = Range(0, 3)

interpreter = ScalarRangeInterpreter(tonality, DiatonicPitch.parse('C:4'), 0, 1)
pitch_function = GenericUnivariatePitchFunction(plf, Position(0), Position(3),
                                                False, interpreter)

constraints = {
    ChordalPitchConstraint(all_notes[0]),
    PitchRangeConstraint([all_notes[0]], PitchRange.create('C:4', 'G:4')),
}
```

```
motif = Motif([all_notes[0]], constraints, 'A')
melodic_form = MelodicForm([motif])
t_reshape = TReshape(score, pitch_function, time_range, melodic_form, False)

results = t_reshape.apply()
```

Fitting to this curve, the resulting melody is shown in Fig. 17.24.

Fig. 17.24 Piecewise linear fitting of scalar tones as scales.

While this geometric approach to reshaping melody looks promising, it must be executed with care. The lines in the above graph were constructed with precision, i.e., lines built with precise slope to get the correct pitch per note duration for linear scales. Having less precision could result in duplicate pitches, as in the sin() example, or wildly harmonically incongruent tones.

These examples made use of a motif only to provide constraints for the transformation. These constraints mainly focused on establishing chordal pitch requirements and limiting the ranges on select pitches. In the following, we return to the sinusoidal curve but this time we introduce several motifs that must be preserved by the transform. We use the following 24 eighth note pattern for input:

```
'{<C-Major: I> iC:4 D E D E E E E C D E D E E E E C D E D E E E E wE}'
```

A closer look allows one to see three identical motifs with the pattern C, D, E, D each starting a new measure. The rest are simple filler notes that adhere to some curve. The melodic form is constructed in the following manner:

```
all_notes = score.line.get_all_notes()

constraints = {
    StepSequenceConstraint([all_notes[0], all_notes[1], all_notes[2], all_notes[3]],
                           [1, 1, -1])
}
motif = Motif([all_notes[0], all_notes[1], all_notes[2], all_notes[3]], constraints)
motif1 = motif.copy_to(all_notes[8])
motif2 = motif.copy_to(all_notes[16])
form = MelodicForm([motif, motif1, motif2])
```

Notice the use of the copy_to() method to replicate the motif in different places in the melody! The StepSequenceConstraint captures the motif figure as diatonic steps.

The gist of all this is that no matter how the reshape transform changes this melody, we want the beginning of each measure to start with that motif, but not necessarily constructed with the same pitches, as long as they adhere to the given motific constraints.

For completion, the code is as follows:

```
# 11 scalar notes to C:4 (0) to G:5 (11) with pitch unit 1/11
interpreter = ScalarRangeInterpreter(tonality, DiatonicPitch.parse('C:4'), 0, Frac-
tion(1, 11))

pitch_function = GenericUnivariatePitchFunction(three_sin, Position(0), Position(3),
False, interpreter)
t_reshape = TReshape(score, pitch_function, Range(0, 3), form, True)
```

The result is shown in Fig. 17.25[57].

Fig. 17.25 Motif preservation on three_sin().

The motifs start off each measure, and the remainder of the notes adhere to the three_sin() curve. The strengths and weaknesses are demonstrated. The motif is preserved even if shifted, e.g., note E, F, G, F in the second measure. However, because the motifs take temporal space during which the curve is not followed, notes outside the motif can be distant from the motif, making for wide jumps.

The harmony is user provided to roughly match the melodic transformation.

17.7 Final Thoughts

The reshape transform looks like as a very powerful and promising technique for shaping melodies as an assist to music composition. It leads one to entertain thoughts of compositional tools wherein one uses a repertoire of standard curves or hand drawn sketches as the seed for constructing melodies, or perhaps using small sketches for minor corrections.

The fulfillment of that vision may lie mainly in constructing an effective user interface with a focus on that kind of interaction. The point of this chapter is that, as a foundation, reshape can be achieved in principle. However, practically there are complications. Mostly these stem from a need for accuracy in constructing the curve especially as seen in the example with scale sequences[58]. Also, between the curve and the melody stands the harmony, and the resulting curve may not be cooperative in pitch selection to a given harmony.

The second issue involves the usage of constraints. One aspect for concern is the need for the user to recognize and establish constraints appropriate to intention, whether due to the recognition of chordal notes, or by the need to identify and implement motific patterns, e.g., pitch step or interval constraints. There is also a concern that the constraint engine may take too long to find solutions, and independently

---

[57] The reader should again note the use of note elisions and ties on neighboring notes with the same pitch.

[58] A smart interface could correct user input curves or provide a limited number of alternatives to clarify the user's intentions.

of that, to efficiently search through results for best solutions. Optimization of the constraint engine is not a topic of this text but is a research top to itself.

Overall, there is something satisfying about seeing a melody arise from a curve specification, and to what that may mean for further music composition tooling.

18 Harmonic Transcription: Preserving Melody over Harmonic Change

The focus on transformation up to this chapter has been on pitch assignment to melodic notes in a variety of melodic disruptive actions such as tonality shifts, inversion, or reshape to a curve. The constraint engine and family of pitch constraints introduced in chapter 14 provide a powerful means for specifying note pitch relationships to be satisfied in a search across pitch assignments over a set of notes. However, the constraint engine and the defined constraints are more a foundational technology, and its usage is situational. For example, we found a usage for the constraint engine and constraints in the design of the reshape transform for the preservation of motif-based constraints.

In this chapter we explore yet another usage of the constraint engine for solving a practical problem. The transformation we consider here involves altering a given melody's pitches to adhere to a newly specified harmony, i.e., chord and/or tonality changes. The challenges center around retaining semblances of the original melody in the face of harmonic changes.

Following an introduction, we explore what is meant by "semblances of the original melody" in a different melody, or in the terminology adopted we ask, "what is melodic similarity?". This involves deriving a set of constraints that define a meaning for melodic similarity. We look at further means for defining the search space for similar melodies to help optimize the search. The harmonic transcription transformation and its api are described, followed by examples.

This work approximately follows the teachings found in [44] [45] [46].

18.1 Introduction

Throughout this chapter, we discuss music in terms of melody and harmony much as we have in prior transformation discussions. The melody is specified as a collection of notes (as in a Line structure) along with an optional set of motif structures. The harmony is specified explicitly as a sequence of harmonic contexts (HarmonicContext objects), each consisting of chord/tonality specifications, each spanning some portion of time, and all collected in an end-to-end non-overlapping sequence of harmonic context objects in a harmonic context track (HarmonicContextTrack object.)

The harmonic transcription transformation involves specifying a different set of harmonic contexts across the melody, and having the melody adjust to the new harmony, but leaving the melody 'sounding similar' to the original melody. Implicit to this qualifying statement is characterizing the qualities that the adjusted melody should have relative to the original melody. In other words, we ask "What melodic invariants characterize a modified melody 'sounding like' the original?" Certainly, we cannot expect the adjusted melody to have the exact same sound. Even if each pitch is adjusted by some constant interval, the sound would be highly similar but not necessarily the same. Similarly, significant changes in harmony could lead to significant affect, sonically, structurally, and emotionally compared to the original melody.

As an example, consider the following melodic segment from the Allegretto in Schubert's Drei Klavier-stucke D946 in Fig. 18.1. In the example we show a portion of the opening, along with a skeletal harmony in Eb-Major provided by the author consisting of the chord sequence I-I-I-IV-I-I-V[59].

Fig. 18.1 Schubert D946 Allegretto original melody.

Suppose we replace the original harmony with different chords and in a different key. For example suppose we move to the C-Major tonality and add more harmonic variety use the chord sequence consisting of I-VDom7-IV-VI-IV-I-V-I. We also wish to retain a semblance of the melody. It is a challenge to re-arrange the melody to fit the new harmony, but the re-arrangement can provide a much more varied sound. One possibility is shown in Fig. 18.2:

Fig. 18.2 Schubert D946 Allegretto melody in C-Major with altered harmony.

Of note in this example is not so much that the new harmony was accommodated, but that the note arrangement in the new melody give it a sound or feeling like the original. Examine the shape of the two melodies. They are similar in the following ways. If sequential pitches in the original are equal they remain equal in the new. The same is true if one is lower or higher than the next. In short, the two melodies have matching contours. Also, importantly, chordal notes of the original melody are chordal in the new. The variance of movement on sequential pitches is different but generally close. The altered original melody in the face of such a revision is called a ***homomorphic melody***, a term reflecting similar but not necessarily identical qualities.

In this chapter we explore the criteria for melodic similarity in the face of harmonic change and see how these are actualized into the harmonic transcription transform. The foundation of the technical approach is to utilize constraints and the pitch constraint engine to develop homomorphic melodies.

---

[59] The harmony cited is approximate to the original.

18.2   Melodic Analysis for Similarity

In the context of harmonic transcription and later in search, we need to analyze melody into concrete details in the context of its harmony. The key elements of such an analysis are to understand each melodic note in its relationship to the underlying harmony, and in its relationship to its neighboring notes. Arguably it is encouraged to distill this information in fine detail above and beyond this immediate application's requirements so that that information can be used later to expand both the original usage, and usages in other applications. In the following sections, we examine two types of melodic analysis that provide useful information to construct constraints to enforce melodic similarity.

18.2.1   Harmonic Role Analysis

A useful melodic analysis is to determine if a note reinforces its harmony's chord, and if a note is a member of the tonality, or neither. Fig. 18.3 shows a typical melodic portion in the context of a given A-Major harmony. We have picked out the harmonic notes, i.e., the melodic notes that are chordal, in red circles. We have also picked out the notes that are scalar, i.e., in this case the notes whose pitches are members of the A-Major tonality (but not chordal) in green circles.

One aspect of melodic similarity between two corresponding melodies is that chordal notes remain chordal and scalar notes remain scalar. With that information one can construct both chordal and scalar pitch constraints to ensure that a transcribed melody (the result of the harmonic transcription transform) has notes that adhere to the same harmonic and tonal roles.

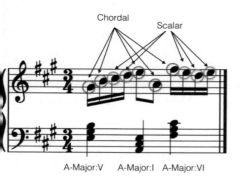

Fig. 18.3 Harmonic role analysis.

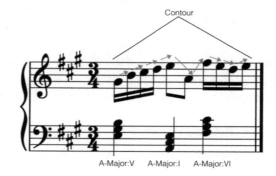

Fig. 18.4 Contour analysis.

18.2.2   Melodic Contour Analysis

A melodic contour captures the rise and fall of pitches in the original melodic line. The rise and fall of adjacent pitches defining a contour can be seen in the example in Fig. 18.4. In melodic analysis, melody notes are analyzed in pairs forward from the first to last to capture the notes' relationship in each pair. There are various ways to capture or define this, but for now, we only consider three possible relationships for two sequential pitches in the melody: the pitches are the same, the first is greater than the second, or the first is lower than the second. From this information, it is easy to construct ComparativePitchConstraints to enforce contours using the pitch constraint engine. One can imagine these as topological constraints, as if the melody were drawn on a rubber sheet which can be stretched along each axis. The gaps between adjacent notes can be larger or smaller but note contour relationships are always invariant.

The algorithm for capturing note contour is straight forward. A code sketch follows:

```
pair_annotation_list = list()
note_list = line.get_all_notes()
for i in range(0, len(note_list) - 1):
    first = note_list[i]
    second = note_list[i + 1]
    pair_annotation_list.append(NotePairInformation(first, second))

class NotePairInformation(object):
    class Relationship(Enum):
        LT = -1
        EQ = 0
        GT = 1

    def __init__(self, first_note, second_note):
        self.__first_note = first_note
        self.__second_note = second_note

        self.__forward_interval = Interval.create_interval(
                                        self.first_note.diatonic_pitch,
                                        self.second_note.diatonic_pitch)

        cd = self.forward_interval.chromatic_distance
        self.__relationship = NotePairInformation.Relationship.GT if cd < 0 \
                        else NotePairInformation.Relationship.LT \
                        if cd > 0 else NotePairInformation.Relationship.EQ
```

The logic is quite straight-forward. Note that the chromatic distance between two notes is used to determine the note pair relationship. The reader is invited to alter the logic to account for rest notes!

18.2.3 Software Design

Turning our attention to software design, Fig. 18.5 shows a design diagram for the melodic analysis described earlier. The design is rather simple, with the analysis producing three lists of encapsulated information described below.

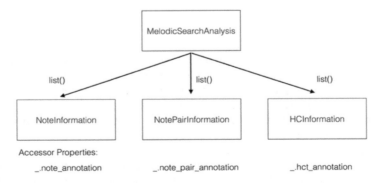

Fig. 18.5 Melodic search analysis design.

Because the object structure is simple, and the calculations are quickly achieved there is no need to incorporate a create/apply methodology as we see in transform design, but rather once created the analysis provides three accessors to the information already prepared.

When the user creates a MelodicSearchAnalysis object it creates three lists of the following types of analysis information:

- NoteInformation: Provides information about the harmonic and tonal roles of each note.
- NotePairInformation: Provides information about each sequential pair of notes regarding their relationship.
- HCInformation: Provides information about each harmonic context (not used in this text).

In the following example, we build a melodic analysis of a small melody and display the details of the note and note pair analysis:

```
l = LineGrammarExecutor()
s = '{qC:4 D:4 [<E-Major: A-Maj> G F A B]}'
line, hct = l.parse(s)


analysis = MelodicSearchAnalysis(line, hct)


note_annotation_list = analysis.note_annotation
for na in note_annotation_list:
    print(na)


note_pair_annotation_list = analysis.note_pair_annotation
for npa in note_pair_annotation_list:
    print(npa)
```

```
[C:4<1/4>-(1/4)] off=0 f=1 hc=h.c.[C-Major, TI [C, E, G], 1/2] scale_degree=0 inter-
val=P:1 is_scalar=True is_chordal=True duration=1/4
[D:4<1/4>-(1/4)] off=1/4 f=1 hc=h.c.[C-Major, TI [C, E, G], 1/2] scale_degree=1 inter-
val=None is_scalar=True is_chordal=False duration=1/4
[G:4<1/8>-(1/8)] off=0 f=1 hc=h.c.[E-Major, TAMaj [A, C#, E], 1/2] scale_degree=None
interval=None is_scalar=False is_chordal=False duration=1/8
...
[C:4<1/4>-(1/4)] off=0 f=1 "< [D:4<1/4>-(1/4)] off=1/4 f=1"
[D:4<1/4>-(1/4)] off=1/4 f=1 "< [G:4<1/8>-(1/8)] off=0 f=1"
[G:4<1/8>-(1/8)] off=0 f=1 "> [F:4<1/8>-(1/8)] off=1/8 f=1"
[F:4<1/8>-(1/8)] off=1/8 f=1 "< [A:4<1/8>-(1/8)] off=1/4 f=1"
[A:4<1/8>-(1/8)] off=1/4 f=1 "< [B:4<1/8>-(1/8)] off=3/8 f=1"
```

18.3   Further Constraining the Search Space

The mentioned constraints on note roles and contours address the melodic shaping essentials for the harmonic transcription transform. However, those constraints may be insufficient if we are left with a very large canvas of pitches and registers in which to work. That is, if each melodic note can assume a pitch from a wide range of pitches, even these constraints may not be enough to adequately contain the constraint engine run time. So, in this section we look for further parameters to help narrow down the pitch search space and limit the search time for obtaining melody results from the harmonic transcription transform.

18.3.1 The Melodic Window

The constraints we consider to further restrict the search space involve defining limiting criterion on the range of pitches in which each melodic note can be assigned a pitch. Towards that end, we define a band of pitches within which all melody note pitch assignments should lie. We begin by defining a window or interval of pitches from which to choose. In this model we specify a lowest pitch called the *WindowAnchorPitch*, and a *WindowHeight* which is the number of semi-tones above the anchor pitch to the highest pitch. This pitch interval is called a *pitch* window. The pitch window taken over time is called a *melodic window*.

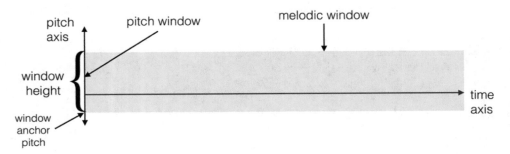

Fig. 18.6 *Pitch window defined by WindowAnchorPitch and WindowHeight.*

Fig. 18.6 shows the pitch window (ref. braces) defined by WindowAnchorPitch and WindowHeight as well as the melodic window. The pitch window on the left pitch axis can be used to create a PitchRangeConstraint defined by the range of the pitch window. With this constraint, all transformed melody notes must have pitches that lie between the lowest and highest pitch of the pitch window. If window height is not specified, as a default, the height of the input melody (number of semitones between the lowest and highest pitch) is used.

18.3.2 Melodic Variance (Tunnel)

Despite the restrictions imposed by the melodic window, the pitch search space can still be too large for efficient search. To limit that search space further, additional parameters can be specified to define a narrow pitch band per note based on an approximate rendering of the melody post transcription. This pitch band is called a *variance tunnel*. Restated, this band is constructed around a speculative shifted impression of the original melodic curve, and the pitch search is limited to within that band.

Referencing Fig. 18.7, the variance tunnel is defined as follows. Assume one can optionally specify the pitches for one or more notes from the melody, e.g., say the melody has a first note C:4 note that we want in the A:4 position in all transcription results. We call that specification, a *tag map*. In our example, the first note, namely C:4, maps to the pitch A:4, or 0—>A:4, where 0 is the index of the first note. Using the first tag only, we can imagine the entire melody shifted by the same interval which we call the *move interval,* in this case a major 6th upward. We call this imagined melody the *tunnel melody*. Finally, we specify a *tunnel half interval*. This is an interval wherein for each note on the tunnel melody, we select from pitches in the range defined above and below that note by the tunnel half interval. The resulting search space is the variance tunnel.

Defining a variance tunnel to limit the pitch search space is not always the best choice for developing results. It may be too limiting, and the user may need a broader search space. However, this approach does help in search time optimization, especially if the source melody is lengthy.

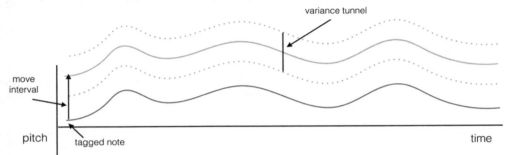

Fig. 18.7 Variance tunnel, a pitch selection limiting constraint based on speculative melodic shift.

The default tunnel half interval is a perfect fifth. As a side note, the melodic search may also be limited by specifying the maximum number of results for the transform.

18.4 The Harmonic Transcription Transform

The api for the harmonic transcription transform follows the create/apply pattern established for all transforms so far discussed. The creation of the THarmonicTranscription object comes about by the object constructor or a static create method.

The THarmonicTranscription constructor has the following arguments:

- source_line: the Line object containing the melody.
- source_hct: the HarmonicContextTrack object for the original harmony for source_line.
- source_melodic_form: An optional MelodicForm object for the melody.

Note that no alternative harmony is specified at this point. That is specified on the apply() method discussed below.

The THarmonicTranscription.create() method is an alternative method for object construction using a textual expression for the source melody and harmony:

- source_expression: textual representation of the source melody and harmony which is parsed using the LineGrammarExecutor described in section 12.2.

Notice that there is no argument for melodic form present as that would be based on the actors in the Line object which has not been created yet at this point of execution[60].

The apply() method notably specifies the alternative harmony to be applied to the source melody, as well as arguments discussed in the prior sections on melodic windows, anchors, and contour variance:

- target_hct: the alternative HarmonicContextTrack that specifies the alternative harmony to apply to the source melody.

---

[60] A solution is to extend the music grammar to specify melodic forms which would be a product of the parsing process.

- window_anchor_pitch: As discussed earlier, the lowest pitch to be considered for pitch as-signment.

- tag_map: a dict mapping source melody actor indices to DiatonicPitches.

- window_height: As discussed earlier, chromatic distance above window_anchor_pitch that defines the pitch window of allowable pitches for assignment.

- num_solutions: An optional specification of the maximum number of solutions (or less) to find before terminating search. Default is -1, unbounded.

- tunnel_half_interval: defines the half tunnel variance, i.e., half-interval for search pitch range on the tunnel melody. Full variance comprises the half interval below to half interval above each pitch on the tunnel melody.

The apply() method returns an MCSResults object. This object contains a list of PMaps (see section 14.3.1) which map melody actors to their reassigned notes. That list of PMaps is accessed through the MCSResults.pitch_results() method.

The THarmonicTranscription transform logic mainly consists of setting up constraints derived from all the arguments that include:

- Constraints derives from melodic analysis on the input melody/harmony.

- Limits define by the melodic window.

- Tunnel variance.

And as well, optionally, limits are applied to the constraint engine run until the number of solutions specified are found, or the search terminates, whichever comes first.

A data/process flow diagram for using the harmonic transform is shown in Fig. 18.8.

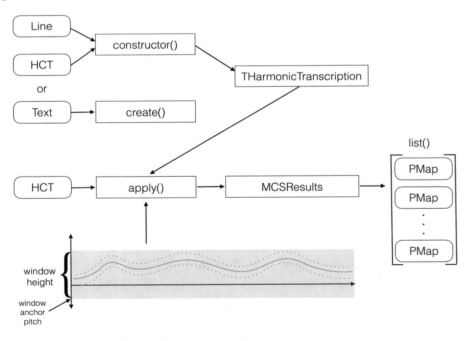

Fig. 18.8 Steps in performing harmonic transcription.

The harmonic transcription transform is complicated for several reasons, included the complex suite of arguments that can be applied, the access to results, and the search time. The examples that follow should clarify argument and process details.

18.5   Examples

For our first example, we consider the opening of the famous Mozart fantasy in C-Minor, K. 475 shown in Fig. 18.9.

For chordal analysis, we chose the i-It-V chord sequence in c (natural) minor. The F# and Ab combination functions as an Italian 6th [47]. This original chord differs from, say, specifying iv with modified F, which is awkward.

Fig. 18.9 Opening Mozart C-Minor Fantasy, K. 475

As an example of harmonic transcription, suppose we alter this chord sequence to the following chordal sequence:

iv (A melodic minor) - i (A natural minor) - (V A melodic minor)

Using harmonic transcription, we get the following as a possibility:

Fig. 18.10 Harmonic transcription of music in Fig. 18.9

This is one solution out of several, and we chose to show this as it represents an interesting alteration of the original, especially with starting with a IV chord along with the strong imitation of the original melody. The interested reader may want to explore other recommended solution.

The source for this example is shown below. Notice the tag setting of D:4 for the first note, and the pitch window defined by the window anchor pitch B:3 and window height being the half-step height of the original melody with a small amount added for variation.

```
from transformation.harmonictranscription.t_harmonic_transcription import THarmonic-
Transcription

source_expression = '{<C-Natural: i> q@C:4 iEb <C-Natural: C-It> F# G Ab C ' \
                    '<C-Melodic: V> iB:3}'

t_sub = THarmonicTranscription.create(source_expression)

target_harmonic_list = [('A-Melodic:iv', Duration(3, 4)),
                        ('A-Natural:i', Duration(1, 4)),
                        ('A-Melodic:V', Duration(1, 8))]
target_hct = build_hct(target_harmonic_list)

tag_map = {0: DiatonicPitch.parse('D:4')}
results = t_sub.apply(target_hct, 'B:3', tag_map, t_sub.height + 5, 100)

results_filter = MinContourFilter(t_sub.source_line, results.pitch_results)
scored_filtered_results = results_filter.scored_results
```

We call out a couple of items that the careful reader may consider pursuing further:

- MinContourFilter is a transform result ranking filter based on minimizing per result the chromatic distances between successive notes as compared to same for the original melody. There are no substantive criteria based on musical qualities, e.g., abnormal jumps, selection of chordal tone/pitch. This is an area the reader my find interesting to explore.

- The logic for build_hct() can be found in the source code. It simply creates an hct and fills in the harmonic contexts.

Our next example is from the 4th movement of the Schubert A Major piano sonata, D.959. We provide the melody, and a simple annotated harmony in Fig. 18.11.

Fig. 18.11 Schubert A Major D.959, 4th movement theme (base provided by author).

As an example of harmonic transcription, we imitate the harmony but in C-Major and use a simple set of chords throughout as in Fig. 18.12.

Fig. 18.12 Fig. 18.11 in harmonic transcription to C-Major.

The code for this example of harmonic transcription is like the prior example:

```
source_expression = '{<A-Major: I> qC#:4 hE qa <:V> qA G# <:I> hA <:ii> q@B iB ' \
                    '<E-Major :viiHalfDim7> qC#:5 A:4 <A-Major:I> hA ig# f# e d}'

t_sub = THarmonicTranscription.create(source_expression)

target_harmonic_list = [('C-Major:I', Duration(1)),
                        ('C-Major:IV', Duration(1, 2)),
                        ('C-Major:V', Duration(1, 2)),
                        ('C-Major:vi', Duration(1, 2)),
                        ('C-Major:V', Duration(1, 2)),
                        ('C-Major:I', Duration(1)),
                        ]
target_hct = build_hct(target_harmonic_list)

tag_map = {0: DiatonicPitch.parse('C:4')}

results = t_sub.apply(target_hct, 'B:3', tag_map, t_sub.height + 5, 100)

results_filter = MinContourFilter(t_sub.source_line, results.pitch_results)
scored_filtered_results = results_filter.scored_results
```

The transform specifies the new set of harmonic contexts. The first note is tagged to C:4 to establish the register. Many results are generated, and as alluded to earlier, filtering based on musical criteria would be an improvement for overall selection.

One can have fun changing harmony and constraints around, even violating traditional harmonic sequencing rules as in Fig. 18.13.

Fig. 18.13 Fig. 18.11 in harmonic transcription.

The harmony for the example in Fig. 18.13 is given by:

```
target_harmonic_list = [('C-Major:V', Duration(3, 4)),
                        ('C-Major:IV', Duration(1, 4)),
                        ('C-Major:I', Duration(1)),
                        ('C-Major:IV', Duration(1, 2)),
                        ('C-Major:I', Duration(1, 2)),
                        ('C-Major:V', Duration(1)),
                       ]
```

The point behind this last example is that the transform does not require observing the original melody's harmonic context time boundaries/durations. However, it is required that the new harmony fully cover the duration of the given melody. While it is fun to play around with differing harmonic sequences, there is no guarantee that the resulting music will be good, only that to a greater than less degree, the melody will adhere to the proposed harmony. The rest of the process, to get the desired sound, is 'musical craft'.

Our last example is an application of the harmonic transcription transform to the Mozart piano sonata in G Major, KV283. Measures 8-10 are show in Fig. 18.14.

Fig. 18.14 Mozart piano sonata in G Major, KV283, 1ˢᵗ movement, measures 8-10.

The author has modified the bass with a simple harmony with an analysis.

This example has more notes than the prior examples and in that sense is longer. We again show how modification with a diversity of chords can have interesting results. The code follows:

```
source_expression = '{<G-Major: I> sD:5 E F# G A B C:6 D <:IV> sC:6 B:5 A G F# E D C
<:I> \
                      sB:4 D:5 B:4 G <:VDom7> A C:5 A:4 F#   <:I> qG}'
t_sub = THarmonicTranscription.create(source_expression)
target_harmonic_list = [('G-Melodic:v', Duration(1, 2)),
                        ('D-Natural:i', Duration(1, 2)),
                        ('D-Major:V', Duration(1, 4)),
                        ('D-Major:IV', Duration(1, 4)),
                        ('A-Melodic:i', Duration(1, 4))
                       ]
target_hct = build_hct(target_harmonic_list)

tag_map = {0: DiatonicPitch.parse('D:5')}
results = t_sub.apply(target_hct, 'F#:4', tag_map, t_sub.height + 4, 20,
                tunnel_half_interval=Interval(3, IntervalType.Major))

results_filter = MinContourFilter(t_sub.source_line, results.pitch_results)
scored_filtered_results = results_filter.scored_results
```

This code is interesting for two reasons. First the new harmonic context sequence has diversity in key and modality types, even measure to measure. The second aspect concerns the half tunnel variance specification. One of the issues with the constraint engine is that when the search space is too large, the search gets trapped in building subsequences of the new melody. Even though the combined tag map and window height is relatively tight, it is not until the tunnel half variance height of a major 3rd interval is specified that solutions appear.

One of the results is shown in Fig. 18.15. Notice that while the transform attempts to secure a scalar nature for the runs, it nonetheless introduces disruptive jumps. Also, the different chord specifications and modality types imposed a different feeling to the measures. Despite these differences, having a result like this provides interesting melodic fuel for composition.

Fig. 18.15 The Mozart music of Fig. 18.14 modified harmonically as described above.

This example leads to an interesting aspect of constraint fitting. Here, one might attempt to eliminate the jumps in the scalar passages by specifying motifs using the StepSequenceConstraint constraint. The problem with this is, for example, that the 6th note in the original melody, B:5, is flagged as chordal by melodic analysis. That limits the 6th note in the modified melody to tones D, F#, or A. However, there are no scalar paths from the first note, fixed to D:5, to any pitch of any of those tones on the 6th note! Consequently, no solutions arise. This example speaks to the difficulty of using constraints for transformation, and that it can be easy, through good intentions, to specify conflicting constraints.

18.6 Final Thoughts

The harmonic transcription transform is in many ways only a beginning to a much more extensive and useful transform. Several features could greatly improve its utility including:

- Allowing for scalar and non-scalar constraints. This includes requesting, for example, that a scalar pitch be 'flatted' or 'sharped' away from its tonality.

- Allowing limits on distances on jumps within a contour, disallowing for example jumps over a perfect 5th, or an octave.

- Overriding constraints created through the melodic analysis. For example, a note can be analyzed as chordal, when in fact its scalar property is only required by the melody.

- Allowing the specification of chordal pitch role, for example being a root, 3rd, 5th, or any other tension, or any one of a possibility thereof through constraints.

- Developing better filters for solution ranking that are more aligned with musical qualities such as voice leading and melodic flow.

- Developing a rule analysis step to locate easily detectable rule conflicts that result in no solutions.

Some of these suggestions can be absorbed into the melodic analysis, which rightfully is an important topic standing on its own. For example, scalar sequences could be detected during analysis for constraints that could retain them as scalar sequences, and not rely on these sequences to be qualified as motifs. The same could be said for arpeggios and the order sequence in which chordal notes are placed in an arpeggio.

There are many possibilities for extending and positioning this transform as a compositional tool. One can imagine a kind of interactive tool for harmonic transcription. This tool could be based a combination of harmonic transcription and reshape. The user would incrementally improve upon the music composition through simple shaping gestures and chord selections, and letting the transforms provide choices that meet the user's intentions.

19 Retrograde: Reversing a Melody

Reversing a theme, motif, or melody as a generative technique for composition ideas is an important tool in a composer's toolbox. The idea behind it is simple. For a given melody, motif, or theme, move each note from the end in turn and move it to the beginning proceeding forward.

In classical music, perhaps the best example of the retrograde usage can be found in Haydn's Symphony 47. In the minuet one finds the theme shown in Fig. 19.1:

Fig. 19.1 Haydn's Symphony 47 Minuet al Roverso.

This is followed immediately with the theme in reverse as shown in Fig. 19.2

Fig. 19.2 Haydn's Symphony 47, reversal of Fig. 19.1.

In the following sections we look closely at retrograde as a music transform. We consider not just how to produce retrograde results of existing music, but analyze issues associated with retrograde. We describe the technical approach, the api, and conclude with examples and final thoughts.

19.1 Introduction

The reader is advised to review section 6.3.3 regarding an algorithm to reverse a melodic line. That algorithm serves as a basis for melody reversal in this chapter.

We begin with the simple example in Fig. 19.3.

Fig. 19.3 Sample melody

D. P. Pazel, *Music Representation and Transformation in Software*, https://doi.org/10.1007/978-3-030-97472-5_19

This is a simple melody in C-Major. Ignoring harmony for now, let's consider its retrograde shown in Fig. 19.4.

Fig. 19.4 Sample melody from Fig. 19.3 in retrograde.

Overall, the result is quite good as a melody. Critically, one could complain that the initial C:4 may be too long in duration. Also, the jump from D:5 to G:4 on entry to the last measure might be judged too large. However, it has potential for use. Clearly, for this example, the retrograde process is not difficult and the result works out well musically which, as we discuss, cannot be generally presumed for retrograde usage.

As a general melodic construction apparatus, retrograde may not be so accommodating. The following are some practical issues in using melody reversal in composition.

1. **Chordal Note Issues:** Reversing a phrase of 4 eighth notes, for example, many times leads to a case where the chordal notes now become non-chordal, and vice versa. That means that using the original harmony, even when reversed, may not sound well paired with the reversed melody.

2. **Off-Beat Issues:** In many cases a melody begins off-beat, that is, the melody begins the initial beat with a rest. Reversing melody in these cases can lead to a sense of unintended incompleteness in the melody. See Fig. 19.5.

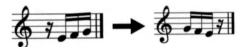

Fig. 19.5 Awkwardness in off-beat reposition.

3. **Asymmetric Boundaries:** Melodies often do not lie fully and aligned within measure boundaries. Often there may be an up-beat to start, and further a melody may end well into a measure. Further the duration of up-beat can be different from the duration on end measure overrun making the melody an asymmetrical retrofit into the music. Reversing a melody with these characteristics is totally off-sync measure-wise and likely beat-wise, especially if the intention is a full in-situ replacement of the original melody.

4. **Harmonic Anomalies:** Just as the melody is reversed, it would be tempting to simply reverse the harmony. While that may work in some cases, in-situ harmonic reversal has several issues. First, the original melody may be in a different key at its end than at start, which when reversed would be an abrupt key change at the start of the reversed melody with the preceding music. The same goes for the succeeding music. Second, typical modulation formulae reversed become very atypical if not rare, e.g., IV V/V V now becomes V V/V IV. If the intention of using secondary chords is key change, the reversal can be problematic to the remainder of the music.

Some issues are exacerbated by trying to use a reversed harmony as a replacement to the original in situ harmony. Part of dealing with these issues is addressing the context for using retrograde, and further setting one's expectations in its usage.

One can for example simply reverse the melody only, ignoring the harmony, and use the reversed melody as fresh melodic material. However, one can use the reversal melody and attempt to use it reversed harmony, warts and all, and use it as fresh melodic material complete with that harmony. One can adapt the reversed melody to the original harmony using harmonic transcription. For that matter, a new harmony can be devised for the melody reversal and adapted using harmonic transcription. The point is that there are many ways to deal with melodic reversal and harmony head-on, largely away from the music context from which it is extracted.

However one attempts to adapt a harmony to the reversed melody there is the additional issue of understanding that beat roles could have changed, and worse, note chordal role designations may now occur on awkward beats.

19.2 The Retrograde Transform

The retrograde transform is developed in a context removed from composition editing. That is, we do not assume a reversed melody is to be implanted in-situ actively by this transform. That is considered an editing issue. We do provide a means for either retaining the original harmony or reversing it, as a convenience for the user using harmonic transcription. If the user wants to use a different harmony, that can be applied post retrograde using harmonic transcription. Finally, an option is provided for adapting the reversed melody to the original harmony. However, we believe that is of limited help, and is merely a user convenience.

19.2.1 The Retrograde Transform Design

The design of the retrograde transform is relatively simple and is largely a re-packaging of the melodic reversal technique described in section 6.3.3, along with a few options for dealing with harmony.

The transform's details are outlined in Fig. 19.6. In the first step, the original line and hct are reversed. Then three cases are considered:

1. Reverse harmony: Return the reversed line and the reversed harmony. No transcription is necessary.

2. Original harmony and no transcription: Return the reversed line and the original harmony

3. Original harmony and transcription: Apply harmonic transcription to the reversed line with the original harmony. Return the transcribed reversed line and the original harmony.

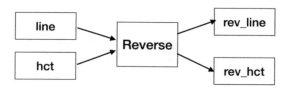

Case: reverse harmony
  return rev_line, rev_hct

Case: no reverse harmony and no transcription
  return rev_line, hct

Case: no reverse harmony and transcription:
  trans_rev_line, _ = transcribe(rev_line, hct)
  return trans_rev_line, hct

Fig. 19.6 Retrograde transform logic

To clarify the third case, a set of transcribed results, based on the reversed line and original harmony, is filtered for best candidate result using MinContourFilter. That best result of reversed melody line along with the original harmony is returned.

19.2.2 The Retrograde Transform API

The retrograde transform api follows the same invocation pattern introduced in the other transforms, namely, a create/apply invocation pattern. The constructor takes only one argument:

- **score**: The input music from which we extract retrograde passages is represented as a LiteScore, see Section 12.3.

The apply() method takes the following arguments:

- **reverse_harmony**: True indicates that the input harmony should be reversed for retrograde results.

- **time_interval**: A numeric interval that cites the whole note time bounds of the music to be extracted in retrograde.

- **transcription**: means that only when we do not reverse_harmony, transcribe the melody to the original harmony using the harmonic transcription transform. Default is True.

- **result_sample_size**: This is the maximum number of solutions that harmonic transcription should generate when the harmony is not reversed. MinContourFilter is used to find the melody that "best matches" the contour of the original reversed melody to fit the original harmony. The larger this number the more computer time and resources are taken.

The return value is a pair consisting of the reversed melody as a line, and the hct as determined by the specified arguments. To clarify, only the section of music bounded by the time interval is returned in retrograde. In the case where the harmony is not reversed and transcription is specified, the result is the top solution as determined by MinContourFilter using the result_sample_size argument.

Note that in the case where transcription is used (again, only if the harmony is not reversed), to facilitate processing, a tag map is made of the first note to the closest matching chord tone of the harmony. This is an optimization step that greatly reduces processing time. The user may change the code and/or simply pass None for the tag map.

To bypass the transcription feature, simply pass reverse_harmony=False and transcription=False. That way the user can do their own harmonic transcription or other harmonization.

19.3 Examples

Our first example considers the melody given at the start of this chapter, along with a very simply harmony. See Fig. 19.7.

Fig. 19.7 Simple melody before retrograding.

Fig. 19.8 shows both the melody and harmony reversed.

Fig. 19.8 Reversed melody and harmony of example in Fig. 19.7.

With no transcription applied, the harmonic match is very good. This is not so much of a surprise since the harmonies align to the same melodic sections as in the original. However, as discussed earlier, that is not always the case.

The code producing this result is[61]:

```
from transformation.retrograde.t_retrograde import TRetrograde

source_instance_expression = '{<C-Major:I> qC:4 D E G <:v> [iD:5 B:4 A G] qC:5 D ' \
                             '<:IV> A:4 iF E hC}'
lite_score = create_score(source_instance_expression, 'piano', (4, 4, 'swww'))

trans = TRetrograde(lite_score)
reversed_line, hct = trans.apply()
```

Finally, we look at this example with the original harmony applied with transcription in Fig. 19.9. Again, not a bad a result, but not the best either. One can observe melodic adjustments between this and the former example, because of the adaptation to the different harmony.

Fig. 19.9 Reversed melody transcribed to original harmony of example in Fig. 19.7.

---

[61] Again, ignore the code for beat specification, i.e., 'swww', which is not covered in this text.

The difference in coding for this example is:

```
reversed_line, hct = trans.apply(False, results_sample_size=500)
```

A more dynamic example comes from a Mozart piano sonata in G-Major, KV283, first movement which we have seen earlier and is shown again in Fig. 19.10. The author has provided a slightly altered harmony to enhance the demonstration of the retrograde transform.

Fig. 19.10 Mozart piano sonata G-Major, KV283, m. 8-9.

Retrograde appears to be most interesting when applied to these types of passages with sweeping scalar or chordal lines. The result of reversing both melody and harmony is shown in Fig. 19.11.

Fig. 19.11 Retrograde melody and harmony of example in Fig. 19.10.

The code for this example is like that presented earlier.

```
source_instance_expression = '{<G-Major:I> sD:5 E F# G A B C:6 D <:IV> C ' \
            'B:5 A G <:VDom7> sF# E D C <:I> B:4 D:5 B:4 G <:VDom7> A C:5 A:4 F# }'
lite_score = create_score(source_instance_expression, 'piano', (3, 4, 'sww'))

trans = TRetrograde(lite_score)
# melody is reversed, harmony is reversed; we do not re-fit the melody to harmony
reversed_line, hct = trans.apply()
```

Finally, as in our first example, we take aim at retaining the old harmony and applying harmonic transcription. See Fig. 19.12.

Fig. 19.12 Retrograde melody transcribed to original harmony in Fig. 19.10

Notice the melodic adjustment made relative to the harmony, as well as the retention of the contour line. While the results are adequate, it appears that the chordal designation of off-beat notes force uneven scalar lines.

19.4 Final Thoughts

Retrograde is likely the most amusing transform presented in this book. Listening to and examining reversed melodies is a great way to uncover new compositional melodic material.

Unfortunately, retrograde is also one of the more problematic transforms for all the reasons mentioned earlier, and as such is less suited for music content replacement or augmentation in the context of an existing composition. Perhaps the most problematic aspect of retrograde concerns the attribution of chordal notes. And whether the harmony is reversed or not, this leads to awkwardness in fitting the melody to harmony.

Readers or adventurous programmers could enhance the transform to accept different harmonic lines or rules for altering chordal note specification, provide different filtering methods, more deliberative automated adjustment, and the like to make for more practical results.

20 Melodic Search and Pattern Substitution

Most if not all document or text editor users are surely familiar with a "find" or "search" feature used to find all instances of a specified text. Similarly, most editor users are familiar with the associated "replace" feature. This feature allows one to swap out, for example, an incorrect word spelling for a correct spelling, using found instances of the incorrect spelling as a guide. In that way corrections are made throughout a document either in one operation or in incremental operations over each incorrect instance.

In this chapter we explore how to define and implement features like "find" and "replace" in the context of musically notated scores. Find and replace are much more complex in a music score setting. As an example, consider searching for a melodic figure, e.g., a simple ascending scalar sequence of sixteenth notes. That melodic figure or one that resembles it (in a sense that will be defined later) may occur in many places in a score but in different tonalities including different modalities and/or modes than the original tonality. Also, one may find a fragment that is to a degree "close" structurally to the search melody but not precisely the same. So, while melodic search is generally like word search, it is more akin to word search allowing for varied spelling, language, and possibly even ambiguous semantics.

Replace is similarly complex. A musical section to be replaced has a harmonic context (tonality and chord) that can be quite varied, requiring the replacement to adapt to a different tonality and harmony. Following the argument above, it's as if in a word processor, each replacement may need to be translated to a different language, based on the language context of the found instance.

In this chapter, we discuss aspects of melodic search and replace (we use the term "pattern substitution"). Observe that melodic search is not a transformation in the sense of the prior chapters, but pattern substitution is transformative. However, pairing these operations is reasonable in a comprehensive music editing discussion. Because these two topics, although related, can be discussed separately, this chapter discusses search and pattern substitution in two sections. Each section considers definition and algorithmic solutions, along with examples.

Because of the complex nature of this topic, the discussion will be limited to several elemental aspects of search and pattern substitution. Further elaboration for consideration in found in the final thoughts section 20.4.

20.1 Melodic Search

A search algorithm for a melodic fragment in a music score involves many nuanced considerations. Putting harmony aside, two melodies can be considered the same even if note per note they are not an exact match. Among considerations is that corresponding consecutive pitches may not have the same degrees of jump, i.e., on the original a note pair may be a perfect 4th apart and on a search candidate,

D. P. Pazel, *Music Representation and Transformation in Software*, https://doi.org/10.1007/978-3-030-97472-5_20

a perfect 5th. For another note, it's tone may be the same as the original note, but in a different register, upper or lower to the original.

Also, one melody may be in a different tonality, modality, or mode from the other. Corresponding notes may differ in harmonic function in that one note may be chordal and the other not. One may be scalar and the other not, and so forth. That is to say that stringent key, modality, or mode identity may not be issues in claiming similarity. For example, an upbeat melody from a major tonality would certainly be considered similar to a sad version of the same melody in a minor tonality.

On the other hand, there are some reasonable qualifications to saying that two melodies are the 'same' (in our discussion, we use the term **homologous**). We expect them to have the same number of notes and note per note we expect them to have the identical durations. Chiefly though, we expect them to sound alike in as much as the two melodies rise and fall the same way. In other terms corresponding note pairs rise or fall together, but not necessarily by identical amounts. Picking up from the harmonic transcription discussion, we say the melodies share a contour.

To provide a more concrete example, consider the melody in Fig. 20.1 in the context of using it as a search pattern in a musical score.

Fig. 20.1 A melodic search pattern.

In searching for this melody in a variety of musical contexts, one could easily consider each measure in Fig. 20.2 homologous to that in Fig. 20.1:

Fig. 20.2 Varied matches to the melodic search pattern in Fig. 20.1.

Notice the variety in pitch jumps, notation style, and even modality changes. Yet each has a striking aural if not visual similarity to the example melody.

Regarding harmony, we don't expect the harmonies of two homologous melodies to match be it root tone for root tone, nor for modality for modality, nor mode for mode. We further do not expect them to match on chord or even relative chord, e.g., for two corresponding chords in search and target instances, one could be a ii and the other a IV. The point behind saying this is that the harmonies, including chords, could be vastly different for two melodies, but the melodies stand homologous nonetheless that in a melodic search, we could still consider such instances as "finds".

To simplify technical presentation here though, we make a couple of assumptions. One is that homologous melodies match in the number of notes and note for note in offset and duration. This is only to simplify discussion. There is no reason to retain such restriction for melodic search. For example, one melody could be quarter notes, and the other in eights.

Another restriction on our approach to search is that the sets of harmonic contexts for two homologous melodies must match in durations, except for the first and last that accounts for pickups and melodic overruns over final measures. While this restriction is not necessary for search per se, we find later that it is important for the replace operation using pattern substitution.

We also assume for our discussion that the search pattern uses a Line to define the notes of the search melody, and a HarmonicContextTrack that specifies the harmony of the search pattern. Throughout this chapter, we refer to these as the *pattern line* and the *pattern hct*. Matching instances are called *targets*.

20.1.1 Melodic Search Options

Taking the considerations from the last section into account, melodic search specification can be very nuanced. Consequently, we opt for specific conditions. For example, one may want an exact find on the melody as given in the pattern line, one may or may not care if scalar notes match scalar degree on target instances, or that chordal notes remain chordal. Towards that end, several options affecting search are defined with the user having the discretion of selecting exactly how the search should be executed.

The following is a list of options regarding note matching on patterns to target that aid the user in specifying the kind of search results desired. These define policies for pattern to target match.

- **note_match_scalar_precision:** scalar tones must match on scalar degree.

- **note_match_chordal:** chordal tones must remain chordal.

- **note_match_chordal_precision:** matching chording tones must have same chordal interval.

- **note_match_non_scalar_precision:** non-scalars must match on interval to tonality root tone.

- **note_match_non_scalar_to_scalar:** allows pattern non-scalar notes to match to scalar notes in target.

- **structural_match:** pattern and target notes must match in beaming, including tuplets.

Similarly, there are options regarding how the pattern and target harmonic contexts should match:

- **hct_match_tonality_key_tone:** pattern and target harmonic contexts must match on specified key tone, but not necessarily on modality.

- **hct_match_tonality_modality:** pattern and target harmonic contexts must match on modality but not necessarily key tone.

- **hct_match_relative_chord:** pattern and target harmonic contexts must match on chord degree relative to tonalities.

The number of options is surprisingly large, and one might add to the list. This points out the many nuances behind melodic search, and that the user of melodic search needs to be quite aware and definitive in what is being asked for in specifying a search.

The many search options for melodic and hct matching are consolidated into a single Python object called GlobalSearchOptions. Doing so makes it easier to track what settings can be and are made. The constructor shows the full set and their default settings.

```
class GlobalSearchOptions(object):

    def __init__(self, structural_match=True,
             hct_match_tonality_key_tone=False,
             hct_match_tonality_modality=False,
             hct_match_relative_chord=False,
             note_match_scalar_precision=False,
```

```
        note_match_chordal=False,
        note_match_chordal_precision=False,
        note_match_non_scalar_precision=False,
        note_match_non_scalar_to_scalar=False):
```

For a melodic search, an instance of this is created and specified in the search.

20.1.2 Melodic Search Technical Details

The level of technical detail involved in melodic is large but straight-forward. So instead of detailing the search algorithm in fine detail, we instead focus on search's larger structural details, and significant details.

Search Setup

The concepts of pattern line and pattern hct were introduced earlier as the input line and hct describing what is being looked for in the search operation. These are the arguments to the MelodicSearch object constructor and saved as object variables as pattern_line and pattern_hct properties. The constructor processes an analysis on the pattern data that details the finer elements of its structure commensurate with melodic search. Melodic search analysis was touched upon earlier in the discussion of harmonic transcription in section 18.2. Briefly there are three collections of information:

- **Note Information:** Per note in pattern line, the scale degree, interval with chord in harmonic context if chordal, interval to key tone, and duration.

- **Note Pair Information:** Per sequential note pairs, their whole note time position difference, the interval between them, and their comparative pitch relationship, e.g., $<$, $==$, $>$. This information captures the melodic contour information.

- **Harmonic Context Information:** Per pattern harmonic context, the duration and relative chord degree to tonality

The results of this analysis are captured in the MelodicSearchAnalysis object that is a convenient service object used throughout melodic search. It is created in the MelodicSearch constructor and used in successive searches. This approach encourages reuse of a complex object, as well as allows one to easily make minor search specification changes through global search options for later search executions[62].

Melodic search is performed by the search() method which takes target_line and target_hct as input arguments. These constitute the notes and harmonic contexts upon which to search for instances of the pattern. It also takes all the search option settings, instantiated and unified in a GlobalSearchOptions object.

Search Algorithm Overview

There are several ways to approach melodic search. One way is to start with note-by-note comparisons of pattern to target input source, and on failure start on succeeding notes. This approach starts a new search on each note and can be wasteful. The approach we discuss is to initially start with searching the target_hct for matches with the pattern_hct, and for each match, see if the notes associated with the target line match note-per-note with the pattern per search options.

The search algorithm is as follows:

---

[62] One should not construe this to mean that one can change search options while a search is executing.

```
def search(self, target_line, target_hct, search_options=GlobalSearchOptions()):
    target_hc_count = 0

    position_answers = list()

    while True:
        hc_start = self.search_hct_incrementally(target_hct, target_hc_count,
                                                 search_options)
        if hc_start is None:
            break
        search_answers = self.search_notes(target_line, target_hct, hc_start[1],
                                            search_options)
        target_hc_count = target_hc_count + 1 if search_answers is None or \
                                        len(search_answers) == 0 \
                                        else hc_start[1] + 1
        if search_answers is not None and len(search_answers) != 0:
            position_answers.extend(search_answers)

    return position_answers
```

This top-level algorithm is clear. The algorithm scans across the target_hct for a full match on the pattern_hct incrementally (once per iteration), and for each match, it attempts a match of the pattern_line notes to the notes on the matched hct segment. If so, the algorithm adds the starting (whole note time) position of the match to the answer list. The target_hct index is bumped appropriately. The method's return value is a list of starting (whole note time) positions of matches.

Finer Details

As mentioned, melodic search is generally a straight-forward process, but there is with much detail below the guiding algorithm presented. In fact, for the sake of improved clarity, the search_notes() method breaks into two similar methods depending on whether or not the pattern_hct is singular (only one harmonic context) or not. That break-down was made for clarity purposes only. Observe that search_notes() delivers a list of matching offsets and not a singular value. As an example, a source matching on an hct with a single hc can have multiple pattern matches at the note level within that hct.

Putting that aside, there are a few details in search that are of interest, and the point of this section is to bring them to attention and discuss some of their details.

HCT Match:

As noted above, the search algorithm is driven by complete matches of the pattern hct in the target hct in the method search_hct_incrementally(). This drives the search process, as with each match, the notes in that part of the target are checked against the pattern notes.

The algorithm in the method search_hct_incrementally() is as follow. We are given the target hct and a start index (target_hc_start_index) into that hc list. Then there are two cases:

1) The pattern HCT is singular, i.e., it has only one hc:

In this case, loop over the target_hct starting with target_hc_start_index and look for the first target hc whose duration is greater or equal to that of the pattern and the global harmonic context search options are met and return that position. This case is special as the pattern starts somewhere in that hc.

2) The pattern hct consists of multiple hc's:

This case is a little more complex. It starts with the same kind of match as with the singular case above, ensuring the first matched hc's duration is greater or equal to the pattern's first hc's duration. However, the last hc of the matched target must have a duration larger than or equal to the last pattern hc's duration. For all other pattern hc's, those hc's must match on duration with the target. In all cases, the target hc's must meet the global hc global search options. See Fig. 20.3.

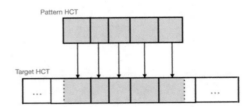

Fig. 20.3 Matching pattern HCT to target HCT.

Structural Match:

In our introductory example, we pointed out how notes can match in pattern search without accounting for beaming depth. If structural_match is set in the global options, then the pattern and target notes must match in their beaming containment structures consisting of beams and tuplets.

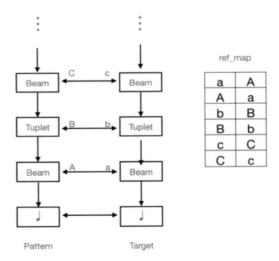

Fig. 20.4 Structural match.

The check for equal containment is relatively easy. See Fig. 20.4. The idea is that, assuming we have the pattern and target notes in order with the name number of pattern and target notes, we simply take pairs of notes, pattern and target, and follow their parentage as far as we can.

There are complications that arise in tracking parentage identity between these two distinct structures. That is handled with a Python dict (ref_map) mapping one structural element, e.g., beam, to the other. If any discrepancies are found along the way, the pattern and target do not match; otherwise, they do. For details, reference the method note_structural_check() in the file melodic_search.py

Pattern Contour Check:

The melodic analysis on the pattern line yields information about sequential pairs of notes and among other information, their relative pitch relationship, e.g., equal, less than, greater than. As part of the note-for-note checks of the pattern relative to target, sequential pairs of target notes are checked for the same pitch relationship as their corresponding pattern note pairs.

20.1.3 Melodic Search API

The api for melodic search is relatively simple. Like the transform api's presented thus far, the focus is on the constructor and a special method, in this case the search() method. The constructor for MelodicSearch takes the following arguments:

- **pattern_line:** The input Line object that only contains the melodic pattern.
- **pattern_hct:** The corresponding harmonic context track for the pattern_line.

The search() method has the following arguments:

- **target_line:** The target line object over which to search.
- **target_hct:** The target harmonic context track over which to search.
- **search_options:** The GlobalSearchOptions object whose setting are observed for the call to search()

The search method returns a list of starting positions (as Position objects) in whole note time, each of which corresponds to the beginning of a found instance of the pattern line/hct on the target line/hct.

20.1.4 Melodic Search Examples

Consider the search pattern in Fig. 20.5. This is a simple melody spanning two keys, first in C-Major, followed by G-Major.

Fig. 20.5 Search Pattern.

We use this as the input pattern in a melodic search using default search arguments on Fig. 20.6.

Fig. 20.6 Search target for pattern in Fig. 20.5.

The search is set up with the following code:

```
from search.melodicsearch.global_search_options import GlobalSearchOptions
from search.melodicsearch.melodic_search import MelodicSearch

lge = LineGrammarExecutor()
pattern = '{<C-Major: I> qC:4 D}'
target = '{qC:4 D <E-Major: v> F# <Ab-Minor: ii> Bb C Db <D-Major: I> D E F#}'
target_line, target_hct = lge.parse(target)

search = MelodicSearch.create(pattern)
answers = search.search_hct(target_hct, GlobalSearchOptions())
```

The result 'answers' is simply a list of position matches. In this case there is one match at Position(1, 2), i.e., at a ½ note into the music. Essentially no matching is done on the HCT, e.g., tonality key- tone. The default search is for contour and structural match.

Alternatively, suppose we want a precise match on tonality key tone on the target in Fig. 20.7.

Fig. 20.7 Search target for pattern in Fig. 20.5 but with search on tonality.

The code difference is:

```
answers = search.search(target_line, target_hct,
                        GlobalSearchOptions(hct_match_tonality_key_tone=True))
```

The result is a successful search with Position(1, 2) as an answer. The reader can verify that there is no answer when searching against the prior target with these conditions.

20.2 The Melodic Pattern Substitution Transform

We turn our attention to the melodic pattern substitution transform. As mentioned, we couched this topic along with search because of their logical and strategic kinship. Most search paradigms found in software tools properly have a substitution/replacement capability, i.e., search and replace. While the two are often paired in application, they can be seen as separate capabilities with melodic pattern substitution discussed separately from search. Our discussion positions melodic pattern substitution as an extension of melodic search. In the following, we describe what we mean by the melodic pattern substitution transform, the approach taken to implement it, the api, and finally examples.

20.2.1 The Foundations of Melodic Pattern Substitution

Much as in our discussion of melodic search, pattern substitution is more complex and nuanced than one might find in other search/replace paradigms. In discussing search, we saw that 'found instances' of the search pattern can be in different tonalities or use different chords than the search pattern, or that while having matching melodic contours the notes may have quite different intervallic relationships to each other. This complicates the issue of how the replacement pattern could be altered towards generating a replacement instance for a found search instance, so that the replacement instance 'makes sense' in its surrounding musical context, e.g., harmony.

We start by introducing foundational elements and terminology for melodic pattern substitution. In melodic search, we have a pattern on which to match. In melodic pattern substitution, we have a pattern that acts as a replacement for each match. So, in this introduction we have:

- **search_pattern:** This defines the melody fragment (and accompanying harmony) for which we search. It has a melody and harmony, which we identify as **search_pattern_line** and **search_pattern_hct** respectively.

- **replacement_pattern:** For each instance of a matched search pattern, the replacement pattern is used as a basis to replace the match. It also has a melody and a harmony, which we identify as **replacement_pattern_line** and **replacement_pattern_hct**.

The search process has already been covered in section 20.1.2. We assume that the search takes place, and each 'find' or found instance, one at a time, is passed to the substitution process described here for replacement. With that in mind, the substitution process has:

- **search_instance:** This term refers to a 'found' instance in a search process using the search_pattern, on some piece of music. As in the above, it also has a melody and a harmony which we identify as **search_instance_line** for the melody and **search_instance_hct** for the harmony.

With this terminology we can now define what melodic pattern substitution means. See Fig. 20.8.

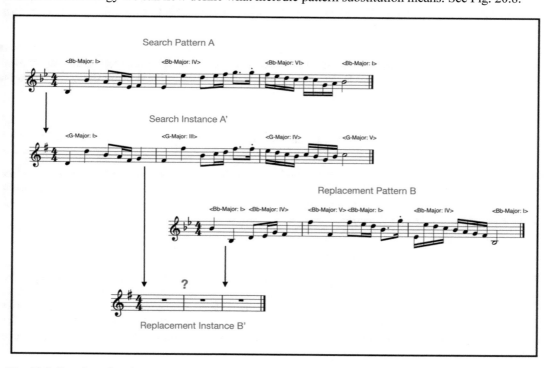

Fig. 20.8 Search and replacement process diagram.

Starting with a search pattern A, we find a search instance A'. A' is a musical segment found in a containing musical piece. B is a provided replacement pattern. The idea is that B will be applied to A' to build a replacement instance B' for A'. The key question in replacement/substitution is "Precisely what should replace A' in the musical piece?".

When likening to word search, B itself would be the replacement as is. However, A' not only has an approximating melody to A, but potentially a different harmony to A, and to B for that matter. So, B could have an entirely different tonality from A'. A wholesale replacement of A' by B itself would likely not fit contextually to its surrounding. So, what should the **replacement instance** B' be?

20.2.2   An Approach to Melodic Pattern Substitution

As we can see, melodic substitution is an entirely different kind of substitution than, say, in word substitution, in that the resulting replacement instance should contextually fit in place of the search instance. It's not only that the harmony needs to be adjusted commensurate to the replacement instance's context. The replacement instance's melody must make sense with the replacement music's harmony. These are two important adaptations of B that should be made to replace A'. Thus,

$$B' = f(A', B) \qquad (20.1)$$

That is, the replacement instance B' is a function of A' and B. The question now becomes "what are the details behind f()?".

The approach we take to pattern substitution in this case is to develop a harmonic context track for B' and leverage harmonic transcription to produce the line for B'. Leveraging harmonic transcription does much of the heavy lifting in that respect.

Following this approach, consider the replacement instance's (B') harmony alone. To make contextual sense of this process, we start with a copy of B's hct and attempt to modify that hct as derivative from the harmony of A'. That is, for the B' hct, we specify a set of rules to build using the B hct based on the A' hct. In short,

$$B' = f(A', B, rules) \qquad (20.2)$$

The idea is that the harmonic contexts of the replacement instance B' is expressed as a function of the harmonic contexts of the search instance A' using a set of rules. f() then uses harmonic transcription in conjunction with the B melody to complete the replacement. We refer to these rules as harmonic context expressions or **HC expressions***.*

20.2.3   Harmonic Context Expression Rules

Referring again to Fig. 20.8, the objective in this section is to describe an approach for building an hct for B', the replacement instance. For our purposes, the number of harmonic contexts to construct for B' is equal to the number of them in the hct of B, i.e., len(B.hct). The search instance A', on the other hand, has as many harmonic contexts in its hct as does for the search pattern A, i.e., len(A.hct). In brief B' is constructed in structure identical to B, but harmonic context details of B' are derived from those of A'.

See Fig. 20.9. The hc's for A' are numbered and referenced @0, @1, ... With that notation, the hc's of A' are referenceable. The HC expressions which we discuss below allow one to construct the hc's for B' as a function of the hc's in A'.hct. The clear utility of the HC expressions is that they work by reference in terms of the harmony defined in the search instance. They also allow sufficient capability to do alterations of harmonic information as needed. We build the replacement instance's harmonic contexts, one by one. That is, we specify a rule set consisting of HC expressions, one each per harmonic context in the replacement instance.

For example, the rule for the first hc in B' is "@3-minor:@5". @3 here refers to the key tone in the third (0-based index) hc in A'. @5 referenced the chord in the fifth hc in A'. Suppose @3 is Ab and @5 is V, the rule reduces to "Ab-minor:V".

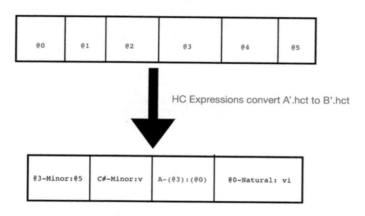

Search Instance A'.hct: len(A'.hct) == len(A.hct)

HC Expressions convert A'.hct to B'.hct

Replacement Instance B'.hct: len(B'.hct) == len(B.hct)

Fig. 20.9 HC expression conversion.

Harmonic context expressions can be quite expressive. Here are a few examples:

```
@0-Natural: vi      # Using HC 0 of search instance, take its key tone but as
                    # natural minor modality and use the vi chord
                    # making, for example, <G-Natural: vi>
@0:v                # HC 0 with chord v making, for example, <G-Major: V>.
(@0)P:5-Melodic:v   # Using HC 0 key tone, shift perfect fifth, as melodic minor
                    # and use a V chord making, for example, <D-Melodic: V>
```

The full replacement instance hct is initially a copy of the replacement pattern's hct. However, each harmonic context is replaced using the search instance's hct and a harmonic context expression. The replacement pattern's hct only provides the number of harmonic contexts and their durations and is otherwise of limited use. The remainder of the information comes from the search instance's hct and the expressions.

The syntax for an HC Expression is sketched here:

```
HC := Key Modality Chord
Key := (Abs_Key | Reference) (Key_Distance)?
Modality := (Abs_Modality | Reference) (Mode_Index)?
Chord := (Chord_Degree | Reference) (Chord_Name)?
```

A few aspects of the above are mentioned:

- Key, Modality, and Chord are referenceable from the search instance's hct, e.g., @5.

- The key can be modified with an interval specification, e.g., (@5)P:5 means a perfect 5th above the key tone specified on hc @5.

- A mode can be specified on the modality, e.g., (@4)(2) means use the modality from @4 but Dorian.

- The chord can be specified by reference, e.g. :@3

20.2.4 The Melodic Pattern Substitution API

The pattern substitution or TPatSub transformation is somewhat complicated by the number and types of arguments it takes. In Fig. 20.10 we present a data flow diagram outlining these arguments and the process of using this transformation.

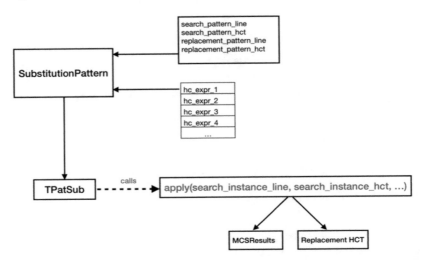

Fig. 20.10 TPatSub API data flow diagram

Most of the arguments are contained in the SubstitutionPattern object which serves as the sole argument to TPatSub. The argument to SubstitutionPattern include:

- **search_pattern_line:** The line used to do the search.

- **search_pattern_hct:** The hct used in the search.

- **replacement_pattern_line:** The line for the replacement pattern.

- **replacement_pattern_hct:** The hct for the replacement pattern.

- **hc-expression_list:** A list of HCExpressions for converting search instance hct's into replacement instance hct's.

The syntax for HCExpressions was covered earlier. To create in instance of HCExpression, merely pass a string representation as an argument to the HCExpression.create() command[63]. If one is interested in seeing an HCExpression producing an hc from a hct, look at its interpret() method. An example of creating an HCExpression and generating an hc is shown below:

---

[63] Alternatively one can use the HCExpression constructor which is a bit more complex than create(). The constructor is not covered in this text.

```
lge = LineGrammarExecutor()
# Build an hct from a grammar expression - do not need line in this case.
s = '{<C-Minor: I> C:4 <D-Major:IV> F A <Bb-Major:V> G D <C-Major:VI> a c b a}'
line, hct = lge.parse(s)


hce = HCExpression.create('(@1)M:6-(@0)')


hc = hce.interpret(hct.hc_list(), Duration(1, 2))
print(hc)

h.c.[B-MelodicMinor, TIVMaj [E, G#, B], 1/2]
```

After the TPatSub object is created, call the apply() method to get substitution results. The arguments to apply() are:

- **search_instance_line:** The search instance's line. Not used but passed for completeness.

- **search_instance_hct:** The search instance's hct, used in conjunction with the HCExpressions to produce a replacement hct.

Other arguments are used to control the harmonic transcription such as window_anchor_pitch, tag_map, window_height, and num_solutions (default as unlimited). We covered these earlier.

The apply() method returns MCSResults and the replacement hct. The user can scan and rank the results in MCSResults and choose one for proper substitution.

20.3 Examples

Consider the simple search pattern in Fig. 20.11:

Fig. 20.11 Simple search pattern.

and the replacement pattern in Fig. 20.12.

Fig. 20.12 Replacement pattern for search pattern in Fig. 20.11.

Recall that for every match on the search pattern, that search instance should be replaced with the replacement pattern adjusted to an hct generated from a combination of the search instance's hct and a set of harmonic context expressions. The following set of harmonic context expressions is used:

```
replacement_hc_expressions = [
    '@0:i',
    '@0:vi',
    '@0:v',
    '@0:i',
    '@0:iv',
    '@0:i',
]
```

These expressions pick up the key tone and tonality of the search instance's first hc (@0) and specifies a chord sequence for the replacement instance {i, vi, v, i, iv, i}.

Consider the search instance in Fig. 20.13.

Fig. 20.13 Search instance based on search pattern Fig. 20.11.

From several alternatives, we show the replacement instance in Fig. 20.14.

Fig. 20.14 Replacement instance for search instance in Fig. 20.13.

Notice that the chords follow the sequence define in the harmonic context expressions. While the resulting melody follows that of the replacement pattern, one can observer several anomalies, especially the larger-than-octave jump at the start of measure two. This could be corrected with the additions of octave constraints. The smoothing of the scale at the end could similarly be achieved with constraints. See section 18.6 for further ideas on improvement by way of further constraints using harmonic transcription.

The code for the above is:

```
t_pat_sub = TPatSub.create(pattern_expression, replacement_expression,
                           replacement_hc_expressions)

tag_map = {0: DiatonicPitch.parse('D:5')}

results, replacement_instance_hct = t_pat_sub.apply(replacement_instance_line,
                                                    replacement_instance_hct,
                                                    'C:4',
                                                    tag_map,
                                                    t_pat_sub.target_height,
                                                    200)
filter = MinContourFilter(t_pat_sub.substitution_pattern.target_pattern_line,
```

```
                              results.pitch_results)
scored_filtered_results = filter.scored_results
```

For a second example, we use the search pattern in Fig. 20.15.

Fig. 20.15 Second example search pattern.

This time the replacement pattern is more complex and shown in Fig. 20.16.

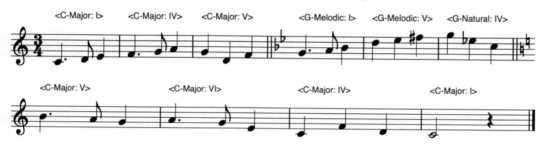

Fig. 20.16 Second example replacement pattern.

Note that this replacement pattern includes several key changes. We accommodate these changes across varied harmonic contexts with the following harmonic context expressions:

```
replacement_hc_expressions = [
    '@0:i',
    '@0:iv',
    '@0:v',
    '(@0)P:5-Melodic:i',
    '(@0)P:5-Melodic:v',
    '(@0)P:5-Natural:iv',
    '@0:v',
    '@0:vi',
    '@0:iv',
    '@0:i',
]
```

Notice that these expressions maintain the modality of the original replacement expressions but force the middle tonality a perfect fifth above the key tone of each search pattern instance. So, consider the search instance in Fig. 20.17.

Fig. 20.17 Search instance based on search pattern in Fig. 20.15.

Again, selecting from several alternatives, we show a replacement in Fig. 20.18.

Fig. 20.18 Replacement for search instance in Fig. 20.17.

The reader should play through this example to see if improvements could be made in the harmony, and how to translate those improvements into HCExpressions.

The code for this example is like that of the first example.

20.4 Final Thoughts

The paradigm outlined of search and replace on musical scores has a surprising number of details. For search alone, there are many options to consider in determining what is important in practice. Along that line, some issues and suggested improvements include:

- For the most part melodic contour search is the basis of melodic search. However, contour alone may be too loose a criterion in that it allows for selecting passages with too wide intervallic gaps. Perhaps a better solution is to amend contour search with a restriction of the size of the gaps, e.g., based on the search pattern for each gap, restrict the pitch search within adjacent intervals. For example, if two notes in the search pattern comprise an upward leap of a perfect fifth, restrict the search between a perfect fourth and minor sixth.

- Ensure the contour search respects scalar and arpeggiated passages. That is, analyze for pure scalar passages in the search pattern and ensure the search instance has a similar scalar passage. Same for note sequences following arpeggiation and octave leaps.

- Constraints based on a note being chordal should be produced with care. There are cases wherein a note is chordal by happenstance, say off-beat and not necessarily a requirement to the melody, and so should not be reflected as a search constraint.

This leads to a question regarding what default search behaviors should be assigned. The problem with having many options is that default search behavior become more difficult to define.

In pattern substitution, the introduction of HCExpressions fills a need to build a replacement harmonic contextual environment based on that of the search instance. Needless to say, while this is a big step forward addressing harmonic contextual issues, it may not be enough. Music is a craft that may need more contextual attention, including potentially a way to reference harmonic qualities of the replacement pattern itself, e.g., the chords, or potentially harmonic information surrounding but outside the search instance itself.

Also, the replacement instance contour construction based on transcription suffers from some of the same issues mentioned in the search criteria above. Pure contour matching criteria is too loose as a sole restricting factor in constructing replacements. Something more like intervallic restricts as mentioned earlier would be useful, as well as a stricter obeyance to scalar and arpeggiated patterns, if not others. These considerations may factor into reducing the transcription search.

Interested readers may want to speculate on or design a user interface for search and replace in a music notation editor. For example, consider search/replace being defined and controlled through a popup-dialog. The user either requests search or search/replace from a menu or selects a melodic phrase and requests search or search/replace from a menu. In either case a dialog appears, with an editable staff for the search melody, which, if it had already been selected in score, would appear in place. If the user selects 'replace' additionally, a separate editable staff appears for that as well wherein the user specifies a replacement melody and an hct based on harmonic expressions, the latter of which could be formulated by selectable elements of a mock search instance hct. And so on.

21 Dilation: Musical Expansion and Contraction

Included amongst the decisions a music creator makes are determining a time signature providing a definition of beat and the number per measure and the tempo with its definition of beat and rate in beats per minute. Once those are set, rhythmic structures can be established and the creative process proceeds. At that point, less often would the time signature be changed especially in the number of beats per measure, as in from 4:4 to 3:4. The same can be said for the tempo beat, say from ♩ to ♩.

However, early on in creating music, one might want to change the time signature beat from say ♩ to ♪, for example. It may be for reasons to accommodate note complexity more neatly for lack thereof. A means to avoid having 1/128th notes for example. A change like this could impact the tempo beat note but in a commensurate way that essentially makes the music sound identical to prior to change. In that way, the music itself does not change, but its representation does.

In this chapter we look at this type of transformation which we call dilation. In doing so we find lessons to be learned in how dilation affects a score and its constituents. We look at changes to time signature, tempo, notes, note structures, as well as harmonic context tracks. We also explore the tradeoffs on composer intentions for speeding or slowing a tempo versus changing beat definition.

The dilation transformation is admittedly a far less used transformation, but its details teach us more about important scoring decisions. To outline, this chapter considers the scoring details involved in dilation and the dynamics amongst those and their trade-offs. We conclude with a few examples.

21.1 A Discussion on Dilation

We begin with an example of applying a dilation transformation to the music in Fig. 21.1.

Fig. 21.1 Music example prior to dilation.

This example has a simple 4:4 time signature with the tempo beat, as in the time signature, being a quarter note. The moderate tempo rate is set at 90 bpm. Suppose the composer is not that happy with this music notationally and wants a more compact and denser score. If he opts to rewrite the same music using an 1/8th note for both the beat and tempo note, the score in Fig. 21.2 takes shape.

© The Author(s), under exclusive license to Springer Nature Switzerland AG 2022
D. P. Pazel, *Music Representation and Transformation in Software*, https://doi.org/10.1007/978-3-030-97472-5_21

Fig. 21.2 Dilation of the music in Fig. 21.1 by a factor of ½.

We find the time signature has changed to 4:8, with the 1/8th note being the beat. Similarly, the tempo beat is now at 1/8th note with a bpm of 90, the same as the original music. The music has not changed in that it sounds identical to the original music in Fig. 21.1. Yet the note durations, tempo, and time signature have changed. A factor of ½ has been applied to all the note durations, as well as the time signature and tempo beats. This is an example of a *dilation transformation*, in this case with a *dilation factor* of ½.

Suppose the composer once again is not satisfied. Given the density of notes, the composer decides that the tempo should be faster, in fact twice as fast. This is shown in Fig. 21.3.

Fig. 21.3 The music in Fig. 21.2 at twice the tempo.

This change can be seen as part of the dilation transform, with the dilation factor being applied to the tempo rate. With this, the composer is satisfied and moves forward with music development.

21.1.1 Dilation Dynamics

For discussion purposes, we introduce the following terminology regarding the dilation transform. Reference Fig. 21.4

- Dilation operates on input in the form of a *source score* (LiteScore) consisting of *source line* (melody) and *source hct* (harmony), as well as time signature and tempo events.

- Dilation uses a positive rational numeric called the *dilation factor* to reduce note durations and relative positions.

- The dilation transform output consists of a *dilated score* (LiteScore) consisting of a *dilated line* (melody) and a *dilated hct* (harmony).

- The source time signature and tempo events are also altered with the dilation factor for adjustments to their beat definitions and tempo rate.

Fig. 21.4 Dilation artifacts and terminology.

The example of dilation given in Fig. 21.1, Fig. 21.2, Fig. 21.3 illustrate several characteristics of this operation that impact consideration of its use. These include:

- The typical dilation factor would be 2 or ½, and most likely would not be used often.

- Aside from note durations and beat changes, the music is identical in almost every other way; the reason for using the dilation transform generally has more to do with scoring layout.

- Dilation impacts the duration of the time signature beat note, as well as tempo beat note.

- Dilation provides an option to automatically change the tempo itself. In fact, as an alternative to dilating the source line, one can "absorb" the dilation factor into the tempo itself (assuming one presumes uniform note duration change indicates a tempo change).

It is apparent that dilation has a dynamic that involves options for not only dilating individual notes, but also for changing beat characteristics, including tempo. This can be quite confusing. However, the interactive behavior between note and tempo dilation can be encapsulated by two Boolean variables or qualifications:

- apply_to_notes: means apply the dilation factor to source line notes as well as all time signature and tempo beat note definitions.

- apply_to_bpm: means apply the dilation factor to the tempo bpm.

This allows a process separation for changing note and beat durations from tempo rate. Table 21-1 summarizes the combined behaviors of these variable settings. In this table $f \equiv duration\ factor$. Also, "-----" indicates "no change".

apply_to_notes	apply_to_bpm	Notes	TS & Tempo Beat	Tempo BPM
Yes	Yes	$duration * f$	$duration * f$	$duration/f$
Yes	No	$duration * f$	$duration * f$	-----
No	Yes	-----	-----	$duration/f$
No	No	-----	-----	-----

Table 21-1   Effects of apply variable settings on results.

The table details the level of control, from having no changes to the input, to changing notes, beats, and bpm of the input score.

Finally consider the legal values for the dilation factor. Our prior example used a setting of ½ which reduced note and beat durations by ½. A setting of 2 is also reasonable, doubling the note and beat values. Traditional music notation is largely based on note durations based on a power of 2, excluding of course tuplets wherein a variety of durations can occur outside the powers of 2.

However, can one imagine applying quite different dilation factors such as 1/3, 3/7, etc. as dilation factors? Do these make sense musically? To address this, let's consider again the music in Fig. 21.1 and apply a dilation factor of 4/7! Assume also that both apply variables in the above table are set to Yes. You get a result that looks like Fig. 21.5.

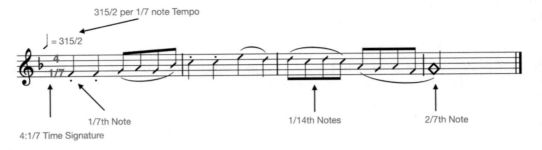

Fig. 21.5 Dilation of music in Fig. 21.1 with a 4/7 dilation factor.

This is certainly a disorienting and unsettling outcome! The time signature is 4 1/7th notes! The tempo is 157.5 BPM on 1/7th tempo beat. And the line consists of 1/7th, 1/14th notes and a lonely 2/7th note, all rendered in a non-standard notation by the author only to remind the reader that these notes have unusual durational values in this example.

In short order, however, the reader should note that there is little too out of the ordinary here. In fact, if you uniformly apply a factor of 7/4 to aspects of the music in Fig. 21.5, you will find that 1/7th notes become ¼ notes, 1/14 notes are eighths, a 2/7th is a ½. The time signature is then 4 quarter notes. So, the music in Fig. 21.5 is very much the music in Fig. 21.1, disguised in a different scale of reference. That is, except for the tempo. On that subject, on sees that a ¼ beat at 90 BPM becomes 157.5 bpm at 1/7 beat. That is far faster than the original because the beat duration has decreased from ¼ to 1/7. This means that instead of 90 BPM (on ¼ notes), we now have 167.5 BPM for 1/7 notes. That is, there are 77.5 more 1/7 beats per minute due to the rescaled beat note.

On the other hand, had we set apply_to_bpm to No, the tempo bpm remains 90 BMP but on 1/7th notes. Now one might argue that all things being equal isn't that in fact the same as the original music. After all, just substitute ¼ for 1/7th, ½ for 2/7th, and 1/8 for 1/14th notes, and we have the original score! One can do that, indeed. However, our paradigm is not one of substitution. In terms of whole note time, 1/7th duration is not the same as ¼ duration. They are different, and one would see clearly that contrast if a quarter note were added to the score in Fig. 21.5. The effective tempo for the lone quarter note would be approximately 51.43.

The case where apply_to_bpm is True and apply_to_notes is False, provides a means to trade off the note duration dilation for absorbing the dilation instead into the tempo rate. It's yet another way to interpret what is wanted from the dilation operation. It's saying to not alter the notes, time signature and tempo beat, but instead put the onus on the BPM to effect the kind of change desired, trading off shortening note durations for a faster tempo in this case.

It is rare to find the kinds of irregular[64] note durations Fig. 21.5 in any music, although irregular note durations comprise an interesting topic. One finds that without any restrictions, music in irregular durations is difficult to configure in beam and tuplet structures, that time signatures and tempo can be difficult to specify in stable or meaningful terms. In contrast though, what is happening in the cases of this chapter, is that a single dilation factor is applied uniformly throughout a score, and for the most part, that keeps all aspects of the score, except beaming and tempo value, organized as a slightly distorted mirror of common Western music scoring.

---

[64] By irregular note durations we mean durations outside of what one finds in common music notation, those being whole, half, quarter, and all manner of powers of 2, plus those that arise from common practice with tuplets, e.g., 1/6th, 1/12th notes.

With that, there is a question on the utility of this transform. We do not address that full on here. However, in running through the four cases of the apply variables, one could clearly find usages for different cases, be it for score spacing with or without tempo alteration. For the purposes of this text however, it is of great interest to clarify the interplay amongst note durations, time signature and tempo beats, and the tempo rate, and how all of that is affected by a single dilation value.

21.1.2 The Dilation Transform API

The API for the dilation transform follows the construct/apply paradigm we set for all the other transforms and is quite simple.

The constructor takes only one argument:

- score – This is a LiteScore meaning it has a line, time signature event sequence, tempo event sequence, and an hct.

The apply() method takes the following arguments:

- dilation_factor: This argument must be a positive fraction or integer. Otherwise, an exception is thrown.

- apply_to_bpm: A Boolean as described earlier. The default is False.

- apply_to_notes: A Boolean as described earlier. The default is False. Note that this factor applies to all notes in the line, as well as the beat notes for time signature and tempo, as well as the hc durations and their positions in the hct.

The apply() method returns a new LiteScore with all changes as given by the arguments.

21.2 Examples

For our first example we have a subsection of the opening of the minuet from Bach's French Suite number II, BWV 813, as shown in Fig. 21.6.

Fig. 21.6 Bach French Suite No. II, BWV 813, opening of Minuet.

Our first application of the dilation transform is to double the notes but retain the BPM. The result is shown in Fig. 21.7

Fig. 21.7 Apply dilation factor 2 to notes but retain BPM on the music in Fig. 21.6.

What the user will find interesting about this music is that when played it sounds precisely like the music in Fig. 21.6. Yet the score is quite different in details.

The code for effecting this dilation is shown below[65]:

```
title = 'Bach, French Suite II BWV 813, MM 1-4 3/4 T.S. 42-46==dotted half f=2 (False,
False)'
bach_line = '{<C-MelodicMinor:i>iG:4 Eb:5 D C B:4 C:5 <:iv> qAb:5 G F iEb:5 D F ' \
            'Eb D C <:V> B:4 A C:5 B:4 A G}'
lite_score = create_score(bach_line, 'piano', (42, Duration(3, 4)),
                                               (3, Duration(1, 4)))


trans = TDilation(lite_score)

#  case 0: apply_to_bpm=False apply_to_notes=True
new_score = trans.apply(Fraction(2), False, True)
```

We quickly mention here that if instead one specifies apply_to_bpm=False and apply_to_notes=False, the resulting score is identical to that passed in. There is no need for an example.

We move to the opening of the first movement of Mozart's piano sonata in A Major, KV 331, shown in Fig. 21.8.

Fig. 21.8 Opening 1ˢᵗ movement Mozart's piano sonata in A Major, KV 331.

Our first example in this case is to use a specification of apply_to_bpm=True and apply_to_notes=False. This means that all note durations remain the same, but the BPM doubles. See

Fig. 21.9 Apply dilation factor ½ to music in Fig. 21.8, but only to BPM.

The code for this dilation is given below:

```
title = 'Mozart, Sonata in A KV331, I, MM 1-4 6/8 T.S. 60==eighth f=1/2 (True, False)'
mozart_line = '{<A-Major:I>i@C#:5 sD iC# qE iE <:VDom7> i@B:4 sC#:5 iB:4 qD:5 iD ' /
              '<:viMin7> qA:4 iA <:V>qB:4 iB <:I> qC#:5 sE D qC# <:V>iB:4}'
lite_score = create_score(mozart_line, 'piano', (60, Duration(3, 8)), (6, Duration(1,
8)))
trans = TDilation(lite_score)
```

---

[65] The method create_score() and print_score() can be found in the file transformation/dilation/dila tion_examples.py

```
# apply_to_bpm=True apply_to_notes=False
new_score = trans.apply(Fraction(1, 2), True, False)
print_score(title, new_score)
```

Of course, this example is somewhat trivial, as it only results in resetting the BPM tempo rate.

A more interesting case involves setting both apply_to_bpm and apply_to_notes to True. In that case all durations change as in Fig. 21.10.

Fig. 21.10 Apply dilation factor ½ to music in Fig. 21.8 to both bpm and notes.

Critically however, the shortened durations feel out of place here, or at best borderline. The 6/16-time signature is relatively rare, and a justification for it here seems weak. The two examples of dilation of this Mozart piece are identically faster and aurally sound the same.

The reader can check that the hct durations and position dilate as well only when apply_to_notes=True.

21.3 Final Thoughts

The dilation transform is interesting in its detailing the connection between note duration reduction/expansion and both tempo and time signature. The four settings of the apply variables summarize these connections. In that regard the dilation transform is useful as a study in music theory.

Practically however this transform is of limited use. It seems rare for a music creator to require such a transform. If one starts with the incorrect time signature for the music, this should be quickly noticed and corrected. Also, dilation factors other than 2 or ½ would be quite rare as the effects would be quite large. And with that, a dilation would only occur rarely in the life of a piece's composition.

Putting that aside, dilations other than binary factors is an interesting topic. Fig. 21.5 easily catches one's attention, even though it is homomorphic to standard notation. The concept of freely using note durations of arbitrary size is tantalizing for composition. As mentioned, many standard musical artifacts such as beams, tuplets, time signature, and tempo do not fit well into compositions with irregular durations. It is a creative area for exploration.

22 The Step Shift Transform and Sequences

In chapter 15, we explored the shift transform whose function is to adjust melody and chords to different root tones, modality, and/or mode. While this transform is quite powerful in adjusting to different key tones, modalities, and modes, there are far simpler cases that often come up in music composition that are not so well addressed by that transform. These are cases wherein we are not so much interested in changing key, but rather in simply moving the melody up or down by a few scalar steps in the established tonality, holding to the same key. This kind of change is based on a number of scalar steps to move as opposed to using an interval. One often sees this kind of transform in examples of sequences characterized by repeated rhythmic, melodic, and harmonic patterns, and no change of key.

This chapter explores this kind of transform which we call the step shift transform. This chapter begins with defining the nature of this transform and providing some examples. We follow with a look at the technical approach towards development of this transform in software. An additional discussion provides details on how secondary chords can be handled by step shift, and the technical approaches behind that change. Finally, we conclude this chapter with a set of examples followed by final thoughts.

22.1 An Introduction to Step Shift

Often in composition, there are repeated melodies that are identical in motion or contour but are off by one or more scalar steps. These patterns often hold attention and anticipation and lead to conclusions, perhaps tonal, or maybe just follow-on sections. Consider the example in Fig. 22.1.

♩ = 70

Fig. 22.1 Simple sequence example involving step sequence.

This example shows a simple melodic pattern or theme in the first measure, that theme is repeated twice, each time beginning a tonal step lower, forming a sequence. Corresponding neighboring notes retain the same number of scalar steps between them as in the theme. The same is true for the bass notes. The first three measures constitute an example of a sequence. Measure one is the main pattern or theme, and it is repeated twice, each time a step lower than the prior.

D. P. Pazel, *Music Representation and Transformation in Software*, https://doi.org/10.1007/978-3-030-97472-5_22

Transforming a melody and/or harmony based on a few scalar steps is called a ***step shift transformation***. It is frequently seen in music. Not only is it effective in leading or transitioning to a different musical section, but it is an effective means for reinforcing musical themes to the listener, or in devising new melodic materials.

In practice melodies are often not only step shifted but modified to add color and texture. Consider the measures from the Mozart sonata in Fig. 22.2. The pickup plus with the next measure and the first beat of the following form a template used to produce two segments comprising the remaining measures. These musical segments are one scalar step shift apart from one another (excluding the C# in the first measure and the bass which is a D ostinato). Note that the first two notes of measure 67 have been altered to provide more texture.

Fig. 22.2 Mozart sonata in G-Major KV 457, I mm. 62-68.

One often finds this is the case, that some notes are altered either rhythmically or in pitch, or with the intention of changing key. The point we make is that the step shift transform, whether used for sequences or not, provides a way to create new melodies or parts thereof, upon which the music creator can improve. For more comprehensive information on sequences, please refer to [21].

In moving forward, we more strictly adhere to the step shift process than shown in Fig. 22.2, and leave alterations to the creative aspect of composition by the music creator.

22.2 Step Shift Dynamics

The basis for the step shift transform is, for a given tonality, the raising or lowering of each note's pitch a given number of tonal steps. We refer to that amount as a ***step increment***. A step increment is an integer which can be positive or negative for raising or lowering respectively. The step shift algorithm is then based on scalar moving each pitch by the step increment. However, there is more to this process than that.

The step shift process involves dealing with several issues, and one that will be discussed later in some depth. First there is the issue of non-scalar tones and how the step shift algorithm should map such tones to different tones. Another issue concerns the impact of the step shift on chords, as found in each harmonic context in the harmonic context track. That is, how should the step shift transform impact chords? In the following, we restrict discussion to diatonic scales, that is, scales of seven tones.

22.2.1 Pitch Remap

The foundation behind this transform is a tone map, which lays out a simple tone-to-tone mapping between the tonality's scale and its scale shifted by the step increment. For example, suppose we have an Eb-Major tonality with a step increment of 3. One obtains the tone map shown on the left of Fig 22.3. That is nothing less than a map between Eb-Major Ionian to Eb-Major Lydian.

Eb-Major	increment=3
Eb	Ab
F	Bb
G	C
Ab	D
Bb	Eb
C	F
D	G

Tone Letter	increment=3
E	A
F	Bb
G	C
A	D#
B	E
C	F
D	G

Fig. 22.3 Mapping Tables for Eb-Major.

However, this table by itself is not terribly practical, especially when one attempts to map altered tones, such as G# or A, for example. A more general approach is to map tone letters (un-altered tones) to corresponding altered tones in the Eb-Major scale. For example, E→A, and A→D#. This complete table is shown on the right in Fig. 22.3. Then alterations can be passed forward. So, for any altered tone, for example G#, using the table we have G→C, and so G#→C#. The process for mapping a pitch is now clear. First, use the tone letter map for the correct tone, alter the tone appropriately, then compute the correct register. Code for mapping the tone and register computations are shown below.

```
def tonal_function(self, tone):
    result_tone = self.tone_map[tone.diatonic_letter]
    alteration = tone.augmentation_offset
    result_tone = DiatonicTone.alter_tone_by_augmentation(result_tone, alteration)
    return result_tone


 def __getitem__(self, pitch):
   if pitch is None:
       return None


   result_tone = self.tonal_function(pitch.diatonic_tone)


   crosses = DiatonicPitch.crosses_c(pitch.diatonic_tone,
                                     result_tone,
                                     True if self._sign(self.increment) >= 0
                                     else False)


   result_register = pitch.octave +
                   self._sign(self.increment) *
                       ((abs(self.increment) // 7) + (1 if crosses else 0))
    return DiatonicPitch(result_register, result_tone)
```

Note that in tonal_function(), after using the map, the correction on tone augmentation is made as discussed earlier. In __getitem__(), the computation of the register is a little complex but the key is knowing if in tonal transition that the C-tone is crossed, indicating a register has been crossed. Note the convenience of implementing __getitem__() allows one to convert pitches using index access notation as follows:

```
fctn_map = PitchRemapFunction(tonality, 3)
p = fctn_map[DiatonicPitch.parse('A#:4')]
```

22.2.2 Simple Chord Remap

Given the process for remapping tones and pitches as described, we move to the impact of step shift on harmony or elements of the harmonic context track. There are many cases wherein the harmony is easily specified such as <G-Major, ii> or similar.

The algorithm for dealing with these cases is quite easy. Chord tones are remapped using the tone remapping functionality just described. Then a chord classifier on these tones is invoked to determine the chord type, then the harmonic context is rebuilt. So, for example, in the case of <G-Major, ii> if the step increment is -1, then the tone set {A, C, E} is mapped to {G, B, D} which is <G-Major, I>.

22.2.3 Secondary Chords

Applying step shift to secondary chords leads to interesting considerations. For a review of secondary chords refer to section 7.3.4. For now, it suffices to recall the general form of this relative chord type.

$$Numerator/Denominator \equiv PrimaryChord/ScaleDegree([modality]) \qquad (22.1)$$

In summary we temporarily suspend the current tonality for another based on the scale degree in the denominator and use the chord relative to that secondary tonality.

In applying a step increment to a secondary chord, we have a choice of applying it to either the numerator or denominator of the secondary chord. Recall that for a harmonic context with a secondary chord, the successor harmonic context is typically in the tonality indicated by the secondary scale degree. The point behind this typical usage of secondary chords is to provide a resolution in the new key, e.g.,

$$< G - Major, V/iii > < G - Major, iii > \qquad (22.2)$$

Suppose, for illustration, we begin by applying an increment of 1 to the numerator. We then have:

$$< G - Major, vi/iii > < G - Major, IV > \qquad (22.3)$$

The result is a curious chord resolution of vi/iii to IV! (Recall that we apply the step shift to all the chords, so the second chord is also affected.) On the plus side though, the change remains a kind of V:I relationship[66] (G chord to C chord). This result is an interesting if an atypical unconventional musical structure.

On the other hand, if instead we apply an increment of 2 to the denominator, we get:

---

[66] In the given example vi/iii from G-Major gives B-MelodicMinor and a diminished chord of {G# B, D}. However, in B-NaturalMinor we have the major chord {G, B, D}. Depending on how one goes it's a kind of V to I relationship.

$$< G - Major, V/V > < G - Major, V > \qquad (22.4)$$

This result is very much in line with traditional usage of secondary chord resolution. In this case, we hold onto the V:I relationship with V in D-Major to V in G-Major (A chord to D chord). The application of applying step increment to the numerator is far less radical than changing the numerator.

However, not every use of secondary chords is for formulating a key change even if temporary. For example, they can be used to add color while staying in the same key. The step shift transform is more about moving pitches to different scale degrees and not about changing key. So, with that in mind, we allow both types of shifts on secondary chords when using the step shift transform. We call these two approaches or policies *secondary shift types*. We have two of them:

- Standard – The case wherein the numerator is incremented/decremented.

- Tonal – The case wherein the denominator is incremented/decremented.

The precise details of the step transform when applied to secondary chords is outlined as follows:

```
if self.secondary_shift_type == SecondaryShiftType.Standard:
  orig_principal_chord_template =
                        secondary_chord.chord_template.principal_chord_template
  # Assume TertianChordtemplate
  new_scale_degree = ((orig_principal_chord_template.scale_degree - 1) +
                                      self.step_increment) % 7 + 1
  new_principal_chord_template = ... # Rebuild TertianChordTemplate.
  secondary_chord_template = ... # Rebuild SecondaryChordTemplate.
  Return SecondaryChord(secondary_chord_template, base_tonality)
else:
  orig_template = secondary_chord.chord_template
  new_degree = ((orig_template.secondary_scale_degree - 1) +
                              self.step_increment) % 7 + 1
```

The essence of this logic is finding which scale degree is modified, numerator or denominator, and used to construct the secondary chord.

22.2.4   The Step Shift API

The step shift api is much like the others in consisting of a constructor and an apply() method. We have an enum for determining which secondary chord policy, as described earlier, should be used:

```
class SecondaryShiftType(enum.Enum):
  Standard = 1    # Change the numerator of a secondary chord.
  Tonal = 2       # Change the denominator of a secondary chord.
```

With that the TStepShift constructor has the following arguments.

- source_line: A source Line of notes.

- source_hct: A source harmonic context track that pairs with the line.

- defaultSecondaryShiftType: The default secondary shift policy to set as default. This can be overridden by the apply() method.

The apply() method for the TStepShift object has the following arguments:

- step_increment: An integer (positive or negative) indicating the number of scale steps and direction of change to apply to each note's pitch and hct.

- temporal_extent: A numerical interval in whole note time indicating the temporal extent that is affected by the transform, both for the source line and hct. (If None, the full source_line and source_hct are used.

- secondary_shift_type: The SecondaryShiftType value to use during the application of the apply() method. If this value is not None, this value overrides the default secondary shift type specified in the constructor.

The return value of apply() is a copy of the hct, but truncated by the temporal extent specified. As for the Line, it is a full copy of the source line, but with the note pitches modified by the step shift only within the temporal extent.

22.3 Examples

Our first example is a simple melody in the first measure transformed into a descending sequence in Fig. 22.4.

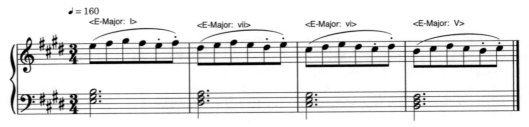

Fig. 22.4 *Step shift used on first measure to build a descending sequence.*

Clearly this is a case of using the first measure and applying step shift iteratively to produce the other three measures. Critically, the derived chords for measures 2-4 may have better alternatives, e.g., V for measure 2. Outside of that the build of the sequential line based on the first measure looks fine.

The code for this example is quite simple:

```
line_text = '{<E-Major:I>iE:5 f# G# F# E f# }'
lge = LineGrammarExecutor()
source_instance_line, source_instance_hct = lge.parse(line_text)
print_score('\n[0]: ', source_instance_line, source_instance_hct)


trans = TStepShift(source_instance_line, source_instance_hct)

new_line, new_hct = trans.apply(-1)
print_score('\n[1]: ', new_line, new_hct)


new_line, new_hct = trans.apply(-2)
print_score('\n[2]: ', new_line, new_hct)


new_line, new_hct = trans.apply(-3)
print_score('\n[3]: ', new_line, new_hct)
```

We now turn to a similar sequence example but using a Standard setting for SecondaryShiftType, and in this case do an upward shift by single steps. See Fig. 22.5

Fig. 22.5 *Step shift example using SecondaryShiftType=Standard.*

This example is not too bad possibly due to the flow generated by the sequence. However, the modulations are quite uncommon, e.g., vii/ii to iii, and vii/ii to IV. We discussed this concern earlier. For this example, the step shift with standard secondary chord shift type used in sequence generation may not be its best use. However, each generated measure may find novel use outside of this sequence setting.

The code is like the prior example, except for the setting of Standard, below:

```
line_text = '{<C-Major:I> (i, 2)[iC:5 E D] <:V/ii> c#:5 b:4 c#:5 e <:ii> f d b:4 a}'
lge = LineGrammarExecutor()
source_instance_line, source_instance_hct = lge.parse(line_text)
print_score('\n[0]: ', source_instance_line, source_instance_hct)
trans = TStepShift(source_instance_line,
                   source_instance_hct,
                   SecondaryShiftType.Standard)

new_line, new_hct = trans.apply(1)
print_score('\n[1]: ', new_line, new_hct)


new_line, new_hct = trans.apply(2)
print_score('\n[2]: ', new_line, new_hct)
```

When we change the secondary shift type to tonal, we get the score in Fig. 22.6.

Fig. 22.6 *Step shift example using SecondaryShiftType=Tonal.*

It should be immediately clear that the benefit of the tonal approach is that we retain the secondary chord paradigm of V/x to x, where x is some scalar tonal displacement.

Tonal step shift becomes more interesting when we apply sequencing to minor keys. For example, here we use the same melody but adapted to a C melodic minor key, as shown in Fig. 22.7.

Fig. 22.7   Step shift example in melodic minor using SecondaryShiftType=Tonal.

A natural minor version of this tonal shift example is shown in Fig. 22.8.

Fig. 22.8   Step shift example in natural minor using SecondaryShiftType=Tonal.

Overall, these last two examples worked out well. They are more colorful than the C-Major example. However, they are far from perfect and could benefit with user alteration using discretion.

Recall that when the secondary minor tonality is left unspecified, the secondary tonality defaults to melodic minor, as in the above examples. So, it is interesting to take the prior example and set V/ii to V/ii-Natural to further see how the results compare to the prior. We get the following shown in Fig. 22.9.

Fig. 22.9   Step shift example from Fig. 22.8 but with the secondary tonality also natural minor.

Indeed, we get more color. Note the use of Eb natural minor in measure 2.

All these examples are based on a shift capability to hold onto the underlying tonality; it never changes throughout. For an example wherein the tonality changes with step shift like behavior, look at section 15.5.4.

22.4 Final Thoughts

The step shift transform is complementary to the shift transform in chapter 15. The shift is focused on either or both of tonality and mode change. The step shift however is focused on retaining tonality and shifting notes by scale degrees. Both transforms also attempt to produce compatible harmony as well.

The concept of the step shift transform is quite easy to visualize. So much so that one could is lured into envisioning a tonality aware score editor application wherein one selects a set of notes and use up/down arrows to move the notes to other notes in their respective tonalities, including non-tonal alterations.

The deeper aspect of step shift lies in disentangling and formalizing approaches to handling secondary chords. This was covered in depth, with many interesting examples.

There is much room for expansion on this concept including:

- Allowing step shift on non-diatonic scales. For example, with pentatonic or hexatonic scales, increments could result in large or uneven intervallic leaps. For octatonic and others, the increment adjustments in tone again vary in contour from the original, but at a finer level. In these cases, though, the key to step transformation is the design of the tone map.

- In this chapter, the chord family was strictly limited to tertian chords. Allowing quartal and secundal chords is a suggested area of improvement.

- Regarding the chord mapping of the step shift, the approach taken was generally the most straight forward. However, these chords may not be the best harmonically for the step shifts. Perhaps more traditional chords sequences might work better, e.g., instead of a iii, use a V, etc., depending on the resulting context.

- The standard secondary shift policy appears to be problematic in resulting in uncommon chord resolutions. This is again another area that could be explored.

Finally, one might be tempted to combine the step shift transform into the Shift transform. As is typical in software there are trade-offs in developing a transform with user unfriendly complexity as a single transform, that alternatively with the separation into two transforms enhances usability with a conceptual separation of function.

23 Final Thoughts

In this brief but interesting journey through music representation and transformation, even when looking in retrospect at all that was covered, there is much yet to explore. It is of interest to explore areas for improvement or new territories as contributions to a vision of technology tools to assist music creators in their work. We consolidate some observations here into final thoughts.

23.1 The Quest for a Broader Musical Synthesis

Early on, an intentional effort was made to expand on oftentimes constrained ideas in music and provide an orderly and logical presentation of concepts. For example, the idea behind the diatonic foundation discussed in chapter 2 was simply to avoid introducing modality and tonality far earlier than needed. This presentation order was intended to provide an apodictic foundation introducing chromatic and diatonic tones as first principles upon which following music theoretic foundations would be built. The notion of whole note time established a standard time measure across scores in lieu of score measures, beats, or other time irregular measurements. This at the same time led to duration and position as flexible musical elements. Intervals led to modality and tonality. The concept of a music note acquired a broader semantic, as arbitrary position and duration values are assigned. The concepts of time signature and tempo are further generalized with arbitrary beat durations.

Further, an attempt was made to add a broader base of tonalities than limiting the discussion to diatonic tonality, using intervals as a foundational concept. With this, we included pentatonic, hexatonic, and octatonic tonalities, as well as crisply distinguishing key tone from modality and mode. Similarly, the chord family was expanded beyond tertian to include quartal and secundal chords. We also expanded on controlled dynamics with the addition of various functions to define dynamics over a timeline.

Much of the discussion in this book focused on melody. Definitionally, we considered the "line" and later motifs and phrases as elements of melody. All the transforms focused primarily on melody. Harmony on the other hand was addressed somewhat abstractly and never realized into notes for bass lines. While the harmonic contexts accurately indicated chords, most of the transforms paid minimal lip service to their operating on them and "punted" on their transformed selves, many times leaving those results as suggested chords. In short there is much more that could be done in chord transformation, especially when considering inversions, added tensions, and even breaking from tertiary forms, that might contribute better in service to melody, and deepen our understand of their contributions.

Putting these short comings aside, one realizes that music theory is a very large topic that is difficult to contain in an organized study. At the same time, a software model design for music aspires towards broad applicability and so a desire to discover a bigger picture for music. It demands inclusion of rich enough structure to encompass much of the world's music and music innovation for which we can only imagine. Along that line are the following thoughts:

D. P. Pazel, *Music Representation and Transformation in Software*, https://doi.org/10.1007/978-3-030-97472-5_23

- The equal-tempered chromatic scale has served well over the centuries. However, more adventurous composers look for more freedoms in this regard. In that spirit, music creators now can find support for microtonal music in many notation applications. There is much to understand about microtonal music and rules or properties for its effective dynamics. There is also a need to understand especially how microtonal fits into or expands upon traditional music theory, which in turn through a software model could serve as a bridge to its accessibility and use by a larger audience of music creators.

- There are many discussions that analyze and draw relatively sharp distinctions between classical (or traditional classical) music and jazz. For illustration purposes, classical theory and jazz theory books are quite different kinds of reading experiences, each with differing focuses related to musical elements. It is beneficial to see these forms of music as less separate but more as two different views within a common theoretical basis and highlight their distinguishing characteristics. In terms of basic musical elements, each contributes an understanding of melody and voice leading as well as chord type and dynamics. In that way, moving these contrasting music views to a music representation in software could expand on current tools and enhance user creativity through these musical landscapes and other differing approaches to the same foundations.

- There is need for a deeper understanding of modern music styles and music structure that would be valuable to aspiring music creators. This understanding includes a clear articulation of principles behind for example, minimalism, atonal, or 12-tone structure. Discussions in this context would include, for example, principles or elements of melody (if there is even one in any meaningful terms) as well as harmony or other voice management principles, and a search for clarity on how chord or chord structures fit together in emerging genera.

These are but a few ideas of areas of expansion in music study, or more to the focus of this book, music representation in software that could make useful gains.

23.2 The Quest for Real-time Synthesis

Several of the transforms presented relied on the rules-based engine introduced early in the transformation part of this book. From the perspective of real-time music tools, several notable problematic aspects on using a rules-based approach in music transformative work include:

- Processing time becomes unpredictable, which with some generality is exacerbated with weakness in or lack of constraints. Understand that the rules engine presented was a prototype meant to assist and demonstrate a transform's feasibility and was not optimally constructed for speed nor for memory efficiency. Efforts to contain these issues would result in a project unto itself.

- The rules engine result consists of a set of solutions. The solutions are collected in no particular order with respect to any quality measure, and so a further filtering step at times was introduced to sort the results as to some measure of quality. That quality is quantified by an objective function that measures solution quality. In our case, it was often a mean-squared difference to some exemplar instance. However, without a standard measure of melodic or harmonic quality the solutions that rise to the top are less likely be the best or even desirable solutions.

In summary, if one wants to use transforms that rely on the rule's engine in real-time music rendering there are problematic considerations. Firstly, there are timing issues that effectively "glitch" the transformative process, and secondly it is unclear if there exist well-founded melodic/harmonic quality measures for purposes of result filtering.

There are several ways to tackle or make progress with these issues.

- Use a production version of a rules-based engine, which is likely to be optimized and therefore faster along with better memory management.

- Develop more constraint rules that tend to restrict the number of solutions, and ensure they are included in a problem's constraint profile.

- Develop an ad-hoc pitch assignment approach that is less a rules engine that sorts through all pitch assignment combinations, but one that does assignment based on a comprehensive knowledge base and logic heuristic related to melodic and harmonic principles.

As one suggestion, perhaps some or all the above can be combined with an AI trained on melody and/or harmony that acts as the arbiter on melodic quality.

It should also be pointed out, as a point for further development, that other music elements could enter a rules-based approach other than melodic rules. Among these are rhythmic, voice-leading, and harmonic rules.

23.3 Automated Score Analysis

Compositional tools for music creators generally lack access to large bases of content. While performers have access to lead sheets or fake books, and audio-based composers have access to countless audio and MIDI content for mixing, composers are left to notation or similar tools that have little access to content in a readily accessible form that would include harmonic or melodic analysis. Granted there is Music XML or MIDI import and other means for transferring music data, but this is just raw input that may require manual editing post import for user-based analysis regarding the harmonic and melodic functions of the individual parts of the music. Sheet music is in print format, and a means from print or image to this kind of input for notational tools is less available or non-existent.

With that it would be useful to have means not only to be able to read notated music such as lead sheets, but to analyze it melodically and harmonically in a way meaningful for compositional tooling. With that kind of accessibility, not just the currently available compositional tools could benefit from the access, but transformative means like those described in this book could be utilized as part of the creative compositional process.

23.4 Forward

Continuing forward, developing a music foundation in software and at the same time developing transformational technologies for composition is a mind-opening and fulfilling experience. It not only leads to interesting forays into music theory and its structure, but also into advanced topics of computer science and algorithms, and into mathematics, as has been demonstrated in the text. We hope the reader has been encouraged by their experiences in reading and working through these discussions. These are a few of the technical possibilities, and we hope to see further progress in coming years.

Appendices

A. Modality Varieties

Continuing with our discourse on modality in Chapter 4, we look at several well-known, familiar modality types, and their specifications.

A.1. Diatonic Modalities

We categorize the diatonic major, minor, and modal modalities. Each has seven tones. For each modality we provide the incremental intervals.

The major modality is well known and already covered in the text.

Major: {P:1, M:2, M:2, m:2, M:2, M:2, M:2, m:2}

For minor scales, the incremental intervals are:

1. Natural Minor: {P:1, M:2, m:2, M:2, M:2, m:2, M:2, M:2}
2. Melodic Minor: {P:1, M:2, m:2, M:2, M:2, M:2, M:2, m:2}
3. Harmonic Minor: {P:1, M:2, m:2, M:2, M:2, m:2, A:2, m:2}

Minor modalities are often used interchangeably in a minor piece of music. The general rule of thumb is to use melodic for ascending notes and natural for descending notes. Although not a firm rule, it is mostly based on semitone resolution of the major 7th to root. The harmonic minor modality provides a hybrid of natural and minor modalities, and in doing so provides a chord set that is a mixture of natural and melodic minor chords.

There are seven modes that are based on the major modality, with Ionian coinciding with major. Each mode is a rotation of that Ionian scale, and in that way, each corresponds to a modal index value on the major scale.

1. Ionian: {P:1, M:2, M:2, m:2, M:2, M:2, M:2, m:2}
2. Dorian: {P:1, M:2, m:2, M:2, M:2, M:2, m:2, M:2]}
3. Phrygian: {P:1, m:2, M:2, M:2, M:2, m:2, M:2, M:2}
4. Lydan: {P:1, M:2, M:2, M:2, m:2, M:2, M:2, m:2}
5. Myxolydian: {P:1, M:2, M:2, m:2, M:2, M:2, m:2, M:2}
6. Aeolian: {P:1, M:2, m:2, M:2, M:2, m:2, M:2, M:2}
7. Locrian: {P:1, m:2, M:2, M:2, m:2, M:2, M:2, M:2}

Usage of these modes are often found in jazz as well as pop tunes. They have a rich and deep history extending to antiquity, a discussion that is beyond the scope of this text.

A.2.   Pentatonic Modalities

Each pentatonic modality is based on five tones, and like the modes are based in turn on a rotation of the incremental intervals. These are:

1.   Major Pentatonic: {P:1, M:2, M:2, m:3, M:2, m:3}

2.   Egyptian: {P:1, M:2, m:3, M:2, m:3, M:2}

3.   Minor Blues: {P:1, m:3, M:2, m:3, M:2, M:2}

4.   Major Blues: {P:1 M:2, m:3, M:2, M:2, m:3}

5.   Minor Pentatonic: {P:1, m:3, M:2, M:2, m:3, M:2}

Note how 3rds provide a means to skip diatonic letters. Pentatonic scales are found in jazz but appear in many other musical contexts.

A.3.   Octatonic Modality

The octatonic modality produces eight tone scales based on alternating 2 and 1 semitone offsets. Since a scale can start with either semitone jump, there are two types of octatonic scales:

1.   Whole-Half: {P:1, m:2, M:2, m:2, M:2, A:1, M:2, m:2, M:2}

2.   Half-Whole: {P:1, M:2, m:2, M:2, A:1, M:2, m:2, M:2, m:2}

Lettering duplication is achieved with the A:1 interval. Octatonic scales are historically modern and are used by modern composers as well as in jazz.

A.4.   Whole Tone Modality

Whole tone modality has six tones, and is based on the pattern:

{P:1, M:2, M:2, M:2, M:2, M:2, d:3}

Notably, the whole tone modality has no leading tone. The d:3 interval provides a means to skip diatonic lettering. Whole tone scales are used by modern composers, as well as in jazz.

A.5.   Blues Modality

The blues modalities we consider have six tone scales. There are two scales with these incremental intervals:

Major Blues: {P:1, M:2, m:2, A:1, m:3, M:2, m:3} (descending)

{P:1, M:2, A:1, m:2, m:3, M:2, m:3} (ascending)

Minor Blues: {P:1, m:3, M:2, m:2, A:1, m:3, M:2} (descending)

{P:1, m:3, M:2, A:1, m:2, m:3, M:2} (ascending)

In practice, for each, the lettering changes based on ascending or descending scales. Although the incremental intervals for ascending and descending are different, the effect is only an enharmonic re-lettering of the same tones.

B.   OrderedMap

The conversion algorithms in class TimeConversion improve on those in sections 5.4 and 5.5 by creating various maps to quickly gain access to precomputed timings. The utility class OrderedMap is used to map whole time position and actual time to time signature and tempo class instances. While Python dictionaries provide mapping capability, they lack a few capabilities for the conversion algorithms to be effective.

One missing capability is to compute a "floor" for key value. That is for a key value, find the closest lower key. As an example, for position, say 235/16, we need to find the immediately lower key position, say 223/8, that maps to the time signature that covers 236/16.

The other useful capability are reverse maps. That is, for a given time signature or tempo to get its position or actual time from the map itself.

OrderedMap is a specialized class that provides those capabilities. While it is designed specifically for the time conversion algorithms, it is general enough to be useful outside that context, and in that sense, it is a general utility class. OrderedMap uses OrderedDict from the Python collections module, plus a sorting operation, to maintain a map with ordered keys.

The floor() operation is a simple binary search across the keys to find the floor. Some students may find using binary search for floor confusing in that it is often used for finding an exact search match on a discrete list of values. However, if you consider the set of segments between keys, finding the exact segment that contains a given point is exactly how binary search is used for the floor operation. By the way, the method floor_entry() returns both the key floor value, as well as the object to which it maps. Also included is ceil() with similar functionality but for finding the closest higher key.

The reverse capability is provided with a simple OrderedDict Python map within OrderedMap. Note that the defined input for mapping should be 1-1 for this to work, i.e. we cannot have keys a, b with a!=b map to the same object.

As a final note on this topic, it is important that the key, that is, Position or Number for time conversion, has comparator operators implemented in addition to __eq__ and __hash__. Having those guarantees that the key sorting, a critical part of OrderedMap's implementation, succeeds.

© The Author(s), under exclusive license to Springer Nature Switzerland AG 2022
D. P. Pazel, *Music Representation and Transformation in Software*, https://doi.org/10.1007/978-3-030-97472-5

C.   The Observer Pattern

We discuss and analyze the dynamics of a simple notification software model consisting of an observable, being an entity with a variety of changeable characteristics, and an observer which monitors observables for changes. When one or more characteristics of the observable entity changes, this model ensures that its observers are notified of those changes, along with specifics about those changes. This notification pattern is important for a software design to maintain data and software behavioral integrity over simple activity, wherein the observable undergoes changes to which the rest of the system must adapt.

This dynamic model is sometimes referred to as publish-subscribe. In some descriptions the observable is referred to as a subject. In any case, the model is essentially the same. For a formal description of the observer pattern, refer to [10].

Implementations of this pattern vary widely depending on requirements. In its simplest form, it consists of a very few basic structures. At its most complex implementations, it deals with issues of concurrency, remote procedure call, observer list integrity, to name a few. For our purposes, we keep the design to the most basic level of detail.

The system described here is based on the code files observer.py and observable.py and represents this design pattern in its most basic form. The observable has the following:

- A list of observers to be notified when the observable changes.

- A way to add/delete observers using methods register() and deregister() on the observable.

- A method to trigger a reaction to state changes, update() that takes a set of arguments that describe the observable's changes for update.

The observer has simple requirements:

- An overridable notification method that is invoked by the observable, informing the observer that a state change has occurred in the observable, and information related to that change.

Fig. C 1 depicts an overview of the observer pattern, with the observable holding a list of observers which are notified when changes occur in the observable.

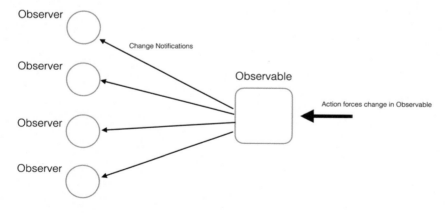

Fig. C 1 – Observer pattern.

© The Author(s), under exclusive license to Springer Nature Switzerland AG 2022
P. Pazel, *Music Representation and Transformation in Software*, https://doi.org/10.1007/978-3-030-97472-5

C The Observer Pattern

The Python Observer and Observable classes can be inherited by other classes, in that way they can be immediately made into Observers or Observables. The usage logic is very simple:

- When the observable's state changes, it calls update()
- Update calls notification() for each observer registered with the observable.
- The observer notification() receives related descriptive data about the change and takes appropriate actions based on the notification and arguments about the observable's changes.

The parameters on the notification() method should provide as much information as possible to the observer about its change. The observer's notification method arguments include:

- *Observable* – A reference to the observable itself.
- *Message_type* – A message type indicator, using any of a number of self-identifying strings that is unique to all possible types of changes to the observable. These message type identifiers should be agreed upon system wide.
- *Message* – A textual message describing the change.
- *Data* – Data about the change. The precise data and its description depend on the message_type.

This signature for the notification method is shown below. Each observer must implement this method.

```python
@abstractmethod
def notification(self, observable, message_type, message=None, data=None):
```

D. Chords

D.1. Tertian Chords

The tertian chords are described in chapter 7. The following defines specific tertian chords considered in this text. The chords categorize to triads, 7-chords, and special cases, e.g., Italian, French, German. These tertian chords are shown below:

Notation	Chord	Notation	Chord
	CMaj Triad: P1, M3, P5		CDimMaj7 7-Chord: P1, m3, d5, M7
	CMin Triad: P1, m3, P5		CDom7Flat5 7-Chord: P1, M3, d5, m7
	CDim Triad: P1, m3, d5		CMajSus2 Triad: P1, M2, P5
	CAug Triad: P1, M3, A5		CSus or CSus4 Triad: P1, M4, M5
	CMaj7 7-Chord: P1, M3, P5, M7		CMaj7Sus2 7-Chord: P1, M2, P5, M7
	CMin7 7-Chord: P1, m3, P5, m7		CMaj7Sus or CMaj7Sus4 7-Chord: P1, M4, M5, M7
	CDom7 7-Chord: P1, M3, P5, m7		CMaj6 7-Chord: P1, M3, P5, M6
	CDim7 7-Chord: P1, m3, d5, d7		CMin6 7-Chord: P1, m3, P5, M6
	CHalfDim7 7-Chord: P1, m3, d5, m7		CIt (Italian) Aug. 6th: m6, P1, A4

© The Author(s), under exclusive license to Springer Nature Switzerland AG 2022

P. Pazel, *Music Representation and Transformation in Software*, https://doi.org/10.1007/978-3-030-97472-5

	CMinMaj7 7-Chord: P1, m3, P5, M7
	CAugMaj7 7-Chord: P1, M3, A5, M7
	CAug7 7-Chord: P1, M3, A5, m7

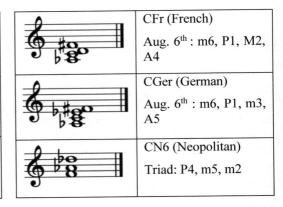

	CFr (French) Aug. 6th : m6, P1, M2, A4
	CGer (German) Aug. 6th : m6, P1, m3, A5
	CN6 (Neopolitan) Triad: P4, m5, m2

D.2.   Secundal Chords

Secundal chords are described in Chapter 7. There are four noteworthy secundal chords. These are major/major, major/minor, minor/major, minor/minor. These secundal chords are shown below:

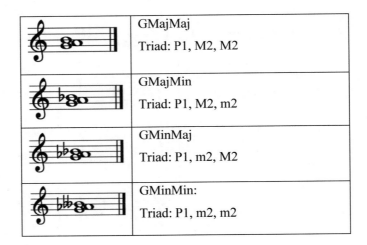

	GMajMaj Triad: P1, M2, M2
	GMajMin Triad: P1, M2, m2
	GMinMaj Triad: P1, m2, M2
	GMinMin: Triad: P1, m2, m2

D.3.   Quartal Chords

Quartal chords are described in Chapter 7. There are three quartal triad chords of note, namely perfect/perfect, perfect/augmented, and augmented/perfect. (The case augmented/augmented results in a duplicate root, and no longer a triad.) These quartal chords are shown below:

	EPerPer Triad: P1, P4, P4

	EPerAug Triad: P1, P4, A4
	EAugPer Triad: P1, A4, P4

E. A Brief Introduction to XML

XML (Extensible Markup Language) is a standardized data format that provides a means for structured data entry and data sharing. The flexibility of XML allows structured data to be easily shared across applications and across platforms. For the purposes of this appendix, we adopt a file-based view of XML, i.e., input as it would appear in a text file.

A more complete presentation on XML can be found in [48].

E.1. Tags, Elements, and Attributes

Data in XML is structured to various identifiable keywords called **markup**. A major markup is **tag**, that identifies a section of data input. The section is demarcated with <tag-name> and </tag_name>. Tags may be enclosed in other tags, making a tree-like structure, e.g.,

```
<section_1>
   ...
   <section_2>
      ...
   </section_2>
   ...
</section_1>
```

Data between a start and end tag is call an **element**. More specifically, element refers to the text between the tag start and end, e.g.

```
<Title>Pride and Prejudice</Title>
```

The start tag itself may include addition keyword-based information called **attributes**, that can add semantic meaning to the tag and element, as is the case with "category" in the following example.

```
<Title category="Fiction" pub="1-28-1813">Pride and Prejudice</Title>
```

A tag may have only attributes:

```
<Articulation name="Marcato"/>
```

Note there is no need for an end tag in this case; it is subsumed into the start tag with the final '/'.

E.2. Data Structuring

An example of how to piece structured data together in XML is:

© The Author(s), under exclusive license to Springer Nature Switzerland AG 2022

D. P. Pazel, *Music Representation and Transformation in Software*, https://doi.org/10.1007/978-3-030-97472-5

```
<Instrument name="Double Bass">
    <Range>
        <Low>c:2</Low>
        <High>c:5</High>
    </Range>
    <Transpose direction="down" interval="P:8"/>
</Instrument>
```

Note how indented tags are used to provide more detailed information about the double bass, with Range and Transpose. Range uses sub-tags to break apart the low and high pitches in reference to the instrument range. The "Transpose" tag uses attributes to provide information about the transpose interval and its direction. It is not necessary to indent tags as shown, but only as a means for presentation clarity.

E.3.   Reading an XML File with Python

Python provides an API for reading an XML file. The API reads the XML file into an internal representation called the Document Object Model or **DOM**, that makes the XML effectively amenable to computer (program) analysis. The API provides an easy means to traverse the DOM tree nodes to get at information details. The following code acquires the DOM tree root:

```
import xml.etree.ElementTree as ET

...

tree = ET.parse(full_file_path)
tree_root = tree.getroot()
```

To access the immediate children, simply loop over the children in the root:

```
for child in tree_root:
    # process child
```

Depending on the node type, you can acquire the information through specific api's. For example,

```
node.tag #provides the name of the tag, e.g., 'InstrumentGroup'
node.get(attr_name) # returns the value of the attribute,
                    # e.g., node.get('name')
```

One must take care in traversing the tree, in as much as the code for traversing the tree must logically follow the structure of the XML DOM it is processing. Programming otherwise, can easily lead to bad information or faults.

F.   Binary Search Trees

This brief look at binary search trees serves as an introduction to search trees. Search trees are structures composed of nodes with key values (and possibly other related values) linked to each other in a tree structure. In a binary search tree, each node has at most two child nodes. Nodes are added to the tree in a way that the following principle is maintained:

For a given node, nodes with a smaller key are found following to the left, and those with larger keys to the right. Identical keys can be either.

A search algorithm traverses the tree nodes and by way of key comparisons attempts to find the node whose search value is a match. When constructed properly, search trees locate values very rapidly. In fact, the result is a search that succeeds on average within $O(\log_2(n))$ where n is the number of nodes in the tree. That is the typical search (on average) and reflects the height of the tree. There are odd cases wherein the search is $O(n)$, should the tree be a sequence of n nodes.

An example of a binary tree and search is shown in Fig. E 1. The diagram shows the search nodes arranged top/down with their key values. Note that the nodes are carefully arranged so that left node values are strictly lower than the parent node key, and similarly, right node values are strictly higher than the parent node key. The top node, 107 in this case, is called the root of the tree.

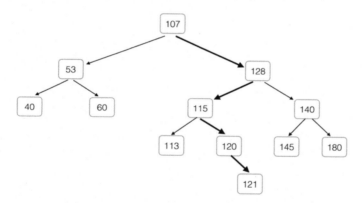

Fig. E 1: Example Binary Tree and Search.

The algorithm for search is simply an iterative path search through the tree, branching left/right per node depending on the search value, until it is found (or not).

```
search(key):
    x = root
    while x && key != x.key:
        x = x.left if key < x.key else x.right
    return x
```

Tracing through the algorithm searching for value 121, one visits in order, the nodes with keys: 107, 128, 115, 120, 121, as shown by the darker path arrows in Fig. E 1. Nodes typically have other attached information, say in additional fields.

© The Author(s), under exclusive license to Springer Nature Switzerland AG 2022
D. P. Pazel, *Music Representation and Transformation in Software*, https://doi.org/10.1007/978-3-030-97472-5

A binary tree is effectively a map. Binary trees are a very efficient and effective structure for a search algorithm. Although a hash table has $O(1)$ access time, binary trees provide two key advantages. They take less space generally, and the values are inherently sorted which can be retrieved with a simple tree traversal.

Algorithms for proper construction and maintenance of a binary tree are beyond the scope of this book. They can be found in [28] or at a number of online sources.

G. Processing Constraints: The Design of a Pitch Constraint Engine

This discussion is based on topics found in chapter 14. To briefly set the context for discussion, we begin with a PMap, the source of which includes all the notes/actors for some melody, and the target for which is a set of contextual notes. Each contextual note has a ContextPolicy with a target harmonic context, a pitch range, but no assigned note, ref. *Fig. 14.3*. We also have a set of constraints or policies, each derived from AbstractConstraint and parameterized on a subset of the PMap's source actors. We seek a solution wherein each PMap's contextual note acquires an assigned note, that is, a note with all the properties of its source note except with a potentially different pitch. Finally, in that solution, all the PMap's actors map to contextual notes whose assigned notes satisfy all the policies.

For our purposes, the process that finds these solutions is called a constraint engine. The technical approach we take to find solutions is called the ***refinement model*** [49] wherein the constraint engine functions as a search engine over a space of possible variables' settings to find solutions[67]. In this section we explore several designs for a constraint engine along this line. Two are obvious, and we provide an analysis of their strengths and weaknesses. The last one is somewhat non-obvious, similarly supplied with an analysis of its strengths and weaknesses.

As we proceed, we will find a few ways to improve performance on traversing the search space. By being a little clever, we can reduce the search, and even cap the search duration, that in many ways allows for a more practical use of the constraint engine on our problem space.

G.1. Two Straight Forward Solutions

To explore the complexity of the constraint engine and for familiarization with the issues therein, we look at two somewhat straight forward solutions on how to process constraints to solutions. However, while each finds solutions, they are at the same time inefficient.

G.1.1 Depth-First Search

The first algorithm we consider is a "vertical" or depth-first search algorithm with backtracking. The idea behind this algorithm is to first collect the set of unassigned actors or ***nodes*** from the starting pmap. Then starting with the first node we iterate through the pitch values that can be assigned to it, and with each assignment, move to a successive unassigned node and assign a valid pitch value to it, and so forth. In this way we dive depth-first through all the unassigned nodes in pitch assignment.

---

[67] An alternative approach to refinement is perturbation, wherein variable values are changed and propagated towards finding solutions.

D. P. Pazel, *Music Representation and Transformation in Software*, https://doi.org/10.1007/978-3-030-97472-5

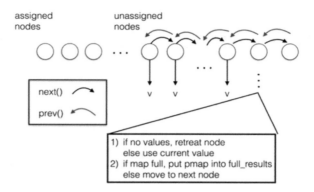

Fig. G 1 Vertical Search

The algorithm for depth-first value assignment is shown in Fig. G.1. The unassigned pmap nodes are shown and are the basis of the algorithm. The algorithm starts with the left most unassigned node, determines its assignable values (pitches), and assigns one. It continues traversing nodes to the right, assigning pitches to nodes as it can. When a node has no value to assign, say because of constraint conflicts, the algorithm retreats to the prior node. Otherwise, it assigns the current value. If all the unassigned nodes are successfully filled, a copy of the pmap is put into the set full_results, and retreats to the prior node for another value. Otherwise, the algorithm moves forward to the next unassigned node. Based on this simple logic, we move back and forth over the unassigned nodes, until all possible pitches for each node have been assigned, while checks are made for full pmap solutions.

Pseudo-code for the depth-first algorithm follows:

```
solve(p_map, policies):
    partial_results = list()
    unsolved_nodes = all p_map unsolved actors, sorted on number solution values
    node_stack # over all unsolved nodes
    value_map # for tracking value loop indices over nodes
    while node != None:
        if node in value_map:
            values = value_map[node]
        else:
            value_map[node] = values = all values that node can take
        v = values.next()
        if v is None:
            remove node from value_map
            p_map[node].note = None
            node = node_stack.prev()
        else:
            p_map[node].note = v
            if p_map is full:
                add p_map to full_results
            else:
                node = node_stack.next()
    return full_results, partial_results
```

Note in the code for this approach that several ancillary data management structures have been added to facilitate the process. One is a Stack class object used to hold unassigned nodes to facilitate traversing left and right over the nodes and checking if the process is at the end of the node list. The other is a value stack that holds for each node all the values it can take, and again facilitating getting the next value, or determining if there is no next value.

The value set for each node is computed by first finding all the constraints in which the node is an actor and finding the pitches for that node that comply to each policy. Be mindful that as the same node is encountered again and again from the left, its values set can be different due to how constraints behave with different assignments to prior actors.

In running this algorithm, you will likely observe that the rate of finding solutions is generally quite slow. There are two principal reasons for this. The main reason is that the nature of the runtime is multiplicative. That is, we go through all value possibilities for each node, which builds up multiplicatively, resulting in a very poor runtime - especially when there are few policies constricting value set size, in which case the cardinality of the nodes' pitch sets can be high. Also adding to the runtime is the continual recalculation of the pitch sets throughout the traversals. While the values stack helps preserves iteration context or state, and contributes positively to the runtime, the recalculation of the value set each time a further node is encountered from the left offsets that gain.

G.1.2   Breadth-First Search and Chains

The second algorithm we discuss is the breadth-first or "horizontal" search algorithm. Like the vertical algorithm, we start with the set of unassigned actors or nodes from the pmap. The gist of this approach is for each unassigned node to generate all pmap instances with that node taking on all possible values, and then using that set as input to build on the next unassigned node, and so forth. Immediately one can see that this causes memory issues, especially when the node value sets have large cardinalities

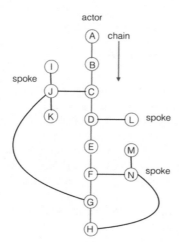

Fig. G 2 Chains and Spokes.

To improve on this approach, and in anticipation of the next section, we introduce the notion of ***chains***. A chain is based on the concept that for a given unassigned actor, that actor is involved in a set of constraints. The union of all the other unassigned actors across those constraints is called the ***chain for that actor***. These unassigned actors are called ***peers*** of the actor. In Fig. G.2, actor A has peers B…H. Also, for example, C has its set of peers A, I, J, K, G, again based on the constraints in which C is an actor. This set of peers intersects with A's and is called a *spoke* of A's peer set. The same for other of A's peers as well, e.g., nodes D and F. In this way, these overlapping chains form a kind of network over many unassigned nodes.

The importance of chains is that intuitively as the actors in a chain get assigned values, the value sets for remaining unassigned actors in the chain reduce to lower cardinality, since the constraints tend to constrict the cardinalities of those value sets. Of course, that depends on the kind of constraints involved. So, as a simple example, if a constraint specifies that an actor must have a pitch in some specific chord, the assignment of one actor to a chordal pitch, means the other peer actors may become more limited in possible value assignments, say, due to a step sequence constraint as described earlier. In that way actor value set cardinalities propagate through peers and ultimately spokes.

Furthermore, if we traverse the unassigned node list over actors with low cardinality value sets first, our multiplicative factors are low, and generally by the time we get to actors with higher cardinality, they should at the point of processing, under optimistic circumstances, have lower value set cardinality due to prior constraint value constriction as just mentioned. In other words, by satisfying actors with low cardinality value sets first, the cardinality of later actor value sets can be lowered in turn.

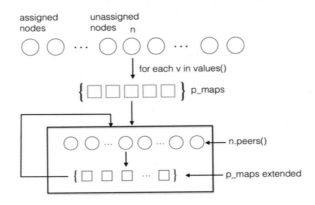

Fig. G 3 Horizontal Search

A visual for the horizontal algorithm is shown in Fig. G.3. For actor n, and for each of its values, a pmap based on the original is made with that actor assigned a value. Then for each of n's peer actors, and for each pmap just created, create yet another pmap for the peer for each of peer's values. That extended pmap now serves as input to the process for the next peer. This process continues for each peer, until the peers are exhausted, the output pmap set growing larger and larger, until all the unassigned peer nodes have been processed. Again, the bet is that as more nodes are assigned pitch values, the cardinality of successive nodes is pruned by the partially filled constraints. Furthermore, the bet is that assigning pitch values to peer sets first, not only restricts the cardinality of value sets, but also cuts down on the unassigned nodes. Thus, the loop over unassigned nodes will skip nodes that have been exhausted by the peer value setting process.

The algorithm for filling chains is shown above, which is an important part of the algorithm. However fill_chain() is not the complete algorithm. The algorithm is driven by a loop over the unassigned nodes Fig. G.3.

This algorithm also does not perform well. There are many duplications of pmaps made, which take time and space, and again the cardinalities of values sets are not pruned as much as one would want especially when there are fewer constraints to process wherein values sets tend to be large.

```
fill_chain(p_map, v_note)
    results = {}
    peers = all of v_note's peers relative to p_map
    v_note_values = all possible values for v_note

    for value in v_note_values:
        p_map[v_note].note = value
        v_note_p_map_set = {p_map}
        for peer in peers:
            peer_results = {}
            peer_values = possible values for peer given p_map
            if len(peer_values) == 0:
                v_note_p_map_set = {}
                break
            for pmap in v_note_p_map_set:
                for pm_v in peer_values:
                    pmap[peer].note = pm_v
                    if pmap is full
                        add pmap to full results
                    else:
                        add pmap to peer_results
            v_note_p_map_set = peer_results
        results = results union v_note_p_map_set
return results
```

G.2. Improvements on the Constraint Solution Algorithm

The prior discussion on constraint solving highlights the concepts that play into a constraint solution algorithm and attempts a few approaches towards solving constraint problems. Along the way, we came across the notion of chains and peers, which figure importantly as we proceed to look for improvements over the prior proposals.

For consideration, we combine the techniques of depth-first search and peer chaining. Here, we more aggressively follow peers in a recursive approach, looking for peer-based pitch assignment as much as we can. Note that for each peer, the policy set may be different but still overlap with other policy sets. By making pitch assignments to peers over more and more policy sets, the algorithm continually provides partial solutions to more and more policies. With that, we are more apt to reduce pitch value set cardinalities for other peers. The result of reducing pitch value candidate cardinality cuts down on the amount of searching, i.e., processing time. The result is likened to that of a chain reaction effect on policy satisfaction and value set cardinality reduction for unassigned peers.

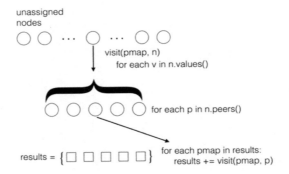

Fig. G 4 Improved Algorithm

A visual explanation of the algorithm is shown in Fig. G.4. As before the algorithm loops over all the unassigned actors of the original pmap. For each unassigned actor, the visit() method is called. Visit() loops over all pitch candidate values for n, and then for each peer, calls visit() recursively, in that way covering spokes recursively. Note that each call to visit() on peers generates a set of pmaps. The first time on the peer loop, {pmap} is processed, and thereafter, the returned results are incorporated into a results set.

The recursive call to visit() provides a means for finding solutions across more policy sets, as mentioned earlier. As a result, pitch value candidate sets could likely be reduced, reducing search and so improving the performance time of the algorithm. Be mindful also, though not explicit in the algorithm, there are checks on actors and peers having already been assigned as a consequence of recursive processing. The pseudo-code for the algorithm visit() is given below.

```
visit(p_map, v_note)
    results = {}
    values = All values for v_note
    for value in values:
        p_map[v_note].note = value
        value_results = {}
        peers = v_note's peers
        if peers is None:
            if p_map is full and valid:
                add p_map to full_results
            else:
                add P-map to value_results
        else:
            for peer in peers:
                if first_time:
                    value_results = visit(p_map, peer)
                else:
                    for r in value_results:
                        r_results = visit(r, peer)
                        value_results = value_result + r_results
            results = results + value_results
    p_map[v_note].note = None
    return results
```

While this algorithm appears to have superior performance, that is not assured. As with many of these approaches, it is quite possible to provide a set of conditions - say by a paucity of policies, or too many unassigned nodes, or a fragmentation of policy groups, that can make the algorithm explode in processing time or memory defying best attempts to prune the search space. Constraint solving is a difficult problem, and the intention of these sections is to show not only what is involved, but that there are many approaches, and that in some ways, perhaps anticipating and analyzing the kinds of problems you want to solve can help with how to approach a solution. With that in mind, analysis of input criteria can help determine if the user can anticipate long processing times and be forewarned. Such an analysis is left for discussion and experimentation.

Additionally, it would be wise to add various threshold value checking to curtail protracted processing. Examples would be limiting the number of solutions, or partial solutions (if that is asked for). Checks on processing time and exiting when the timing threshold is exceeded is always a good capability to include. The reader should check with the code base to see how some of these details may be handled.

Again, the interested reader should look over historical solutions and practices in this area [40] [37] [38].

Bibliography

[1]   S. Abrams, D. Oppenheim, D. Pazel and J. Wright, "Higher-level Composition Control in Music Sketcher: Modifiers and Smart Harmony," in *Proceedings of ICMC*, Beijing, China, 1999.

[2]   S. Abrams, R. Fuhrer, D. Oppenheim, D. Pazel and J. Wright, "A Framework for Representing and Manipulating Tonal Music," in *Proceedings of ICMC 2000*, Berlin, Germany, 2000.

[3]   D. P. Pazel, S. Abrams, R. M. Fuhrer, D. Oppenheim and J. Wright, "A Distributed Interactive Music Application using Harmonic Constraint," in *ICMC 2000*, Berlin, 2000.

[4]   A. Martelli, A. Ravenscroft and S. Holden, Python in a Nutshell: A Desktop Quick Reference, O'Reilly Media, 2017.

[5]   M. Urban, J. Murach and M. Murach, Murach's Python Programming, Mke Murch & Associates, 2016.

[6]   "Python 3.9.1 Documention," [Online]. Available: https://docs.python.org/3/.

[7]   B. D. McLaughlin, G. Pollice and D. West, Head First Object-Oriented Analysis and Design, O'reilly Media, 2006.

[8]   R. C. Martin, Clean Code: A Handbook of Agile Software Craftsmanship, Pearson, 2008.

[9]   G. Booch, J. Rumbaugh and I. J. Booch, The Unified Modeling Language User Guide (Object Technology Series) 2nd Edition, Addison-Wesley, 2005.

[10]   E. Gamma, R. Helm, R. Johnson, J. Vlissides and G. Booch, Design Patterns: Elements of Reusable Object-Oriented Software, Addison-Wesley, 1994.

[11]   "Pythagorean tuning," [Online]. Available: https://en.wikipedia.org/wiki/Pythagorean_tuning. [Accessed February 2021].

[12]   K. Gann, "Just Intonation Explained," [Online]. Available: https://www.kylegann.com/tuning.html. [Accessed February 2021].

[13]   "Werckmeister temperament," [Online]. Available: https://en.wikipedia.org/wiki/Werckmeister_temperament. [Accessed February 2021].

[14]   "Twelve-Tone Musical Scale," [Online]. Available: https://thinkzone.wlonk.com/Music/12Tone.htm. [Accessed February 2021].

[15]   "A440 (pitch standard)," [Online]. Available: https://en.wikipedia.org/wiki/A440_(pitch_standard). [Accessed February 2021].

[16]   "re - Regular expression operations," [Online]. Available: https://docs.python.org/3/library/re.html.

[17]   I. N. Herstein, Abstract Algebra, 3rd Edition, Wiley, 1996.

[18]   N. Jacobson, Basic Algebra I, 2nd Edition, Dover Publications, 2009.

[19]   N. Jacobson, Basic Algebra II, 2nd Edition, Dover Publications, 2009.

[20]   "Tuplets/Grouplets," [Online]. Available: http://learnmusictheory.net/PDFs/pdffiles/01-01-07-TupletsGrouplets.pdf. [Accessed April 2021].

[21]   W. Piston, Harmony, Norton, 1978.

Bibliography

[22]   V. Persichetti, Twentieth-Century Harmony, Norton, 1961.

[23]   "Ranges of Orchestral Instruments," [Online]. Available:
http://www.orchestralibrary.com/reftables/rang.html. [Accessed May 2021].

[24]   "music theory online: phrasing and articulation," [Online]. Available:
http://www.dolmetsch.com/musictheory21.htm#slurstaccato. [Accessed May 2021].

[25]   "Creating a singleton in Python," [Online]. Available:
https://stackoverflow.com/questions/6760685/creating-a-singleton-in-python. [Accessed Ma
2021].

[26]   "XML Schema Tutorial," [Online]. Available:
https://www.w3schools.com/xml/schema_intro.asp. [Accessed May 2021].

[27]   "JSON - Introduction," [Online]. Available:
https://www.w3schools.com/js/js_json_intro.asp. [Accessed May 2021].

[28]   T. H. Corman, C. E. Leiserson and R. L. Rivest, Introduction to Algorithms, The MIT
Press, 1993.

[29]   "Red/Black Tree," [Online]. Available:
https://www.cs.usfca.edu/~galles/visualization/RedBlack.html. [Accessed May 2021].

[30]   T. Kientzle, A Programmer's Guide to Sound, Addison-Wesley, 1997.

[31]   "Official MIDI Specifications," [Online]. Available: www.midi.org/specifications.
[Accessed May 2021].

[32]   "https://pypi.org/project/mido/," June 2021. [Online].

[33]   "Antlr," [Online]. Available: https://www.antlr.org/. [Accessed July 2021].

[34]   "Magenta," [Online]. Available: https://magenta.tensorflow.org/. [Accessed July 2021].

[35]   C. Ruding and J. Radin, "HDSR," 22 Nov 2019. [Online]. Available:
https://hdsr.mitpress.mit.edu/pub/f9kuryi8/release/6. [Accessed July 2021].

[36]   M. Bramer, Logic Programming with Prolog, 2nd Edition, Springer, 2013.

[37]   F. Rossi, P. van Beek and T. Walsh, Handbook of Constraint Programming, Elsevier
Science, 2006.

[38]   R. Dechter, Constraint Processing, Morgan Kaufmann, 2003.

[39]   "SWI Prolog," [Online]. Available: https://www.swi-prolog.org/. [Accessed July 2021].

[40]   "generic constraint development environment," [Online]. Available:
https://www.gecode.org/. [Accessed July 2021].

[41]   "OptaPlanner," [Online]. Available: https://www.optaplanner.org/. [Accessed July 2021].

[42]   "python-constraint 1.4.0," [Online]. Available: https://pypi.org/project/python-
constraint/. [Accessed July 2021].

[43]   "A composer is setting portraits of cats and dogs to music, and they are jut beautiful," 12
July 2021. [Online]. Available: https://www.classicfm.com/discover-music/composer-
setting-cat-dog-portraits-to-music/. [Accessed August 2021].

[44]   S. R. Abrams and et al., "System and Method for Applying a Role and Register
Preserving Harmonic Transformation to Musical Pitches (Expired 8/10/2007)". USA Patent
5936181, 13 May 1998.

[45]   S. R. Abrams and et. al., "System and Mathod for Approximate Shifting of Musical
Pitches while Maintaining Harmonic Function in a given Context (Expired 1/4/2008)". USA
Patent 6011211, 25 March 1998.

[46]   S. R. Abrams and et. al., "System and Method for Applying Harmonic Change to a Representation of Musical Pitches while Maintaining Conformity to a Harmonic Rule-Base (Expired 1/18/2008)". USA Patent 6015949, 13 May 1998.

[47]   "38: What is an Italian sixth?," [Online]. Available: https://www.ars-nova.com/Theory%20Q&A/Q38.html. [Accessed September 2021].

[48]   J. Fawcett, D. Ayers and L. R. E. Quin, Beginning XML 5th Edition, WROX, 2012.

[49]   "Constraint Programming," [Online]. Available: https://en.wikipedia.org/wiki/Constraint_programming. [Accessed July 2021].

[50]   [Online]. Available: https://www.steinberg.net/en/company/technologies/vst3.html. [Accessed June 2021].

[51]   M. Spivak, Calculus, 4th Edition, Publish or Perish, 2008.

Printed in the United States
by Baker & Taylor Publisher Services